Herbert Fry

London in 1880

illustrated with bird's-eye views of the principal streets, also its chief suburbs and environs

Herbert Fry

London in 1880
illustrated with bird's-eye views of the principal streets, also its chief suburbs and environs

ISBN/EAN: 9783337182496

Printed in Europe, USA, Canada, Australia, Japan

Cover: Foto ©Andreas Hilbeck / pixelio.de

More available books at **www.hansebooks.com**

LONDON IN 1880.

ILLUSTRATED WITH

BIRD'S-EYE VIEWS OF THE PRINCIPAL STREETS.

ALSO

ITS CHIEF SUBURBS AND ENVIRONS.

BY

HERBERT FRY,

EDITOR OF THE 'ROYAL GUIDE TO THE LONDON CHARITIES,'
'HANDBOOK TO NORMANDY,' 'THE ROAD TO PARIS,' ETC.

London:
DAVID BOGUE,
3, ST. MARTIN'S PLACE, TRAFALGAR SQUARE, W.C.
NEW YORK: SCRIBNER, WELFORD, & CO.
1880.

LONDON:
PRINTED BY WILLIAM CLOWES AND SONS,
STAMFORD STREET AND CHARING CROSS.

PREFACE.

In the following pages I have endeavoured to provide, for one shilling, the most attractive and useful Handbook to London, which, after many years of labour and consideration, I could compress within a necessarily limited space. If it be compared with similar Handbooks, I think it may be found to possess some advantages over them. If, without comparison, it be accepted upon its own merits, I shall be the more fortunate and gratified.

I have to express my thanks to Mr. Sulman for having successfully carried out my plan for the illustrations, which, being original, I hereby notify my intention to protect from piracy as far as I am able.

I hope to publish a new edition of this book annually—as I do of the 'Royal Guide to the London Charities'—I therefore expect to have the opportunity of adding to, and improving hereafter, what I have herein written; and, with that view, I shall esteem it a great favour if any kind reader will forward to me, at the publishers', any data or corrections for future editions.

HERBERT FRY.

LIST OF ILLUSTRATIONS.

		PAGE
1.	From Charing Cross through Whitehall to Westminster	20
2.	The Strand, from Charing Cross to Fleet Street	49
3.	Fleet Street and Ludgate Hill to St. Paul's and Cheapside, &c.	72
4.	Cannon Street to the Mansion House, the Tower, &c.	94
5.	From Charing Cross through Pall Mall to Pimlico	116
6.	Regent Street, from Waterloo Place to Portland Place	127
7.	St. James's Street and Old and New Bond Streets	132
8.	Piccadilly, from the Haymarket to Hyde Park Corner	138
9.	Oxford Street, from the Marble Arch to Tottenham Court Road	165
10.	New Oxford Street, and Holborn, to Smithfield and Cheapside	176
11.	The Poultry to Bishopsgate Street, and to Whitechapel	219
12.	From London Bridge, through the Borough, to Newington Butts and St. George's Fields	237
13.	The Thames from the Tower to Westminster	248

MAP OF LONDON IN 1880.

INDEX.

Abchurch Lane, 96.
Abney Park Cemetery, 290.
Abbey Mills Pumping Station, 253.
Academy, Royal, of Arts, 145.
—————— Music, 171.
Acton, 271.
Adelaide Gallery, 51.
Adelphi Terrace, 52.
———, Dark Arches of, 53.
———, Society of Arts, 53.
———, Adam Street, 53.
———, James Street, 53.
———, John Street, 53.
———, Robert Street, 53.
Addle Hill, 115.
Admiralty, 20.
Agar Street, 51.
Agricultural Hall, 234.
Air Street, 140.
Albany, The, 142.
Albemarle Street, 147.
Albert Embankment, 47.
——— Hall, 164.
——— Memorial, 164.
———, Statues of Prince, 164, 196, 294.
——— Suspension Bridge, 252.
Aldersgate, 213.
Aldgate, 228.
——— Pump, 229.
Alexandra Palace, 271.
——— Park, 271.
Almack's, 133.
Almonry, Royal, 21.
———, Westminster, 29.
Alsatia, 80.
Amen Corner, 86.
American Consulate, 314.

Amwell, 271.
Anerley, 271.
Antiquaries, Society of, 144.
Apollo, Oracle of, 73.
Apothecaries' Company, 85.
—————— Garden, 250.
—————— Hall, 85.
Apsley House, 152.
Aquarium, Royal, 40.
Arabella Row, 126.
Arcade, Burlington, 146.
———, Lowther, 51.
———, Royal Opera, 117.
Archæology, Society of Biblical, 136.
Archery, Society of, 131.
Arches, Court of, 216.
Architects, Royal Institute of British, 136.
Architectural Association, 136.
Architecture, 88.
Argyll Street, 129.
Arlington Street, 148.
Armourers' Company, 220.
Artillery (Hon.) Company, 232.
———, Woolwich, 269.
Arts, Society of, 53.
——— Society for Encouragement of, 136.
Arundel House, 67.
——— Marbles, 67.
——— Street, 67.
Ascot, 271, 295.
Asiatic (Royal) Society, 148.
Astronomical (Royal) Society, 144.
Athenæum, The, 61.
Athletic Sports, 288.
Audit Office, 63.
Austin Friars, 227.
Ave-Maria Lane, 86.

Index.

BACON, Lord, born, 51.
—— at Gray's Iun, 191.
Baker Street, 168.
Bull's Pond, 271.
Bagnigge Wells, 192.
Balham, 271.
Bankside Stews, 239.
—— Theatres, 259.
Bank of England, 221.
    Bullion Office, 222.
    Weighing Office, 222.
    Bank Note Machinery, 222.
    Government Dividends, 222.
Baptist Chapels, 298.
Barber Surgeons' Company, 215.
Barclay's Brewery, 260.
Barebones, Praise God, 79.
Barking, 272.
—— Outfall, 253.
Barnard's Inn, 192.
Barnes, 272.
Barnet, 272.
Barnsbury, 272.
Bartholomew Fair, 200.
—————— Close, 201.
Bartholomew's, St., Hospital, 201.
Bath House, 150.
—— Street, 207.
—— in the Thames, 258.
Battersea Bridge, 252.
———— Park, 252.
———— Sub Tropical Garden, 252.
———— Pier, 252.
———— Railway Bridge, 252.
Battlebridge, 271.
Bay Tree Tavern, 96.
Bayswater, 167.
Beaufort Buildings, 60.
Bedford Head Tavern, 56.
—— House, Strand, 55.
—— Row, 187.
—— Square, 177.
——, Statue of Duke of, 184.
Belgravia, 153.
—————— Origin of Name, 153.
Berkeley Square, 149.
—————— Street, 149.
Bermondsey, 240.
'Bermudas', 8.
Bethlehem Hospital, 245.

Bethnal Green, Beggar of, 272.
—————— —, Columbia Market, 273.
—————— —, Museum, 272.
—————— —, Victoria Park, 273.
Bevis Marks, 228.
'Big Ben', 42.
Billingsgate Fish Market, 262.
Birdcage Walk, 28.
Bishopsgate, 229.
Blackfriars, 83.
—————— Bridge, 83.
—————— Railway Stations, 83.
Blackheath, 269.
Blackwall, 269.
—————— Docks, 269.
Blind, School for Indigent, 245.
Bleeding Heart Yard, 194.
Bloomfield, Robert, 219.
Bloomsbury Square, 184.
—————— Street, 177.
Blue Coat School, 205.
'Boar's Head,' Eastcheap, 96.
Bond Street Loungers, 137.
—————, New, 136.
—————, Old, 135.
Board of Works, 4, 124.
Borough, The, 240.
—————— Market, 242.
——————, Old Inns in, 242.
Botanic (Royal) Gardens, 131.
Boxhill, 274.
Bow Bells, 217.
—— Church, 216.
——, Stratford le, 273.
—— Street, 59.
—————— Police Court, 59.
Bread Street, 215.
Brentford, 274.
Brentwood, 274.
Break Neck Steps, 198.
Brewer Street, 128.
Bridewell Palace, 81.
—————— Prison, 81.
Bridgewater House, 123.
British Museum, 178.
—————— Reading-room, 182.
Brixton, 274.
Broad Sanctuary, 28.
Broad Street, Old, 227.
Bromley, 274.

rompton Cemetery, 153.
——— Hospitals, 153.
——— Road, 153.
rook Street, 137.
rownlow Street, 187.
rownrigg, Mrs., 79.
roxbourne, 275.
ruton Street, 136.
uckingham Palace, 124.
——————————— Hotel, 126.
——————————— Road, 125.
——————————— Stables, 125.
——————— Street, 51-2.
ucklersbury, 220.
ullhead Court, 207.
unhill Fields Cemetery, 232.
unyan's, John, Grave, 232.
urlington Arcade, 146.
——————— Gardens, 145.
——————— House, 142.
ushy Park, 275.
ury Street, 135.
utcher's Row, 71.
utcher Hall Lane, 207.
utton's Coffee House, 58.
——————— Lion's Head, 58.
yron, Lord, 151.
———, Born, 170.

AB Fares, 319-322.
abmen, 4.
ade, Jack, 95, 214, 261.
alves' Head Club, 116.
amden Road, 175.
——————— Town, 175, 275.
——————— Vet. College, 275.
amberwell, 247.
ambridge, Duke of, 151.
——————— House, 150.
ancer Hospital, 153.
andlewick Street, 94.
annon Street, 94.
——————— Bridge, 259.
——————— Railway Terminus, 94.
——————— Hotel, 94.
anonbury Place, 236.
——————— Tea Gardens, 236.
——————— Tower, 236.
anterbury Hall, 48.

Carey Street, 70.
Carlton House Terrace, 119.
Carlisle House, 173.
Carlyle, Thomas, 250.
Castelnau, 284.
Catherine Street, 62.
Cato Street Conspiracy, 169.
Cattle Market, Metropolitan, 202.
——————————, Foreign, 267.
——— Show, Islington, 235.
Cavendish Square, 170.
Cecil Street, 53.
Cemeteries—
　Abney Park, 290.
　Brompton, 153.
　Bunhill Fields, 232.
　Highgate, 236.
　Kensal Green, 167.
　Norwood, 288.
　Nunhead, 289.
　Woking, 295.
Centlivre, Mrs., 117.
Central Criminal Court, 198.
Chalk Farm Road, 175.
Chancellor of Exchequer's Office, 27.
Chancery, Court of, 190.
——————— Lane, 78.
Change Alley, 227.
Chapels, 297-8.
　Hanover, 129.
　Lambeth Palace, 256.
　Regent Street, 127.
　Royal, 25, 62, 123.
　Spurgeon, Mr., 246.
　Tenison, Archbishop, 129.
　Unitarian, 69, 298.
　Vere Street, 170.
　Whitfield's, 174.
Charing Cross, 7.
——————— Q. Eleanor's Cross, 51.
——————— Hospital, 51.
———————, King's Mews, 8.
——————— Pillory, 7.
——————— Post Office, 50.
——————— Railway Terminus Bridge, 51.
——————— Hotel, 50.
——————— Steamboat Pier, 51.
——————— Swimming Bath, 258.
Charles Street, 127.

Charles I., 7, 22, 23, 122.
Charles II. at Whitehall, 23.
——————— in the Mall, 124.
Charlies, Old, 21.
Charlton, 269.
Charterhouse, 211.
——————— Chapel, 212.
———————, Col. Newcome at, 212.
——————— School, 212.
——————— Street, 202.
Chaucer at Charing Cross, 8.
——————— The 'Tabard,' 243.
Cheapside, 214.
——————— Cross, 214.
——————— Conduit, 214.
——————— Standard, 214.
Chelsea—Beaufort Row, 249.
———————, Botanic Garden, 250.
———————, Bun House, 249.
——————— Bridge (Old Battersea), 250.
———————, Cheyne Walk, 249.
——————— Church (Old), 249.
——————— China, 250.
——————— Embankment, 250.
——————— Pier, 249.
———————, Royal Hospital, 250.
———————, ——————— Military Asylum, 251.
———————, Don Saltero's Museum, 249.
——————— Philosopher, 250.
———————, Sir Thomas More, 249.
——————— Suspension Bridge, 252.
———————, Sloane, Sir Hans, 249.
———————, Turner, J. M. W., 250.
Chemical Society, 144.
Cheshunt, 275.
Chigwell, 275.
Childs's Bank, 73.
Chipping Barnet, 272.
Chiswick, 275.
——————— Churchyard, 276.
——————— House, 276.
Christchurch, 206.
Christie and Manson's, 133.
Christ's Hospital, 205.
——————— Lenten Suppers, 206.
Churches, &c.—
Allhallows, Barking, 97.

Churches, &c.—*continued*.
Allhallows, Bread Street, 215.
———————, Lombard Street, 223.
All Saints, Margaret Street, 129.
All Souls, 130.
Bow, 216.
Catholic Apostolic, 298.
Christ Church, 206.
City Temple, 196.
Foreign, 297.
Hanover Chapel, 129.
Irvingite, 298.
Presbyterian, 298.
Roman Catholic, 298.
St. Alban's, Wood Street, 215.
———————, Holborn, 193.
St. Andrew's, Holborn, 195.
——————— by the Wardrobe, 83.
———————, Undershaft, 228.
St. Anne's, Soho, 172.
St. Bartholomew, Great, 200.
———————, Less, 201.
St. Benet, 97.
St. Botolph, 231.
St. Bride's, 80.
St. Catherine Cree, 228.
St. Clement's Danes, 67.
St. Dunstan's in the East, 96.
——————— in the West, 78.
St. Edmund, 223.
St. George's Cathedral, 246.
———————, Bloomsbury, 184.
———————, Hanover Square, 171.
——————— Burial Ground, 167.
———————, Southwark, 244.
St. Gregory, 93.
St Helen's, 230.
St. Giles's, Cripplegate, 213.
——————— in the Fields, 176.
St. James's, Piccadilly, 141.
———————, Clerkenwell, 204.
———————, Chapel Royal, 123.
St. John's in the Tower, 102.
St. Leonard's, 231.
St. Luke's, Chelsea, 249.
St. Magnus, 115.
St. Margaret's, Westminster, 29.
St. Mark's, Kennington, 247.

Churches, &c.—*continued.*
St. Martin's-in-the-Fields, 10.
——— -, Ludgate, 84.
St. Mary, Aldermary, 94.
———, Abchurch, 96.
———, Islington, 235.
——— le Bow, 216.
——— le Strand, 65.
——— Magdalen, 94.
——— Overy, 241.
——— Woolnoth, 223.
St. Michael's, Cornhill, 227.
St. Mildred's, 94.
St. Nicholas, 94.
St. Olave's, 240.
St. Pancras, New, 192.
———, Old, 192.
St. Paul's Cathedral, 87.
———, Covent Garden, 56.
St. Peter and Vincula, 106.
———'s, Cornhill, 227.
St. Saviour's, 241.
St. Sepulchre's, 196.
St. Stephen's, Walbrook, 221.
St. Swithin, 94.
St. Vedast, 211.
Savoy, Chapel Royal, 62.
Scottish Episcopal, 141.
Temple Church, 75.
Whitehall, Chapel Royal, 25.
Cibber, Colley, 117.
City Companies, 240.
——— M.P.'s, 6.
——— of London School, 215.
——— of Westminster M.P.'s, 6.
——— Temple, 196.
——— Walls, 228.
Clapham, 276.
——— Common, 276.
——— Junction, 276.
———, Macaulay at, 276.
———, Plough Inn, 276.
——— Sect, 276.
———, Tom Hood's School, 276.
Clapton, 277, 284.
Claremont, 283.
Clarence House, 123.
Clarges, Nan, 52.
——— Street, 150.
Clement's Inn, 68.
——— ———, Justice Shallow at, 68.

Cleopatra's Needle, 54.
Clerkenwell, 204.
——— Green, 204.
——— -House of Correction, 204.
Cleveland Row, 132.
Clifford's Inn, 79.
Clothworkers' Company, 97.
Clubs—
Army and Navy, 119.
Arthur's, 132.
Arts, 171.
Arundel, 54.
Athenæum, 119.
Beaconsfield, 121.
Boodle's, 134.
Brooks's, 134.
Burlington Fine Arts, 128.
Carlton, 120.
Cocoa Tree, 133.
Conservative, 132.
Crichton, 56.
Devonshire, 134.
East India United Service, 120.
Egerton, 132.
Garrick, 19.
Grafton, 136.
Guards, 121.
Hanover Square, 171.
Hogarth, 175.
Junior Army and Navy, 136.
——— Athenæum, 151.
——— Carlton, 120.
——— Garrick, 56.
——— St. James's, 134.
——— United Service, 127.
Marlborough, 119.
National, 27.
Naval and Military, 151.
New University, 134.
Oriental, 171.
Orleans, 292.
Oxford and Cambridge, 121.
Pall Mall, 127.
Raleigh, 127.
Reform, 119.
Re-union, 56.
Royal Thames Yacht, 148.
Savage, 56.
Scientific, 128.
St. James's, 151.
St. Stephen's, 257.

Clubs—*continued*.
Stafford, 128.
Thatched House, 132.
Temple, 67.
Travellers', 119.
Turf, 150.
Union, 10.
United University, 116.
—— Service, 118.
Wanderers', 119.
Westminster, 148.
Whitefriars, 67.
Whitehall, 27.
White's, 135.
Windham, 120.
Coaches, 148.
Coal Exchange, 263.
Cobden, Richard, 117.
Cockney, 217.
Cock Lane Ghost, 199.
Cocker, Grave of, 244.
Cockpit Gate, 28.
Cockspur Street, 117.
Coffee-house, The First, 227.
Coffee-houses, Wits', 57, 69.
College, Heralds', 85.
—— (Royal), of Physicians, 10.
—— (Royal), of Surgeons, 189.
Colney Hatch, 277.
Colonial Office, 27.
Columbia Market, 273.
Commercial Docks, 266.
Commissionnaires, 301.
Conduit Mead, 170.
—— Street, 129.
Congregational Chapels, 298.
Constitution Hill, 150.
Consulates, 314.
Cookery, National School of, 163.
Co-operative Societies,—
    Army and Navy, 126.
    ————, Junior, 127.
    Civil Service Co-operative, 139.
    Civil Service Supply, 19, 52.
Copenhagen Fields, 277.
Cork Street, 136.
Corn Exchange, 97.
Cornhill, 226.
——, Standard at, 226.
Corsica, King Theodore of, 172.
Coutts's Bank, 52.

Covent Garden, 56.
———————, Evans's, 57.
———————, Floral Hall, 57.
——————— Market, 56.
——————— Theatre, 59.
Coventry House, 151.
Crane Court, 80.
Cranbourne Street, 19.
Craven House, 66.
Craven Street, 50.
Creed Lane, 86.
Cremorne, 250.
Cricket Grounds—
    Lord's, 166.
    Kennington Oval, 247.
    Prince's, 153.
Cripplegate, 213.
Crockford's Gaming-house, 134.
Crossnesss, 253.
Crosby Hall, 229.
Cromwell, Oliver, in King Street, 28.
————, at Whitehall, 23.
————, Married, 213.
————, Buried, 35.
————, Gibbeted, 165.
————, Head of, 42.
Crown Jewels, 105.
Crutched Friars, 97.
Crystal Palace, 277.
————————, Picture Gallery, 280.
————————, Aquarium, 280.
Cuckold's Point, 262.
Custom House, 263.
———————- Dues, 3.

DAILY Chronicle, 77.
—— News, 77.
—— Telegraph, 77.
Dalston, 280.
Danes Inn, 66.
Datchet, 295.
Davies Street, 170.
Dean Street, Soho, 172.
Dean's Yard, 28, 39.
De Foe, at 'Tom's', 58.
————, in the Pillory, 72.
————, in Cornhill, 227.
————'s Grave, 233.
Deptford, 267.
————, Foreign cattle depot, 267.
Devereux Court, 69.

Index. xi

vil Tavern, 73.
vonshire Gems, 150.
——— House, 149.
———, Kemble Collection of Plays, 150.
:kens on City Churches, 97.
—— and Thackeray, 193.
—— at Fox-under-the-Hill, 54.
—— in the Borough, 243-4.
—— in Golden Square, 128.
rty Dick, 228.
cks (London), 264.
ctors' Commons, 86.
ver Street, 149.
wgate, 115.
wn Street, 157.
wning Street, 26.
ulton's Pottery, 254.
ainage, 252.
ummond's Bank, 20.
ury Court, 65.
ury Lane, 59.
idley Street, 177.
ke of York's Column, 124.
————— School, 251.
ke Humphrey, Dining with, 87.
ke Street, Adelphi, 52.
————, Piccadilly, 142.
————, Oxford Street, 169.
lwich, 280.
—— College, 280.
—— Gallery, 281.
rham House, 52.

LING, 281.
st India Docks, 269.
gware Road, 166.
monton, 281.
yptian Hall,
—————, Mansion House, 220.
—————, Piccadilly, 146.
anor's (Q.) Cross, 51.
ephant and Castle Station, 246.
gin House, 151.
zabeth (Q.), Statue of, 79.
—— and Bishop, 194.
—— and Essex, 111.
y Chapel, 194.
- Place, 194.
ibassies, 314.
field, 282.

Engine Street, 151.
Epping, 282.
Epsom, 282.
Frith, 283.
Esher, 283.
Essex, Earl of, 111.
—— House, 69.
—— Street, 69.
————— Chapel, 69.
Euston Square Terminus, 303.
Eton College, 283.
Evans's Supper Rooms, 56.
Exchange, Coal, 263.
————, Corn, 97.
————, Royal, 224.
————, Stock, 226.
Exchequer Office, 27.
Execution Dock, 261.
Exeter Change, 62.
Exeter Hall, 60.

FARRINGDON Market, 81.
————— Street, 81.
————— Station, 83.
Fenchurch Street Terminus, 229.
Fenian Conspiracy, 204.
Fetter Lane, 79.
————— Chapel, 80.
————— Whitehorse Inn, 80.
Field Lane, 195.
Field of Forty Footsteps, 175.
Finchley, 286.
Finsbury, 232.
————— Park, 283.
Fire of London, 238.
Fish-market, 262.
Fishmongers Company, 238.
————— Hall, 239.
Fleet Ditch, 81.
—— Market, 81.
—— Marriages, 82.
—— Prison, 82.
—— River, 82.
—— Street, 72-81.
Fletcher, John, 242.
Floral Hall, 57.
Flower Market, 57.
Folly Theatre, 51.
Foreign Cattle-depot, 267.
————— Churches, 297.
————— Office, 26.

Foster Lane, 210.
Founder's Court, 227.
Foundling Hospital, 185.
Foxe, John, 213.
Fox Court, Gray's Inn Lane, 192.
Friday Street, 215.
Friends' Meeting Houses, 298.
———— Burial Ground, 233.
Fry, Mrs., at Newgate, 198.
Fruit Market, 56.
Fulham, 284.
————, Bishop of London's House, 284.
Fulwood's Rents, 191.
Furnival's Inn, 193.

GAIETY Theatre, 62.
Gainsborough's House, 120.
Gallery of Illustration, 127.
Garrick, David, 203.
————, died, 52.
———— Street, 19.
Gardens—
  Botanic, 131.
  Chelsea Botanic, 250.
  Royal Horticultural, 163.
  Kew, 287.
  Zoological, 131.
Gas, 4.
General Post-office, 209.
Geographical Society (Royal), 145.
Geological Society (Royal), 144.
———— ———— Museum and School, 140.
George Street, Strand, 52.
———— ————, Hanover Square, 171.
Gerard Street, 173.
German Gallery, 130.
———— Hospital, 280.
German Reed's Entertainment, 130.
Giltspur Street, 198.
———— ———— Compter, 199.
Great Cumberland Street, 168.
———— Marlborough Street, 129.
———— Portland Street, 171.
———— Surrey Street, 246.
Glasshouse Street, 128.
Globe Newspaper, 61.
Gloucester House, 151.
Gog and Magog, 218.
Golden Square, 128.
Goldsmith, Oliver, 75.

Goldsmith, at Surgeons' Hall, 84.
————, at Green Arbour Cou 198.
————, at Canonbury, 25 ;.
Goldsmiths' Company, 210.
Goswell Road, 213.
Government Offices, 20, 26, 27.
Gower, John, 241.
Gower Street, 177.
Gracechurch Street, 97.
Grafton Street, 136.
Gravesend, 270.
Gray's Inn, 191.
————, Lord Bacon at, 191.
———— Chapel, 191.
———— Hall, 191.
———— Road, 192.
———— Lane, 192.
————, Verulam Buildings, 1
Grecian Coffee-house, 69.
Great Eastern Railway, 302.
———— Northern Railway, 302.
———— Western Railway, 166, 302
'Great Tom,' 43.
Great Fire, 238.
———— Plague, 129, 195.
Great Russell Street, Bloomsbu 174.
———— ———— ————, Covent G den, 57.
———— Turnstile, 187.
Greek Street, Soho, 173.
Greenhithe, 284.
Green Park, 150.
Greenwich, Bellot Obelisk, 267.
———— Hospital, 267.
———— Chapel, 268.
———— Observatory, 269.
———— Park, 269.
————, Merchant Seame Hospital, 268.
————, Steamboat Pier, 267
————, Royal Naval Colle 268.
————, Whitebait Dinners, 2
Gresham College, 231.
———— Lectures, 231.
Grimaldi, 235.
Grocers' Company, 220.
Grosvenor Canal, 252.
———— Gallery, 136.

Index.

Grosvenor House Collection, 137.
———— Place, 126, 153.
———— Square, 169.
———— Street, 137.
Grote, George, 128.
Grub Street. 214.
Guildhall, 218.
———— Library, 219.
———— Museum, 219.
Gutter Lane, 215.
Guy Faux, 253.
Guy's Hospital, 242.
Gwynne, Nell, 65, 121, 190.

HABERDASHERS' Company, 215.
Hackney, 284.
———— Coaches, 284.
Haggerstone, 284.
Half Moon Street, 150.
Hamilton Place, 151.
Hammersmith, 284.
Hammam Turkish Baths, 135.
Hampstead Heath, 175.
———— Road, 175.
Hampton Court, 284.
Hanging Sword Alley, 80.
Hanover Chapel, 129.
———— Court, Long Acre, 19.
———— Square, 171.
———— Street, 129.
Hanway Street, 174.
Hanwell, 285.
Harewood House, 170.
———— Place, 170.
Harrow School, 286.
———— Road, 166.
Hart Street, Bloomsbury, 184.
Haymarket, 138.
———— Theatre, 117.
Hatcham, 284.
Hatfield, John, 43.
Hatton Garden, 194.
Haverstock Hill, 175.
Haydon, B. R. 147.
Haynau, Marshal, 260.
Hedge Lane, 17, 116.
Hendon, 286.
Henley Regatta, 287.
Henry VII.'s Chapel, 34.
Henry VIII. at Whitehall, 22.
Heralds' College, 85.

Hercules' Pillars, 151.
Hertford, Marquis of, Villa, 131.
Her Majesty's Theatre, 117.
Herne Hill, 287.
Hertford House, 169.
Hicks's Hall, 203.
Highbury, 236.
Highgate Hill, 236.
———— Cemetery, 236.
————, Sworn in at, 236.
High-level Sewers, 253.
Hogarth, William, 18, 187.
————, Grave of, 276.
Holborn Bars, 193.
———— Circus, 196.
————, High, 184.
———— Hill, 196.
————, Middle Row, 192.
———— Viaduct, 196.
Holland House, 155.
Holles Street, 170.
Holloway, 236.
Holywell Street, 67.
———— Lane, 231.
Home Office, 27.
Homerton, 284.
Honey Lane, 214.
Hood, Tom, 219, 276.
Horns Tavern, 247.
Hornsey, 236.
Horse Guards, 25.
Horselydown, 240.
Horsemonger Lane Gaol, 244.
Horticultural Society, 163.
Hotels—
    Alexandra, 153.
    Bath, 148.
    Buckingham Palace, 126.
    Cannon Street Terminus, 94.
    Charing Cross Terminus, 50.
    ————, Grand Hotel. 49.
    Covent Garden—
        Bedford, 57.
        Clunn's, 57.
        Evans's, 57.
        Hummums, 57.
    Fischer's, 136.
    Furnival's, 193.
    Golden Cross Hotel, 50.
    Great Northern Terminus, 302.

Hotels—*continued*.
  Great Western Terminus, 302.
  Grosvenor, 126.
  Hatchett's 149.
  Holborn Viaduct, 196.
  Inns of Court, 187.
  Langham, 130.
  Limmer's, 136.
  London Bridge Terminus, 241.
  Long's, 136.
  Morley's, 10.
  Queen's, Clifford St., 136.
  —— St. Martin's-le-Grand, 210.
  Midland Railway Terminus, 302.
  Saracen's Head, 196.
  St. James's, 149.
  Star and Garter, 290.
  Westminster Palace, 40.
Houndsditch, 229.
Hounslow, 287.
House of Commons, 44.
  —— Lords, 43.
Howard Street, 67.
Hoxton, 231.
Humane Society, 10.
Hungerford Bridge, 51.
  —— Market, 51.
Hunter, John, 18, 153.
  ——, William, 139.
Hurlingham, 284.
Hyde Park, 154.
  —— Gates, 154.
  ——, Lady's Mile, 154.
  ——, Rotten Row, 154.
  ——, Serpentine, 154.
  ——, Statue of Achilles, 154.
  ——, the Ring, 165.

INDIA Office, 27.
Inland Revenue Office, 63.
Inns of Chancery, 66, 68, 79, 192, 193.
  —— Court, 74, 190, 191.
Inns, Old—
  Angel, Islington, 234.
  ——, Strand, 67.
  Bell, 207.
  Belle Sauvage, 84.
  Bull and Mouth, 210.
  Crown and Anchor, 67.

Inns, Old—*continued*.
  Elephant and Castle, 246.
  George and Blue Boar, 185.
  Hercules Pillars, 151.
  Jack Straw's Castle, 175.
  Oxford Arms, 207.
  Peacock, 234.
  Plough, Clapham, 276.
  Red Lion, 184.
  Saracen's Head, 196.
  Tabard, 243.
  White Hart, 243.
  White Horse Cellar, 149.
  —— Inn, 80.
Ironmongers' Co., 229.
Islington, 234.
Isle of Dogs, 267.
Isleworth, 287.
Italian Church, 297.
  —— Legation, 315.
  —— Opera, 59, 117.
  —— Organ-grinders, 193.
  —— Plaster-cast Makers, 193.

JACK Cade, 95, 214, 261.
Jenny's Whim, 126.
Jermyn Street, 134.
Jewish Synagogues, 297.
Jewin Street, 213.
Jews, first, in London, 219.
Joe Miller, 68.
Johnson, Dr. S., and Cock Lane Ghost, 199.
  ——————, at Thrale's Brewery, 260.
  ——————, at Church, 67.
  ——————, at 'Mitre,' 77.
  ——————, in Fleet Street, 77.
  ——————, at St. John's Gate 203.
Jonson, Ben, at School, 7.
  ——————'Devil,' 73.
  ——————, as a Mason, 190.
  ——————, "Sons of," 74.

KEAN, Edmund, 150.
  ——, Charles, 172.
Kennington, Gallows at, 247.
  —— Common, 247.
  ——, 'Horns Tavern,' 247.
  —— Oval, 247.

Kennington Park, 247.
Kensal Green Cemetery, 167.
Kensington, 154.
————— Gardens, 154.
—————, Holland House, 155.
————— Palace, 154.
—————, South, Museum, 155.
Kentish Town Road, 175.
Kew, 287.
—— Gardens, 287.
—— Palace, 287.
Kilburn, 166.
Kilmarnock, Lord, 114.
King Edward VI., 81.
————————— Street, 207.
King William Street, Strand, 51.
———————————, City, 96.
King Street, St. James's, 132.
—————, Cheapside, 218.
—————, Westminster, 27.
King's College, 64.
————————— Hospital, 64.
————————— School, 64.
King's Cross, 192.
—————Gate Street, 184.
————— Mews, 8.
Kingsland, 288.
—————, Road, 231.
Kit Kat Club, 71.
Knightsbridge, 153.

ɹACON and Ollier's, 136.
ɹadbroke Grove Road, 167.
ɹady's Mile, 154.
ɹambeth, 254.
—————, Albert Embankment, 47.
————— Bridge, 254.
—————, Doulton's Pottery, 254.
————— Ferry, 254.
—————, Lollard's Tower, 256.
————— Palace, 255.
————————— Chapel, 256.
————————— Library, 256.
—————, St. Mary's Church, 254.
ɹamb's Conduit Street, 185.
ɹangham Place, 130.
————— School for Artists, 130.
ɹansdowne House, 150.
ɹant Street, 244.
ɹaw Courts, 69.
ɹawrence Pountney Hill, 115.

Leadenhall Street, 227.
————— Market, 228.
Leather Lane, 193.
————— Trade, 240.
————— Sellers' Co., 230.
Leicester Square, 17.
————— Exiles, 18.
————— House, 18.
Lewisham, 288.
Leyton, 288.
Leytonstone, 288.
Life-Guards, 26.
Lillie Bridge, 288.
Limehouse, 267.
————— Reach, 267.
Lincoln's Inn, 190.
————— Chapel, 190.
————— Fields, 187.
————— Hall, 190.
————— Library, 190.
—————, New Court, 191.
—————, Old Buildings, 190.
Linnæan Society, 144.
Lion's Head, Button's, 58.
Little Britain, 207.
Lloyd's, 225.
Locket's Ordinary, 117.
Lock Hospital, 286.
Lollard's Tower, 93, 256.
Lombard Street, 223.
London, Land in, 3.
————— Bridge, 260.
————— House, 241.
————— Railway Terminus, 240.
————— Docks, 264.
————— Hospital, 229.
————— Institution, 232.
————— Library, 120.
————— Stone, 95.
————— Road, 245, 246.
————— University, 145.
————— Walls, Old, 228.
————— and Brighton Railway, 40, 126, 240.
————— North Western, 184, 303.
————— South Western, 303.
————— Chatham and Dover, 83, 126, 303.
Long Acre, 19.

Long Lane, 202.
Low-level Pumping-house, 252.
Lord Mayor's Banquets, 218.
—————— Day, 220.
—————— Show, 217, 220.
Lord's Cricket Ground, 166.
Lost in London, 4.
Lothbury, 227.
Lovat, Lord, 114.
Lovelace, Richard, 81.
Lower Thames Street, 115.
Lowther Arcade, 51.
Ludgate, 84.
—————— Hill, 84.
—————— Street, 84.
—————— Viaduct, 83.
Lyon's Inn, 66.

MACCLESFIELD, Countess of, 192.
Maddox Street, 136.
Magdalen Hospital, 291.
Magna Charta, 290.
Maiden Lane, 55.
Maida Vale, 166.
Main Drainage, 252.
Mall, The, 124.
Manchester Square, 169.
—————— Street, 170.
Mansion House, 220.
——————, Egyptian Hall, 220.
—————— Station, 94.
—————— Police Court, 220.
Marble Arch, 165.
Mark Lane, 97.
Marlborough House, 121.
—————— (Great) Street, 129.
—————————————— Police Court, 129.
Marshalsea Prison, 244.
Martyrs in Smithfield, 200.
Marvell, Andrew, 55.
Marylebone, 170.
—————— Lane, 170.
—————— Road Station, 168.
—————— St. Old Church, 170.
—————— New Church, 170.
Massinger, Philip, 242.
Maundy Money, 21.
May Meetings, 60.
Maypole, 65.
Meat Market, 202

Mercers' Co., 219.
Merchant Taylors' Co., 212, 240.
Macaulay, Lord, 88, 276.
Metropolitan Board of Works, 4, 124.
—————— Boroughs, 6.
—————— Cattle Market, 202.
—————— School Board, 5.
—————— Main Drainage, 252.
—————— Meat Market, 202.
—————— Police, 4, 21.
—————— Railway, 303.
—————— Tabernacle, 246.
Meux's Brewery, 174.
Mews, King's, 8.
Middlesex Hospital, 172.
Midland Railway Terminus, 303.
Milk Street, 215.
Mildmay Park, 288.
Military Asylum (Royal), 251.
Milbank Penitentiary, 254.
Milton, John, born, 215.
——————, Christened, 216.
——————, in Westminster, 40.
——————, Spring Gardens, 117.
——————, St. Bride's Churchyard, 81.
——————, Married and Buried, 213.
Milton Street, 213.
Milwall, 267.
—————— Docks, 267.
Mincing Lane, 97.
Minories, 228.
Mint, Royal, 114,
—————— Street, 244.
Mitchell's Library, 135.
Missionary Museum, 232.
Money Order Office, 210.
Monmouth, Duke of, 112.
—————— Street, 177.
Montagu House, Old, 178.
Montague House, 258.
Monument, The, 237.
——————, Nelson's, 9.
——————, Crimean, 118.
——————, Duke of York's, 124.
Moore and Burgess Minstrels, 141.
More, Sir Thomas, Born, 215.
——————, at Chelsea, 249.
——————, at New Inn, 66.
——————, Executed, 107.
——————, Head of, 107.
Morning Advertiser, 77.

Morning Chronicle, 65.
———— *Post*, 61.
Morris, Captain, 120.
Mortlake, 288.
Mudie's Library, 178.
Museum, Bethnal Green, 272.
————, British, 178.
————, Geological, 140.
————, Guildhall, 219.
————, India, 228.
————, Missionary, 232.
————, Natural History, 163.
————, Royal Architectural, 40.
————, Royal College of Surgeons, 189.
————, Sir J. Soane's, 188.
————, South Kensington, 155.
———— Street, 178.
————, United Service, 25.
Music Halls—
　Canterbury, 48.
　Evans's, 57.
　Middlesex, 60.
　North Woolwich, 270.
　Oxford, 174.
　Pavilion, 139.
　Rosherville, 270.
　Royal, Holborn, 184.
　South London, 245.
　Winchester, 244.
Music, Royal Academy of, 171.
Muswell-hill, 288.
Myddelton, Sir Hugh, 235.

NAPOLEON III.'s Lodgings, 133.
Nash, the Architect, 130.
National-Gallery, 11.
———— Opera House, 27.
———— Portrait Gallery, 162.
———— School of Cookery, 163.
Natural History Museum, 163.
Naval College, 268.
Nell Gwynne, 65, 121, 190.
Nelson, Lord, Column, 9.
———— Tomb, 91.
———— to Wellington, 91.
New Bond Street, 136.
Newcastle House, 205.
———— Street, 66.
Newgate Market, 207.
———— Prison, 198.

Newgate Gallows, 197.
———— Street, 197.
New Inn, 66.
Newington Butts, 247.
———————— Tabernacle, 247.
Newland, Abraham, 222.
Newman Street, 172.
New Oxford Street, 176.
Newport Market, 19.
New River, 235.
New Road, 233.
Newton, Sir Isaac, 18.
Nine Elms, 316.
Nonsuch House, 260.
Norfolk Street, 67.
Northumberland Avenue, 49.
———————— House, 49.
———————— Lion, 50.
———————— Street, 50.
Norwood, 288.
———— Cemetery, 288.
————, Gipsy Hill, 288.
————, Lower, 288.
————, Upper, 288.
Notting Hill, 167.
Nunhead Cemetery, 289.

OMNIBUSES, 4, 304–14.
Obelisk, Cleopatra, 54
————, Surrey side, 246.
Observatory, Royal, 269.
October Club, 28.
Of Lane, 52.
Old Bailey, 84.
————, Breakneck Steps, 198.
———— Sessions House, 84, 198.
Old Bond Street, 135.
—— Broad Street, 227.
—— Change, 215.
—— Jewry, 219.
—— London, 5.
—— Palace Yard, 40.
—— Street, 213.
—— Swan Stairs, 115.
O. P. Riots, 59.
Opera Houses, 59, 117.
————, National, 27.
————, Royal Italian, 59, 117.
Orchard Street, 168.
Organ grinders, 193.
Otway, Grave of, 68.

b

Oval, Kennington, 247.
Oxford Market, 171.
———— Music Hall, 174.
———— Street, 165.
————————, New, 176.

PADDINGTON Railway Terminus, 166.
Pall Mall, 116.
————, Game of, 124.
———— East, 116.
———— *Gazette*, 50.
Palsgrave Place, 69.
Panopticon, 19.
Pantheon, 171.
Panyer Alley, 86.
Parcels Delivery Co., 301.
Park Crescent, 130.
—— Lane, 165.
—— Street, 168.
Parks—
　Battersea, 252.
　Busby, 275.
　Green, 150.
　Greenwich, 269.
　Hyde, 154.
　Kennington, 247.
　Kensington, 154.
　Kew, 287.
　Regent's, 131.
　Richmond, 289.
　St. James's, 123.
　Victoria, 273.
　Windsor, 295.
Parliament, Houses of, 42.
———————— Street, 27.
Partridge's Almanac, 54.
Paternoster Row, 208.
———————— Square, 207.
Paul's Cross, 93.
—— Walkers, 87.
—— Wharf Pier, 258.
Peckham Rye, 289.
Peele's Coffee House, 79.
Pentecost Lane, 207.
Pentonville, 234.
Percy Chapel, 174.
Pest-field, 129.
Peterborough House, 20.
Petticoat Lane, 229.
Physicians, Royal College of, 10.
Piazza, Covent Garden, 57.

Piccadilly, 138.
———— Circus, 139.
———— Hall, 138.
———— Saloon, 139.
Picket Place, 71.
Picton, Sir Thomas, 167.
Pillory, The, 7, 41, 72, 188.
Pimlico, 126.
———— Railway Terminus, 126.
Pindar, Sir Paul, 231.
Pirates gibbeted, 262.
Presbyterians, 298.
Primrose Hill, 131.
Prince's Cricket Ground, 153.
———— Street, 129.
Printing House Square, 85.
Picture Galleries—
　Academy Royal, 145.
　Agnew's, 135.
　British Artists, 116.
　Crystal Palace, 280.
　Danish, 137.
　Doré, 136.
　Dudley, 147.
　Dulwich, 281.
　French, 136.
　Grosvenor, 136.
　Hampton Court, 284.
　Lady Artists, 129.
　National, 11.
　———— Portrait, 162.
　South Kensington, 160.
　Water Colours, Society of
　　Painters in, 116.
　————————, Institute of
　　Painters in, 121.
　Private Galleries:
　　Apsley House, 152.
　　Ashburton Collection, 150.
　　Bridgewater House, 123.
　　Buckingham Palace, 124.
　　Grosvenor House, 137.
　　Hertford, 169.
　　Stafford House, 123.
Plague of London, 129, 195.
Playhouse Yard, 83.
Plumstead, 289.
Pool, The, 261.
Pope's Head Alley, 223.
Police, Metropolitan, 21.
Polytechnic Institution, 130.

Population, 2.
Portland Place, 130.
──── - Street Railway Station, 171.
Porridge Island, 8.
Portman Square, 168.
──────── Street, 168.
Post Office, Charing Cross, 10.
────────, Dead Letters, 210.
────────, General, 209.
──────── Orders, 209.
──────── Savings Banks, 209.
──────── Telegrams, 209, 299.
Postal Districts, 299.
──── Regulations, 299.
Poultry, The, 219.
────, Compter, 219.
Praise God Barebones, 79.
Prisons—
   Bridewell, 81.
   Clerkenwell, 204.
   Cold Bath Fields, 192.
   Fleet, 82.
   Giltspur Street, 199.
   Holloway, 82.
   Horsemonger Lane, 244.
   Marshalsea, 244.
   Milbank, 254.
   Newgate, 198.
   Queen's Bench, 244.
Privy Council Office, 27.
Pudding Lane, 237.
Punch, 77.
Purfleet, 289.
Putney, 289.
Pye Corner, 199.
Pyx, Trial of The, 114.

"Q., OLD," 151.
Quakers' Meeting Houses, 298.
Quebec Street, 168.
Queen Anne's Mansions, 40.
──── Street (Great), 184.
──────── (Little), 184.
──── Square, Bloomsbury, 184.
──── Victoria Street, 220.
Queen's Head Passage, 207.
──── Tobacco-pipe, 264.
Queenhithe, 115.

RACES—
   Ascot, 271.
   Epsom, 282.

Races—*continued*.
   Henley Regatta, 287.
   Sandown Park, 283.
   University Boat, 289.
Rag Fair, 229.
Railway and Booking Offices, 139.
──────── Termini, 302-3.
Raleigh, Sir Walter, 41.
────────, His Study, 52.
Ranelagh Gardens, 251.
Raphael's Cartoons, 23.
Rathbone Place, 174.
Record Office, 79.
Red Lion Inn, 184.
──────── Square, 185.
──────── Street, 185.
Regalia, 105.
Regent Circus, Piccadilly, 127.
────────, Oxford Street, 171.
Regent Street, 127.
Regent's Quadrant, 128.
──────── Park, 131.
Regicides, Execution of, 7.
──────── Exhumed, 165.
Registrar-General's Office, 63.
Restaurants—
   Argyll, 139.
   Blanchard, 128.
   Café Royal (Nicols), 128.
   Criterion, 139.
   Crosby Hall, 229.
   Gatti's, 51.
   Holborn, 184.
   Monico, 128.
   Pall-Mall, 127.
   St. James's, 140.
   Simpson's, 60.
   Verrey, 128.
Reynolds, Sir Joshua, 18.
Richardson, Samuel, 80.
Richmond, 289.
──────── Hill, 289.
──────── Park, 289.
────────, Pembroke Lodge, 289.
────────, Sheen Lodge, 289.
────────, Star and Garter, 290.
────────, Thatched Lodge, 289.
────────, White Lodge, 289.
Roehampton, 290.
Rogers, Samuel, 132.
Rolls Chapel, 78.

Rolls Court, 78.
Roman Bath, 64.
—— Catholic Churches, 298.
—— London, 5.
Rookery, St. Giles's, 176.
Rosamond's Pond, 124.
Rosherville Gardens, 270.
Rotherhithe, 266.
Rotten Row, 154.
Rothschild's, Piccadilly, 152.
————, St. Swithin's Lane, 96.
Royal Academy of Arts, 145.
—————— Music, 171.
—— Albert Hall, 164.
—— Almonry, 21.
—— Aquarium, 40,
—— Asiatic Society, 148.
—— Astronomical, 144.
—— Botanic Gardens, 131.
—————— Society, 131.
—— College of Physicians, 10.
—————— Surgeons, 189.
—— Free Hospital, 192.
—— Exchange, 224.
—— Geographical Society, 145.
—— Geological Society, 144.
—— Horticultural Society, 163.
—— Humane Society, 10.
—— Institution, 147.
—— Military Asylum, 251.
—— Italian Opera, 59, 117.
—— Music Hall, 184.
—— Naval College, 268.
—— Observatory, 26.
—— Society, 143.
—————— of Antiquaries, 144.
—— Veterinary College, 275.
Runnimead, 290.
Russell, Lord William, 78, 188.
———— Square, 184.
———— (Great) Street, Bloomsbury, 174.
———— (Great) Street, Covent Garden, 57.

SACRED Harmonic Society, 60.
Sackville Street, 142.
Saddlers' Company, 214.
Saffron Hill, 195.
St. Albans, The City of, 290.
St. Bartholomew's Hospital, 201.

St. Chad's Well, 271.
St. George's Circus, 244.
————— Fields, 244.
————— Hall, 130.
————— Hospital, 153.
————— Road, 246.
St. James's, Court of, 122.
————— Hall, 140.
————— Market, 127.
————— Palace, 122.
————— Place, 132.
————— Park, 123.
————— Station, 40.
————— Square, 120.
————— Street, 132.
————— Vestry Hall, 142.
St. John's Gate, 203.
————— Square, 203.
————— Street, 202.
————— Road, 202.
————— Wood, 166.
St. Katherine's Docks, 264.
————— Hospital, 131.
St. Martin's Court, 18.
————— Lane, 19.
————— le Grand, 209.
St. Mary Axe, 228.
St. Paul's Cathedral, 87.
————— Churchyard, 93.
————— Clock Room, 92.
————— Cross, 93.
————— Geometrical Staircase, 92.
————— Library, 92.
—————, Old, 87.
————— School, 93.
————— Walkers, 87.
—————, Whispering Gallery, 92.
St. Stephen's Hall, 43.
St. Swithin's Lane, 96.
St. Thomas's Hospital, 47.
Salisbury House, 53.
————— Street, 53.
————— Square, 80.
Salter's Company, 96.
Sam's Library, 132.
Sanctuary, Westminster, 28.
Sandown Park, 283.
Savage, Richard, 192.
Savile House, 18.
—— Row, 128.
Savoy, Chapel Royal, 62.

Index.

Savoy Conference, 62.
—— Palace, 62.
Schomberg House, 120.
Schools of Art and Design, 163.
Scotland Yard, 20.
Scottish Corporation, 80.
Sermon Lane, 86.
Serjeant's Inn, Chancery Lane, 78.
————, Fleet Street, 78.
Serpentine, 154.
Sewers, High-level, 253.
————, Low-level, 252.
Seven Dials, 176.
—— Sisters Road, 291.
Shakespeare, Edmund, 241.
————, W., Statue of, 19.
———— at Bankside, 259.
———— Blackfriars, 83.
————'Mermaid,' 216.
Shaver's Hall, 138.
Shadwell, 267.
Sheepshanks' Collection, 161.
Shepherd's Bush, 167.
Shire Lane, 71.
Shoe Lane, 81.
Shooter's Hill, 269.
Shore, Jane, 93.
Shoreditch, 231.
Sidney Alley, 18.
Sion College, 213.
Sir Hugh Myddelton, 235.
Skinners' Company, 240.
Sloane, Sir Hans, 249, 250.
—— Square, 153.
—— Street, 153.
Smith, Captain John, 197.
Smithfield, 200.
———— Martyrs, 200.
———— Markets, 202.
Snow Hill, 196.
————, Saracen's Head on, 196.
Snaresbrook, 290.
Soane, Sir J., Museum, 188.
Society of Antiquaries, 144.
———— Archery, 131.
———— Arts, 53.
————, Astronomical, 144.
————, Chemical, 144.
————, Royal Geological, 144.
————, Royal Geographical, 145.
————, Royal Horticultural, 163.

Society, Royal Humane, 10.
————, Royal Linnæan, 144.
————, Royal, 143.
————, Sacred Harmonic, 60.
Soho Bazaar, 173.
—— Fields, 173.
—— Square, 172.
Somerset House, 63.
Somers Town, 192.
Southall, 290.
Southampton Buildings, 78.
———————— House, 78.
———————— Row, 184.
———————— Fields, 175.
———————— Street, Strand, 55.
Southcote, Joanna, 170.
South Kensington Museum, 155.
———————— Railway Station, 155.
Southwark, Borough of, 240.
———— Bridge, 259.
———— Park, 290.
Speed, The Historian, 213.
Spenser, Edmund, 28.
Spitalfields, 231.
Spring Gardens, 117.
Sports, Athletic, 288.
Spurgeon's, Mr., Tabernacle, 246.
Stafford House, 123, 273.
———— Street, 136.
Staines, 290.
Stamford Hill, 292, 313.
Standard, Cheapside, 214.
————, Cornhill, 226.
———— Newspaper, 77.
Staple Inn, 192.
Stationers' Hall, 86.
———————— Court, 208.
Statistics of London, 2, 3, 4.
Statues—
Achilles, 154.
Albert, Prince, 164, 196, 294.
Anne, Queen, 89.
Bedford, Duke of, 184.
Bentinck, Lord G., 170.
Brunel, I. K., 67.
Burgoyne, Sir J., 119.
Canning, George, 46.
Charles I., 7.
Charles II., 251.
Clyde, Lord, 117.

Statues—*continued*.
  Cobden, Richard, 117.
  Cumberland, Duke of, 170.
  Derby, Earl of, 46.
  Elizabeth, Queen, 79.
  Father Thames, 64.
  Fox, C. J., 184.
  Franklin, Sir John, 119.
  George III., 64, 117.
  —— IV., 10.
  Guards' Crimean Memorial, 118.
  Havelock, Sir H., 10.
  Henry VIII., 201.
  Herbert, Lord, 120.
  James II., 25.
  Jenner, Dr., 154.
  Mill, J. S., 67.
  Napier, Sir C., 10.
  Nelson, Lord, 9.
  Outram, Sir F., 258.
  Palmerston, Lord, 46.
  Peabody, Mr., 225.
  Peel. Sir R., 46, 208.
  Pitt, William, 171.
  Richard I., 46.
  Shakespeare, 19.
  Victoria, Queen, 224.
  Wellington, Duke of, 152, 225.
  ——————, in St. Paul's, 90.
  William III., 120.
  —— IV., 96.
  York, Duke of, 124.
Steamboat Piers, 316.
—————, Margate, 262.
Stepney, 267.
Sterne, Lawrence, 135.
——, his Death, 135.
——, his Grave, 167.
Stews, Bankside, 239.
Stock Exchange, 226.
Stocksmarket, 219.
Stockwell, 274.
Stoke Newington, 290.
————— Cemetery, 290.
Storey's Gate, 28.
Strafford, Earl of, 98.
Stratton Street, 150.
Strand, 49.
—— Lane, 64.
——, New Exchange, 52.

Stratford, 273.
—— Place, 170.
Streatham, 291.
——————, Magdalen Hospital, 291.
——————, Thrale House, 291.
Sub-tropical Garden, 252.
Subway, Thames, 263.
Suffolk Street, 116.
Surbiton, 291.
Surgeons, Royal College of, 189.
Surrey Docks, 266.
—— Prison, 244, 292.
—— Street, 67.
—— (Great) Street, 246.
——-side Boats, 258.
—— Turnpike Gates, 247.
—— Zoological Gardens, 246.
Sutherland House, 273.
Sutton, Thomas, 211.
Swallow Street, 141.
Swimming Bath in Thames, 258.
Swiss Cottage, 166, 310.
Swithin's Lane, 96.
Sydenham, 291.
Synagogues, 297.

Tabernacle, 175, 246.
Tattersalls, 153.
Taverns—
  Adam and Eve (Old), 174.
  Baytree, 96.
  Boar's Head (Old), 96.
  Belvedere, 234.
  Blue Posts, 136.
  Coal Hole, 60.
  Cock, 76.
  Czar's Head, 97.
  Dolly's, 207.
  Fountain, 60.
  Fox-under-the-Hill, 54.
  Freemasons, 184.
  Horns, 24.
  Mermaid (Old), 216.
  Mischief, 172.
  Mitre (Old), 77.
  Napier, 191.
  Old Dog, 67.
  Simpson's, 60.
  Turk's Head (Old), 174.
Tavistock Square, 184.
Taylor, Waterpoet, 19.

Teddington, 291.
Telegraph Offices, 207.
Temple Bar, 72.
——— Pillory, 72.
——— Church, 75.
——— Gardens, 75, 76.
———, Inner, 74.
———, Middle, 74.
———, Gateway, 74.
———, Outer, 69.
——— Railway Station, 67.
Tenison's, Archbishop, Chapel, 129.
——————— Grammar School, 18.
Tennyson, Alfred, 76, 91.
Tenterden Street, 171.
Thames, The, 248.
——— Ditton, 291.
——— Embankment, 47, 250, 257.
——— Steam Ferry, 266.
——— Street, Lower, 115.
———————, Upper, 115.
——— Subway, 263.
——— Tunnel, 265.
Thavie's Inn, 194.
Theatres (Modern)—
  Adelphi, 53.
  Alcazar, 18.
  Alhambra, 18.
  Astley's, 47.
  Britannia, 231.
  Court, 153.
  Covent Garden, 59.
  Criterion, 139.
  Drury Lane, 59.
  Duke's, 191.
  East London, 229.
  Folly, 51.
  Gaiety, 62.
  Grecian or Eagle, 233.
  Globe, 66.
  Haymarket, 117.
  Hengler's Circus, 171.
  Her Majesty's, 117.
  Holborn, 191.
  Imperial (Aquarium), 40.
  Lyceum, 61.
  Marylebone, 166.
  National Standard, 231.
  Olympic, 66.
  Opera Comique, 67.

Theatres (Modern)—*continued.*
  Park, 275.
  Philharmonic, 234.
  Prince of Wales's, 175.
  Princess's, 171.
  Royalty, 172.
  St. James's, 132.
  Sadler's Wells, 235.
  Strand, 67.
  Sanger's (late Astley's), 47.
  Surrey, 246.
  Vaudeville, 53.
  Victoria, 48.
Theatres (Old)—
  Bankside, 259.
  Blackfriars, 83.
  Curtain, 231.
  Duke's, 190.
  Red Bull, 204.
  Whitefriars, 80.
Thistlewood, 169.
Thrale, Mrs., 291.
Threadneedle Street, 221.
Throgmorton, Sir Nicholas, 228.
Thumb, Tom, 147.
Thurtell, 66.
Tilbury Fort, 291.
Tilt Yard (Old), 25, 124.
Times Newspaper, 85.
Tokenhouse Yard, 227.
Tom's Coffee House, 57.
Tooley Street, 240.
———————, Three Tailors of, 240.
Tooting, 291.
Tothill Fields, 126.
Tottenham, 291.
——— Cross, 291.
——— Court Road, 174.
Tower, The, 99.
  Barracks, 106.
  Beauchamp Tower, 102.
  Bell Tower, 102.
  Bloody Tower, 102.
  Bowyer Tower, 103.
  Byward Tower, 101.
  Council Room, 102.
  Devereux Tower, 103.
  Horse Armoury, 104.
  Jewel or Martin Tower, 103.
  Middle Tower, 101.

xxiv   *Index.*

Tower—*continued.*
   Queen Elizabeth's Armoury, 102.
   Regalia Tower, 105.
   Salt Tower, 103.
   St. John's Chapel, 102.
   St. Peter's ad Vincula, 107.
   Traitor's Gate, 101.
   Wakefield Tower, 102.
   White Tower, 102.
Tower Hamlets, 6.
—— Hill, 97.
——————, Scaffold on, 97.
—— Royal, 94.
—— Subway, 263.
Toxophilite Society, 131.
Trafalgar Square, 8, 9.
———————— Fountains, 8.
Treasury, 26.
Trinity House, 114.
Turkish Baths, 135.
Turnham Green, 275.
Turnpike Gates abolished, 247.
Turnstile, Great, 187.
Tussaud, Madame, 168.
Twickenham, 292.
————, Orleans Club, 292.
————, Pope's Villa, 292.
————, Strawberry Hill, 292.
Tyburn Lane, 165.
—— Tree, 165.
Tyler, Wat, 200, 214, 239.

UNDERGROUND Railway, 303.
Unitarian Chapels, 69, 298.
United Service Museum, 25.
University Boat Race, 288.
—————— College, 177.
—————— School, 177.
—————— Hospital, 177.
—————— of London, 145.
Uxbridge, 292.
—————— Road, 167.

VAUXHALL, 253.
—————— Bridge, 253.
—————— Bridge Road, 126.
——————————— Tramway, 314.
—————— Gardens, 254.
Vere Street, 170.
—————— Chapel, 170.

Veterinary College, 275.
Vicar of Bray, 220.
Victoria Docks, 267.
—————— Embankment, 257.
—————— Park, 273.
—————— Railway Stations, 40, 126.
—————— Street, 40, 126, 258.
—————— Tower, 43.
Vigo Street, 128.
Villiers Street, 51, 52.
Vine Street Police Station, 141.
Vintners' Company, 258.
Virginia Water, 295.
Voltaire, 56.

WALBROOK, 221.
Walham Green, 292.
Wallace, Sir Richard, 169.
————, Sir William, 200.
Wallingford House, 20.
Walthamstow, 292.
Walworth, 292.
————, Sir W., 238.
Wandsworth, 292.
Wapping, 265.
————, Judge Jeffreys at, 113.
———— Old Stairs, 266.
War Office, 120.
Ware, 282.
Warwick Lane, 206.
Watch-face, Story of, 64.
Watchmen, Old, 21.
Watergate, 51.
Waterloo Banquet, 152.
—————— Bridge, 62.
—————— House, 117.
—————— Place, 127.
—————— Railway Terminus, 62.
—————— Road, 62.
Watling Street, 94.
Watts, Dr. Isaac, 233.
Waxworks, Madame Tussaud, 168.
——————, Mrs. Salmon, 77.
Weighhouse Chapel, 115.
Wellington Barracks, 106, 124.
——————, Duke of, in bed, 152.
——————, at his Club, 118.
——————, Tomb of, 91.
—————— Street, Strand, 61.
Welsh Harp, 286.

Wesley, Charles, 233.
———, John, 233.
———, Mrs. S., 232.
West India Docks, 267.
Westminster, 28.
——————— Abbey, 31.
——————————Chapter House, 33.
———————————, Jerusalem Chamber, 39.
———————————, Poets' Corner, 33.
————————— Almonry, 29.
————————— Aquarium (Royal), 40.
—————————, Big Ben, 42.
————————— Bridge, 46.
———————————— Road, 47.
———————————— Steamboat Pier, 257.
——————————— Railway Station, 257.
—————————, Dean's Yard, 39.
—————————, Great Tom, 43.
————————— Hall, 41.
————————— Hospital, 28.
————————— Palace Yard (New), 40.
————————————— (Old), 40.
————————— Pillory, 41.
—————————, Queen Anne's Mansions, 40.
————————— Sanctuary, 28.
————————— School, 39.
——————————————— Memorial, 39.
—————————, St. Stephen's Hall, 43.
————————— Sessions House, 28.
—————————, Victoria Clock Tower, 42.
Whitcomb Street, 17, 116.
Whitebait Dinners, 269.
Whitechapel, 229.
Whitefriars, 80.
——————— Theatre, 80.
Whitehall, 22.
————, Henry VIII. at, 22.
————, Charles I. at, 23.
———————— II. at, 24.
————, Cromwell at, 23.
————, James II. at, 24.
————, Destruction of, 24.
————, Chapel Royal, 25.
———— Gardens, 27.

Whitehall Street, 151.
" White Milliner," 53.
Whitfield's Tabernacle, 175.
Whittington's Almshouses, 236.
————————— and Bow Bells, 216.
Wigmore Street, 170.
Wills and Probate Office, 63.
Willis's Rooms, 133.
Will's Coffee-house, 57.
Wimbledon, 292.
Winchester House, 227.
——————— (Great), Street, 227.
Windmill (Great), Street, 139.
Windsor, 292.
————, Albert Chapel, 293.
———— Castle, 293.
————, Home Park, 294.
————, Herne's Oak, 295.
————, Long Walk, 294.
————, St. George's Chapel, 293.
———— Castle Stables, 294.
Wits' Coffee-house, 58.
Woking Cemetery, 295.
————— Royal Dramatic College, 295.
Woodbridge Street, 204.
Wood Street, 215.
—————, Compter, 215.
Woolwich, 269.
————— (North), Gardens, 270.
Woolwich Arsenal, 269.
—————, Royal Artillery Barracks, 269.
————————— Dockyard, 269.
————— Steamboat Pier, 270.
————— Royal Military Repository, 270.
Wormwood Scrubs, 296.
Wren, Sir Christopher, 88.
—————————————, his Trowel and Mallet, 88.
Wren, Sir Christopher, his Grave, 91.
—————————————, Macaulay's praise of, 88.
Wyat, Sir Thomas, 84.
Wych Street, 66.

YORK's, Duke of, Column, 124.
———————————, School, 251.
York House, 51.
——— Stairs, Water-Gate, 51.

ZOOLOGICAL Gardens, 131.

THE GRAND HOTEL, TRAFALGAR SQUARE
(On the Site of the former Northumberland House).
THE VERY CENTRE OF LONDON.

This magnificent Hotel will be completed early next year (1880), to comprise the most important and attractive features of the great Continental and American Hotels, with a home-like comfort and repose, which will be its special characteristic.

LONDON IN 1880.

"I have seen the greatest wonder which the world can show to the astonished spirit. I have seen it, and am still astonished,—and ever will there remain fixed indelibly on my memory the stone forest of houses, amid which flows the rushing stream of faces of living men with all their varied passions, and all their terrible impulses of love, of hunger, and of hatred,—I mean London."—HEINRICH HEINE.

ACCORDING to Herschel, the great astronomer, London is the centre of the terrestrial globe; we know it to be the centre of commerce, of wealth, of intellectual and moral life. As "all roads led to Rome," when she was mistress of the world, so now every thinker and worker, every artist, every inventor, seems to turn to London, and find his best home or market here, where the multitudinous transactions of mankind are concentrated and carried on. In this vast metropolis there are to be seen individuals, families, tribes of pretty nearly every race on the habitable globe, of nearly every tongue and dialect, of every colour and complexion, of every creed, religion, persuasion, and opinion—howsoever eccentric. We can say of London, more truly than Gibbon could claim for pagan Rome, that she is the centre of religious toleration, the common temple of the world. The freedom of our city is bestowed on all the gods of mankind, and without preference for race or creed we adopt virtue and merit, whether in ourselves or strangers. Each of our millions of denizens is fulfilling, or supposed to be fulfilling, some duty or errand, following some calling, or learning to follow it. The idlers, who, whether from predilection or obligation, take no share in the work of London, have their marked characteristics, the beggars theirs, and the thieves also. Of the thousands who rise in the morning knowing not how they are going to earn a breakfast, nor where they shall lay their heads at night, it may be said that a large proportion would certainly starve anywhere but in this amazing metropolis, where the crumbs which fall from so many hundreds of thousands of tables are to be picked up by those who are on the alert to watch for them, and to benefit themselves by the habits, foibles, vices, fortunes and misfortunes of their neighbours. The city sparrow, who lives upon the unregarded refuse of the streets, fattens beneath his smoke-begrimed feathers; and in like manner does many a crossing-sweeper in London earn more and thrive better than a labourer in the country.

The history of the world can show us no such city as London. For better for worse it is unparalleled. Its statistics are all upon such a gigantic scale that if they were related of some remote and foreign place we should stand amazed at the revelation of them. Even figures can scarcely convey to the mind the full meaning of London facts, until they are aided by comparison or contrast. As, for instance, in the matter of population. This enormous collection of human beings was estimated by the Registrar-General in 1876 as amounting, within the Metropolitan area, to 3,489,428; and within the 15-mile radius to 4,200,000 souls. In 1878 the number had increased to 4,500,000. If we take the population statistics of other great cities we shall find that the greatest city contains less than half the above number, and the others are far behind.

In 1876 the population of Paris was	. . . .	1,851,792
,,	,,	New York and Brooklyn	1,496,000
,,	,,	Berlin	980,000
,,	,,	Vienna	676,000

Every year the increase continues—London adds annually to her population 75,000 persons—equal to all the inhabitants of some large provincial towns—nearly as many as all Huddersfield, more than all Wolverhampton. In London there have been reckoned more Roman Catholics than in Rome, more Jews than in all Palestine, more Scotchmen than in Aberdeen, more Welshmen than in Cardiff, more Irishmen than in Belfast. Six hundred thousand persons daily enter and leave the comparatively small area (632 acres) of the City of London proper, where every inch of ground is ardently contended for, and where recently (in Lombard Street) land fetched a price equal to two millions an acre. Besides the numerous railways which pour into London the produce and the fuel from all quarters of the kingdom, this great city is supplied by a fleet of 1000 colliers, manned by 10,000 seamen. The London Custom House Dues equal those of all the other places in the kingdom. Liverpool is a great port, scarcely to be paralleled elsewhere, and its Custom Dues are between two and three millions sterling per annum; but London Custom House Dues for the same period amount to twelve millions. The total rateable annual value of the parishes and districts comprised within the Metropolitan area doubled itself in the twenty years ending 1876, when it had reached £23,111,313. We continue to increase, and at an accelerated pace, for during 1877 there were built 14,410 new houses, 270 new streets, and two new squares. London has been computed to cover an area of 122 square miles. Its 7400 streets, placed end to end, would extend to 2600 miles; its 1100 churches and chapels would not hold a tithe of its inhabitants. They require and occupy 528,798 dwelling-houses; their refreshment is provided for by 7500 public-houses and 1700 coffee-houses; they consume annually 2 million quarters of wheat, 400,000 oxen, 1½ million of sheep, 130,000 calves, 250,000 pigs, 8 million head of poultry and game, and 400 million

pounds of fish. Their drinking is upon the same vast scale
180 million quarts of malt liquor, 31 million quarts of wine
18 million quarts of spirits. A million gas-lamps light Lon
don streets, and 6½ million tons of coal are needed annuall
for warmth, for cookery, &c. The omnibus and cab traffic c
London is upon the same scale. The number of passenger
carried by the London General Omnibus Company (wh
have not all the omnibuses) was last half-year about 2
millions. The Company possess 580 omnibuses, each earn
ing on an average over £18 per week, at an average far
of 2½d. each passenger, over a distance of 6,132,707 miles
The Cabmen of London are upwards of ten thousand, an
earn between 3 and 4 millions per annum. To protect th
millions of human beings and their untold millions c
property, London employs a comparatively small number c
guards. The Metropolitan Police, at the end of 187?
numbered only 10,446, consisting of 25 superintendent
279 inspectors, 1078 sergeants, and 9064 constables, costin
about a million per annum. To these must be added th
City Police Force, which costs about £100,000 per annum
The Police Commissioners' Report mentions that ther
were 65 adults and 23 children lost and missing in 1877
of whose fate nothing had been learnt; but these were bu
the remnants of a total of 8483 lost children, and 321
adults, all the others having been found. The vice an
crime of London are, unfortunately, in proportion to it
size and wealth ; the crime generally amounts to one-thir
of all the crime in the kingdom. Its places of Amusemen
are numerous and varied, including about 40 Theatres an
over 400 Music-halls, Concert-rooms, Harmonic Meeting
nightly entertaining 302,000 persons. Its expenditure o
Public Improvements has of late years been considerable
Since 1856, when the Metropolitan Board of Works wa
first established, the Board has raised, and spent, nearl
21 millions sterling ; while the Corporation of London ha
contributed also immense sums for the same purpose. Th

Metropolitan School Board has had, of course, an enormous work to do, and it has spent millions in but half a dozen years. The results of all this expenditure are gradually developing themselves. The abodes of vice and crime and dirt are being cleansed or rebuilt; the inconvenient, narrow and crooked thoroughfares, choked with an ever increasing traffic, have been enlarged; and new streets opened up, so that, in many quarters of Town, the features of but twenty years ago have been so altered and improved that it would be difficult for any one so long absent from London to understand, at a first glance, the character of the metamorphosis.

If we desire to trace the history of this microcosm (it is not merely a dozen cities rolled into one), we shall have to go back to before the Roman era. There was a town here before the Romans came, which the Britons knew as Caer-Ludd, or the City of Lud. The present name is derived from the Latin *Londinium*, mentioned by Tacitus as "a city not indeed dignified by the title of a colony, but frequented by a large number of merchants, and by many ships entering its port." The Romans built the old City Walls and Forts, and fixed the position of the City Gates. They made Watling Street, the great highway from south to north; they reared fine buildings, and brought the civilization of the world to London; but when they retired, after nearly five hundred years' occupation, they seem to have left behind them no adequate impression upon the people. The Anglo-Saxons were but barbarians, compared with the Roman legions, and they destroyed, or left to decay, the structures which were the legacy of Rome. William the Conqueror brought with him the arts and sciences which the Normans had acquired in the South of Europe, and from his time began a new era of improvement. He built the White Tower, and granted a Charter to the Corporation of the City of London, which secured and enlarged old privileges, afterwards still further strengthened by the Great Charter. In all the history of England, London is to be seen, as of course, occupying a prominent place; and it is not too much to say that her influence has been almost always exercised beneficially for the public weal. London has ever appeared foremost of the champions for liberty and progress, and in every good work among the suffering populations of the world. Let her immense and numerous charities witness for her both at home and abroad. She neither forgets the poor, the sick, the helpless at her gates; nor does she hesitate to bestow her thousands—even her hundreds of thousands—upon the famine-stricken natives of India and China, or upon the helpless and suffering people ruined by European wars. But that we must not overweight these pages with statistics, it would be a useful task to furnish a summary of the Religious, the Educational, and the Sanitary labours of London; to tell of her pauperism, and her sickness, by the side of her wealth and her improving healthiness; but this is beyond our present function. Let us note, however, that, politically, London is scarcely so powerful as her numbers entitle her to be. The *City of London* sends four Members to Parliament; the *City of Westminster*, only two Members; the Metropolitan Boroughs, viz., Marylebone, Finsbury, Tower Hamlets, Hackney, Chelsea, Southwark, Lambeth, and Greenwich, return two Members each. Of other topics we shall proceed to speak as they transpire in the course of our wanderings through the Streets of London.

By way of beginning, we select *Charing Cross* as a starting-point, inasmuch as we believe that this will be found most convenient to the greater number of those Visitors to London who can spare time and can take interest in the sights and scenes of to-day, as well as in the memories and the relics of this ancient and historical Metropolis.

CHARING CROSS AND STATUE OF CHARLES I.

CHARING CROSS derives its name from a Cross erected here (1291-94), in the village of Charing, by Edward I. in memory of his wife Eleanor. "Wherever," it is said, "Eleanor's corpse rested on its transit from Grantham to Westminster Abbey, Edward erected a cross in memory of her." A stone cross, from the design of Cavalini, subsequently replaced the original wooden one, and lasted till 1647, when it was demolished, by order of the Long Parliament. The site was next used as a place of execution. On this spot, before King Charles's Statue was erected upon it, were executed, Hugh Peters, chaplain of Oliver Cromwell; Jones, Scrope, Harrison, and many others of the regicides. *Charing Cross Pillory* was among the most famous, or infamous, of the many that formerly stood in London. The Pillory was a wooden frame fixed upon a scaffold, and so arranged that the offender's head and hands were held fast, and he was thus publicly exhibited. The use of the Pillory in this kingdom was abolished by Parliament in June 1837. The *Statue of Charles I.* was cast by Le Sœur, for the Earl of Arundel, in 1633; the pedestal was by Grinling Gibbons, but the statue was not erected at Charing Cross until 1674. "The sovereign now faces Whitehall, as in triumph, yet, behind the Banqueting-house, lurks a statue of another of this unfortunate race who lost his throne for attempting to renew the dictatorial spirit which cost his ancestor his head."

Ben Jonson was born in Hartshorn Alley, Charing Cross, near Northumberland Street, Strand; he was a scholar in St. Martin's Court, and afterwards of Westminster School.

TRAFALGAR SQUARE, NATIONAL GALLERY, AND LEICESTER SQUARE.

UPON the site now occupied by Trafalgar Square—pronounced by Chantrey to be " the most favourable that could be found or imagined for any national work of art," and by Sir Robert Peel, "one of the finest sites in Europe"—stood, three hundred years ago, but a few small houses, which formed part of the Village of *Charing*. On the northern side of Trafalgar Square, where the National Gallery now stands, the *King's Mews* were situated, from the time of Edward I. In the reign of Richard II., Sir Simon Burley kept the King's Falcons at Charing Cross; and Geoffrey Chaucer, our first English poet, was "Clerk of the King's works and the Mews at Charing." In the reign of Henry VIII. the Mews were converted into stables, and in 1732 the stables were rebuilt, but they were subsequently altogether removed, in order to make room for the erection of the *National Gallery*, by W. Wilkins, R.A., in 1834-38, at a cost of £96,000. At the bottom of the present St. Martin's Lane were the squalid courts and rookeries mentioned in the literature of Ben Jonson's times, as the "*Bermudas*" and "*Caribbees*," and, in Dr. Johnson's era, known as *Porridge Island*.

The *Fountains, &c., in Trafalgar Square*, were designed by Sir Charles Barry. The water is supplied from two Artesian wells; one in *Orange Street*, Leicester Square, 300 feet deep, and the other in front of the National Gallery, 395 feet deep, connected at the depth of 170 feet by a tunnel,—to contain 70,000 gallons. Water is spouted from these fountains thirteen hours a day in summer, and seven hours in winter; the height of the jets varies with the weather, from

The Nelson Column.

25 to 40 feet from the ground, at the rate of 500 gallons a minute.

TRAFALGAR SQUARE (named in honour of Nelson's last victory, which destroyed the French and Spanish fleets, and effectually put an end to Napoleon's intended invasion of England) was planned by Barry, upon the site of the yard of the old Royal Mews. The *Nelson Column*, erected on the south of the Square by public subscription, aided by the Government, was designed by Mr. Railton. It is said to be of the exact proportion of a column of the Corinthian Temple of Mars Ultor at Rome. It is of Portland stone, 145 feet in height, and was erected 1840-43. Upon a circular pedestal on the *abacus* is a colossal statue of Nelson, 17 feet high, with a coiled cable on his left, sculptured by E. H. Bailey, R.A. The figure was carved out of three massive stones, of which the largest weighed thirty tons; the capital of the column is of bronze obtained from cannon captured by Nelson. The pedestal has upon its four sides the following bronze reliefs: *North* (facing the National Gallery), *Battle of the Nile*, designed by W. T. Woodington. Nelson, wounded in the head, is being carried by Captain Berry into the cockpit, the surgeon is about to quit a wounded sailor to attend upon him. "No," said Nelson, "I will take my turn with my brave fellows." *South* (facing Whitehall), *Death of Nelson at Trafalgar*, designed by C. E. Carew. Nelson is being carried from the quarter-deck by a marine and two seamen. "Well, Hardy," said Nelson to his captain, "they have done for me at last." "I hope not," was the reply. "Yes, they have shot me through the backbone." Beneath the relief: "England expects every man will do his duty." *East*, (facing the Strand), *Bombardment of Copenhagen*, designed by Mr. Ternouth. Nelson is seen sealing his dispatch to send it by a flag of truce; in the foreground are the wounded, in the distance Copenhagen in flames. *West* (facing Pall Mall), *Battle of St. Vincent*, by Watson. Nelson is seen on board the San Josef receiving the swords of the Spanish admirals, which an old man-of-war's-man carries off under his arm. Four lions in bronze, designed by Sir Edwin Landseer assisted by Baron Marochetti, guard the foot of this national memorial to her greatest naval hero. Upon either side of the Nelson Column are to be seen Statues to our military commanders,—*Sir Charles Napier* and *Sir Henry Havelock;* and at the north-east corner of the Square is the equestrian statue of *George IV.*, by Sir Francis Chantrey.

The west side of Trafalgar Square is occupied by the *Union Club*, built (1824) from designs by Sir R. Smirke, R.A., as was also the ROYAL COLLEGE OF PHYSICIANS adjoining to it. This College was founded in 1518 by Linacre (physician to Henry VII. and VIII., and the friend of Erasmus, Latimer, and Sir Thomas More), and was removed hither in 1825 from Warwick Lane, Newgate Market. An order for admission to the College of Physicians may be obtained from any Fellow; i.e., from any eminent London Physician. There are many interesting and valuable portraits and relics of ancient and honoured members of the medical profession to be seen here. At the south-east corner of Trafalgar Square, and immediately over Charing Cross Post Office, stands the well-known *Morley's Hotel;* a little higher up (No. 4) is the Office of the *Royal Humane Society;* and at the north-east corner is the handsome *Church of St. Martin's-in-the-Fields.* This edifice (occupying the site of a smaller church built here by Henry VIII.) was completed in 1726, from the designs of Gibbs. George I. laid, by proxy, the foundation stone, and presented this, the Royal parish, with its organ. St. Martin's Church is built in the florid Roman or Italian style, and has a very fine western Corinthian hexastyle portico. The east end is truly elegant. In the Registry of this church were entered the births of Royal children born at Buckingham Palace, which is within this parish.

Farquhar, the dramatist; Roubiliac, the sculptor; the Hon. Robert Boyle; John Hunter, the surgeon; Nell Gwynne, and Jack Sheppard, were buried here.

THE NATIONAL GALLERY

Occupies the north side of Trafalgar Square, and has a frontage of 500 feet, in the centre of which is a portico with eight columns of the Corinthian order, which were removed hither from Carlton House, when that residence of the Prince Regent was taken down. The Entrance to the Gallery is by a flight of steps at each side of the portico, and the whole building is surmounted by a dome; but the edifice is altogether too low, in comparison with the buildings near it, and it is considered unworthy of the great national purpose for which it is maintained. The Gallery is open to the public on Mondays, Tuesdays, Wednesdays, and Saturdays, and on Thursdays and Fridays to students only. The hours are ten to five, or dusk, from October until April 30 inclusive, and from ten to six, from April until the middle of September. The Rooms are wholly closed during October. The National Gallery dates its origin from the purchase, by Lord Liverpool's Government in 1824, of the Collection of thirty-eight pictures, of the late J. J. Angerstein, Esq., for £57,000,—Parliament having granted £3000 beyond that sum, to include expenses. The first exhibition took place in Mr. Angerstein's house, in Pall Mall, May 10, 1824. Sir George Beaumont bequeathed sixteen pictures to the National Collection in 1826; the Rev. W. Holwell Carr bequeathed thirty-five pictures to it in 1831; William IV. presented six, in 1836; Lord Farnborough bequeathed fifteen, in 1838; Richard Simmons, Esq., bequeathed eleven, in 1846. Up to this date, the National Gallery contained only forty-one pictures of the British School, but, in 1847, Robert Vernon, Esq., gave one hundred and fifty-seven, all but two of which were of the

British School. In 1854, Lord Colborne bequeathed eight pictures; in 1856 the Collection was enriched by one hundred finished oil pictures, and some thousand drawings and sketches, bequeathed by J. M. W. Turner, R.A.; Jacob Bell, Esq., bequeathed twenty pictures, in 1859; the Queen presented twenty-two, in 1863. In 1871 the Cabinet Collection, chiefly of Dutch Masters, made by the first Sir Robert Peel, was purchased for £75,000. In 1875 Mr. Wynn Ellis bequeathed to this Collection about one hundred and fifty of his finest pictures. Of the entire number of one thousand and thirty works in this Gallery, three hundred and eighty-seven have been purchased by the Nation, at a total cost, to the end of 1876, of £356,013. The Gallery, since the removal of the Royal Academy to Burlington House in 1869, extends throughout the building and contains eighteen rooms, of which Nos. I., II., III., V., VII. and VIII. contain pictures of the *British School* of Painting; IV. and VI. contain the *Turner* Collection; in IX. are works of the *French School;* X., XIII., XIV. and XVII. of the *Italian School;* XI. the *Wynn Ellis* gift; XII. the *Dutch and Flemish;* XV. a select cabinet collection; XVI. the *Peel* Collection; XVIII. the *Spanish School.* The names of the painters and of the subjects appear upon the frames of the pictures.

The following is a list of the Masters represented in the National Gallery, with the number of their works as given in the catalogue. The hyphens between the figures indicate that the intermediate numbers are included.

BRITISH SCHOOL.

Allan, Sir W., R.A., 373.
Armitage, E., R.A., 759.
Barker, Thos., 792.
Beaumont, Sir G. H., 105, 119.
Beechey, Sir W., R.A., 120.
Bird, E., R.A., 323.
Bonheur, Rosa, 621.
Bonington, R. P., 374.
Boxall, Sir W., R.A., 601.
Briggs, H. P., R.A., 375, 376.
Calcott, Sir A. W., R.A., 340-348.
Clays, P. J., 814, 815.
Clint, Geo., 377.
Collins, W., R.A., 351, 352.

Constable, John, R.A., 130, 327.
Cooke, E. W., R.A., 447, 448.
Cooper, T. S., R.A., 435, 436.
Copley, J. S., R.A., 100, 733, 787.
Creswick, T., R.A., 429.
Crome, John (Old Crome), 689, 897, 926.
Cruikshank, G., 795.
Danby, F., A.R.A., 437.
Daniell, T., R.A., 899.
Douglas, W., R.S.A., 617.
Dubufe, C. M., 457.
Dyckmans, J. L., 660.
Eastlake, Sir C. L., P.R.A., 397-399, 898.
Egg, A. L., R.A., 444.
Etty, W., R.A., 356-366, 614.
Fraser, Alex., 453.
Frith, W. P., R.A., 615.
Gainsborough, T., R.A., 80, 109, 308-311, 678, 683, 684, 760, 789, 925.
Geddes, Andrew, A.R.A., 355.
Good, T. S., 378, 917-919.
Goodall, F., R.A., 450, 451.
Gordon, Sir J. W., R.A., 743.
Haghe, Louis, 456.
Hart, Solomon A., R.A., 424.
Haydon, Benjamin R., 682, 786.
Herbert, J. R., R.A., 425.
Herring, John F., 452.
Hilton, William, R.A., 178, 333-338.
Hogarth, William, 112-118, 675.
Hoppner, John, R.A., 133, 233, 900.
Horsley, J. C., R.A., 446.
Howard, H., R.A., 349.
Huysman, J., 125.
Jackson, John, R.A., 124, 171, 326.
Johnston, Alex., 449.
Jones, Geo., R.A., 389-392, 800, 801.

Kaufmann, A., R.A., 139.
Kneller, Sir Godfrey, 273.
Lance, Geo., 441-443.
Landseer, Chas., R.A., 408, 610, 612.
Landseer, Sir E., R.A., 409-415, 603-609.
Lane, T., 440.
Lawrence, Sir T., P.R.A., 129, 136, 142, 144, 188, 324, 325, 785, 922.
Lee, Fredk. R., R.A., 418, 419, and Cooper, 619, 620.
Leslie, C. R., R.A., 402, 403.
Linnell, John, 438, 439.
Linton, William, 1029.
Loutherbourg, P. J., R.A., 316.
Maclise, D., 422, 423.
Martin, John, 793.
Morland, Geo., 1030.
Müller, W. J., 379.
Mulready, W., R.A., 393-396.
Nasmyth, Patrick, 380, 381.
Newton, G. S., R.A., 353, 354.
O'Neill, G. B., 618.
Opie, John, R.A., 784, 1026.
Phillips, Thomas, R.A., 183, 339.
Pickersgill, F. R., R.A., 445.
Pickersgill, H. W., R.A., 416, 417, 791.
Poussin, Charles, 810.
Redgrave, R., R.A., 428.
Reynolds, Sir J., P.R.A., 78, 79, 106, 107, 111, 128, 143, 162, 182, 185, 305-307, 681, 754, 885-892.
Rippingille, E. V., 454, 455.
Roberts, David, R.A., 400, 401.
Romney, Geo., 312.
Scott, Samuel, 313, 314.
Seddon, Thos., 563.
Shee, Sir M. A., P.R.A., 367, 368, 677.
Simpson, 382.
Singleton, H., 1027, 1028.

Sleap, J. A., 676.
Smirke, Robt., R.A., 761–765.
Stanfield, Clarkson, R.A., 404–407
Stothard, Thos., R.A., 317–322.
Stuart, Gilbert, 217, 220, 229.
Thomson, H., R.A., 350.
Thomson, Rev. J., 731.
Tschaggeny, C. P., 738.
Turner, J. W. M., R.A., 369–372, 458–562, 813.
Uwins, Thomas, R.A., 387, 388, 730.
Ward, E. M., R.A., 430–432, 616.
Ward, James, R.A., 385, 386, 688.

Webster, Thos., R.A., 426, 427.
West, Benjamin, P.R.A., 121, 126, 131, 132, 315. 799.
Wilkie, David, R.A., 99, 122, 231, 241, 328–332, 894, 921.
Williams, Edward, 123.
Williams, Penry, 433, 434, 662.
Wilson, Richard, R.A., 108, 110, 267, 301–304.
Witherington, W. F., R.A., 420, 421.
Wright, J., of Derby, 725.
Wyatt, Henry, 383, 384.

FOREIGN SCHOOLS.

Albertinelli, 645.
Allori, 21.
Alunno, 247.
Angelico, Fra G., 582, 663.
Bakhuizen, 204, 223, 818, 819, 1000.
Barocci, 29.
Basaiti, 281, 599.
Bassano, J., 173, 228, 277.
Bellini, 189, 280, 726, 808, 812, 694, 234, school of.
Beltraffio, 728.
Benvenuto, 909.
Berchem, 240, 820, 1005, 1006.
Bibiena, 936.
Bissolo, 631.
Bles, De, 718, 719.
Boccaccino, 806.
Bol, 679.
Bono, 771.
Bonsignori, 736.
Bordone, 637, 674.
Borgognone, 298, 779, 780.
Both, 71, 209, 956–959.
Botticelli, 226, 275, 782, 915, 916.

Bourdon, 64.
Bouts, 783.
Bramantino, 729.
Bronzino, 650, 651, 670, 704.
Canaletto, 127, 163, 937–942.
Caravaggio, 172.
Carnovale, Fra, 769.
Carpaccio, 750.
Carracci, Agostino, 147, 148.
Carracci, Annibale, 9, 25, 56, 63, 88, 93, 94, 198.
Carracci, Ludovico, 28.
Casentino, Jacopo di, 580.
Champaigne, 798.
Cima da Conegliano, 300, 634, 816.
Cimabue, 565.
Claude de Lorraine, 2, 5, 12, 14, 19, 55, 58, 61, 1018.
Clouet, 662.
Coques, 821, 1011.
Cornelissen, 657.
Correggio, 7, 10, 15, 23, 37, 76.
Costa, 629, 895.
Cranach, 291.

Credi, 593, 648.
Crivelli, 602, 668, 724, 739, 788, 807, 906, 907.
Cuyp, 53, 797, 822-824, 960-962.
Dalmasio, 752.
De Hooge, 794, 834, 835.
De Keyser, 212.
De Koning, 836, 974.
Dietrich, 205.
Dolci, Carlo, 934.
Domenichino, 48, 75, 77, 85.
Dossi, 640.
Dou, Gerard, 192, 825, 968.
Duccio, 566.
Dujardin, 826-828, 985.
Dürer, Albert, 245.
Dyckmans, 600.
Elzheimer, 1014.
Emmanuel, 594.
Engelbertz, 714.
Ercole da Ferrara, 73.
Forli, M. da, 755, 756.
Francia, 179, 180, 638.
Fyt, 1003.
Gaddi (School of), 215, 216, 579.
Garofalo, 81, 170, 642, 671.
Giolfino, 749.
Giorgione, 41, 269.
   Ditto (School of), 930.
Giotto, 276.
   Ditto (School of), 568.
Gozzoli, 283, 591.
Greuze, 206, 1019, 1020.
Guardi, 210.
Guercino, 22.
Guido, 11, 177, 191, 193, 196, 214, 271.
Hackaert, 829.
Hals, 1021.
Hobbema, 685, 830-833, 995, 996.

Holbein, 772.
Hondecoeter, 202, 1013.
Huchtenburg, 211.
Huysman, C., 954.
Huysman, J., 125.
Justus of Padua, 701.
Kneller, Sir G., 273.
Lancret, N., 101-104.
Lanini, 700.
Lely, Sir P., 1016.
Libri, G., 748.
Liesborn, von, 260, 261.
L'Ingegno, 702.
Lingelbach, J., 837.
Lippi, Filippino, 293, 592, 598, 927.
Lippi, Fra F., 248, 586, 589, 666, 667.
Lochner, S., 705.
Lombard, L., 266.
Looten, Jan, 901.
L'Ortolano, 669.
Lotto, 699.
Maas or Maes, N., 153, 159, 207.
Mabuse, J. de, 656, 946.
Mantegna, A., 274, 902.
Mantegna, F., 639.
Maratti, C., 174.
Margaritone, 564.
Marziale, M., 803, 804.
Masaccio, 626.
*Master of Cologne, 707.
Master of Lyversberg, 706.
Matsys, Q., 295, 944.
Mazzolini, L., 82, 169, 641.
Melone, A., 753.
Memling or Hemling, 686, 709, 747, 943.
Messina, A. de, 673.
Metsu, G., 838, 839, 970.

---

* An anonymous artist, said to have been a pupil of Albert Dürer.

Michel Angelo, 8, 790, 809.
Mieris, F. van, 840.
Mieris, W. van, 841.
Mola, 69, 160.
Montagna, B., 802.
Morando, P., 735, 777.
Moretto, Il, 299, 625, 1025.
Moro, A., 184.
Morone, F., 285.
Moroni, G., 697, 742, 1022-1024.
Mostert, J., 713.
Moucheron, F. de, 842.
Murillo, B. E., 13, 74, 176.
Neefs, P., 924.
Netscher, G., 843-845.
Orcagna, A. di C., 569, 570-578.
Oriolo, G., 770.
Ostade, A. J. van, 846.
Ostade, I. van, 847, 848, 963.
Pacchiarotto, J., 246.
Padovanino, 70, 933.
Palmezzano, 596.
Pannini, 138.
Parma, L. da, 692.
Parmigiano, 33.
Patinir, J. de, 715-717, 945.
Perugino, Il, 181, 288.
Peruzzi, B., 167, 218.
Pesellino, F., 727.
Piero della Francesca, 585, 665, 758, 908.
Piero di Cosimo, 698.
Pinturicchio, B. di, 693, 703, 911-914.
Pisano of Verona, 776.
Poelenburg, 955.
Pollajuolo, A., 292, 296, 781, 928.
Pontormo, J. da, 649.
Pordenone, Il, 272.
Potter, Paul, 849, 1009.
Potter, Peter, 1008.
Poussin, C., 810.
Poussin, G., 31, 36, 68, 95, 98, 161.

Poussin, N., 39, 40, 42, 62, 65, 91, 165.
Previtali, A., 695.
Raphael or Raffaello, 213, 168, 27, 661, 744, 929.
Rembrandt, H., 43, 45, 47, 51, 54, 72, 166, 190, 221, 237, 243, 289, 672, 757, 775, 850.
Ricci or Rizzi, S., 851.
Rigaud, H., 903.
Romanino, G., 297.
Romano, G., 225, 624, 643, 644.
Rosa, Salvator, 84, 811, 935.
Rosselli, C., 227.
Rottenhammer, J., 659.
Rubens, P. P., 38, 46, 57, 59, 66, 67, 157, 187, 194, 278, 279, 852, 853, 948.
Ruysdael, J., 627, 628, 737, 746, 854, 855, 986-991.
Salviati, 652.
San Daniele, 778.
San Severino, 249.
Santa Croce, 632, 633.
Santi, G., 751.
Sarto, A. del, 17, 690.
Sassoferrato, 200, 740.
Savery, R., 920.
Schalken, G., 199, 997-999.
Schiavone, G., 630, 904.
Schoen, M., 658.
Schoorel, J. Van, 720, 721.
Sebastiano del P., 1, 20, 24.
Segna, 567.
Signorelli, 910.
Solario, A. da, 734, 923.
Spagna, Lo, 282, 691.
Spagnoletto, Lo, 235, 244.
Spinello Aretino, 581.
Steen, Jan., 856.
Tacconi, F., 286.
Teniers, D. (the elder), 949, 950, 951.

The National Gallery. 17

Teniers, D. (the younger), 154, 155, 158, 242, 805, 817, 857–863, 952, 953.
Terburg, G., 864, 896.
Tintoretto, 16.
Titian, 3, 4, 32, 34, 35, 224, 270, 635, 636.
Treviso, G. da, 623.
Tura, C., 590, 772, 773, 905.
Uccello, P., 583.
Unknown, 195, 932, 947, 1012, 1017.
Van Deelen, D., 1010.
Van der Cappelle, 365, 964–967.
Van der Goes, 710, 774.
Van der Helst, B., 140.
Van der Heyde, J., 866, 992–994.
Van der Meire, G., 264, 696.
Van der Neer, A., 152, 239, 732, 969.
Van der Plaas, 175.
Van der Weyden, R., 664.
Van der Weyden, R. (younger), 653, 654, 711, 712.
Van de Velde, A., 867–869, 982–984.
Van de Velde, W. (younger), 149, 150, 870–876, 977–981.

Vandyck, A., 49, 50, 52, 156, 680, 877.
Van Eyck, Jan, 186, 222, 290.
Van Eyck, M., 708.
Van Huysum, 796.
Van Orley, B., 655.
Vanos, Jan, 1015.
Velasquez, D. de, 197, 232, 741, 745.
Veneziano, B., 287.
Veneziano, D., 766, 767.
Vernet, C. J., 236.
Veronese, Paolo, 26, 97, 268, 294, 931.
Vinci, Leonardo da (School of), 18.
Vivarini, A., 768.
Vivarini, B., 284.
Walscappelle, J., 1002.
Weenix, Jan, 238.
William of Cologne, 687.
Wils, Jan, 1007.
Wouwerman, P., 878–882, 975, 976.
Wynants, Jan., 883, 884, 971–973.
Zelotti, B., 595.
Zoppo, M., 597.
Zurbaran, F., 230.

"In the reign of Charles II.," wrote Leigh Hunt, "*Hedge Lane* (now *Whitcomb Street*, at the north-west corner of Trafalgar Square) and the Haymarket, were still real lanes and passages to the fields. In Elizabeth's time you might set out from the site of the present Pall Mall, and, leaving St. Giles's Fields on the right, walk all the way to Hampstead without encountering a dwelling-place. Lovers plucked flowers in Cranbourne Alley, and took moonlight walks in St. James's Market."

LEICESTER SQUARE has been long noted as the centre of a portion of London occupied by foreign refugees. After each continental upheaval new faces are to be ob-

served here by those who know the neighbourhood. The
exiles of the Great French Revolution have long since gone
to their rest. Of those of 1848 but few remain, many
having returned home with the re-establishment of a
Republic. The Communists are now where the Republicans were. The Square takes its name from *Leicester
House*, built by Robert Sidney, Earl of Leicester, on the
north side, early in the seventeenth century. After him,
also, *Sidney Alley* was named. Leicester House changed
hands, and became the "pouting place" of the Prince of
Wales, afterwards George II., who had been turned out of
St. James's for taking his mother's part against his father.
The Duke of Cumberland, who fought at Culloden, was
born in Leicester House in 1611. Frederick Prince of Wales,
in his turn, quarrelled with his father in 1737, came hither,
and died here, 1751. Leicester House was considerably
enlarged by the addition of Savile House, and this was a
royal residence until the family removed to Carlton House
in 1766. Upon the site of Savile House it is proposed
to erect a grand Theatre of Varieties, Restaurant, and
Café, to be named *The Alcazar*.

William Hogarth's house stood on the site where *Archbishop Tenison's Schools* now stand, and in it he died. The
Polish hero Kosciusko lived in the house afterwards, and
the Countess Guiccioli, known for her association with
Lord Byron. Sir Joshua Reynolds lived at No. 47
(now Puttick and Simpson's), and his studio is now their
auction-room. Sir Isaac Newton lived at the corner of
St. Martin's Court, and passed, as he said, "the happiest
years of his life in the Observatory at that house," now
unhappily destroyed. Dr. Burney and his celebrated
daughter lived afterwards in the same building. John
Hunter, the famous surgeon, lived in the house south of
the *Alhambra Theatre*, and there began his collection in
1785, which has now grown into the Museum of the Royal
College of Surgeons. The *Alhambra* is a handsome theatre

and music-hall, chiefly devoted to burlesque and comic opera. The edifice was originally built and named the Royal Panopticon of Science and Art. Leicester Square owes its present handsome appearance to Mr. Albert Grant, who, at his own expense, cleared it of rubbish, set up a fountain and seats, planned its flower-beds, and provided a pleasant halting-place for a tired pedestrian in the very heart of London. Busts of the four worthies of Leicester Square now appropriately ornament it at each corner, viz., Newton, Hogarth, Hunter, and Reynolds, and in the centre is a statue of Shakespeare, copied from the one in Westminster Abbey. *Newport Market* reminds us that Lord Newport *(temp.* Chas. I.) had his mansion here. *Cranbourne Street* is named from the minor title of the Marquis of Salisbury, its owner. *Garrick Street* beyond it is a comparatively new street, chiefly known as the site of the *Garrick Club*, founded 1831, and containing a highly interesting collection of theatrical portraits. "Aldridge's," in *St. Martin's Lane*, is perhaps the most important (next to Tattersall's) of the Horse Auction Stables in the Metropolis.

LONG ACRE, which runs directly east of Cranbourne Street to the top of Drury Lane (whence it is proposed to make a new street eastwards in continuation of it), was at one time a fashionable street, but is now chiefly noted for its numerous coachbuilders' shops. Even these, however, of late years seem to be following their patrons westward. In Phœnix Alley, afterwards *Hanover Court*, on the south side of Long Acre, lived Taylor the water poet, who there kept an alehouse named the 'Mourning Crown.' This, however, he changed under the Commonwealth for 'Taylor's Head,' with the motto:

"There's many a head stands for a sign ;
Then, gentle reader, why not mine?"

At 67, 68, Long Acre, is the chief store of the *Civil Service Supply Association*.

WHITEHALL TO WESTMINSTER AND LAMBETH.

STANDING before the Statue of Charles I. with our face towards the Houses of Parliament, we shall recall some of the historical associations of this wonderfully interesting locality, "where every step we take is upon ground sacred to a hundred memories." The street was formerly much narrower than at present. Drummond's bank, on the right hand, now being rebuilt, was set back years ago, "full forty feet more to the west," upon an open square called Cromwell's Yard; wherein it has been said that Cromwell once lived. Hogarth's 'Night' shows the position of the street before it was widened.

Farther down, upon the right-hand side, we see *The Admiralty*, built (1726) by Ripley, upon the site of Peterborough (afterwards called Wallingford) House,—from which Archbishop Usher attempted to view the execution of Charles I.; "for, it was said, from the leads of Wallingford House they could plainly see what was being enacted before Whitehall. The primate, who could not stand the sight, fainted, was taken down and put to bed." There have been only three personages, since 1688, who have held the post of Lord High Admiral—Prince George, the husband of Queen Anne, 1702-8; Earl of Pembroke, 1709 and the Duke of Clarence, afterwards William IV., in 1827-8. The First Lord of the Admiralty possesses a fine residence, in connection with these official premises, £4500 a year, and the whole of the patronage of the Navy.

Opposite to the Admiralty is *Scotland Yard*, which is said to have derived its name from an ancient palace of the Scottish kings, who came hither to do homage for their fief

SOCIETY FOR PROMOTING CHRISTIAN KNOWLEDGE.

NEW PUBLICATIONS.

THE HOME LIBRARY.
Crown 8vo., cloth boards, 3s. 6d. each.

GREAT ENGLISH CHURCHMEN; or, Famous Names in English Church History and Literature. By W. H. DAVENPORT ADAMS.

MILITARY RELIGIOUS ORDERS OF THE MIDDLE AGES. The Hospitallers, the Templars, &c. By the Rev. F. C. WOODHOUSE, M.A.

NARCISSUS: A Tale of Early Christian Times. By the Rev. W. BOYD CARPENTER, M.A.

(*Three other Volumes of this Series have already appeared.*)

THE FATHERS FOR ENGLISH READERS.
Fcap. 8vo, cloth boards, 2s. each.

GREGORY THE GREAT. By the Rev. J. BARMBY, B.D.

ST. AMBROSE; his Life, Times, and Teaching. By the Rev. R. THORNTON.

SAINT BASIL THE GREAT. By the Rev. RICHD. TRAVERS SMITH, B.D.

THE VENERABLE BEDE. By the Rev. G. F. BROWNE.

(*Other Volumes of this Series on the APOSTOLIC FATHERS, the APOLOGISTS, ST. JEROME, and ST. AUGUSTINE, have already appeared.*)

NON-CHRISTIAN RELIGIOUS SYSTEMS.

CONFUCIANISM AND TAOUISM. By ROBERT K. DOUGLAS, of the British Museum, and Professor of Chinese at King's College, London. With Map. Fcap. 8vo., cloth boards, 2s. 6d.

(*Other Volumes of this Series on HINDUISM, BUDDHISM, and ISLAM, have already appeared.*)

CONVERSION OF THE WEST.

THE SLAVS. By the Rev. G. F. MACLEAR, D.D. With Map. Fcap. 8vo., cloth boards, 2s.

(*Other Volumes of this Series on the ENGLISH, the NORTHMEN, and the CELTS and GERMANS, have been already published.*)

ANCIENT HISTORY FROM THE MONUMENTS.
Fcap. 8vo., cloth boards, 2s.

SINAI: from the Fourth Egyptian Dynasty to the Present Day. By HENRY S. PALMER, Major R.E., F.R.A.S.

ASSYRIA: from the Earliest Times to the Fall of Nineveh. By the late GEORGE SMITH, Esq., of the British Museum.

BABYLONIA (The History of). By the late GEORGE SMITH, Esq. Edited by the Rev. A. H. SAYCE.

EGYPT: from the Earliest Times to B.C. 300. By S. BIRCH, LL.D., &c.

PERSIA: from the Earliest Period to the Arab Conquest. By W. S. W. VAUX, M.A.

GREEK CITIES AND ISLANDS OF ASIA MINOR. By W. S. W. VAUX, M.A.

MANUALS OF HEALTH.

THE HABITATION IN RELATION TO HEALTH. By F. S. B. FRANCOIS DE CHAUMONT. Fcap. 8vo., limp cloth, 1s.

(*Four other Volumes of this Series have already appeared.*)

COMMENTARY ON THE OLD AND NEW TESTAMENTS.
Crown 8vo., cloth, each Vol. 4s.

OLD TESTAMENT.—Vol. I. containing the Pentateuch. Vol. II., containing the Historical Books, Joshua to Esther. Vol. III., containing the Poetical Books, Job to Song of Solomon. Vol. IV. will be ready shortly.

THE APOCRYPHA in the press.

NEW TESTAMENT.—Vol. I., containing the Four Gospels. Vol. II., containing the Acts, Epistles, and Revelation.

Among the Commentators are the Bishops of BEDFORD, SALISBURY, ELY, ROCHESTER, LINCOLN, BATH AND WELLS, Canon BARRY, &c., &c.

LONDON: NORTHUMBERLAND AVENUE, CHARING CROSS, S.W.; 4, ROYAL EXCHANGE, E.C.; AND 48, PICCADILLY, W.

VICTORIA STREET.

111, *Metrop. Drinking Foun. and Cattle Trough Association*

PARLIAMENT STREET

DOWNING STREET.

ABINGDON STREET.

PARLIAMENT STREET.

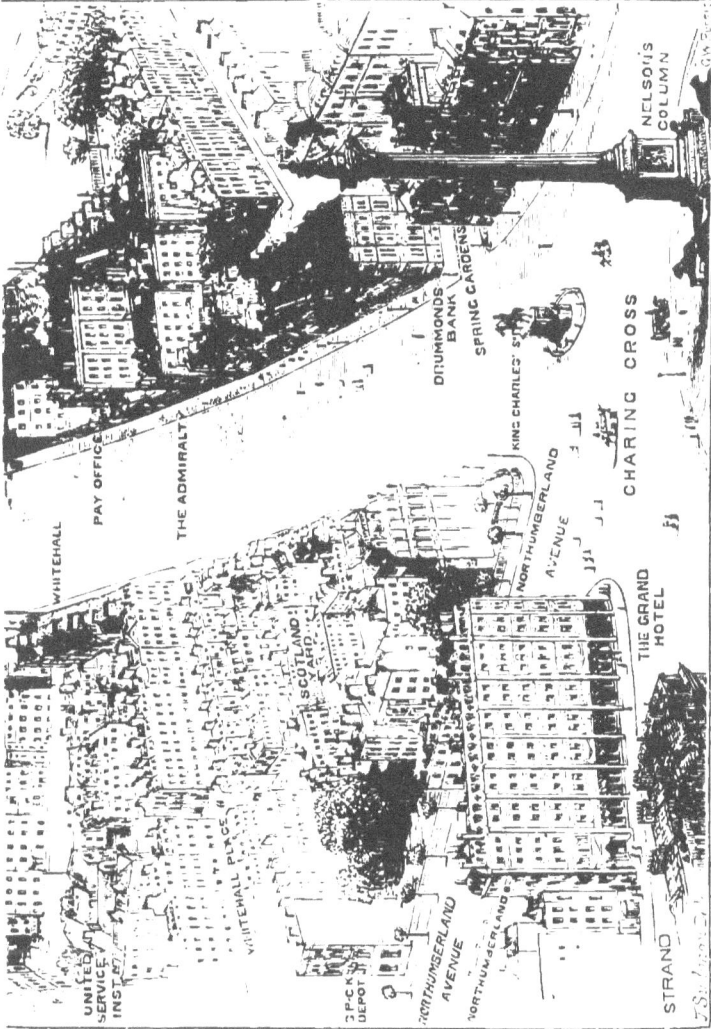

FROM CHARING CROSS THROUGH WHITEHALL TO WESTMINSTER.

NORTHUMBERLAND AVENUE.

*Central Dep*t of The Society for Promoting Christian Knowledge.*

THE STRAND.

in Cumberland. Scotland Yard is now known far and wide as the headquarters of the Metropolitan Police; yet it has some claims to be considered classic ground. Milton, when he was Secretary to Cromwell, lodged in Scotland Yard, and his son died whilst he resided here. Inigo Jones, Sir J. Denham, and Sir Christopher Wren, filled the office of Crown Surveyors, in Scotland Yard. Vanbrugh built a house here which Swift deigned to write satiric poems about. With reference to the present *Metropolitan Police* force, one may quote the following: "Till the last year of the reign of Charles II., when Heming contracted to supply a lamp before every tenth door, the streets were left in profound darkness. Thieves and robbers plied their trade with impunity. Dissolute young men amused themselves for many generations, swaggering about, breaking windows, upsetting sedan-chairs, beating quiet men, &c. The Muns and Tityre Tus were succeeded by Hectors, and these were followed successively by Nickers, Hawkubites, and Mohawks. Watchmen to the number of 1000 were supposed to guard the city at night, each inhabitant having to take duty in turn; but few left their homes in obedience to their summons, and many of these preferred the alehouse to the streets." The old watchmen named "Charlies" were abolished by Sir Robert Peel's Government, in 1829, and the present Police system instituted. Policemen obtained the *soubriquet* of "Peelers," and "Bobbies," from the populace, as indicative of their origin. The *Thames Police* are specially set apart for protecting property on the river from the depredations of so-called river-pirates.

The office of the *Royal Almonry* is in Middle Scotland Yard; where the Easter, Whitsuntide, and Christmas distributions take place; but on Maundy-Thursday the Royal Alms are bestowed in the Whitehall Chapel Royal—amongst as many poor as the years of Her Majesty's life—food, clothing, and silver money. Maundy-money is always now from the Mint. Of the adjoining tract of ground called

WHITEHALL,

Extending to the Thames on one side and St. James's Park on the other, many volumes of historical value might be written. From the era of Wolsey, who inhabited, as Archbishop of York, the palace which stood on this ground, then known as *York Place*, we might find ample interest in marking the tide of life which flowed round Whitehall. Upon the fall of Wolsey, in 1529, York Place came into the hands of Henry VIII., who was so pleased with it that he made it his own residence, and changed its name. (See Shakespeare's *Henry VIII.*, act iv. scene 1 :—

" You must no more call it York Place—that is past,
For since the Cardinal fell that title's lost,
'Tis now the King's, and called Whitehall.")

Henry VIII. married Anne Boleyn in a closet of Whitehall, and here celebrated their coronation. Here Henry took Hans Holbein into his service. Holbein painted many pictures, and built for Henry a magnificent *Gatehouse*, opposite the entrance to the Tilt-yard, which gate was removed in 1750, to be re-erected in the great Park at Windsor—the stones having been all numbered for the purpose—but the handsome structure was never rebuilt. Henry VIII. died at Whitehall, 1546. Edward VI. held a Parliament here. Mary, and afterwards Elizabeth, are described as proceeding from Whitehall to Westminster, Richmond, &c., by water. James I. rebuilt the *Banqueting-house* by the aid of Inigo Jones, and that building, the only part of old Whitehall which still remains, is justly regarded as one of the finest and most remarkable edifices in the metropolis. In the Cabinet Room of Whitehall, by means of Rubens (who painted the ceiling of the Banqueting-house), Charles I. collected four hundred and sixty of the finest masterpieces of Titian, Correggio, Giulio

The Execution of Charles I.

Romano, Raphael, Guido, Parmigiano, and others, which were seized by the Roundheads, sold, and dispersed. Many of the so-called superstitious pictures were actually destroyed by fire. The list of the pictures, destroyed and saved, may be found in Walpole's 'Anecdotes of Painting.'

Charles I. was beheaded in front of the Banqueting-house, Whitehall, facing the present Horse Guards. "He was led along the galleries to the Banqueting-house, through the wall of which a passage was broken to the scaffold. A man in a closed visor stood ready to perform the office of executioner. After the King's brief address to the few who could hear him, and his last words with Bishop Juxon, the King laid his head upon the block and the executioner struck it off at a blow. Another visored official picked it up and immediately held it forward, all dripping with blood for the crowd to see, and exclaimed, "This is the head of a traitor."

Cromwell was the next tenant of Whitehall. He has been described as having preached here, soon after the death of the King, sermons to the people of three hours' length. The Protector was, however, far from being such an enemy to the fine arts as some of those friends of his who wrought havoc upon Charles's gallery of pictures. Cromwell rescued and brought back many of the masterpieces, including amongst others the magnificent Cartoons of Raphael, which are now at the South Kensington Museum. Cromwell expired, Sept. 3, 1658, in Whitehall, in the midst of one of the most terrific storms that had visited England for many years. Richard Cromwell held his brief sway at Whitehall; and here Monk held power, as *locum tenens*, for the anxiously expected Charles II.

With the Restoration the festivities of Whitehall revived, but they were of a grosser sort than even those of Queen Elizabeth. Evelyn's description of King Charles's last Sunday in Whitehall is wonderfully graphic: "The King, sitting and toying with his concubines, Portsmouth, Cleaveland, and Mazarine, &c.; a French boy singing love-songs in those glorious galleries; whilst about twenty of the great courtiers, and other dissolute persons, were at basset, round a large table, a bank of at least £2000 in gold before them. Six days after was all in the dust." Charles II. died at Whitehall, Feb. 6, 1685, and his successor was immediately proclaimed at Whitehall-gate. James II. here washed the feet of the poor on Maundy-Thursday; and he rebuilt the chapel for Romish worship. When he quitted Whitehall, Dec. 18, 1688, he left it never to return.

Two fires subsequently destroyed the palace, of which all that now remains is the Banqueting-house,—converted into a Chapel Royal in the reign of George I., and re-altered, in 1829 and 1837, by Smirke; but they say it has never been consecrated. Macaulay thus describes " the destruction of the most celebrated palace in which the sovereigns of England have ever dwelt." " On the evening of the 4th of January, 1698, a woman—the patriotic journalists and pamphleteers of the time did not fail to note that she was a Dutch woman—who was employed as a laundress at Whitehall, lighted a charcoal fire in her room and placed some linen round it. The linen caught fire and burned furiously. The tapestry, the bedding, the wainscots were soon in a blaze. The unhappy woman who had done the mischief perished. Soon the flames burst out of the windows. All Westminster, all the Strand, all the river, were in commotion. Before midnight, the King's apartments, the Queen's apartments, the Wardrobe, the Treasury, the office of the Privy Council, the office of the Secretary of State, had been destroyed. The two chapels perished together; that ancient chapel, where Wolsey had heard mass in the midst of gorgeous copes, golden candlesticks, and jewelled crosses; and that modern edifice, which had been erected for the devotions of James, and had been embellished by the pencil of Verrio and the chisel of Gibbons. . . . No trace was left of that celebrated gallery, which had witnessed so many balls and pageants. . . . During some time men despaired of the Banqueting-house. The flames broke in on the south of that beautiful hall and were with difficulty extinguished. . . . Before the ashes of the old palace were cold, plans for a new palace were circulated and discussed. But William, who could not draw his breath in the air of Westminster, was little disposed to spend a million on a house which it would have been impossible for him to inhabit." The *Chapel Royal, Whitehall*, is open for Divine Service every Sunday, and may be seen on week days from ten to four o'clock.

The *Statue of James II.*, by Grinling Gibbons, still stands, as we have said, where it was set up, at the back of the Chapel Royal; a new road, recently made through Whitehall, connects this quarter with the Thames Embankment. *The United Service Institution Museum*, in Whitehall, open to visitors from eleven to four in winter, till five in summer, except on Fridays, is worth seeing. Many interesting relics are here on view; and upon the first floor is exhibited Captain Siborne's Model of the Battle of Waterloo, containing 190,000 metal figures.

The HORSE GUARDS stands opposite the Chapel of Whitehall. Behind it is a large enclosed space (the site of the *Old Tilt-yard*), between the present offices of the Admiralty and the Treasury, which is memorable as the scene of the tournaments and pageants of the Courts of Henry and Elizabeth. The modern guard-house and buildings contain offices and audience-room for the Commander-in-Chief, &c. [for *War Office*, see Pall Mall], and consist of a centre and two pavilion wings, with a turret and clock, the west front opening into St. James's Park by a low archway. On either side of the entrance facing Whitehall, a mounted cavalry soldier sits as sentry daily from 10 to 4. The guard is relieved every morn-

The Government Offices.

ing at a quarter to 11. "The marching and counter-marching of the guards, drawn from the cavalry barracks at Knightsbridge and the Regent's Park, is a picturesque scene, as the troop passes through the parks; their stately cuirassed and helmeted figures, and the splendour of their accoutrements, rendering them the most magnificent household troops in Europe." The *Life Guards*, who now form two regiments, were distributed in the time of Charles II. (the date of their formation) into three troops, each of which consisted of 200 carbineers, exclusive of officers. "This corps," says Macaulay, "to which the safety of the King and royal family was confided, had a very peculiar character. Even the privates were designated as gentlemen of the Guard. Many of them were of good families, and had held commissions in the Civil War. Their pay was far higher than that of the most favoured regiments of our time, and would in that age have been thought a respectable provision for the younger son of a country squire. Their fine horses, their rich housings, their cuirasses and their buff coats, adorned with ribands, velvet, and gold lace, made a splendid appearance in St. James's Park. Another body of household cavalry, distinguished by blue coats and cloaks, and still called *The Blues*, was quartered in the capital." The *Horse Guards Clock* has an excellent reputation as a correct time-keeper.

Other Government offices, built in the Italian style at a cost of half a million, by Sir Gilbert G. Scott, extend from the Horse Guards, south, into *Downing Street*, and consist of the—

TREASURY. There has been no Lord High Treasurer since 1612. The Prime Minister is First Lord of the Treasury. His official income is £5000 per annum.

FOREIGN OFFICE, 14 Downing Street. Here the Cabinet Councils are generally held, as also Foreign Princes and Ministers of State received. The Grand Staircase and Conference Room are very magnificent. *Passports* are granted here. The Secretary of State for Foreign Affairs receives £5000 per annum.

HOME OFFICE. Here is conducted the business of the Secretary of State for the United Kingdom, or the Home Department. His official income is £5000 per annum.

COLONIAL OFFICE, 13 Downing Street. Here is the office of the Secretary of State for the 44 colonies of Great Britain. His official income is £5000 per annum.

INDIA OFFICE. This is the office from which the affairs of our vast Indian Empire are regulated by a Secretary of State for India, assisted by a Council. His official income is £5000 per annum. The East India Company came to an end in 1860.

EXCHEQUER OFFICE, 11 Downing Street. The business of this office is conducted by the Chancellor of the Exchequer, whose duty it is to regulate the imposition of taxes, and to provide for a revenue of over 70 millions sterling per annum. His official income is £5000 per annum. Cabinet Councils are sometimes held here.

The *Privy Council Office* is also in Downing Street.

Upon the east side of Whitehall, opposite the new Government offices, are WHITEHALL GARDENS, the residence of many of the nobility, including the Duke of Buccleugh, Lord Beaconsfield, &c., also the *National Club-house* for Protestant members of the Church of England; and immediately beyond is a short street (at the corner of which is the *Whitehall Club-house* for members of the scientific professions), which forms one of the approaches to the new *National Opera House*, whose chief frontage will be towards the Thames Embankment. In preference, however, to following a direct course through *Parliament Street*, we will bear a little to the right, look down *Charles Street*, Westminster, as we go by, noting it as the headquarters of recruiting-sergeants, and thus pass into *King Street*, Westminster, now a poor mean street, but full of historical interest. This was the ancient thoroughfare to Westminster; in the time of Henry VIII. the *Cockpit Gate* was at its north end. In King Street, Edmund Spenser, the poet, took lodgings at a tavern, after his last return from Ireland, " that he might be near the Court"; and on January 16, 1599, died there, according to Ben Jonson, " for lack of bread." Cromwell took horse from his house in King Street, 1649, with a retinue of gallant men for his life-guard, to Windsor, *en route* for Ireland. In King Street, also, lived Sackville, Earl of Dorset; the Poet Carew; Dr. Sydenham, and others. The *October Club* of High Tories (1712) met at the Bell Tavern, in King Street.

Opposite the south end of King Street is Westminster Abbey, with the church of St. Margaret's standing by its side. The visitor will obtain from this point, perhaps, the most remarkable of all the views in London. The venerable Abbey, with Henry VII.'s Chapel, is before him; on his left are the Houses of Parliament, Palace Yard, and Westminster Bridge, leading over to Lambeth; on his immediate right is *Storey's Gate*, leading to *Birdcage Walk*, St. James's Park; and between that Gate and the Abbey lies the *Broad Sanctuary;* with *Dean's Yard* and Westminster School beyond.

WESTMINSTER HOSPITAL and WESTMINSTER SESSIONS HOUSE stand upon the site of the ancient SANCTUARY OF WESTMINSTER, the only one of the Ancient Sanctuaries in the metropolis of which the name still exists. The right of sanctuary, or the protection of criminals and debtors from arrest, was retained by Westminster after the Dissolution of the Monasteries in 1540 ; and the privilege (which was not abolished until James I., in 1623) caused the houses within the precinct to be let for high rents. The Church was removed in 1750, to give place to a Market House, which was pulled down fifty years later, to make way for the *Sessions House*, or Westminster Guildhall, as it is sometimes called, erected by Cockerell, 1805. In Westminster Sanctuary, Elizabeth, Queen of Edward IV., took refuge when the victorious Warwick was marching on London to dethrone her husband; and here she gave birth to Edward V. To the west of the Sanctuary stood the *Almonry* of Westminster, in which was set up the first printing-press ever used in England, viz., that by William Caxton, in 1474.

The Parish Church of *St. Margaret's, Westminster*, dates from the time of Edward I., but was rebuilt *temp.* Edward IV. It has appeared to some persons unaccountable that this Church should have been erected so near to the Abbey, in a position to obstruct the view of Henry VII.'s beautiful chapel. But whether it was originally set up to provide for the parochial, as distinguished from the ecclesiastical, uses of the adjoining Abbey or not, certain it is that its removal would now be a most pitiable mistake, upon both historical and æsthetical grounds. This being the Church of the House of Commons, all the Fast-day Sermons were preached here during the Commonwealth ; and, on September 25, 1642, the *Solemn League and Covenant* was read from the pulpit of St. Margaret's, and taken by both Houses of Parliament, by the Assembly of Divines, and the Scots Commissioners. Here Hugh Peters urged the Commons to bring Charles I. to " condign, speedy, and capital punishment." Here Case censured Cromwell to his face, and afterwards attacked General Monk, by saying, " There are some who would betray three kingdoms for filthy lucre's sake," then throwing his handkerchief into the pew where the General was sitting. Recent renovations have altered the internal appearance of the edifice, at the expense of old galleries, and memorials and pews. It is no longer the " little Church " of St. Margaret of Antioch, but one of the handsomest of Perpendicular churches, having an exquisitely beautiful nave of 130 feet, arcaded in eight bays and a half, also a fine panelled-oak roof. The East Window, representing the Crucifixion, is considered the most perfect of the ancient stained glass windows in London, and was pronounced by Winston the most beautiful work of glass-painting he was acquainted with. This window has a history as full of vicissitudes as that of a hero of fiction. It was made at Gouda, in Holland, for the magistrates of Dort, who intended presenting it to King Henry VII. for his Chapel in Westminster Abbey; but after that king's death it was sent to Henry VIII., who gave it to Waltham Abbey. Here it remained until the Dissolution, when it was removed by the last abbot for safety to his private chapel at New Hall. The Villiers family came into possession of New Hall, and removed the window out of the way of destruction and buried it underground, whence at the Restoration General Monk again set it up in New Hall chapel. There it remained till the chapel was demolished by a subsequent possessor, a Mr. John Olmins, who, however, preserved the window as an object of *virtu*, and, not finding a purchaser, cased it up for many years. At length it was bought for 50 guineas by Mr. Conyers, of Copped Hall, Essex, and sold by his son in 1758 for 400 guineas to the churchwardens of St. Margaret's. The churchwardens had scarcely put it up before they were denounced and prosecuted by the Dean and Chapter of Westminster for erecting "a superstitious image or picture." After seven years' litigation the churchwardens won their suit, and the stained-glass window was allowed to rest in what one may hope to be its final position. The glass painting represents the Crucifixion—angels receiving the blood-drops from the Redeemer's wounds; an angel bears off the soul of the repentant thief to Paradise; a demon hurries that of the impenitent thief to Hell. Angels are seen in the six upper compartments, bearing severally the Cross, the Sponge, the Crown of Thorns, the Hammer, the Rods, and the Nails. In the lower compartment is Arthur, Prince of Wales, eldest son of Henry VII., and above him St. George and the red and white rose; on the left is Katharine of Arragon, the bride of Arthur, as well as afterwards of his brother Henry VIII., and above her the figure of St. Cecilia, with a ripe and juicy pomegranate, the emblem of Granada. There were originally in this church side-chapels or altars to St. Margaret, St. George, St. Katharine, St. Erasmus, St. John, and St. Cornelius. The old brass Memorials were sold in 1644 at 3*d*. and 4*d*. a pound ; the most noteworthy modern Brass (1845) is that to Sir Walter Raleigh (who was buried in the chancel of this church after his execution in Palace Yard, near by); also a Tablet to Caxton, the first English printer; a Slab to Harrison, author of 'Oceana'; a Monument, with epitaph, by Pope, to Mrs. E. Corbet; and to Captain Sir P. Parker, with epitaph by Byron. In St. Margaret's churchyard were buried in a pit many of the bodies of the Cromwellians, which at the time of the Restoration were exhumed from their resting-places in Westminster Abbey; such as those of the mother of Oliver Cromwell, Admiral Blake, Sir. W. Constable (one of the judges who tried Charles I.), and John Pym. Here lie also the poet Skelton, Nicholas Udall, Sir William Waller, the Parliament General, Hollar, the engraver (near the north-west corner of the tower), the notorious Colonel Blood, who tried to steal the regalia, &c. Sir Charles Barry, who built the new Houses of Parliament, recommended that St. Margaret's Church should be restored, to harmonise with the surrounding edifices, or should be removed altogether; but, so far, the great architect's opinion has been unattended to—perhaps it ever may be. The *Overseers' box*, with silver mountings, engraved by Hogarth and others, with various historical and other designs, is of some interest.

WESTMINSTER ABBEY

Stands upon the site of a Temple dedicated to Apollo. The first Christian church erected here was founded by Sebert, King of the East Saxons, 610, "to the honour of God and St. Peter," and it is still known as the Collegiate Church of St. Peter, Westminster. King Edward the Confessor wholly rebuilt the Church of West Minster, in which he was buried, but no portion of the present Abbey belongs to Edward's time, unless, perhaps, some part of the foundations, or it may be the Chapel of the Pyx, in the dark cloister near the South Transept. King Harold and William the Conqueror were crowned in Westminster Abbey, and every succeeding sovereign to the present day. Henry III. rebuilt the Abbey, but it was burnt down almost immediately after. Edward I. and II. restored it. In the reign of Edward III. Abbot Littlington added several buildings to it, including the Jerusalem Chamber. In 1502 Henry VII. erected, upon the site of a Chapel to the Virgin, which he pulled down, the magnificent structure dedicated also to Mary, but generally known as Henry VII.'s Chapel, and styled by Leland "the miracle of the world." Among its profuse and delicate decorations one may note the "portcullis chained" (the symbol of the House of Beaufort, and since of Westminster); the rose of England, barbed and seeded; the Tudor *fleur-de-lis*. The length of Westminster Abbey is 416 feet; length of transept, 203 feet; length of choir, 155 feet. Its height is 101 feet 8 inches; height of towers, 225 feet. The North Transept is remarkable for its pinnacled buttresses, its triple porch, its clustered columns, and its great rose window 90 feet in circumference. The Interior shows the wonderful effects of "long-drawn aisle and fretted vault." Henry III.'s portions of this Abbey, especially the Choir, are considered to be the most perfect specimens of the Lancet, Early English, and Pointed styles. The Early English style is the best seen in the North Transept and South Aisle of the Nave, and in the narrow, Lancet-shaped arch in one compartment of the Nave. The Decorated style is shown in the western side of the Nave; the Perpendicular, at its very best, in Henry VII.'s Chapel—" a sublime monument without a parallel of the consummate skill and genius of the architects of old." Of the stained glass, the most ancient is in the north and south windows, the clerestory windows, the east window of Henry VII.'s Chapel and the Jerusalem Chamber; the remainder is modern, viz. the great West window, the large Rose window, and the Marygold window, in the South Transept. The Western Towers of the Abbey had not been completed even down to the time of Sir Christopher Wren. That great architect pulled down the unfinished structures, and erected the present towers in a Grecianised Gothic style, incongruous and unsatisfactory; but he, too, after twenty-five years' labour, left his work unaccomplished, for, although he commenced a central spire, " he left off before it rose so high as the ridge of the roof."

The chief entrances to Westminster Abbey are by the western and northern doorways. We will, however, enter as visitors frequently prefer to do, by the door in the South Transept at *Poets' Corner*. Here we shall find ourselves at once surrounded by the memorials of all the great and honoured worthies of English Literature. Here is the tomb of *Geoffrey Chaucer*, the father of English poetry; and of *Edmund Spenser*, author of the 'Faerie Queen'; a statue of *William Shakespeare*, erected in the reign of George II. (the poet rests at Stratford-on-Avon); of *Michael Drayton*, &c.; also memorial busts and tablets of *Ben Jonson, Samuel Butler*, the author of 'Hudibras'; *Sir William Davenant, Abraham Cowley, John Dryden, L. Shadwell, John Philips* (author of the 'Splendid Shilling'), *Matthew*

Prior, Gay, Handel, Addison, Thomson, Goldsmith, Gray, Mason, Southey, Campbell; and below, close by, repose the remains of *Grote, Thirlwall, Macaulay, Thackeray,* and *Charles Dickens.* In the South Transept, and beyond the Poets' Corner, is a monument to *Isaac Casaubon* (1614); to *Camden,* the antiquarian; to *St. Evremond;* to *John, Duke of Argyll;* to *Handel,* by Roubiliac; to *Booth* (actor); *Mrs. Pritchard* (actress); to *David Garrick,* by Webber; and grave-stones over *Old Parr, Chiffinch,* '*Prue*' second wife of Steele, *Macpherson,* and *W. Gifford.*

From Poets' Corner we pass onward to look at the Chapels, of which there are twelve in this Abbey,—usually shown by the Vergers to groups of twenty or thirty visitors at a time, in the following order:—

1. *St. Benedict's*— Tombs of *Langham,* Archbishop of Canterbury, d. 1376; the *Countess of Hertford,* d. 1598; *Cranfield,* Lord High Treasurer to James I. d. 1645.

2. *St. Edmund's*—Tombs of *William de Valence,* Earl of Pembroke, half-brother of Henry III., d. 1296; *John of Eltham,* son of Edward II., d. 1334; *William of Windsor* and *Blanche de la Tour,* children of Edward III.; portrait brasses of *Eleanor de Bohun,* Duchess of Gloucester, and *Robert de Waldeby,* Archbishop of York, d. 1397; *Frances,* Duchess of Suffolk, mother of Lady Jane Grey, and a statue of *Lady Elizabeth Russell,* who used to be, most absurdly, described by the Vergers as having died by the prick of a needle.

3. *St. Nicholas'*—At the entrance is the grave of *Spelman,* the antiquary; monuments to the Wife of Lord Protector Somerset (d. 1578); to *Mildred* and *Anne,* wife and daughter of Lord Burghley (1588-9); brass to *Sir Humphrey Stanley* (d. 1505); altar-tomb of *Sir George Villiers* (1619).

4. *Henry VII.'s,* or the Virgin Mary's Chapel, consists of a nave and two aisles, with five chapels at the east end. In the nave are the *Stalls of the Knights*

of the Bath, who were installed in this chapel till 1812;—the Dean of Westminster being still Dean of the Order, which ranks next after that of the Garter. The Tombs in centre of the chapel are those of *Henry VII. and his Queen* Elizabeth, considered by Lord Bacon one of the stateliest and daintiest tombs in Europe. *South Aisle:* Tombs of *Margaret,* mother of Henry VII.; of the *Mother of Darnley,* husband of Mary Queen of Scots, whose tomb is also here; of *George Villiers, Duke of Buckingham,* assassinated by Felton; also of his two sons (one the profligate Duke), buried below; also of the first Wife of Sir R. Walpole. *North Aisle:* Tombs of *Queen Elizabeth* and *Queen Mary,* buried in the same grave; *James I.* and *Anne of Denmark,* and their infant daughter, also their son, *Prince Henry;* the *Queen of Bohemia* and *Arabella Stuart; Duke and Duchess of Richmond, temp.* James I., and *La Belle Stuart;* Monument of *Monk,* Duke of Albemarle; Sarcophagus containing supposed bones of *Edward V.* and his brother *Richard,* murdered in the Tower; monuments of *Saville, Marquis of Halifax,* d. 1695; *Montague, Earl of Halifax,* d. 1715; *Sheffield, Duke of Buckingham; Duke of Montpensier,* brother to Louis Philippe, King of the French. Next is the grave of *Addison. Charles II., William and Mary,* and *Queen Anne,* lie in a vault at the end of the south aisle. *George II. and his Queen, Frederick Prince of Wales,* father of George III., and the *Duke of Cumberland,* hero of Culloden, lie in a vault in the central aisle. In the recess at the east end of the chapel *Oliver Cromwell* was buried, but his body was exhumed from this grave and sent to Tyburn gallows, see pp. 165, 185.

5. *St. Paul's*—Tombs of *Sir Thomas Bromley,* Queen Elizabeth's Chancellor; *Lord Bourchier,* Standard-

bearer to Henry V. at Agincourt; *Sir Giles Daubeny; Viscount Dorchester;* and *Lord Cottington.* Also colossal statue of *James Watt,* engineer. *Archbishop Usher* was buried in this chapel.

6. *Edward the Confessor's*—In the centre is the Shrine of *Edward the Confessor* (in the rear of the high altar of the Abbey), erected by Henry III.; Tombs of *Edward I.*, d. 1307 (*'malleusScotorum'*); of *Henry III.*, d. 1272; of *Eleanor, Queen of Edward I.;* of *Henry V.* (whose head cast in solid silver was stolen at the Reformation, but whose helmet, shield, and saddle are to be still seen over his tomb); of *Edward III.,* and his Queen, *Philippa,* with the "monumental sword that conquered France"; of the Children of Edward III., Edward IV., and Henry VII.; of *Richard II. and his first Queen;* of *John de Waltham,* Bishop of Salisbury, Richard's High Treasurer. This Chapel is divided from the choir by a Shrine, having a frieze containing fourteen sculptures, representing the Incidents in the life of Edward the Confessor. Near the screen are the two *Coronation Chairs* still used at the Coronation of the Sovereign of this kingdom; one of them contains the famous stone of Scone, on which Scottish Kings were crowned—a reddish grey sandstone (believed by some to have been Jacob's Pillow), 26 by 16¾ inches, and 11 inches thick, which Edward I. carried off with him from the Abbey of Scone, Scotland, in token of his conquest of that country. The Scots held that wherever it was carried the supreme power would go with it. The other Coronation chair was made for the coronation of Mary, Queen of William III.

7. *St. Erasmus',* which contains little of importance, leads to

8. *St. John the Baptist,* in which are the tombs of many of the early *Abbots of Westminster,* also of *William*

de Colchester; A. Carey, Lord Hunsdon, first cousin and Chamberlain to Queen Elizabeth; *Thomas Cecil, Earl of Exeter*, and his two wives (the second Countess commanded that she should not appear upon her husband's left side, so her place is still vacant); and a monument to *Colonel Popham*, the only one to an officer of the Parliamentary Army allowed to remain; his body was taken away with those of Cromwell, Ireton, Bradshaw, and Blake, see p. 35.

9. *Abbot Islip's*, in which is an effigy of the Abbot himself, as also the Vault of the *Hatton* family. Near the chapel is the monument to *General Wolfe*, with a *bas-relief* of the landing at Quebec.

In the *East Aisle of the North Transept* is the celebrated tomb of *Sir Francis Vere;* also Roubiliac's monument to *Mr. and Mrs. Nightingale*, where Death appears launching his dart at the wife, who sinks back into the arms of her husband—her right arm and hand are considered the perfection of monumental art.

In the *Choir* are the tombs of *King Sebert*, of *Edmund Crouchback*, second son of Edward III., and his Countess; also of *Aymer de Valence, Earl of Pembroke;* and of *Anne of Cleves*, wife of Henry VIII.

The *North Transept* contains some remarkable monuments of comparatively recent date. Here are Bacon's *Lord Chatham;* Nollekens's group of the *Three Captains*, mortally wounded in Rodney's naval victory, 1782; Roubiliac's *Sir Peter Warren;* Rysbrach's *Admiral Vernon;* Flaxman's *Lord Mansfield; Warren Hastings;* Westmacott's *Mrs. Warren and Child;* Chantrey's *Canning, F. Horner,* and *Sir J. Malcolm;* Gibson's *Sir Robert Peel; John Philip Kemble; Sir W. Follett.* Under the pavement lie *Chatham, Pitt,* and *Fox, Castlereagh, Grattan, Lord Colchester,* and *Wilberforce;* and in the north aisle of the choir, leading to the nave called *Musicians' Corner*, lie *Purcell* and *Arnold, Dr. Blow, Dr. Burney,* and *Dr. Croft.*

The Chapter-house and Crypt, recently restored at a heavy expense by Sir Gilbert G. Scott, were built by Henry III. The entrance is near Poets' Corner. It is an elegant octagon of English Gothic style, supported by massive buttresses. For 300 years the House of Commons met in this Chapter-house, and here must have occurred almost all the great struggles for liberty against the Crown, even up to the time of the Reformation, for the Parliament sat here down to the time of Henry VIII. In 1547 the Commons moved to the Chapel of St. Stephen, vacant by the suppression of the Collegiate Chapel of St. Stephen's, Westminster. The Records and Domesday Book formerly preserved in this Chapter-house were in 1860 removed to the Rolls Court, Chancery Lane.

The *Nave* of the Abbey contains every kind of memorial, bust, statue, tablet, tomb. In the pavement is a stone to *Rare Ben Jonson*, here buried on his feet (his skull was seen in 1840, about a foot below this stone, and his body in an upright posture); here also are a memorial to *Tom Killigrew* and his Son; monuments to Wives of Sir Samuel Morland; to *Sir P. Fairborne;* to *Sir William Temple;* to *Sprat;* to *Atterbury;* to *Sydney, Earl of Godolphin;* to *Heneage Twysden;* to *Colonel Townshend;* to Secretary *Craggs;* to *Congreve,* by *Henrietta, Duchess of Marlborough;* and Lough's statue of *Wordsworth.* The following monuments are to be seen under the organ screen: Rysbrach's *Sir Isaac Newton; James, first Earl Stanhope;* Roubiliac's *Marshal Wade, General Fleming,* and *General Hargrave;* Read's *Admiral Tyrrel;* Flaxman's *Captain Montague;* Westmacott's *Spencer Perceval, William Pitt,* and *C. J. Fox;* Bailey's *Lord Holland; General Lawrence; Major André,* executed by the Americans, 1780, as a Spy.

South Aisle of Choir—Monuments of *W. Thynne* and *Thomas Thynne;* Le Sœur's bust of *Lord Chief Justice Richardson; Dr. South; Sir Cloudesley Shovel; Dr. Busby; Sir Godfrey Kneller; Dr. Isaac Watts* (buried in Bunhill Fields); *Dr. Burney;* and a bust of *Paoli.*

Cloisters—In the South Cloister are Monuments of several *Abbots of Westminster;* in the East Cloister is one to *Sir Edmondsbury Godfrey;* also tablets to the *Mother of Addison;* and to *General Withers.* In the West Cloister are memorials of *George Virtue; T. Banks, R.A.; Woollett,* engraver; and *Dr. Buchan.* In the East *Ambulatory* lie *Aphra Behn* (1689), *Henry Lawes, Betterton, Tom Brown, Mrs. Bracegirdle,* and *Samuel Foote.*

The *Jerusalem Chamber* on the south-west of the Abbey, and near the Cloister doorway, may be seen upon applying at the porter's lodge. It dates from 1386, and was so named from the coloured glass, brought from Jerusalem, which decorates it. In it died Henry IV.; the death of this King, as described by Shakespeare, is singularly dramatic:—

KING HENRY. Doth any name particular belong
 Unto the lodging where I first did swoon?
WARWICK. 'Tis called Jerusalem, my noble Lord.
KING HENRY. Laud be to heaven! even there my life must end.
 It hath been prophesied to me many years
 I should not die but in Jerusalem;
 Which vainly I supposed the Holy Land:—
 But bear me to that chamber; there I'll lie,
 In that Jerusalem shall Harry die.

Westminster Abbey is open to the public daily (Sundays included) for Divine Service, at 10 A.M. and 3 P.M.; and it can be viewed between 11 and 3, and in summer, from 4 till 6. There is no charge for admission to the Nave, Transepts, and Cloisters; but 6d. is charged for admission on any other week day than Monday, to the Choir and the Chapels.

WESTMINSTER SCHOOL, or ST. PETER'S COLLEGE, is in *Dean's Yard*, near the western entrance to the Abbey. In front of Dean's Yard is a *Memorial Column* to the scholars of Westminster School who died in the Crimean war. This College was founded by Queen Elizabeth, 1560, to consist of a Dean, twelve Prebendaries, twelve Almsmen, and forty Scholars, with a master and an usher. Such was the original foundadation; but Westminster School contains about 200 scholars, of whom day scholars pay 25 guineas per annum; boarders, 75 to 85 guineas. The forty Queen's Scholars, elected by open competition (about ten yearly, at Whitsuntide), from boys who have been a year at the School, and who were under fifteen on 25th March, pay £30 per annum for board and education. Six School Exhibitions, worth £20 to £50 per annum, are competed for at Easter. In the ancient College Hall, before Christmas, are given performances of the Latin plays of Plautus, Terence, &c., for which Westminster scholars have long been noted.

At the right-hand corner of *Victoria Street* (which leads to the Victoria Station, of the London, Brighton and South Coast, and London, Chatham and Dover Railways) is *Westminster Palace Hotel*, one of the largest at this end of the town. The *Royal Aquarium* is scarcely a stone's throw from the Hotel, and in the same building as the Aquarium is the *Imperial Theatre* for the performance of comedy, &c., also a number of stages for other performances; a *Restaurant* on a large scale, &c. The *Royal Architectural Museum* is at 18 Tufton Street.

Observe the lofty structure, of Mr. H. A. Hankey, at the end of this street, providing suites of chambers, as well as club accommodation for families of the wealthier classes. Upon part of the site of this building, known as *Queen Anne's Mansions*, stood 19 York Street, Westminster, a house in which John Milton resided while Latin Secretary to Oliver Cromwell; here he was first overtaken with blindness, and here he began 'Paradise Lost.' Jeremy Bentham bought and lived in the house and afterwards lent it to Hazlitt. *St. James's Park Station* is in this street.

NEW PALACE YARD, Westminster, is the space enclosed within the gilded railings in front of Westminster Hall. It was in *Old Palace Yard*, south-west of the Houses of Parliament, that the Pillory stood, and where *Sir Walter Raleigh* was beheaded in 1618. At the southeast corner of Old Palace Yard stood the house through which the Conspirators in the Gunpowder Plot carried their powder-barrels into the vault, and in the same yard Guy Fawkes, Winter, Rookwood, and Keyes, were executed, in 1606. In the present New Palace Yard, Perkin Warbeck was set in the stocks, 1498; Stubbs and his servant had their hands cut off for libelling Queen Elizabeth; Leighton was pilloried and publicly whipped; William Prynne was pilloried, and his *Histrio-Mastrix* burnt; Titus Oates was pilloried, 1685.

WESTMINSTER HALL was added by William Rufus to the ancient Palace of Westminster, and he held his first Court in it, 1099. It was repaired and raised in height by Richard II., whose device, a White Hart, *couchant*, still appears on the stone mouldings. The Hall is 290 feet long by 68 feet wide, and 92 feet high, and now forms the vestibule to the *Houses of Parliament*, and to the *Courts of Law*, which were originally within the Hall itself. Parliament assembled in Westminster Hall as early as 1248. In Westminster Hall the High Courts of Justice have been held for seven and a half centuries. In it the Coronation feasts were always given. Here King Edward III. entertained his prisoner, King John of France; here Sir William Wallace was tried and condemned. Here patrolled, with a "straw in their shoes, to denote their quality," the ruffian "men of straw," who were ready to sell their testimony to the first comer; here were tried and condemned Protector Somerset and Sir Thomas More, also the Earl of Strafford, whose motto was 'Thorough.' Here sat the High Court of Justice which tried and condemned Charles I.—the King sitting covered, and the Naseby banners hanging over his head. Here Cromwell was inaugurated Lord Protector, June 26, 1657. At Westminster Hall Gate Charles II. was proclaimed, May 8,

1660. Upon the south gable were set the heads of Cromwell, Ireton, and Bradshaw. Cromwell's head remained there for twenty years. Here the Seven Bishops were acquitted in the reign of James II. Here were tried Dr. Sacheverell and the rebel lords of 1745; Lord Byron, for killing Mr. Chaworth; Lord Ferrers, for murder; and the Duchess of Kingston, for bigamy. Here Warren Hastings' seven years' trial took place, and Lord Melville's, in 1806, besides many more of historical note. The interior of Westminster Hall was, until the middle of the last century, filled with shops and stalls, principally of booksellers. Many books, tracts, and pamphlets before that time bear the imprint of Westminster Hall. The Courts of Law at the side of the Hall will shortly be removed to the Strand. They were last rebuilt by Sir John Soane.

Adjoining to the Courts of Law is the site of the ancient *Houses of Lords and Commons*, which were accidentally destroyed, October 16, 1834, by some officials employed to burn the used wooden tallies of the Court of Exchequer, and who, in doing so, overheated the flues and set fire to the woodwork of the library. Westminster Hall was saved with difficulty, and the Abbey itself was at one time in danger.

THE NEW HOUSES OF PARLIAMENT were built upon the site of the old Palace of Westminster, and of St. Stephen's Chapel, by Sir Charles Barry, the whole pile covering eight acres, and having four principal fronts, of which the river frontage is 940 feet long. The edifice contains 11 open quadrangular courts, 500 apartments, and 18 official residences, besides the Royal State Apartments, the Houses of Lords and Commons, and the Central Hall. The style of the building is Tudor (Henry VIII.), with portions of the Halls of the Netherlands. The *Clock Tower*, with *Big Ben* for a bell, is 40 feet square and 320 feet high. Here an electric light burns when Parliament is sitting. The bell, 'Great Tom of Westminster,' was at one time as noted as 'Big Ben' is now. It was 'Great Tom' (not

St. Paul's bell, as some state) that the sentinel heard strike thirteen. The story goes that John Hatfield, in the reign of William and Mary, was tried and condemned by court-martial for falling asleep whilst on duty as a sentinel upon the terrace of Windsor Castle. He pleaded innocence, and alleged that he had heard 'Great Tom' at midnight strike thirteen; a statement disbelieved both on account of the distance, and the improbability. But several persons came forward and swore that the clock did strike thirteen, and the man was pardoned. The *Victoria Tower* is 75 feet square and 340 feet high, and its entrance archway to the House of Lords is 65 feet high. The chief approach for the public to the Houses of Parliament is through Palace Yard and Westminster Hall, up the broad flight of steps at the farther end into *St. Stephen's Hall*, on either side of which are ranged statues of our greatest statesmen; Hampden, Selden, Fox, Chatham, Clarendon, Grattan, Falkland, Walpole, and Mansfield; and thence into the *Octagon Hall*, 80 feet high, and having a beautifully groined stone roof. From the Octagon Hall the right-hand passage leads to the House of Lords; the left, to the House of Commons.

The Royal Entrance by the Victoria Tower leads to the Norman Porch decorated with statues of the Norman kings, thence to the *Robing-Room*, which faces the river, and is decorated with frescoes by Dyce, R.A. The *Victoria Gallery*, 110 feet long, 45 feet wide, and 45 feet high, also decorated with frescoes, gilded ceiling, and stained-glass windows, contains frescoes by Maclise, R.A., of the *Meeting of Wellington and Blucher*, after the Battle of Waterloo; the *Death of Nelson*, &c., &c. Her Majesty passes through this gallery, and the Prince's Chamber, to the House of Lords, when she goes to open Parliament; and tickets are to be obtained upon such occasions from the Lord Chamberlain to view the procession.

THE HOUSE OF LORDS is a magnificent chamber, extremely rich in gilding and colour, wrought metal, and carved work. It is 97 feet long, 45 feet high, and 45 feet wide, and was opened April 15, 1847. On either side of the *Throne*, but upon a less elevated dais, is a chair for the Prince of Wales and the personage next in honour. The *Woolsack* (covered with crimson cloth corresponding in colour with the other seats of the House) is in front of the Throne, and hereon sits the Lord Chancellor. The Peers are ranged on either side, or upon the cross benches. The *Reporters' Gallery*, with the *Strangers' Gallery* behind it, face the Throne. Frescoes in six compartments, three at either end, decorate the walls. The subjects illustrated are, the *Baptism of Ethelbert*, by Dyce, R.A.; *Edward III. conferring the Order of the Garter on the Black Prince*, and *Henry, Prince of Wales, committed to prison for assaulting Judge Gascoigne*, both by Cope, R.A.; the *Spirit of Religion*, by Horsley, R.A.; and the *Spirit of Chivalry* and the *Spirit of Law*, by D. Maclise. The twelve stained-glass windows are lighted at night from the outside. On the cornice below the Gallery are the arms of the Sovereigns and of the Chancellors of England, since Edward III.

THE HOUSE OF COMMONS, 62 feet in length by 45 feet in breadth and 45 feet in height, is not so gorgeous in colour as the House of Peers, but it is, nevertheless, a fine apartment. The *Speaker's Chair* in the Commons fills the place which in the Upper House is occupied by the Throne. Over the Speaker's Chair is the *Visitors' Gallery*. The surrounding galleries are arranged for the Members, for Reporters, and for the public, who are admitted by Members' orders. The *Members' Entrance* is either by the public approaches, or by a private door and staircase from the *Star Chamber Court*, so called from its occupying the site of the old much-dreaded Star Chamber. The *Upper Waiting Hall* contains a number of frescoes from scenes by eight British poets, including: *Griselda*, from Chaucer, by Cope, R.A.; *Lear and his daughter*, from Shakespeare, by Herbert; *Ithuriel's Spear*, from Milton, by Horsley;

St. Cecilia, from Dryden, by Tenniel. In the *Peers' Corridor*, beginning upon the left hand, on the way to the House of Commons, are the following eight frescoes: *Burial of Charles I.; Expulsion of Fellows at Oxford for refusing to subscribe to the Covenant; Defence of Basing House, attacked by Roundheads; Charles I. erecting his Standard at Nottingham; Speaker Lenthall opposing the Arrest of the Five Members by Charles I.; Departure of London Train-bands to relieve Gloucester; Embarkment of the Pilgrim Fathers for New England; Lady Russell taking leave of her Husband before his Execution.* In the *Commons' Corridor* are the following eight frescoes: *Alice Lisle concealing the Fugitives after the Battle of Sedgemoor; The Last Sleep of Argyll; William and Mary receiving the Crown from Parliament in the Banqueting-house, Whitehall; Acquittal of the Seven Bishops, temp. James II.; General Monk declaring in favour of a Free Parliament; Landing of Charles II. at Dover; The Execution of Montrose; Jane Lane assisting Charles II. to escape from his pursuers.* In the *Peers' Robing-room* is a fresco by Herbert, of *Moses bringing the Commandments from Mount Sinai*. It is said to be impossible now to burn down the Houses of Parliament. If by accident a fire should occur, it would only destroy the furniture and fittings, but the flooring, walls, and roof would remain intact. The New Houses of Parliament cost about two millions; their chief demerit arises from the decay of the stone with which they were built.

Admission to view both Houses, and all the public portion of the Palace of Westminster, is to be obtained every Saturday during the session, upon application at the Chamberlain's office, in the court near the Victoria Tower. Admission to hear the Debates—in the House of Lords, by a Peer's written order; in the House of Commons, by the written order of a Member. The doors are opened at 4, but, upon a night when the Debate is expected to be interesting, the stranger should be in attendance much before that hour, for the Strangers' Galleries are but small, and strangers are admitted according to priority of arrival. The Speaker takes the chair at 5, when prayers are read and business begins. The best nights for Debates are Mondays or Fridays. On Wednesday the House only sits till 6 P.M.

Baron Marochetti's equestrian statue of *Richard Cœur de Lion* is in Palace Yard; and statues of *Canning*, *Peel*, *Palmerston*, and *Derby*, are set up in Parliament Square.

Westminster Bridge, said to be the widest bridge in the world, and certainly one of the handsomest structures in London, was built upon the site of a former bridge, 1856-62, by Mr. Page, to connect Westminster with Lambeth. It is 85 feet wide (the roadway, 53 feet, foot-ways, 15 feet each), 1160 feet long, and consists of seven arches of iron (the centre arch being of 120 feet span, and 22 feet above high water), resting upon stone piers, with foundations 30 feet below low-water mark. The roadway rises only 5 feet 4 inches at the centre arch. It was upon the former bridge that the lonely and unaided poet Crabbe walked meditating suicide; and, from the same place at early morning, the view suggested Wordsworth's well-known sonnet :—

> "Earth has not anything to show more fair ;
> Dull would he be of soul who could pass by
> A sight so touching in its majesty ;
> This city now doth like a garment wear
> The beauty of the morning ; silent, bare,
> Ships, towers, domes, theatres and temples lie
> Open unto the fields and to the sky,
> All bright and glittering in the smokeless air.
> Never did sun more beautifully steep,
> In his first splendour, valley, rock, or hill ;
> Ne'er saw I, never felt a calm so deep !
> The river glideth at its own sweet will,
> Dear God, the very houses seem asleep,
> And all that mighty heart is lying still."

St. Thomas's Hospital. 47

Upon the Lambeth side of the Bridge is the entrance to *St. Thomas's Hospital*, an ancient Foundation by Richard, Prior of Bermondsey, in the year 1213, for Converts and Poor Children. Remodelled in 1215 by Peter de Rupibus, Bishop of Winchester, for Canons regular; it was surrendered to Henry VIII., in the 30th year of his reign, and purchased by the Citizens of London in 1544, and opened for the reception of patients in November, 1552, under Charter from the Crown. The Hospital remained on its old site in the borough of Southwark, near to London Bridge, from its foundation, until the year 1862, when the South-Eastern Railway Company obtained possession of the premises, and the Hospital was removed to a temporary location at Newington, Surrey. The new Hospital Buildings (of which the Foundation Stone was laid by the Queen, on the 13th May, 1868) were opened by Her Majesty on the 21st June, 1871, and are arranged for about 600 beds. The gross income of the Hospital, chiefly derived from rents, aided by donations, is about £45,000; but from this a large deduction has to be made, leaving about £33,000 for Hospital purposes. The *Albert Embankment* runs in front of the Hospital.

ASTLEY'S AMPHITHEATRE (now Sanger's Theatre Royal) stands in Westminster Bridge Road, not many yards beyond the entrance to St. Thomas's Hospital. It derived its original name from its first proprietor, Philip Astley, a cavalry soldier of handsome build and an expert rider, who, after his discharge from the army, took to equestrian performances in an open piece of ground in St. George's Fields. Here he made a little money, which was increased by £60, the produce of a diamond ring which he had the good fortune to find one day at the foot of Westminster Bridge, and built therewith his first theatre, opened in 1780. This, and two other theatres which succeeded it, were burnt down on this site. Andrew Ducrow, son of Peter Ducrow, of Bruges, was 'Flemish Hercules' at

Astley's, and one of its most successful riders. The present edifice contains both a stage for dramatic purposes and a circle for horsemanship. Admission from 6d. Pit 1s. 6d.

Canterbury Hall and Fine Arts Gallery, one of the largest of London Music Halls, is situated in Westminster Bridge Road, near the part spanned by the Railway Bridge. It is open from 11 A.M. to 12 at night. Concert begins at 7 P.M. Admission 6d.

Upon the south-east side of Westminster Bridge Road are the *Lambeth Baths*, more famous for its Temperance Meetings and social assemblies of working people than even for its sanitary appliances. When the water has been drawn out of the spacious bath, the place serves for a lecture and concert room. Here all kinds of simple amusement, in the way of songs, chorused by the people, newspaper readings, "spelling-bees," and temperance meetings, are held regularly through the year. Near Westminster Bridge Road, by the Railway Bridge, runs a thoroughfare leading eastwards to Waterloo Bridge Road, and familiarly known as the *New Cut*. The stranger, who may take the trouble to make his way through this street on Saturday night or Sunday morning, would see one of the busiest scenes in London. This is then the market for the poorest classes of the district, and the whole street is alive with people; costermongers, quack medicine vendors, and all manner of dealers in all kinds of wares and articles. The excuse for all this traffic on Sunday—and it is scarcely to be overruled—is, that the poor buyers have no place to keep their food if they bought it before the very moment they are ready to consume it.

The *Victoria Palace Theatre*—or, in popular parlance, "the Vic"—is a large edifice famous for melodramas and farces of the most pronounced kind. It can hold 2000 persons, and is situated in *Waterloo Bridge Road*, Lambeth.

PLATE II.

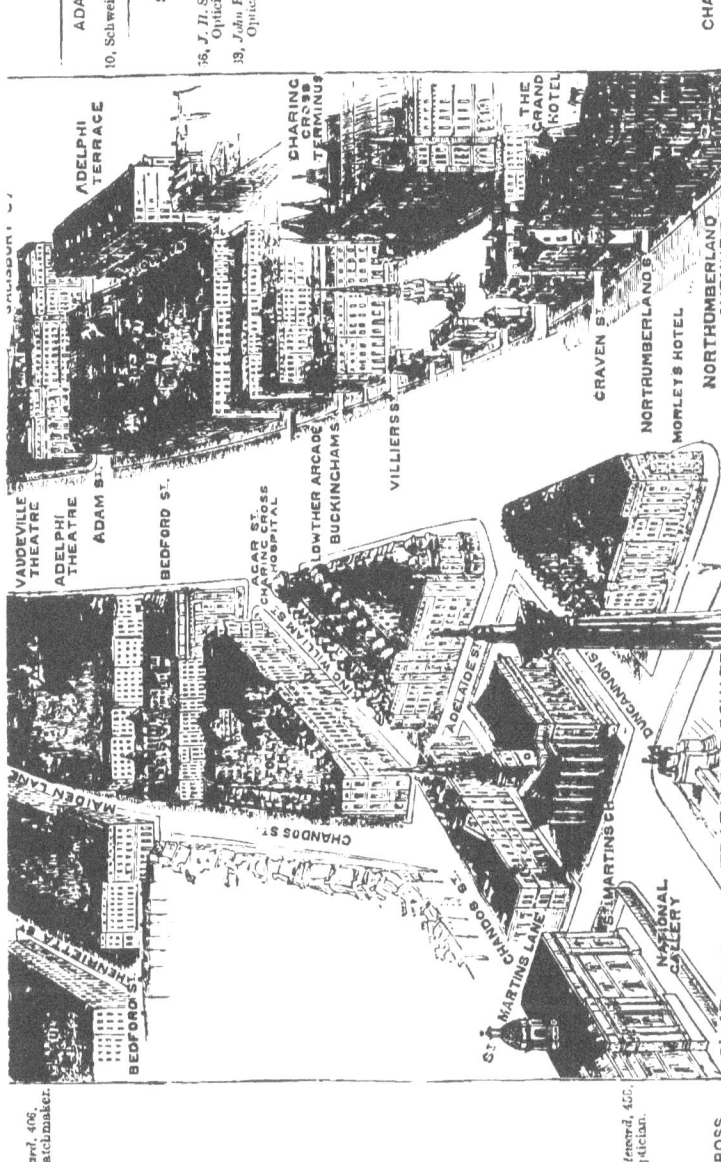

THE STRAND,

FROM CHARING CROSS TO FLEET STREET.

ADAM STREET.

10, Schweitzer's Cocoatina.

STRAND.

16, J. H. Steward, Optician.
39, John Browning, Optician.

THE STRAND.—FROM CHARING CROSS TO FLEET STREET.

STANDING with our backs to the Nelson Column and facing east, we shall observe upon our right hand the *Northumberland Avenue*, with the *New Grand Hotel* at the corner of it; this is the new thoroughfare to the Thames Embankment, for the sake of making which *Northumberland House*, the family mansion of the Duke of Northumberland, which stood here since 1603, was pulled down in 1876, at a cost of £500,000, and other expenses incurred amounting to £150,000 more. The land sold for building purposes will, however, doubtless repay much of the expenditure, and other great advantages will be obtained by opening up the Avenue; for it is said that, whereas the average time occupied by a Hansom cab in travelling from Charing Cross to the Mansion House, by way of the Strand, is 22 minutes, the journey by the Embankment takes but 12 minutes.

NORTHUMBERLAND HOUSE was the last of the many old palaces of the nobility which once graced the Strand, and had been the residence of the ancestors of the Dukes of Northumberland for two centuries and a half; its well-known Strand front, surmounted by a lion, the crest of the Percys, dated from about 1605, and is best represented perhaps in the painting by Canaletto, engraved by Bowles, 1753. There was a rather valuable collection of pictures to be seen here, but these of course were removed by their owner before the demolition of the house (the necessity for which was much regretted). Suffice it for the visitor that we indicate where the mansion, of no great historical or architectural interest, once stood. Of the

Northumberland House Lion many jokes used to be made, but perhaps the best was that by a humourist who undertook for a wager to persuade passers-by that the lion wagged his tail. He stood very intently looking up at the lion; took out a telescope, and appeared highly interested. The action was observed by an idler or two, who of course stopped to see what might happen, and gazed accordingly; the crowd increased, till at length the Strand became impassable; the greatest curiosity was manifested about nobody knew what—several persons asserted that they had seen the lion's tail wag; and even after the crowd was eventually dispersed, a few curious and pertinacious people hung about under doorways to satisfy themselves about the new phenomenon. A London crowd will gather quickly and for nothing. The wise pedestrian knows this; at once buttons up his coat, to protect his pockets, and passes on. Opposite the site of Northumberland House is the *Charing Cross Post Office*, at which letters and papers for the country can be posted half an hour later than at district post-offices.

In *Northumberland Street* is the office of the *Pall Mall Gazette* newspaper. At 27 *Craven Street*, lived Dr. Benjamin Franklin, in 1771, while representing in this country the interests of his American fellow-colonists. In front of the *Golden Cross Hotel*, in the Strand, once a well-known hostelry and place of departure for old mail-coaches, Mr. Pickwick is described as having been assailed by the hackney-coachman, and to have been thereupon taken under the protection of Mr. Jingle. Next door to the hotel is an old house of business, Messrs. Gardner's, which has been established in the Strand for a century and a quarter.

CHARING CROSS RAILWAY STATION is the West-end terminus of the South-Eastern Railway, and the *Charing Cross Hotel* is one of the largest in London. The Station occupies the site of Hungerford Market, which was demolished to make way for it, and the railway-bridge is

The Lowther Arcade.

partly supported upon the piers of the old Hungerford Suspension Bridge (built for foot-passengers only), which was taken away and set up across the Avon at Clifton, near Bristol, soon after this bridge was built in 1863. There is still a way for foot-passengers over the Charing Cross railway-bridge, by a staircase entered from *Villiers Street*—at the bottom of which street is the *Charing Cross Station of the Underground Railway*, and beyond it, the *Charing Cross Steamboat Pier*. In front of the Charing Cross Railway-station (S. E. Railway) stands a handsome copy of the *Cross* erected to the memory of Queen Eleanor, which used to be seen near here, in the centre of the village of Charing. Opposite the station is *Agar Street*, in which is the chief entrance to *Charing Cross Hospital*, erected in the Grecian style by Decimus Burton in 1831. This is an important institution, increasing in value with the wants of an increasing population, and is one of the medical schools of London. At the south west corner of Agar Street, there is an Electric Telegraph office. In *King William Street*, Strand, running west from Agar Street, is the little theatre once known as Woodin's Polygraphic Hall, afterwards as Charing Cross Theatre, and more recently as the *Folly Theatre;* a small house, but far from unpopular. *Lowther Arcade*, named after Lord Lowther, a former Chief Commissioner of Woods and Forests, consists of 25 shops for toys. The rooms once named the *Adelaide Gallery*, at the north end, is now a café—*Gatti's. Villiers Street*, on the south of the Strand, was named after the Dukes of Buckingham, whose mansion once stood here, and which originally formed part of *York House*—the residence of the Archbishop of York in Queen Mary's time, and afterwards the home of Lord Bacon, who was born in it, January 22, 1561. The beautiful *York Stairs*, or *Water Gate*, said to have been built by Inigo Jones, at the bottom of *Buckingham Street*, will give us some idea of the style of York

House, to which it belonged, and of which it is the sole relic. Peter the Great lodged at No. 15 Buckingham Street, Strand. S. Pepys lived at the house then opposite to it. *George Street*, *Villiers Street*, *Duke Street*, *Buckingham Street*, and *Of Lane*, which once connected them, perpetuate the memory of George Villiers, Duke of Buckingham—

> "Who in the course of one revolving moon,
> Was chemist, fiddler, statesman and buffoon."

In *Bedford Street* is a Civil Service Co-operative Supply Store.

Passing *Coutts's Bank*, a dreary-looking edifice, whose cellarage, however, filled with valuable property, extends far back into the ADELPHI, we turn down *Adam Street*, *Adelphi*, and find ourselves in the rear of those houses in the Strand, upon a handsome terrace overlooking the Embankment and the Thames. David Garrick died here at No. 5, *Adelphi Terrace*. The *Adelphi*, occupies part of the site of *Durham House*, once extending from the Strand to the river.

DURHAM HOUSE was the scene of the marriage of Lady Jane Grey; from hence she was escorted to the Tower. The use of Durham House was granted by Queen Elizabeth to Sir Walter Raleigh. Aubrey describes *Raleigh's Study* to have been "on a little turret that looked into and over the Thames, and had the prospect which is as pleasant perhaps as any in the world, and which not only refreshes the eyesight, but cheers the spirits, and (to speak my mind) I believe enlarges an ingenious man's thoughts." Upon the site of the stables of Durham House was built by the Earl of Salisbury the *New Exchange*, opened by James I. It was an open paved arcade, and above were shops occupied by perfumers, milliners, &c. Nan Clarges, a sempstress here—daughter of the blacksmith who lived in Maypole Alley and reared the Maypole—managed to captivate Monk, and became Duchess of Albemarle.

Frances Jennings, Duchess of Tyrconnell, when reduced in circumstances, took up her place at a stall in this Exchange—sitting in a white mask and white dress, and was therefore known as the *White Milliner*. She was soon discovered and provided for. The name of the Adelphi is derived from four architects, brothers (ἀδελφοί), named Adam, who built vast arches over the site of Durham House, and erected streets above them upon a level with the Strand, which they named after themselves, *John, Robert, James, and William Streets*. The *Dark Arches of the Adelphi* had long an evil reputation as the night-resort of thieves, but gas-light and police supervision have abolished the evil. The rooms of the *Society of Arts* are in John Street, Adelphi; they are open free, daily, from 10 to 4, except Wednesday and Saturday.

Opposite to the Strand end of Adam Street, Adelphi, is the *Adelphi Theatre*, a well-known and popular house of entertainment, first built by Scott, and known as the *Sans Pareil*, opened November, 1806; named the *Adelphi Theatre*, in 1820, by Rodwell and Jones. They transferred it to Terry and Yates. The latter joined Mathews the elder, and afterwards sold it to Mr. B. Webster, who rebuilt it in 1858. It has been chiefly noted for melodrama and farce, and for the acting of John Reeve, Wright, P. Bedford, Webster, Toole, Mrs. Keeley, Madame Celeste, and Miss Woolgar.

The *Vaudeville Theatre*, but a few doors east of the Adelphi Theatre, was built in 1872, and has enjoyed enormous popularity, as the scene of Mr. H. J. Byron's most popular comedies. No such hold of a stage was ever taken by a play, as by his comedy at this house, of 'Our Boys.'

Opposite the Vaudeville Theatre is *Salisbury Street*, which, with *Cecil Street* close by, occupies the site of *Salisbury House*, once the residence of the great Sir Robert Cecil. Salisbury House was subsequently divided into two houses, known as Great and Little Salisbury House, both of which were removed to make way for Cecil Street and Salisbury Street, rebuilt by Mr. Payne, the architect. In Salisbury Street lived a once noted man, *Partridge*, who combined, with his ordinary business of a shoemaker, the study of astrology, and realised a reputation by his almanacks, which he would not have achieved by his boots. Partridge also sold pills and other medicines in Salisbury Street, and transmitted the good-will of his businesses to his widow, who after his death continued the publication of the almanack, and the manufacture and sale of pills, &c., at the sign of the Blue Ball, in Salisbury Street. The chief feature of Salisbury Street for the last twenty years has been the *Arundel Club*, founded 1859, for literary men and artists, whose club-house is at No. 12, the last edifice in the street, upon the left-hand side of the way. From the balcony of this club one used to look below upon a busy scene of coal-heavers and their barges at the neighbouring wharf; just beyond was the pier for the halfpenny steamboats—to and from which a continual stream of passengers seemed to flow uninterruptedly, except perhaps a few who eddied, so to speak, round the picturesque old tavern known as the 'Fox under the Hill.' The Thames Embankment now occupies the site of the wharf; the river, once so near, has retired with the barges and the coals, and mine host of the 'Fox,' to a respectful distance; but the relics of the old tavern, before which Charles Dickens remembered himself as a boy resting from his labours at the neighbouring blacking factory in Hungerford Stairs, and watching the coal-heavers dancing to the sound of street music, are not yet demolished.

The Egyptian Obelisk named *Cleopatra's Needle* is placed upon the Thames Embankment at the foot of Salisbury Street. It is 70 feet high, and 8 feet wide at the base, weighs 200 tons, and is formed of granite. It was presented by Mohammed Ali to the British Government, and

Maiden Lane. 55

for many years it lay unclaimed in the sand at Alexandria along with a similar monolith; such obelisks were usually placed in pairs outside of Egyptian temples. The cost and difficulty of removing it to England were surmounted in 1878, the former by the munificence of Mr. Erasmus Wilson, who gave £10,000 for its removal, the latter by the skill of Mr. Dixon, C.E., who triumphed over every obstacle by his practical engineering science. This huge block of granite, after being lifted and placed in the cylinder-barge in which it was to be floated to England, had a most tempestuous voyage. The Steamboat which towed the Obelisk only escaped destruction by cutting it adrift in the Bay of Biscay, and for days nothing was to be heard of it. At length a passing vessel picked up the strange-looking object, a veritable—

"Monstrum horrendum, informe, ingens,"

and earned salvage thereon. Mr. Dixon's genius had secured the buoyancy of the huge bulk, and through him England's title of possession was fully substantiated. The scenes on the pyramidion represent the monarch Thothmes III., under the form of a sphynx with hands, offering water, wine, milk, and incense to the gods, Ra and Atum, the two principal deities of Heliopolis. The inscriptions give the names and titles of the deities, the titles of Thothmes III., and the statement of each of his special gifts.

SOUTHAMPTON STREET, on the north side of the Strand (named after Lady Rachael, daughter of the Earl of Southampton, and wife of Lord William Russell), leads directly to Covent Garden. At the foot of Southampton Street stood BEDFORD HOUSE, the town mansion of the Earl of Bedford. Half-way up the street, upon the left, is *Maiden Lane*, upon a second floor in one of the houses of which lodged Andrew Marvell, when M.P. for Hull, and it was here that he refused to accept a bribe of £1000 from the King. J. M. W. Turner, the great English painter, was born at the corner of Hand Court, Maiden Lane. Voltaire lodged, when in London, at the sign of the 'White Peruke,' Maiden Lane. The *Bedford Head Tavern*, in Maiden Lane, maintained until recently its associations with literature, art, and the drama, by means of the well-known *Re-union Club*, which for many years met here, but which is now transferred to rooms in the Adelphi Terrace, near the *Savage Club*, the *Junior Garrick*, the *Crichton*, and other clubs.

Passing northwards, up Southampton Street, we come upon—

COVENT GARDEN, a place of great celebrity and interest, which derives its name from the Convent Garden of Westminster, that once occupied not only this site, but the entire space from St. Martin's-in-the-Fields to Long Acre. After the dissolution of the Monasteries, the Garden was granted, with other lands, by Edward VI. to his uncle, the Lord Protector Somerset, but after the Protector's attainder it reverted to the Crown, and was given, in 1552, to John, Earl of Bedford. In 1634 Inigo Jones built for the then Earl of Bedford the church of *St. Paul's, Covent Garden*, which, except the portico, was totally burnt down in 1795. The present edifice was erected by John Hardwick, upon the same plan and proportions as the original. In and around it were buried Samuel Butler, the author of 'Hudibras;' the notorious Robert Carr, Earl of Somerset; Sir Peter Lely; Wycherley, the dramatist; Grinling Gibbons, Mrs. Centlivre, Dr. Arne, Dr. Armstrong, Sir Robert Strange, T. Girtin (the father of the school of English Water Colours), Macklin, the actor, Dr. Wolcot, &c. *Covent Garden Market-house* was built in 1830, and has been much improved within the last year or two, during which time the whole square has been undergoing a process of rebuilding. The visitor, who wishes to see Covent Garden Market at its busiest time, should go thither about six o'clock in the morning, of a Tuesday, Thursday, or Saturday; but the middle row is at all times an interesting sight, no matter what the time of year; for you may be always sure of seeing in it the finest fruit and flowers that skill can produce and that money can buy. The old song gave good advice which said—

"If ever you go to London town,
Just take a peep at Covent Garden."

Besides the great historical associations in which the district is so rich, Covent Garden has ample attractions in its own wonderful cornucopia; but we can only find space to note a few of the former. Hogarth's well-known print of 'Morning' shows St. Paul's Church, Tom King's Coffee-house under the portico, and the mansion close by, built for the Earl of Orford, and now long known as Evans's Hotel—in the rear of which are the noted concert and supper-rooms called *Evans's*, where Thackeray, Jerrold, Albert Smith, Mayhew, Mark Lemon, and others used to rendezvous. In a line with Evans's Hotel frontage ran the great *Piazza*, just taken down, in front of the numerous old hotels—the Bedford, Clunn's, the Tavistock, &c. In the north-east corner is the entrance to the *Floral Hall*, connected with the Italian Opera-house, Covent Garden. Upon the east side there used to be also a piazza in front of the *Hummum's Hotel*, but this was done away with many years ago.

In *Great Russell Street*, Covent Garden, were the three celebrated Coffee-houses, 'Will's,' 'Tom's,' and 'Button's.' WILL's was the house on the north side of Great Russell Street, at the corner of Bow Street (then the Bond Street of London). It is well to remember what an important influence coffee-houses exercised upon public opinion, in Queen Anne's time, before newspapers existed. "There were coffee-houses, where medical men might be consulted; Puritan coffee-houses, where no oath was heard; Jews' coffee-houses, for money changers; and

Popish coffee-houses, where, as good Protestants believed, Jesuits planned over their cups another Great Fire and cast silver bullets to shoot the King (Wm. III.)." Persons at that time commonly asked of such and such a one not where he lived, nor what was his address, but whether he frequented the 'Grecian' or the 'Rainbow.' WILL's was The Wits' coffee-house, where Dryden had his arm-chair in winter by the fireside, in summer in the balcony; the company met on the first floor and there smoked. Ward says that "the young beaux and wits, who seldom dared approach the principal table, thought it a great honour to have a pinch from Dryden's snuff-box." "Nowhere," says Macaulay, "was the smoking more constant than at 'Will's,' that celebrated house sacred to polite letters. There the talk was about poetical justice, and unities of place and time. There was a faction for Perrault and the Moderns, a faction for Boileau and the Ancients. Under no roof was a greater variety of figures to be seen. There were earls in stars and garters, clergymen in cassocks and bands, pert Templars, sheepish lads from the University, translators and index-makers in ragged coats of frieze." BUTTON's was Addison's house, "over against 'Tom's.'" Here met Pope, Steele, Swift, Arbuthnot, &c., and here Philips hung up the birchen-rod with which he threatened to chastise Pope for a bitter epigram. At 'Button's' was set up the *Lion's Head* to receive letters and papers for the *Guardian.* Pope describes Addison as having "usually studied all the morning, then met his party at 'Button's,' dined there, and stayed for five or six hours and sometimes far into the night. I was of the company for about a year, but found it too much for me. It hurt my health, so I quitted it." Tom's was at 17 Great Russell Street, the north side of the way. Daniel De Foe, in 1722, wrote of this house: "After the play the best company generally go to 'Tom's' and 'Will's' coffee-houses near adjoining, where there is playing at Picket and the best of conversation till midnight." 'Tom's' was a favourite resort of Dr. Johnson, Sir Joshua Reynolds, Garrick, &c.

A little farther up *Bow Street* is the *Police Court*, and beyond it the ROYAL ITALIAN OPERA-HOUSE, occupying the site of old *Covent Garden Theatre*, which was built 1732, by Rich, the celebrated actor. Garrick played in it in 1746. In 1803 John Kemble became proprietor and stage manager. In September 1808, it was burnt down, and twenty persons killed. It was rebuilt by R. Smirke, R.A., and reopened December 31, 1808, at increased prices, which enraged the people. Riots ensued in favour of the old prices (which became known as the *O. P. Riots*), and after seventy-seven nights the manager succumbed. In 1817 John Kemble retired, and Charles Kemble in 1840. Charles Mathews, Madame Vestris, and Macready, subsequently leased the theatre, and later the Anti-Corn Law League used it for its meetings and Bazaar. In 1847 it was converted into the Royal Italian Opera-house. In 1856, while being used for a masquerade by Professor Anderson, the so-called Wizard of the North, it was burnt down. It was rebuilt by Mr. E. M. Barry, and reopened as an Italian Opera-house in 1858. The former opera-house was the one in which Grisi and Mario, Viardot, &c., achieved their great success; the latter has had for its chief artistes Patti and Albani. It holds about 2000 persons. The bas-reliefs on the Bow Street front were by Flaxman.

But a few yards from the bottom of Bow Street, eastwards, is the *Theatre Royal, Drury Lane*, the oldest in London (1812), and the fourth erected upon this site. The first Drury Lane Theatre, built for T. Killigrew, under a patent of Charles II., and opened 1663, was burnt down in January, 1671–2. It was rebuilt by Sir Christopher Wren, and opened with a prologue by Dryden, 1674. Rich, Steele, Doggett, Wilks, Cibber, and Booth were successively patentees. Garrick succeeded them, and in 1747 opened with a prologue by Dr. Johnson.

Garrick here took leave of the stage, June 10, 1776. Sheridan followed, and in 1788 John Kemble. In 1791 the theatre was taken down, rebuilt, and re-opened, 1794. It was burnt down in 1809, rebuilt by B. Wyatt, and reopened, October 12, 1812, with a prologue by Lord Byron. The 'Rejected Addresses,' by Horace and James Smith, were written *apropos* of this opening. At *Drury Lane Theatre* appeared Nell Gwynne, 1666; Booth, 1701; Mrs. Siddons, 1775; J. P. Kemble, 1783; H. Mellon, Duchess of St. Albans, 1795; Edmund Kean, 1814. Macready here took farewell of the stage, February 26, 1851. The *Middlesex Music Hall* is in Drury Lane.

Retracing our steps through Covent Garden and Southampton Street, we will now return to the Strand, at the point from which we left it.

BEAUFORT BUILDINGS, on the south side of the Strand, occupy the site of an ancient mansion known by different names, but eventually as *Worcester House*, after its then owner, the celebrated Marquis of Worcester, author of the 'Century of Inventions.' His eldest son became Duke of Beaufort, and the mansion, *Beaufort House*. Here was married by Protestant rites at midnight, in September 1662, the Duke of York, afterwards James II., to Anne Hyde, daughter of the Earl of Clarendon. The mansion underwent some changes, was reduced in size, and the smaller house was burnt down. Upon the site, Beaufort Buildings (in which once lived Henry Fielding the novelist) suffered a similar fate not long since. *Simpson's Tavern and Divan* occupy the site of the *Fountain Tavern* described by Strype, and noted for its political club. *Fountain Court* took its name from the tavern. Here was the *Coal Hole*, one of Edmund Kean's tavern haunts, and the scene of later orgies under Nicholson, the so-called Lord Chief Baron of the Judge and Jury entertainment.

Exeter Hall, famed for its May Meetings of Religious Societies and for the *Sacred Harmonic Society's Oratorio*

Concerts, stands opposite. On its front is the Greek word ΦΙΛΑΔΕΛΦΟΙ (loving brethren). The Great Hall, which holds over 3,000, was opened in 1831; in the lobbies of Exeter Hall are various offices of philanthropic and other societies. The narrow frontage of Exeter Hall, like those of several other public buildings in the Strand, by no means corresponds with the size of the adjoining edifice. A list of the May Meetings is given away at the Hall.

The *Lyceum Theatre* will be found a few yards farther west; its chief entrance is in Wellington Street. It was built in 1765 as an academy for a society of artists. After many vicissitudes it was opened in 1809 as the English Opera House; was rebuilt in 1816 and destroyed by fire, again rebuilt and again opened for English opera in 1834. It was re-decorated for Madame Vestris in 1847. The Sublime Society of Beef Steaks, otherwise the *Beef Steak Club*, held their meetings in a room at this theatre, dining every Saturday from November to June off beef steaks, cooked upon a gridiron, and served with arrack punch. The Society was founded at Covent Garden Theatre, by Rich and Lambert, who, there in the painting-room, used to cook their own steaks and invite an occasional dropper-in to partake with them. The number of members increased at length to 25, of whom George IV., then Prince Regent, was one, and the celebrated Captain Morris was the poet laureate. Within a year or two of the present time the whole of the paraphernalia of this club, including its silver gridiron, its plate, its ornaments, furniture, pictures, &c., were all sold by auction at Christie and Manson's and realised over £650. The *Lyceum Theatre* has of late years flourished under Mr. Bateman's management, and more recently under that of Mr. H. Irving.

In *Wellington Street* is the office of the *Morning Post* newspaper, founded in 1772, and known as the organ of the fashionable world. Here also is the office of the *Athenæum*, and at 110, Strand, the Evening *Globe*.

The SAVOY was so called from a palace built in 1245, by Peter, Earl of Savoy and Richmond (uncle of Eleanor, the wife of Henry III.), in which John, King of France, lived during his captivity, and died soon after his release. The chapel of *Mary le Savoy* was the chapel of the Hospital of St. John the Baptist, and is the only relic of the old palace. It is a building of the late Perpendicular style, with a rich fine ceiling, and is historically remarkable as the scene of the *Savoy Conference* for the revision of the Liturgy at the Restoration of Charles II. Fuller was at this time lecturer of the Savoy, and Cowley was a candidate for the office of Master. Twelve bishops took part in the Conference on behalf of the Established Church, and Calamy, Baxter, and Reynolds for the Presbyterians. George Withers, poet (d. 1667); and the Earl of Feversham (d. 1709), who commanded James II.'s troops at Sedgemoor, were buried here, without monuments.

WATERLOO BRIDGE (named from the number of suicides from it, "the English Bridge of Sighs") was built by Rennie, and opened, June 18, 1817, the second anniversary of the battle of Waterloo, by a grand procession headed by the Prince Regent and the Dukes of York and Wellington. The bridge is built of granite, "in a style of solidity and magnificence never before known." It consists of nine semi-elliptical arches, each of 120 feet span and 35 feet high. It cost a million of money, including the approaches, or by itself £400,000, and proved a poor speculation to the company that built it. It is now made free. The Terminus of the South Western Railway is in *Waterloo Bridge Road*.

Upon the opposite or north side of the Strand is the *Gaiety Theatre*, built on the site of old *Exeter Change*, in 1868, by Mr. J. C. Phipps, for Mr. J. Hollingshead. The performances consist of comedy, farce, operetta, burlesques, and extravaganzas. Commence usually at seven. The chief entrance is in the Strand, but there is a side entrance in *Catherine Street*. Prices of admission are from 6d. upwards.

Somerset House.

SOMERSET HOUSE, in the Strand, stands upon the site of the old Palace, built by the Lord Protector Somerset, at an immense cost, and occupied by the wives of James I., Charles I., and Charles II., as described by Samuel Pepys. The present building was begun, in 1776, by Sir William Chambers, and completed in 1786, all but the west wing, which was finished by Mr. Pennethorne in 1852. The style of Somerset House is Italian, "refined to a degree scarcely excelled by Palladio himself." The exterior is the perfection of masonry, the sculptors employed in its decoration were Carlini, Wilton, Geracci, Nollekens, Bacon, Banks, and Flaxman. The Entrance archway from the Strand has been much admired, and the Terrace front in the Venetian style, facing the Thames, 800 feet in length, enriched with columns, pilastered pediments, &c., is regarded as one of the noblest works of the kind in London. The building is in the form of a quadrangle, and contains a large number of Government offices. The learned societies, which at one time (as well as the Royal Academy of Arts) were accommodated with rooms at Somerset House, have been removed to Burlington House, Piccadilly. The chief Government offices at Somerset House are the *Audit Office*, where the accounts of the kingdom and colonies are audited, the *Office of Registrar-General of Births, Deaths, and Marriages*, the *Office of Inland Revenue*, a centre for the receipt from district collectors of all taxes, stamp, money, legacy, and excise duties, and the *Wills and Probate Office*, removed here in 1874, from Doctor's Commons near St. Paul's, and which occupies the south side of the quadrangle. Here all Wills are proved (since 1861 they may be proved without a solicitor) and administration granted; the calendars may be searched for one shilling; the original of a will be seen for one shilling; and the wills of living persons may be deposited. The wills of Shakespeare, Newton, Dr. Johnson, and of nearly all the great Englishmen of past times, are to be seen here.

The Inland Revenue Department has rooms below the level of the street, wherein all the mechanical work is done, such as the stamping of documents, patent medicine labels, postage envelopes, post cards, and postage and receipt stamps. The bronze *Statue of George III.*, and the figure of *Father Thames* in the quadrangle, were by John Bacon, and cost £2000. The *Story of the Watch-face* (which is to be seen a little above the entrance to the office of Stamps and Taxes) must once again be told. The tradition is that a workman employed on the building fell from a scaffolding and was saved from being killed by the ribbon of his watch, which caught in a piece of projecting stonework and broke his fall. The labourer was supposed to have let it remain there in memory of his miraculous escape. The story is fabulous. The watch-face was placed there as a meridian mark for a transit instrument in one of the windows of the Royal Society.

KING'S COLLEGE AND SCHOOL occupy a part of Somerset House, which was left unfinished by Sir William Chambers and was completed by Sir R. Smirke, extending from the entrance in the Strand to the east wing of the river front, and containing, besides theatres, lecture-room, museum, library, and chapel, the residences of the Principal and the Professors. Over the lofty Strand entrance are the arms of the College, and the motto, " Sancte et sapienter,"—Holily and wisely. The Institution, a proprietary one, was founded in 1828. The School is for lads between nine and sixteen. The other departments of the College are the Theological, General Literature and Sciences, Applied Sciences, and the Medical; in connection with which last was established, in 1839, *King's College Hospital*, in Portugal Street, Lincoln's Inn Fields, now one of the most important Hospitals in London. A limited number of matriculated students are resident in the College.

In *Strand Lane*, which formerly led to a landing stairs called Strand Stairs, is an old *Roman Spring Bath.* The cold clear water in it was believed to be derived from the neighbouring well of Holywell Street, famed for its miraculous cures.

Opposite Somerset House, No. 332, used to be the office of the old *Morning Chronicle*, once the rival of the *Times*. The *Morning Chronicle* reckoned among its staff many of the foremost men of the period—as James Perry; J. Campbell, afterwards Lord Chancellor, who began upon it his London career, and was its theatrical critic in 1810, as Hazlitt was afterwards. In it Dickens obtained early fame by his *Sketches by Boz*. Coleridge and Thomas Campbell were contributors. Black and Mackay were also upon its editorial staff, as was later the present writer.

The *Maypole*, in the Strand, stood upon the site of the present churchyard of St. Mary-le-Strand, opposite Maypole Alley, "where Drury Lane descends into the Strand." The Maypole set up here at the Restoration, in lieu of one which had been removed by the Puritans, was 134 feet high, with a crown, vane, &c., richly gilt, at the top of it, and a balcony about the middle of it. with the King's arms, "far more glorious, bigger and higher than ever any one that stood before it." It was broken by a high wind in 1672, and in 1713, being old and decayed, was taken down. Samuel Pepys mentions a May-day incident of Drury Court: "To Westminster" (May 1, 1667), "in the way meeting many milkmaids with their garlands upon their pails, dancing, with a fiddler before them, and saw pretty Nelly (Gwynne) standing at her lodging-door in Drury Court, in her smock sleeves and bodice, looking upon me; she seemed a mighty pretty creature."

The church of *St. Mary-le-Strand* was built by James Gibbs (the architect of the church of St. Martin's-in-the-Fields), in 1714-17. It consists of two Orders, in the upper of which the lights are placed; the wall of the lower being solid, to keep out noises from the street. There was at first no steeple designed for this church, only a campanile or turret;

F

but a column, 250 feet high, in honour of Queen Anne, was to have been set up by the same architect, 80 feet westward of the church. The Queen died, the idea of the column to her was abandoned, and Gibbs was ordered to erect a steeple instead of the campanile."

In *Newcastle Street*, named after the ground landlord, John Holles, Duke of Newcastle, is the *Globe Theatre*, erected upon the site of old *Lyon's Inn;* once an inn in Chancery, but more recently let out in small residential chambers, in one of which lived Weare, the victim of Thurtell:—

> " They cut his throat from ear to ear,
> His brains they battered in;
> His name was Mr. William Weare,
> He dwelt in Lyon's Inn."

The Globe Theatre is one of the numerous recent additions to the theatres of London. Its terms and hours of admission are the same as those of other Strand theatres.

Wych Street is an old thoroughfare (Via de Aldwyche) from the Strand to Drury Lane (named after the family mansion of Sir W. Drury), still containing some picturesque gabled houses. The *Olympic Theatre*, at its west end, was originally built on the site of *Craven House* (the residence of Lord Craven), by Philip Astley, as a circus for horsemanship. It was burnt in 1849, and rebuilt. Many actors and actresses of repute have appeared here— Elliston, Keeley, C. Kean, Vestris, Nisbett, Foote, Liston— among the latest, F. Robson, who drew all London hither. The prices and hours of admission are similar to those of the neighbouring theatres. In Wych Street is the chief entrance to *New Inn*, whereat Sir Thomas More studied before he entered himself of Lincoln's Inn. He afterwards described " New Inn fare, wherewith many an honest man is well contented."

Danes Inn, at the end of Wych Street, consisting of residential chambers, was recently built on the site of the

Old *Angel Inn*, whose covered galleries and waggon-yard dated from 300 years ago.

Holywell Street was named from a well, said to have been situated under the *Old Dog Tavern*. It is still one of the most picturesque of the streets of London, many of the old lofty gabled houses yet remaining. It has long been noted for its old book-stalls, and for questionable literature; but its chief business seems of late to be in new cheap books, at a 25 per cent. discount off the published prices. Holywell Street has, by one or two of its bookselling tenants, been named Booksellers' Row, Strand; but the old name, not perhaps more honoured, is better known.

In the Strand, about this point, and nearly facing each other, are two small theatres; the *Strand Theatre*, famous for burlesques (once Punch's Playhouse); and a new theatre known as the *Opera Comique*, but chiefly noted for its English performances of the school of Opera Bouffe.

Between *Surrey Street* (in which Congreve died, 1729), *Norfolk Street, Howard Street* (in which lived Mrs. Bracegirdle), and *Arundel Street*, stood ARUNDEL HOUSE, or PALACE (taken down in 1678), wherein the Earl of Arundel collected the celebrated Arundelian Marbles, afterwards given to the University of Oxford. In Arundel Street, on the site of the old *Crown and Anchor*, was built the Whittington, now the *Temple Club*. The *Whitefriars Club* of literary men, &c., meet at the Temple Club-house. At the foot of Arundel Street is the entrance to the *Temple Station of the Underground Railway*, to the Mansion House, &c., and at this part of the Thames Embankment have been set up *Statues of Isambard Brunel, Esq.*, the engineer, and *John Stuart Mill, Esq.*, the great political economist.

St. Clement's Danes' Church, frequented by Dr. Johnson, in which, as Boswell says, he repeated the responses with tremulous energy. A tablet to his memory appears where he sat, No. 18 pew, in the north gallery. St.

Clement's was so named because the Danes, left in the kingdom after the Conquest, lived compulsorily between Ludgate and Westminster, and built a church here called *Ecclesia Clementis Danorum*, the Clement referred to being, some think, Clement the martyr Pope, third Bishop of Rome. The anchor which forms the symbol of the Church and of *Clement's Inn* was, it is said, derived from the anchor attached to the Bishop's body when he was cast into the sea. St. Clement's anchor is therefore not the symbol of hope, but of destruction. The body of old St. Clement's Church was taken down and rebuilt 1682, to the old tower, by Edward Pierce, under the gratuitous direction of Sir C. Wren. In 1719 Gibbs added the present tower and steeple. In the church were buried Rymer, compiler of the *Fœdera*; Otway and Nat. Lee; and, in the churchyard, in Portugal Street, hard by, Honest Joe Miller, of facetious memory.

Clement's Inn, one of the Inns of Chancery once attached to the Inner Temple, and named from the parish church, is used now chiefly for chambers and offices, but formerly only by students-at-law. Shakespeare has immortalised this Inn, in connection with Justice Shallow (Henry IV.):

"*Shallow*. I was once of Clement's Inn; where I think they will talk of mad Shallow yet.

"*Silence*. You were called lusty Shallow then, cousin.

"*Shallow*. By the mass, I was called anything; and I would have done anything indeed, and roundly too. There was I and Little John Doit of Staffordshire, and Black George Barnes of Staffordshire, and Francis Pickbone and Will Squele, a Cotswold man; you had not four such swinge-bucklers in all the Inns of Court again.

* * * * * *

"*Shallow*. Nay, she must be old; she cannot choose but be old; certain she's old, and had Robin Nightwork by old Nightwork, before I came to Clement's Inn.

"*Falstaff*. We have heard the Chimes at midnight, Master Shallow."

* * * * * *

Clement's Inn.

"*Shallow.* I remember at Mile-end-green (when I lay at Clement's Inn), I was then Sir Dagonet in Arthur's show.

* * * * * *

"*Falstaff.* I do remember him at Clement's Inn, like a man made after supper of a cheese-paring."

The Chimes are still heard at midnight, as Falstaff heard them; but they are now "grown hoarse with age and sitting up."

Essex Street and *Devereux Court*, upon the south side of the Strand, formerly known as the Outer Temple, were named after Robert Devereux, Earl of Essex, the favourite of Queen Elizabeth; on this site stood *Essex House*. Dr. Johnson established a Club, called 'Sam's' at the *Essex Head Tavern*. *Essex Street Chapel* is the oldest Unitarian Chapel in London. The *Grecian Coffee-house*, kept by a Greek, in *Devereux Court*, was mentioned in No. 1 of the 'Spectator': —"My face is likewise very well known at the Grecian;" and here it is said two friends quarrelled so bitterly over a Greek accent they went out into Devereux Court and fought a duel, in which one was killed on the spot.

Palsgrave Place was the site of the *Palsgrave Head Tavern*, named after the Palsgrave Frederic, afterwards King of Bohemia, affianced at Whitehall to the Princess Elizabeth, 1612.

The COURTS OF LAW, or PALACE OF JUSTICE, are being erected, by Mr. G. E. Street, on the north side of the Strand, to a little beyond the line of Temple Bar and of old Shire Lane—(so called "because it divideth the City from the Shire)," and extending back to Carey Street, Lincoln's Inn. In 1880, or 1881, it is hoped that these buildings will be sufficiently complete to allow of all the Divisions of the High Court of Justice and both branches of the Supreme Court being assembled under one roof. The Eastern part of the building, containing the wing for Masters, Registrars, Chief Clerks, and the like, has been already finished; the remainder of the seven acres is being gradually covered. When the structure is further advanced, there will be seen from the Strand a Portland stone edifice of 500 feet long, and about 80 feet in height, pierced with Gothic windows, and set off by gables and pinnacles. On the City side of the site of Temple Bar will stand a great campanile, or bell tower, 160 feet high. In the centre of the main building the gable will have a height of 130 feet, and contain a great rose window, above the main window of the central hall, which will be 230 feet long, 40 feet wide, and 80 feet high. At each end of this new *salle des pas perdus* will be a marble gallery, like the wooden galleries at the end of the Halls of Trinity College, Cambridge. At the north end of the Central Hall there will be a corridor running east and west the whole length of the building; while another corridor, continuing the direction of the central hall, will lead out into *Carey Street*, past two jury halls, as large as courts, and a refreshment room for the members of the Bar, with kitchen, cellar, larder, robing-room, &c. The level of Carey Street at this northern front of the building will be 17 feet above the Strand, and 12 feet higher than the central hall. The Chief Entrance from the Strand will be under an arch of 50 feet, on either side of which will be Gothic traced windows with the lancet arch; and above the windows will be recesses for sculpture. Through the central arch will be reached an entrance porch. A second porch will succeed to this, from which will rise steps leading to the south gallery of the central hall and to the level of the courts; for the eight courts round the central hall are to be above its level, while the floor of the hall will be 4 or 5 feet higher than the Strand. The long Strand and Carey Street fronts will be formed by two buildings, of which the westernmost, called the Main building, will contain the Courts and the Central Hall. The Eastern building is joined to the Main building by a narrow front to the Strand, and by a like erection, without depth, at the Carey Street end; but except for these two communications, the two wings will be separated from each other by an open space called the Quadrangle. This quadrangle will be more than twice as large as the central hall; it will be paved, either wholly or in part. The Carriage Entrance will sweep into it from the Strand between two smaller arches for pedestrians. From the quadrangle, which will give light and air to both buildings, many entrances will lead into each. The Eastern building will be different in style from the other, and the brown Portland stone, which in the other part of the building holds all the prominent positions, will here be largely relieved by red brick. In addition to the eastern tower in front, there will be a tower of equal height at the north-eastern end, with smaller towers elsewhere. On one of these heights the tutelary statue of Justice is to stand, as an embodiment of the purpose of the edifice. From the tower in Fleet Street a Janus clock, facing two ways, now shows conspicuously from the east and from the west, in the style (well suited to London) of the clock of St. Mary-le-Bow in Cheapside. Including staircases, corridors, halls, and rooms, there will be 800 apartments in the main edifice, and 300 in the eastern building. The contract price was about £700,000. The land upon which these courts are being built cost Parliament £1,453,000. It was occupied of late years by some of the dingiest and most wretched tenements in London, and very few noteworthy houses or streets have been removed in clearing the ground. Mention, however, may be made of *Butcher's Row*, afterwards the site of *Picket Place*; also of *Shire Lane*, above referred to, noted as the birthplace of Sir C. Sedley, and the abode of Ashmole, the astrologer, alchemist, and antiquary; of Isaac Bickerstaff, the 'Tatler;' of Christopher Kat, at whose house originated the *Kit-Kat Club*, of Protestant politicians.

FLEET STREET, LUDGATE CIRCUS, LUDGATE HILL, LUDGATE STREET, ST. PAUL'S CHURCHYARD.

TEMPLE BAR, recently demolished, was one of the City gates marking the boundaries of the City of London and at this point separating it from the City of Westminster; and was built by Sir C. Wren in 1670, after the fire of 1666 which destroyed a previous "Bar." It opened, not immediately, into the City itself, which terminated at Ludgate, but into " the liberty or freedom thereof." Each façade of Temple Bar had four Corinthian pilasters, an entablature, and arched pediment. On the west, in two niches, were statues of Charles I. and Charles II. in Roman costume; on the east, in similar niches, statues of James I. and Queen Elizabeth—all by Bushnell, who died in 1701. In the centre of each façade was a window lighting an apartment over the Bar, rented by Messrs. Child, the neighbouring bankers. Above the centre of the pediment, upon iron spikes, were formerly placed the heads and limbs of persons executed for high treason.

> "Fast, fast, the gallants ride in some safe nook to hide,
> Their coward heads predestined to rot on Temple Bar."

Upon the visit of the Sovereign to the City, it was customary to keep the gates closed till admission was formally demanded; they were then thrown open, the City sword was surrendered by the Lord Mayor to the Sovereign, who thereupon returned it to the Lord Mayor. Daniel De Foe stood in the pillory at Temple Bar for libel on the Government, while the people drank his health and hung the pillory with flowers. Temple Bar had long been in a very tottering condition, its removal recently was a matter of necessity; it were well, however, one would think, that

SAVE AT LEAST 25 PER CENT.
CLOTHING AT TRADE PRICE.
PUBLIC SUPPLY STORE,
271 & 272, HIGH HOLBORN, (*Next door to Inns of Court Hotel.*)
CITY BRANCH: 82, FLEET ST., (*2 Minutes' walk from Ludgate Circus.*)
Proprietors, CHAS. BAKER & CO.,
West of England Manufacturers. (Established 1864.)

RULES.

1st.—All GOODS to be paid for in Cash before they are removed from the Store.

2nd.—No TICKETS required, and no Extra Charge whatever is made on Wholesale Trade Price Marked in Plain Figures on each Garment.

3rd.—ALL GOODS NOT APPROVED are exchanged or the Cash returned as the customer desires; if made to order it makes no difference in this respect.

GENTLEMEN'S CLOTHING DEPARTMENT.—Price List.

Cloth Trousers (very durable)		4/11	5/11	6/11	7/11	8/11 10/9
Trousers and Vest (very durable)			12/11	14/11	16/11	19/11
Business Suits, complete (very durable)		18/11	21/-	25/-	29/6	35/-
Gentlemen's Serge Suits, Indigo Dye, complete			21/-	29/6	37/6	
Morning or Business Coats, superior Cloth		12/11	14/11	16/11	19/11	
Morning Coat and Vest, superior Black Diagonal Cloth			29/6	35/-	39/6	
Super Black Frock and Morning Coats, either Plain or Diagonal			19/11	25/-	29/6	
Vests only, superfine Black Cloth, Plain or Diagonal			4/11	5/11	6/11	
Black Trousers, very superior make		8/11	10/9	12/11	14/11	

Black Cloth Garments are manufactured from celebrated West of England Broad Cloth and Doeskins.

Gentlemen's Diagonal Overcoats, all Wool	16/11	and 19/11
" Superior Cloth and best Lining, warm and durable	21/-	and 24/6
Very Superior Overcoats, extra quality Linings		29/6
Blue and Black Nap Overcoats, warm and durable	16/11	and 19/11
Very Superior Nap and Beaver Overcoats, extra quality Linings	24/6	and 29/6

All our good quality Nap and Beaver Overcoats are warranted Fast Colour Indigo Dye.

GENTLEMEN'S BESPOKE DEPARTMENT.—No Extras charged on these Prices.

Trousers to measure, from all Wool, Scotch Cheviots, West of England Tweeds, Homespuns, &c., warranted shrunk, and very durable	10/-	12/6	14/11	
Suits complete to measure, from All-Wool Scotch Cheviots, Real West of England Tweeds, Blue Serge (Indigo dye) Homespuns, &c., warranted shrunk, and very durable, well made, and fashionably cut, lined with Silk, Italian, and good Trimmings. No extras	39/6	44/6	49/6	54/6 59/6

These Prices are for Jacket Shape Suits. If required with Morning Coats, Tweeds, 4s., and Diagonals, 7s. 6d. more per Suit.

Morning or Business Coat and Vest to measure, well and fashionably made, from superior All-Wool, Diagonal, or plain Black Broad Cloth, lined with Silk, Italian, and bound with real Mohair Braid	35/-	39/6	49/6
Frock or Dress Coats to measure, very superior, from real West of England Black Broad Cloth, thoroughly well made and trimmed, lined with Silk Italian. No extras	34/6	39/6	44/6 49/6
Vests to measure, to match Frock or Dress Coats	8/6	9/11	12/6
Overcoats to measure, from superior Diagonal and other fashionable cloths, warranted shrunk and thoroughly well made, lined	29/6	39/6	49/6

First-class Cutters being always employed on the premises, a good fit, style, &c., can be relied on, the Firm's aim being to supply well-made, durable, and fashionable garments, rather than cheap, inferior articles.

Patterns of Cloth, Price Lists, Fashion Plates, and Self-measurement Form post-free.

JUVENILE DEPARTMENT.

Dark useful Knickerbocker Suits, complete				1/11	2/6	2/11
" " Durable Cloth, Braided		3/11	4/11	5/11	6/11	7/11 8/11
Very Superior Cloth, Richly Braided	10/9	12/11	14/11	16/11	19/11	24/6
Blue Serge Sailor Suits, complete	3/6	3/11	4/11	5/11	6/11	7/11 8/11
" " Superfine Fine Serge, Richly Braided		11/9	12/11	14/11	16/11	
Boys' Velvet Suits, newest styles			12/11	18/11	24/11	
Youths' Durable Trouser Suits, 7 to 10 years	10/9	12/11	14/11	18/11	24/6	
" " " " 14 to 15 years		15/9	18/11	24/6	29/6	
Youths' Serge Trouser Suits, Indigo Dye, complete			14/11	16/11	19/11	
Youths' Ulsters and Chesterfield Overcoats	6/11	8/11	10/9	14/11	16/11	21/-
Youths' Trousers, very durable, well made and lined			3/11	4/11	5/11	6/11
Odd Knickers made from Remnants of Cloth, very cheap and durable				1/11	2/11	3/11

SPECIAL NOTICE.—GENTLEMEN'S AND YOUTHS' SHIRTS AT TRADE PRICE.

PLATE III.

CHEAPSIDE.

J. Pigott, 110,
My Tailor, My Hatter, My Hosier

Wilcox & Gibbs, 150,
Automatic Silent Sewing Machine.

ST. PAUL'S CHURCH-YD.

Religious Tract Society's
Retail Depot, 65.

LUDGATE HILL.

John Hudson, 6,
The City Lilliputian Glove &
Hosiery Warehouse.

Lindsey & Sons, 82,
Surgical Instrument Maker

Hope Brothers, 44-46,
Tailors & Outfitters

Grand Café Restaurant de Paris

FLEET STREET.

CHEAPSIDE.

ST. PAUL'S CHURCH

LUDGATE HILL

15-17, M. Clark & Co.,
Ladies' Under-Clothing,
Juvenile Dress Warehouse

45, Sherwood & Vernes,
Provision Stores.

The "Bodega" Ludgate
Wine Merchants.

FLEET STREET

FLEET STREET AND LUDGATE HILL,
TO ST. PAUL'S AND CHEAPSIDE, &c.

Bickford & Mehling, 180 & 181,
The American Novelty Stores.

this the last of the boundary gates of the City, with more historical interest than perhaps any other, should be re-erected upon a fitting site. Passing this no longer visible boundary we find ourselves in FLEET STREET, so called from the river Fleet which used to run between it and Ludgate Hill, and empty itself into the Thames at Blackfriars. The first house on the City side of the Bar, south, is Child's Banking House dating from 1620, and built on the site of the *Devil Tavern* (named in compliment to the neighbouring church of St. Dunstan and that muscular Christian's victory over the fiend), where Ben Jonson reigned, as Dryden afterwards did at Will's. The Apollo room at the *Devil* was immortalised in verse, and the "oracle of Apollo" was Rare Ben Jonson himself. Over the door of the entrance to the Apollo room were the following lines:—

"Welcome all who lead or follow,
To the oracle of Apollo—
Here he speaks out of his pottle,
Or the tripos, his tower bottle;
All his answers are divine;
Truth itself doth flow in wine.
Hang up all the poor hop drinkers!
Cries old Sim, the king of skinkers; *
He the half of life abuses,
That sits watering with the Muses.
Those dull girls no good can mean us.
Wine it is the milk of Venus,
And the poet's horse accounted,
Ply it, and you all are mounted.
'Tis the true Phœbian liquor,
Cheers the brain, makes wit the quicker;
Pays all debts, cures all diseases,
And at once the senses pleases.
Welcome all who lead or follow
To the oracle of Apollo."

---

* Simon Wadloe, the host of the 'Devil,'—about whom was written the song of 'Old Sir Simon the king.'

"I myself, simple as I stand here, was a wit in the last age. I was created Ben Jonson's son in the 'Apollo,'" boasts Oldwit, in Shadwell's play of *Bury Fair*. A few steps from Child's Bank is the entrance to Middle Temple Lane, and a little farther down Fleet Street is the gateway of the Inner Temple; it will be well, then, to furnish here a few particulars of these two famous Inns of Court.

THE TEMPLE was so named from the Knights Templar, who removed their abode hither from Thavies Inn, Holborn, in 1184, and who were succeeded (upon the forfeiture of their estates by the Pope) by the Knights Hospitallers of St. John of Jerusalem. From these the Inner and Middle Temples were demised to certain students of the Common Law, and the Outer Temple to Walter Stapleton, Bishop of Exeter and Lord Treasurer, who was afterwards beheaded. The lawyers retained their hold upon the Temple at the dissolution of the monasteries, and James I. confirmed them in their claims by granting the Temple to the Benchers of the two Inns of Court and their successors for ever. The Entrance *Gateway to the Middle Temple* from Fleet Street was built by Sir C. Wren in 1684. *Middle Temple Hall*, towards the bottom of Middle Temple Lane, was built in 1572, and is said to have been the first building in which Shakespeare's *Twelfth Night* was played. The roof of this hall has been specially praised as a fine example of Elizabethan architecture, and the carved screen and music-gallery in the *Renaissance* style have been much admired. There are here some portraits and marble busts of considerable interest.

The *Inner Temple Hall*, by Smirke, is of smaller architectural note. Proceeding to it from Fleet Street down *Inner Temple Lane* we shall pass *Dr. Johnson's Buildings*, so named in memory of the great lexicographer, who lived at No. 1 in this lane; at the foot of the lane we shall come upon the magnificent western doorway of the *Temple Church*,—one of the four circular churches built by

Temple Church.

the Knights Templar in 1185 after their return from the second crusade, the other three being at Cambridge, Northampton, and Maplestead in Essex. The style is partly Romanesque and partly Early English Gothic. The Round is the only remaining portion of the ancient building of the Templars; the Choir, in pure Lancet style, was almost rebuilt in 1839–42. The Church is divided into three parts by clustered marble columns, and the groined roof is richly coloured in arabesque and decorated with sacred emblems. Oliver Goldsmith was buried east of the choir in 1774; in testimony of which a tablet appears in a recess on the north side of the choir. Goldsmith was not of the Temple, but he had chambers in it, first on the staircase of the Inner Temple Library, then in King's Bench Walk, and last at 2, Brick Court, where he died. Upon the pavement of the Church are figures of crusaders sculptured out of freestone. The attitudes are all different, but the effigies are all recumbent with the legs crossed. The best authorities assign five of them as follows:—Geoffrey de Magnaville, Earl of Essex, A.D. 1144; William Mareschall, Earl of Pembroke, 1219; Robert Lord de Ros, A.D. 1245; William Mareschall, junior, 1231; and Gilbert Mareschall, 1241, Earls of Pembroke. Here are also tombs of the learned Selden, Plowden, Hooker, Gibbon the historian, and several busts and other memorials of less note. North-east of the choir is the house of the Master of the Temple, as the preacher of the church is called. Hooker and Sherlock were among the Masters of the Temple. The Choral Service of the Temple, and the high reputation of the present Master attract many visitors to this church. The "Round" is open to all, but the Choir is reserved for benchers and students and for persons presenting a bencher's order. The cloisters adjoining Temple Church were built by Sir C. Wren. The *Temple Gardens* are beautiful green retreats from the midst of a dirty noisy city, and, to a stranger turning in suddenly from Fleet Street, are a peculiarly agreeable surprise. Shakespeare has made these Gardens for ever famous by his scene descriptive of the origin of the Wars of the Roses: there are no roses nowadays in Temple Gardens; the smoke will not let them grow.

SUFFOLK.   Within the Temple Hall we were too loud—
            The garden here is more convenient.
                    *   *   *   *
PLANTAGENET. Since you are tongue-tied and so loath to speak,
            In dumb significants proclaim your thoughts.
            Let him that is a true-born gentleman,
            And stands upon the honour of his birth,
            If he suppose that I have pleaded truth,
            From off this briar pluck a white rose with me.
SOMERSET.   Let him that is no coward nor no flatterer,
            But dare maintain the party of the truth,
            Pluck a red rose from off this thorn with me.
                    *   *   *   *
WARWICK.   This brawl to-day
            Grown to this faction in the Temple Gardens,
            Shall send, between the red rose and the white,
            A thousand souls to death and deadly night.

Of the well-known armorial bearings of the Inner Temple, a *Pegasus*—of the Middle, a *Lamb*—it has been said ironically of the lawyers.

"The *Lamb* sets forth their innocence,
The *Horse* their expedition."

Nearly opposite Middle Temple Lane, and upon the north side of Fleet Street, is the *Cock Tavern*, once a noted place for steaks and stout and fine old port; and, as such, made memorable by Tennyson, whose address to the "plump head waiter at the 'Cock'" to "fetch a pint of port," exhibits a sense of humour for which the Laureate has not generally been fully credited:—

"High over roaring Temple Bar,
    And set in heaven's third story,
I look at all things as they are,
    But through a kind of glory;

> Headwaiter, honoured by the guest
> Half-mused or reeling ripe,
> The pint you brought me was the best
> That ever came from pipe."

No. 17 Fleet Street, a hairdresser's shop, is advertised, without evidence, as "formerly the Palace of Henry VIII. and Cardinal Wolsey." Mrs. Salmon, the Madame Tussaud of her time, who had her wax-work exhibition here about 1795, described it as "once the Palace of Henry, Prince of Wales, son of James I.," a statement corroborated by an enriched plaster-ceiling in the first floor front room, inscribed P. (triple-plumed) H., which, with part of the carved wainscoting, seems to belong to the period of James I.

Fleet Street still maintains the closest associations with literature. It is famous for the number of its newspaper offices. Here, besides multitudes of weekly papers and periodicals, are published the *Daily News*, the *Daily Telegraph*, the *Morning Advertiser*, the *Standard*, the *Daily Chronicle*, *Punch*, &c.

"Dr. Johnson," says Leigh Hunt, "is the *Genius loci*, the presiding spirit of Fleet Street. He was conversant for the greater part of his life with this street, was fond of it, frequented its *Mitre Tavern* above any other in London, and has identified its name and places with the best things he ever saw and did. Here he walked and talked and shouldered wondering porters out of the way, and mourned and philosophised and was a 'good-natured fellow' (as he called himself), and roared with peals of laughter till midnight echoed to his roar." When Boswell replied to Dr. Johnson's question as to Greenwich Park, "Is not this very fine?" "Yes, sir, but not equal to Fleet Street;" Johnson heartily responded, "You are right, sir!" Johnson lived in Fleet Street, first in Fetter Lane, then in Boswell Court, then in Gough Square, then in Inner Temple Lane, then in Johnson's Court, and for the longest period in Bolt Court, where he died. In Gough Square he wrote part of his Dictionary.

CHANCERY LANE, considered the principal legal thoroughfare in London, extends from Fleet Street, past Lincoln's Inn to Holborn, opposite Gray's Inn. Isaak Walton lived here in what was in his time the seventh house from Fleet Street on the left. Opposite is *Serjeants' Inn, Chancery Lane*, rebuilt by Sir Robert Smirke in 1838; the old Hall still remains, but has recently been sold and converted to new uses. (*Serjeants' Inn, Fleet Street*, was the residence of serjeants'-at-law, *temp.* Henry VI.) Farther north upon the left of Chancery Lane is a fine old *Gateway to Lincoln's Inn*, of the time of Henry VIII., and on the opposite side of the street is the Rolls Yard, in which is *Rolls Court*, presided over by the Master of the Rolls. In *Rolls Chapel*, where formerly the Rolls or Records were kept, is a fine monument of Italian work, of the sixteenth century. On the site of Southampton Buildings stood *Southampton House*, the residence of the unfortunate Lord William Russell. It was in passing this house on his way to the scaffold, that he was for a moment unmanned by the recollection of his domestic happiness herein, but recovering himself, he said, "The bitterness of death is now passed." Wentworth, Lord Strafford was born in a house nearly opposite Southampton House.

Returning to Fleet Street we observe the Church of *St. Dunstan's-in-the-West*, built by J. Shaw 1831-33, but set back 30 feet from the site of the former church—three doors from which stopped the great fire of 1666. The old church was noted for its clock, which struck the quarters by two wooden figures of savages, life-size, standing within an alcove, each having a club in his hand. To these Cowper likens a lame poet,

"Where labour and where dulness hand in hand,
Like the two figures of St. Dunstan's, stand."

The clock and figures were bought when the old church was taken down, and removed to the grounds of the Marquis of Hertford, Regent's Park, where they are still to be seen. The present Church of St. Dunstan's is in the latest Pointed style, and has a lofty tower surmounted by an elegant lantern, 130 feet high, of Ketton stone. Over the entrance porch are the heads of Tyndale, the Reformer, and Dr. Donne, the poet, once vicar of this church. The Statue of Queen Elizabeth seen here was removed from Ludgate, having survived the Great Fire of London. The interior of St. Dunstan's is very elegant.

By the side of St. Dunstan's Church is the entrance to *Clifford's Inn*, one of the old Inns of Chancery, now let out in chambers. The Hall of Clifford's Inn is Modern Gothic. Harrison, the regicide, was clerk to an attorney in Clifford's Inn. " There are three things to notice in Clifford's Inn: its little bit of turf and trees, its quiet, and its having been the residence of Robert Pultock (probably a briefless barrister), author of ' Peter Wilkins.' "

FETTER LANE, named from the Faitors or beggars who infested this quarter. *Peele's Coffee-House* at the corner, was until recently noted for its files of newspapers, both town and country, which are, however, now no longer preserved here. In this street lived the leatherseller, Praisegod Barebones, and his brother, Damned Barebones, this being the contraction for his full name, which was, " If-Christ-had-not-died-I-had-been-Damned-Barebones." Mrs. Brownrigg, who murdered her apprentice in 1767, lived at No. 16.

> " She whipp'd two female 'prentices to death,
> And hid them in the coal hole."

Strange labyrinths of courts lie between Chancery, Fetter, and Shoe Lanes. The *Public Record Office*, built by Pennethorne, between Chancery and Fetter Lanes, 1856, is a capacious fireproof building, containing the most complete national archives in the world, including the original 'Old Domesday Book, or Survey of England made by William the Conqueror.' There is a convenient Reading-Room at the Record Office, to which there is no difficulty in obtaining admission. The *White Horse Inn*, in Fetter Lane, was one of the most famous of the old coaching-houses. *Fetter Lane Chapel* is a Nonconformist place of worship of some historical note; of late years chiefly remarkable as the scene of the ministry of the eloquent and able Rev. Caleb Morris.

CRANE COURT was noted for the mansion in which the Royal Society met from 1710 till 1782, and for the room, preserved intact, in which Sir Isaac Newton sat as president of that society. The house was bought by the Scottish Corporation when the Royal Society, in 1782, removed to Somerset House, but was almost totally destroyed by fire in 1877.

Passing down BOUVERIE STREET, on the south side of Fleet Street, we shall come to WHITEFRIARS, formerly the site of a Convent of Carmelites or White Friars, founded 1244. The Hall of the dissolved monastery became the *Whitefriars Theatre*. The precinct retained the privileges of sanctuary, and these were confirmed by James I. in 1608. It, in consequence, became the asylum of debtors and thieves, and obtained the cant name of *Alsatia*, suggesting the scene of Shadwell's 'Squire of Alsatia,' the characters of which dared not stir out of Whitefriars. In Sir Walter Scott's 'Fortunes of Nigel,' are depicted the manners and customs of Alsatia. *Lombard Street* still exists, as well as *Hanging Sword Alley* named from a tavern called the 'Hanging Sword,' mentioned by Stowe.

Richardson, the novelist, lived in SALISBURY SQUARE or COURT, as it was then called, and wrote 'Pamela' there. Nichols says he was "the son of a joiner, and was educated (but little) at Christ's Hospital."

ST. BRIDE's steeple is one of the most beautiful of Wren's

works, though not so perfect as he made it, for it was shortened in a storm and not rebuilt. "As to its illuminated clock," Leigh Hunt joked, "which seems to remind the jovial that they ought to be at home, we are loth to object to anything useful, and in fact, we admit its pretensions; yet, as there is a time for all things, there would seem to be a time for time itself," &c. At the west end of this church was buried, Richard Lovelace, the most elegant of cavaliers, who sang—

> "Stone walls do not a prison make,
> Nor iron bars a cage,
> Minds innocent and quiet take
> That for a hermitage."

Milton once lodged in St. Bride's Churchyard.

By the side of St. Bride's, or St. Bridget's Church, is a passage leading down towards the western side of Bridge Street, Blackfriars. Near this site stood formerly the *Palace* and subsequently the *Prison of Bridewell*, named from the well of St. Bride's near by, granted by Edward VI. for the purpose mentioned in the following lines, which used to be seen under a portrait of His Majesty in old Bridewell Chapel:—

> "This Edward of fair memory the Sixth
> In whom with greatness, goodness was commixt,
> Gave this Bridewell, a palace in old times
> For a chastising house of vagrant crimes."

SHOE LANE leads to Holborn Hill, past St. Andrew's Workhouse, in the burial-ground of which (now Farringdon Market) Chatterton was buried. *Fleet Market*, formerly held upon the ground of the now clear and open Farringdon Street, was removed towards Shoe Lane, and has been since known as *Farringdon Market*. *Fleet Ditch* flowed beneath what is now called Farringdon Street to the Thames. The little river *Fleet* took its rise in the hills of Hampstead, passed through Kentish and Camden Town, on through the Bagnigge Wells Road and Clerkenwell Fields, where it was joined by the water from the Wells, and thence to the bottom of Holborn or Old Bourne (indicating its junction with another stream). The Fleet was crossed by Holborn and Fleet Lane bridges. Its character is depicted by Pope in the 'Dunciad.'

> "To where Fleet ditch, with disemboguing streams,
> Rolls the large tribute of dead dogs to Thames,
> The king of dykes, than whom no slime of mud
> With deeper sable blots the silver flood."

The ditch has been so thoroughly covered over, that no sign now exists by which passers-by would observe any token of its existence.

Fleet Prison was abolished in 1846, after a history of nearly eight centuries. Its site is partly occupied by the *Memorial Hall*, built by Nonconformists, in memory of the victims of religious bigotry who were incarcerated here in the reign of Queen Mary and of Charles I. Hither were sent, in the former reign, Bishop Hooper, who but quitted the Fleet for the stake and the fire at Gloucester. Many of the political victims of the Star Chamber were sent to Fleet Prison, including Prynne, and Lilburne—who led the forlorn hope in their time in favour of the noble liberty since acquired—of unlicensed printing. After the abolition of the Star Chamber, the Fleet Prison was used for debtors only. The prison was destroyed by fire in the riots of 1780, and the prisoners were liberated by the mob, but it was rebuilt immediately after in a long brick pile, parallel with Farringdon Street; above the entrance was the figure '9', and the polite form of addressing debtors confined in this prison was "at No. 9, Fleet Market." Fleet Marriages were not put an end to until 1754. "How impossible it would be now," says Leigh Hunt, "in a neighbourhood like this, for such nuisances to exist as a fetid public ditch, and scouts of degraded clergymen asking people to 'walk in and be married.' Yet such was the case a century ago. They performed the ceremony inside the prison to sailors and others for what they could get. The parties retired to a gin-shop to treat the clergyman, and there and in similar houses the register was kept of the marriages."

At the north end of Farringdon Street is a railway station of the London, Chatham and Dover Line.

BRIDGE STREET, BLACKFRIARS, leading to *Blackfriars Bridge* (rebuilt by Cubitt, 1864–9 at a cost of 320,000*l.*), is a continuation, so to speak, of Farringdon Street. The district known as BLACKFRIARS extends from Ludgate Hill to the Thames, and derives its name from a monastery of Dominican Friars (*Frères*), founded here in 1276. In the church of this monastery many parliaments and other great meetings took place, and in the mansion attached thereto, the Emperor Charles V. of Spain was lodged by Henry VIII. after the Dissolution. Here was held the Parliament which decided upon Henry's divorce from Katherine of Arragon, and that which condemned Wolsey. Richard Burbage took advantage of the privilege of sanctuary belonging to the district, to build a playhouse in the Blackfriars precinct when he was ejected from the City. Shakespeare had a share in this Theatre, which is for ever memorable in literature as the House wherein many of the great dramas of our greatest poet were first produced. The site is still called PLAYHOUSE YARD. The great fire of London destroyed the fine buildings of Blackfriars; the church of *St. Andrew by the Wardrobe* (named from a building that once stood here, the Royal Wardrobe) stands in the place of old Blackfriars Church. In Bridge Street is the *City Station* of the London, Chatham and Dover Railway, which crosses the Thames by a bridge running near and parallel to Blackfriars Bridge; the line also spans the foot of Ludgate Hill by a *Viaduct*, dividing the view of St. Paul's from the bottom of Fleet Street.

LUDGATE HILL extends from LUDGATE CIRCUS to *St. Martin's Church*, Ludgate, which was rebuilt by Wren after the Great Fire of London, and is considered to contribute to a fine architectural effect, backed by the campanile towers and majestic dome of St. Paul's. In this old church was the following quaint epitaph:

Earth goes to	} Earth {	As mold to mold.
Earth treads on		Glittering in gold.
Earth as to		Returns here shold.
Earth shall to		Goe ere he wold.
Earth upon	} Earth {	Consider may.
Earth goes to		Passed away.
Earth though on		Is stout and gay.
Earth shall from		Passe poor away.

LUDGATE STREET connects St. Paul's Churchyard with Ludgate Hill. The old City Gate called Ludgate stood between the present sites of St. Martin's, Ludgate, and the London Coffee House; the name of Ludgate has been ascribed to King Lud, 66 B.C., but is more probably due to the Flud or Flood-gate of Fleet river. The *Gate*, which was used as a prison for debtors of the City of London, was much injured by the Fire of London, 1666, and was taken down altogether 1760-62. On Ludgate Hill, opposite the Gate was ended the rebellion of Sir Thomas Wyat, who here, after his adherents had forsaken him, flung himself on a bench opposite the *Belle Sauvage Inn*, and began to repent his rashness and lament his folly.

The OLD BAILEY derives its name from the *ballium*, or outer space near the wall of Ludgate, and reached from Ludgate Hill past Newgate prison to Newgate Street. Its position as respects the ancient wall of the City could be traced in some massive stonework near Seacoal Lane, at the bottom of Breakneck Steps. The *Old Bailey Sessions House* stands upon the site of *Surgeon's Hall*, where Oliver Goldsmith went up for examination and was rejected by the examiners, December 21, 1758. (See p. 198.)

Apothecaries' Hall and Heralds' College.

Through a narrow thoroughfare under an ancient archway upon the southern side of Ludgate Street, is a lane often crowded with carts and pedestrians, leading to *Printing House Square*, the site of the King's printing house in the days of the Stuarts, and now of the offices of the *Times* newspaper, where a roll of paper, three or four miles long, is printed off nightly at the rate of a hundred *Times* per minute. Admission to view the machinery and offices is sometimes granted upon written application to the *Times* Printer. The new offices for advertisements front Queen Victoria Street. *Apothecaries' Hall* built for the Apothecaries' Company, with laboratories and warehouses for medicines, are close by. This Company is fifty-eighth upon the list of City Companies, and they have for their arms Apollo slaying the Python, with the motto from the legend as given by Ovid," *Opiferque per orbem dicor*." " Through the world I am spoken of as a helper." Of this edifice Garth wrote—

> "Nigh where Fleet Ditch descends in sable streams,
> To wash his sooty Naiads in the Thames,
> There stands a structure on a rising hill,
> Where tyros take their freedom out to kill."

HERALDS' COLLEGE, or the College of Arms, now in Queen Victoria Street, received its first charter of incorporation from Richard III. It has consisted since 1622 of thirteen officers, viz., three kings-at-arms—Garter, Clarencieux and Norroy; six heralds — Lancaster, Somerset, Richmond, Windsor, York, and Chester; and four pursuivants—Rouge Croix, Blue Mantle, Portcullis, Blue Dragon—holding their places by appointment of the Duke of Norfolk as Hereditary Earl Marshal. The mode of obtaining a grant of arms is by a petition to the Earl Marshal, prepared on behalf of the applicant by some member of the Herald's College, setting forth that the memorialist cannot prove his title to arms, and praying for an authorisation to bear armorial ensigns. A warrant is issued and a patent made out, exhibiting a painting of the armorial ensigns granted under the application, and describing in official terms the proceedings and the correct blazon of arms granted. This patent is registered in the books of the Herald's College. Thus a man may write *Armiger* after his name, at a cost of seventy-five guineas. There are several wonderful curiosities at Herald's College, including a pedigree of the Saxon kings, from Adam.

DOCTORS' COMMONS, which lies between Knightrider Street and St. Paul's Churchyard, was so called from the Doctors of Civil Law dining here together four days in each term. The recent transfer of the Will Office from Doctors' Commons to Somerset House considerably reduced the legal business of this locality.

STATIONERS' HALL COURT, Ludgate Hill. "It is worth anybody's while," says Leigh Hunt, "to go to Stationers' Hall to see the portraits of Steele, Prior, and Richardson." All publications have to be registered here, in order to protect them under the Copyright Act; and hence arises the phrase so frequently seen on prints, music, &c., "Entered at Stationers' Hall."

PATERNOSTER ROW (see p. 208), AVE MARIA LANE, CREED LANE, SERMON LANE, AMEN CORNER, are said to have been so named from the number of rosary or paternoster makers and text writers who dwelt there, and sold horn books of the alphabet, with the Creed, Lord's Prayer, &c., added thereto. In the most easterly of narrow passages from Paternoster Row to Newgate Street called PANYER ALLEY is a stone built into the wall of one of the houses on the east side, carved to represent a wicker basket or pannier with a boy on the top of it. Beneath is the inscription—

"When you have sought the city round,
Yet still this is the highest ground."

ST. PAUL'S CATHEDRAL.

THE present magnificent edifice, by Sir Christopher Wren, the most prominent feature of London, is the third church dedicated to St. Paul which has been reared upon this site—originally, we are told, the place of a temple in honour of Diana. The first church was built A.D. 610, and lasted till the time of William the Conqueror—it was burnt down in 1087. The second was the one usually known as *Old St. Paul's*, and was 690 feet in length, 130 in breadth, and its spire, 520 feet high, was equal to that of the present Cross with the Monument superadded. Old St. Paul's was used by the young gallants of the time, described as "Paul's Walkers." The proverb of "dining with Duke Humphrey," originated in the use, by the poorer frequenters of Old St. Paul's, of a tomb said to have been the burial-place of Duke Humphrey of Gloucester. Those who strolled about in want of a dinner used his tomb as a resting-place, and were therefore described as dining with Duke Humphrey. Old St. Paul's was remarkable for its splendid shrine and magnificent robes, crosses, jewels, and plate, its chapels, altars, and its numerous clergy. Henry VIII. swept its wealth into his treasury. In the time of the Commonwealth, Old St. Paul's was turned to several "base uses;" the Parliamentary soldiers played at ninepins in the churchyard; they sawed timber in sawpits dug in the body of the church, and stabled their horses in another part of it. Inigo Jones's lofty and beautiful portico was converted into milliners' shops and lodgings, and the statues on the top were knocked down and broken to pieces. In the Great Fire of 1666, the church was reduced to a heap of ruins. It was eight years before the site was cleared for the present St. Paul's, the first stone of which was laid on the 21st of June 1675, by the Architect and his lodge of Freemasons; the trowel and mallet then used are preserved in the Lodge of Antiquity, of which Sir Christopher Wren was Master. The entire Cathedral was completed in 1710, i.e. in 35 years; under one architect, Sir Christopher Wren, one master mason, Mr. T. Strong, and one bishop, Dr. H. Compton, at a cost of £747,954. Wren received £200 per annum for his services, and for this, said the Duchess of Marlborough, " he was content to be hoisted in a basket three times a week, to the top of St. Paul's, at a great hazard." Sir Christopher lived to a good old age, ninety years, and it is said his chief delight, as an old man, was to be carried once a year to look at his noble work. His epitaph in Latin now rescued from the vaults of the church where no one could see it, and placed in gold letters over the choir, is—

"Subtus conditur hujus ecclesiæ et urbis conditor Ch. Wren qui vixit annos ultra nonaginta, non sibi sed bono publico. Lector, si monumentum requiris, circumspice." Which may be translated: "Beneath is buried Ch. Wren, architect of this Church and City, who lived for more than ninety years, not for himself, but for the public good. Reader, if thou seekest his monument, look around."

" The reader," says Leigh Hunt, " does look around, and the whole interior of the Cathedral, which is finer than the outside, seems like a magnificent vault over his single body."

Macaulay writes, " In architecture, an art which is half a science, an art in which none but a geometrician can excel, an art which has no standard of grace but what is directly or indirectly dependent on utility, an art of which the creations derive a part at least from mere bulk, our country could boast at the time of the Revolution of one truly great man, Sir Christopher Wren; and the fire which laid London in ruins, destroying 13,000 houses

St. Paul's Cathedral.

and 89 churches, gave him an opportunity unprecedented in history of displaying his powers. The austere beauty of the Athenian portico, the gloomy sublimity of the Gothic arcade, he was, like most of his contemporaries incapable of emulating, and perhaps incapable of appreciating; but no man born on our side of the Alps has imitated with so much success the magnificence of the palace churches of Italy. Even the superb Louis XIV. has left to posterity no work which can bear a comparison with St. Paul's."

The Cathedral has been thus described. Exterior: The ground plan is that of a Latin cross, with lateral projections at the west end of the nave. Length from east to west 550 feet, width 125 feet, except at the west end, where the campanile towers are each 222 feet high, and the chapels beyond make the principal front facing Ludgate Hill, 180 feet in width; the height to the top of the cross is 370 feet. The upper part of the exterior is of the Composite, the lower of the Corinthian order; the surface is Portland stone. At the west end a noble flight of steps ascends to a doubled portico, terminated by a pediment, in the tympanum of which is sculptured the Conversion of St. Paul; on the apex is a colossal figure of St. Paul, and on the right and left St. Peter and St. James. Beneath the portico are the doors, above which there is a marble group, St. Paul preaching to the Bereans. All the figures, as well as the *Statue of Queen Anne* on the pedestal in front of the building, were sculptured by Bird. Each dome has a gilt pine-apple at the apex; the south tower contains the clock, the north the belfry, and in the west faces are statues of the Four Evangelists. At the northern and southern ends of the transepts the lower order Corinthian is continued into porticos of six fluted columns standing on the segment of a circle, and crowned with a semi-dome. The interiors of the nave and choir, are each designed with three arches longitudinally springing from piers strengthened as well as decorated on their inner faces by an entablature whose cornice reigns throughout the nave and church. The entrances from the transepts lead into vestibules, each communicating with the centre and its aisles, formed between two massive piers and the walls at the intersections of the transepts with the choir and nave. The eight piers are joined by arches springing from one to the other so as to form an octagon. The choir contains some of the finest carvings in the world—by Grinling Gibbons. The side aisles or oratories were added to the nave as first planned by Wren—it was said, by order of the Duke of York, afterwards James II., who wished "to have them ready for the Popish service, when there should be occasion." Wren remonstrated with tears, but in vain. The Monuments are remarkable as memorials rather than as works or art. "In general, while civil eminence has been commemorated in Westminster Abbey, St. Paul's has been made a Pantheon for our heroes." The following are the chief statues: *Howard*, the philanthropist (sometimes from his keys mistaken for St. Peter), *Dr. Johnson*, both by Bacon; *Sir Joshua Reynolds*, by Flaxman; *Sir William Jones*, the Orientalist, by Bacon; *Lord Nelson*, by Flaxman; *Lord Cornwallis*, by Rossi; *Sir Ralph Abercrombie* and *Collingwood*, by Westmacott; *Lord Howe*, by Flaxman; *Lord Heathfield*, by Rossi; *Sir John Moore*, by Bacon; *Sir W. Hoste*, by Campbell; *Major-General Gillespie*, by Chantrey; *Lord Rodney*, *Captains Morse* and *Rivers*, by Rossi; *Captain Westcott*, by Banks; *General Ponsonby*, by Baily; *Generals Gore* and *Skerrett*, by Chantrey; *Earl St. Vincent*, by Baily; *General Picton*, by Gahagan; *Admiral Duncan*, by Westmacott; *General Dundas*, by Bacon; *Dr. Middleton*, by Lough; *Bishop Heber*, by Chantrey; *Sir Astley Cooper*, by Baily; and *Dr. Babington*, by Behnes: also two fine works by Chantrey, in memory of *Colonel Cadogan* and *General Bowes*. The *Duke of Wellington's Monument* occupies the west chapel in the south nave aisle. In the crypt, south aisle, is the grave of *Sir Christopher Wren;* near him lie *Sir Joshua Reynolds, Barry, Opie, West, Fuseli, Lawrence,* and last, not least, *J. M. W. Turner. Nelson's Tomb* is in the middle of the crypt. He was buried in a sarcophagus said to have been made for Henry VIII. at the expense of Cardinal Wolsey. Nelson's coffin was made out of the mainmast of *L'Orient*—a present to Nelson from his friend Captain Hallowell, of the *Swiftsure,* after the Battle of the Nile, with the statement that it was sent "so that when you are tired of this life you may be buried in one of your own trophies." Nelson's flag was to have been buried with his coffin, but just as it was about to be lowered, the sailors who had borne him to the tomb, moved as if by one impulse, rent the flag in pieces, so that each might keep a fragment. *Lord Collingwood* lies, as he requested, near Nelson, and opposite, *Lord Northesk.* The *Duke of Wellington's Tomb* is in the east crypt, and near him sleeps the brave *General Picton,* of Waterloo fame. The Laureate's lines respecting the burial of Wellington and Nelson in this crypt, beginning with Nelson's inquiry are here recalled to us—

"Who is he that cometh like an honoured guest,
With banner and with music, with soldiers and with priest,
With a nation weeping, and breaking on my rest?"

"Mighty seaman this is he,
Was great by land as thou by sea;
Thine island loves thee well, thou famous man,
The greatest sailor since the world began;
Now to the roll of muffled drums
To thee the greatest soldier comes;
For this is he,
Was great by land as thou by sea."

Mylne, the architect of Old Blackfriars Bridge, and *Rennie,* builder of Waterloo Bridge, also *Dance,* the architect, and *Dr. Boyce,* musician, all lie in this crypt, in which are preserved the following monuments, which belonged to Old

St. Paul's: *Dean Colet*, founder of St. Paul's school, *Sir Nicholas Bacon*, *Sir Christopher Hatton*, and *Dr. Donne*.

The WHISPERING GALLERY is reached from an angle under the dome by 260 easy steps. There, a low whisper from one side is carried to the opposite side with great distinctness.

The LIBRARY in the gallery over the southern aisle contains many thousands of valuable books and MSS. relating to Old St. Paul's. The GEOMETRICAL STAIRCASE of 110 steps was built by Wren for private access to the Library from the Gallery. In the MODEL ROOM is to be seen Wren's Original Design for St. Paul's. The CLOCK ROOM is in the south-west tower. THE CLOCK was made by Bradley in 1708, and is remarkable for its size and good workmanship. It has two dial-plates (south and west) each fifty-one feet in circumference, and the numerals are 2 feet $2\frac{1}{2}$ inches in height, the minute hands are 9 feet 8 inches long, and weigh 75lbs. each, and the hour hands are 5 feet 9 inches long, and weigh 44lbs. each. The Clock goes eight days, and strikes the Great Bell, which has been heard in the silence of midnight twenty miles off. The INNER DOME, painted by Sir James Thornhill, portrays the events in the history of St. Paul. The STONE GALLERY is outside the base of the dome. The OUTER GOLDEN GALLERY is at the summit of the dome, and the INNER GOLDEN GALLERY at the base of the lantern, whence the ascent is made by ladders to the Ball and Cross. From the OUTER GOLDEN GALLERY may be obtained at early morning, the most perfect view of London possible. "In high winds the creaking and whistling resemble those of a ship labouring in a storm." Visitors are admitted to St. Paul's without fee, daily, except during Divine Service, but the following fees are paid for admission to the portions of the Cathedral not open to the public. Whispering and Stone and Golden Galleries, 6*d*. each. Library, Great Bell, and Geometrical Staircase, 6*d*. Clock, 2*d*. Crypt, 6*d*., or total 3*s*. 2*d*. Choral service is performed at a quarter before

St. Paul's Cathedral.

ten in the morning, and a quarter past three in the afternoon. Morning prayer daily at eight o'clock. Divine service on Sundays at 10.30 A.M., 3.15 P.M., and 7 P.M. Dr. Stainer presides at the organ, a splendid instrument, under the dome. The *Chapter-house* of St. Paul's is in St. Paul's Churchyard opposite the north door of the Cathedral.

ST. PAUL'S CHURCHYARD is itself but a small area of a little over two acres, containing no memorials of interest. In the adjoining thoroughfare, known under the same name, are some of the busiest shops of London. On its east side is *St. Paul's School*, founded by Dean Colet in 1509 for 153 boys (all free) of every nation, country, and class, between nine and nineteen years of age—the number of 153 being derived from the 11th verse of St. John, chap. xxi., "Simon Peter went up and drew the net to land full of great fishes, an hundred and fifty and three." The education comprises classics, mathematics, and French. Admission to the school is obtained by means of presentations in the gift of the Master, Wardens, and Court of Assistants of the Mercers' Company. There are no school fees. The average cost of books is about £1 per annum. There are numerous exhibitions to the Universities connected with this school. Of the eminent men who were scholars at this school may be mentioned John Milton, Leland the antiquary, the great Duke of Marlborough, Samuel Pepys, and Halley the astronomer. Towards the corner of St. Paul's Churchyard leading to Cheapside, stood, as we have said, *Paul's Cross*, a campanile, or bell-house (to summon people to the Folkmote), which was taken down in the time of Henry VIII. Before *Old Paul's Cross*, Jane Shore was made to do penance in a white sheet with taper in her hand. Upon the south-west side of the Cathedral stood the parish church of *St. Gregory*, over which was the LOLLARD'S TOWER,—infamous, like its namesake at Lambeth, for the ill-treatment of so-called heretics.

CANNON STREET, EASTCHEAP, THE TOWER, THAMES STREET, &c.

AT the south-eastern corner of St. Paul's Churchyard begins a large wide thoroughfare running east, and now named CANNON STREET (said to be a corruption of Candlewick Street), in which the wax-chandlers dwelt who supplied Catholic churches with tapers, &c. *St. Mildred's Church*, Bread Street, *St. Nicholas*, and *St. Mary Magdalen* in Old Fish Street, were all by Sir C. Wren. *St. Mary Aldermary* faces the *Mansion House Station of the Underground Railway.*

WATLING STREET, said to be derived from Atheling (noble), forms part of the direct old Roman road from Dover through London to the north. TOWER ROYAL is a name indicating the site of an old royal palace, in which the widow of the Black Prince was residing when the rebels under Wat Tyler broke in upon her. BUDGE ROW was named from the sellers of Budge or lambskins who dwelt there. The *Cannon Street Railway Station* is the City terminus of the South Eastern Railway, which by means of the Cannon Street bridge over the Thames communicates every five minutes with Charing Cross or with London Bridge, and joins the South Western Railway at Waterloo Station, half-way to Charing Cross. The *Cannon Street Railway Hotel* is one of several large and commodious railway hotels built of late years in London for the use of travellers, and found to be, generally, admirable investments of capital. Opposite the Station is the *Church of St. Swithin*, rebuilt by Wren and since modernised. Dryden was married here in 1663 to Lady Elizabeth Howard.

LONDON STONE is to be seen fixed into the south end of

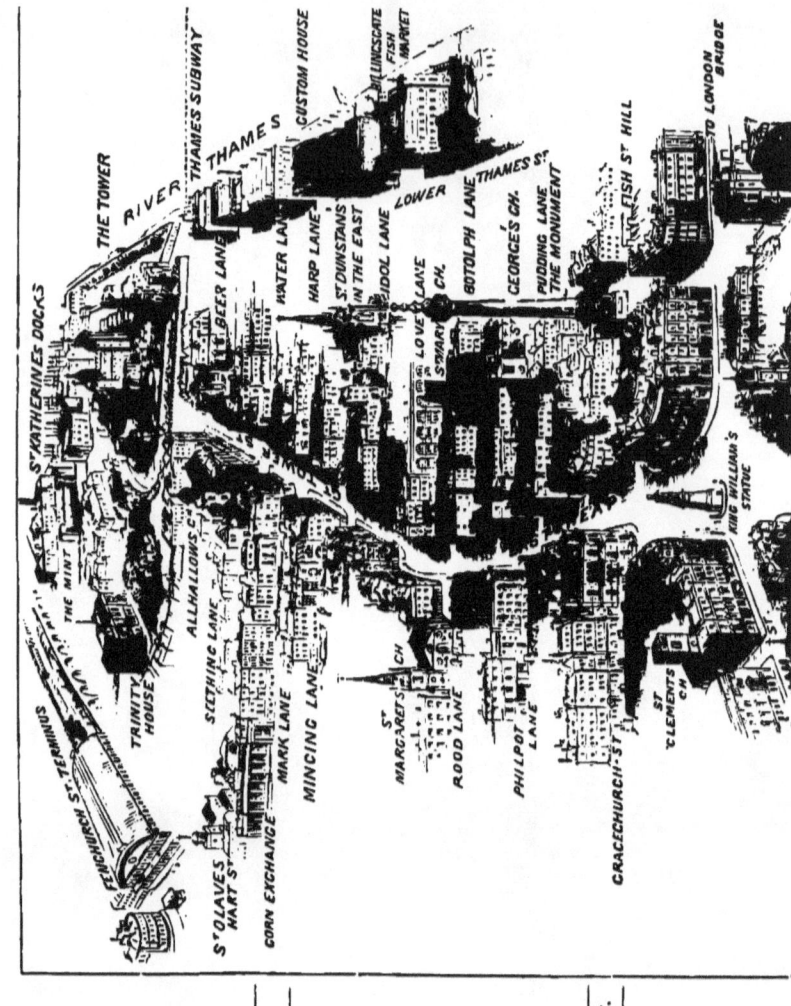

CANNON STREET,
TO THE MANSION HOUSE, THE TOWER, &c.

St. Swithin's Church, facing the Cannon Street Station. It formerly stood on the south side of the street, as stated by Stowe; but it was removed in 1798, being regarded as a nuisance and obstruction. But for the interposition of a neighbouring printer, Mr. Malden, of Sherborne Lane, it is probable that this most ancient relic of Roman London would have been totally destroyed at that time. It was, however, set in a large stone case and built as we see it into the outer wall of St. Swithin's. London Stone was the Milliarium or central milestone, from which all other milestones marked distances, even as the Milliarium in the Forum was the centre from which all Roman roads radiated. In Stowe's time, *London Stone* was "fixed in the ground, fastened with bars of iron, and otherwise so strongly set that if carts do run against it through negligence, the wheels be broken and the stone itself unshaken." Strype describes this stone as much worn, "but a stump remaining before the fire of London," but "it is now for the preservation of it cased over with a new stone." Shakespeare in 'Henry VI.,' act iv. sc. 6, describes Jack Cade entering Cannon Street with his followers in triumph, and, "striking his staff on London Stone," saying, "Now is Mortimer lord of the city. And here, sitting upon London Stone, I charge and command, that of the city's cost, the conduit run nothing but claret wine this first year of our reign. And now henceforth it shall be treason for any that calls me other than Lord Mortimer." When looking at this old fragment of the past, and remembering that it has been here for a thousand years, that it is perhaps the most perfect historical relic of the Roman occupation, being in fact the "quorna or umbilievs castri Londinensis," and that it has been recognised as such, or as, at all events, one of the most ancient of London landmarks, by every historian, dramatist, and antiquarian known to English literature, we shall consider London Stone as one of the most interesting of old world relics.

In ST. SWITHIN'S LANE is the *Hall of the Company of Salters;* also the *Counting-House of `Baron Rothschild,* the great millionnaire and financier. The latter house may be easily distinguished from its neighbours; it stands a little back from the street upon the west side. At the northern end of St. Swithin's Lane upon the east side is a noted house for cheap city luncheons, the *Bay Tree,* in the old smoking-room of which one may see much of the ways and manners of the poorer class of city speculators.

ABCHURCH LANE is named from the parish of *St. Mary Abchurch or Upchurch. St. Dunstan's-in-the-East,* restored by Wren, is near Eastcheap.

The *Boar's Head* in EASTCHEAP (rendered for ever memorable by Shakespeare as the scene of Falstaff and Prince Henry's roysterings), was burnt down in the Great Fire. It stood upon the site occupied now by the *Statue of William IV.,* at the end of King William Street. There is proof that in Shakespeare's time the *Boar's Head Tavern* in Eastcheap existed, and was of some repute, for Robert Harding, Alderman of London, who died in the 11th year of the reign of Queen Elizabeth, is recorded to have been seised of a "messuage, sive tenem. sive tabern. called the Boare's Head lying in East Cheape in the parish of St. Michael in Crooked Lane, London, in the tenure of Edward Betham." The Tavern was rebuilt after the Great Fire, and had over its central door a boar's head carved in stone. Goldsmith, Boswell and Washington Irving have each given us an ideal picture of this ancient hostelry. Many a traveller to London, before and since, has set himself to find some relic of the old 'Boar's Head' in Eastcheap, where Falstaff swallowed his "intolerable quantity of sack to but a ha'porth of bread." So long as a house stood upon the ground, it was possible for fancy to supply some comfort to the Eastcheap pilgrim. William IV.'s Statue to such a one must seem a mockery and a wrong.

GRACECHURCH STREET formerly written Gracious Street,

but also, and more properly Grasschurch Street, from the parish church of *St. Benet*, called Grasschurch, because of the herb-market there kept. Mark Lane is noted for its *Corn Exchange*.

MINCING LANE, named after the Minchuns or nuns of St. Helen, is the tea-merchants' quarter. The *Hall of the Clothworkers Co.* is on the east side of Mincing Lane. Samuel Pepys was Master of the Company in 1677, and presented to it a richly chased silver "Loving Cup," still used upon festive occasions.

CRUTCHED FRIARS is named from a Priory of crutched (cruxed) or crossed Friars which formerly stood here.

From Gracechurch Street through Little Eastcheap and Great Tower Street we shall best reach the Tower of London. The *Church of Allhallows, Barking* (so called from its founders, the nuns of Barking Abbey), is at the end of the last-named street, and contains some fine examples of brass memorials, and one or two altar tombs of great antiquity. In this church were buried several of those personages who had been beheaded on Tower Hill. Of such Old City Churches, with their various peculiar features, Dickens wrote as follows: "In the churches about *Mark Lane* there was a dry whiff of wheat, and I accidentally struck an airy sample of barley out of an aged hassock in one of them. From Rood Lane to Tower Street and there about, there was sometimes a subtle flavour of wine; sometimes of tea. One church near Mincing Lane smelt like a druggist's drawer. Behind the Monument the service had a flavour of damaged oranges, which a little farther down the river tempered into herrings, and gradually turned into a cosmopolitan blast of fish." The 'Czar's Head' public-house near Tower Hill was named after Peter the Great, who is said to have frequented it with his companion soakers and smokers.

TOWER HILL is a large open space of great historical note. On the site of the present garden of Trinity Square, stood the wooden scaffold whereon many most eminent persons were beheaded, including Bishop Fisher and Sir Thomas More, Cromwell Earl of Essex, Henry Howard Earl of Surrey, Thomas Lord Seymour, of Sudely, the Protector Somerset, John Dudley Earl of Northumberland, Lord G. Dudley, Sir Thomas Wyat, Wentworth Earl of Strafford, Archbishop Laud, Algernon Sydney, Duke of Monmouth, Earl of Derwentwater and Lord Kenmuir, Lords Kilmarnock and Balmerino, and last of all Simon, Lord Lovat in 1747. Since that time there has been no beheading in this kingdom, nor any execution upon Tower Hill. Of the few other historical associations of this quarter, may be mentioned the fact that Edmund Spencer was born (1552) near here; William Penn was born (1644) in a court then upon the east side of Tower Hill; Otway, the poet, died, it is said of hunger, at the 'Bull' public-house; and, "in a by-cutler's shop of Tower Hill," says Sir Henry Wotton, "Felton bought a tenpenny knife (so cheap was the instrument of this great attempt) with which he assassinated the Duke of Buckingham." *Postern Row*, which marks the site of the old Postern gate and the boundary wall of the City, once had an evil reputation as the favourite lurking-place for crimps and press-gangs. A portion of the old Roman wall is still to be seen upon the eastern side of Tower Hill.

THE TOWER OF LONDON.

[Admission from ten to four; free on Mondays and Saturdays, upon other days 6d. for the Armoury and the White Tower, and 6d. for the Crown Jewels. The entrance is near the end of Lower Thames Street, and here the tickets for admission are obtained.]

THE Tower of London has a history, which, like that of the kingdom itself recedes into the dim distance of tradition. There is little doubt that for many centuries before the Conquest, an important structure stood on this site. Shakespeare but repeats the tradition that Julius Cæsar reared the pile. Heywood says:

> "Cæsar himself
> That built the same, within it kept his court,
> And many kings since he; the rooms are large,
> The building stately and for strength besides,
> It is the safest and the surest hold you have."

William the Conqueror built the White Tower or Keep in 1078. William Rufus and Henry I. added St. Thomas's Tower over Traitor's Gate. Henry III. largely improved it, and made it into a palatial dwelling. Edward III. imprisoned in it Baliol, Bruce, Wallace, and John, King of France. Richard II. occupied the Tower during the Wat Tyler insurrection; in the upper chamber of the White Tower he abdicated his sovereignty in favour of his cousin, Henry Bolingbroke. Shakespeare describes Richard as saying upon this occasion:—

> "With mine own tears I wash away my balm;
> With mine own hands I give away my crown;
> With mine own tongue deny my sacred state;
> With mine own breath release all duteous oaths,
> All pomp and majesty I do forswear."

Henry IV. imprisoned here Prince James, son of Robert III. of Scotland, and beheaded his brother-in-law, the Earl of Huntingdon. Henry V. brought hither his captives from Agincourt, and hence sent the leader of the Lollards, the good Lord Cobham, to the stake at St. Giles's. Henry VI. died here, under circumstances which suggested that he had been murdered by Richard of Gloucester. The Duke of Clarence fell the next victim, then Hastings, and then the two infant princes, Edward V. and Richard of York. The last of the Plantagenets, Edward, son of the murdered Duke of Clarence, was beheaded here, for no offence save being the heir of his father. Perkin Warbeck went hence to Tyburn, where he was deservedly hanged. In Henry VIII.'s reign the Tower was specially busy and occupied, and, if it were possible to exceed in blackness the records of the murders just recited, the open and legalised executions of this reign must be held to have done so. The best blood of England poured forth lavishly on the slightest pretence during this period upon the scaffold of Tower Hill, or upon the more private block on the green by St. Peter's at Vincula, inside the Tower. After the victims to Henry VIII.'s claims to be his own Pope, came those who suffered for not properly comprehending the new orthodoxy; such as Anne Askew, who was racked in the Tower before she was burnt in Smithfield—Lord Chancellor Wriothesley himself having pulled off his coat to give the poor creature an extra wrench. Bloody Mary imitated her father but mildly so far as the Tower is concerned—her chief victims being the Lady Jane Grey and her adherents. Good Queen Bess imprisoned many persons here, but executed only a few, and those chiefly to assert her supremacy in Church and State. James I. filled the Tower dungeons with the Gunpowder Plot conspirators, and these were all duly sent out of the world after undergoing the traitors' penalty of being hanged and disembowelled alive. James's reign was stained by comparatively few other atrocities in the Tower—the principal being the poisoning of Sir Thomas Overbury. In Charles I.'s reign began a new chapter of Tower History. After Sir John Eliot had suffered incarceration and death; one after another of the king's chief supporters, Strafford, Laud, and others, went the old way of the scaffold. Charles II. is answerable for little beyond his revenge taken on the regicides; but James II. found ample use for this time-worn instrument of tyranny, although he did not cut off so many heads as his predecessors, for the times had improved a little. It is not, perhaps, too much to say that James II.'s imprisoment of the six bishops in the Tower led to the destruction of his sovereignty, for it gave the deathblow to the doctrine of "passive obedience" in the minds of many a staunch upholder of the divine right of kings. The few victims who followed after this reign, were sacrificed to the *manes* of the House of Stuart, whose cause they too ardently espoused; the last Tower executions were of the adherents of the Young Pretender.

The parts of the building exhibited to the public, by means of the Beef-eaters (Buffetiers) or Yeomen of the Guard—old soldiers who still wear the handsome costume which was made for them at their institution by Henry VII., may be thus described :—

We enter under the MIDDLE TOWER, defended by gates and a portcullis. Next is the BYWARD TOWER, the chief entrance to the external line of fortifications. We pass over the moat which surrounds the whole building, and which, now used as a garden, might be flooded at high water, if need be, for defence. TRAITOR'S GATE or ST. THOMAS'S TOWER—

"That gate misnamed through which before
Went Sidney, Russell, Raleigh, Cranmer, More"—

is seen towards the river. It was the principal entrance for those prisoners who were brought hither by water, but is no longer in use. Almost opposite Traitor's Gate is the BLOODY TOWER, wherein were murdered, by command of Richard III., the infant princes, Edward V. and the Duke of York, sons of Edward IV. Near by is the RECORD or WAKEFIELD TOWER, where the Records used to be kept. Passing onwards we come to the BELL TOWER, the Governor's House, not now exhibited. Here were imprisoned, Queen Elizabeth when Princess, Lady Lennox, grandmother of James I., Bishop Fisher, and subsequently Guy Faux, and the Gunpowder Plot conspirators.

THE WHITE TOWER, the most ancient part of the fortress, was erected for William the Conqueror by Gundulph, Bishop of Rochester, noted for his architectural skill, 1079–80. It has three lofty stories, and vaults below, each story having one large room and two smaller ones. The smallest apartment on the first floor, called *Queen Elizabeth's Armoury*, has a doorway communicating with a cell 10 feet long by 8 feet wide, but unlighted except from the door. Sir Walter Raleigh is said to have been imprisoned in these rooms, and to have herein written his 'History of the World.' There are inscriptions near the door of the cell of Rudstone, Fane and Culpepper, adherents of Sir Thomas Wyat in his rebellion 1553. Above is ST. JOHN'S CHAPEL, "one of the finest specimens of Norman architecture in England," but long unused for religious purposes. Upon the next floor is the *Council Room and Banqueting Hall*, where the Kings of England held their Court at the Tower, but which is now used for storage of small arms, arranged in various ingeniously contrived groups and devices.

BEAUCHAMP TOWER was named after Beauchamp, Earl of Warwick, imprisoned here in the reign of Richard II., 1397. At the entrance, is the name of Marmaduke Nevile, one of the Neviles who conspired against Queen Elizabeth in favour of Mary Queen of Scots, and near it are three wheat sheaves (arms of the Peverels), also a crucifix, a bleeding heart, a skeleton, and the name 'Peverel.' Over the fireplace is an inscription by Philip Howard, Earl of Arundel, an ardent Roman Catholic who fell under Queen Elizabeth's displeasure for his welcome of the Spanish Armada. On the right of the fireplace are sculptured a device and inscription by John Dudley, Earl of Warwick; a lion and bear grasping the ragged staff are seen, and four lines beneath referring to the Earl, and his three brothers who were imprisoned for their attempts to make Lady Jane Grey (married to Lord Guilford Dudley) queen. Near the north-western recess is an inscription in Latin—" Deo servire, penitentiam inire, fato obedire, Regnare est. A. Poole, 1564, IHS." "To serve God, to be repentant, to be submissive to fate, is to reign;" and another in English, "A passage perilous maketh a port pleasant," A°. 1568. Arthur Poole, Æ. suæ (in the year of his age), 37. Under the former inscription is the word IANE—the royal name of Lady Jane Grey, who was not (as some have asserted) imprisoned here, but "at Master Partridge's lodgings," probably the rooms of one of the Tower officials. Neither was Anne Boleyn imprisoned here, but in the Palace of the Tower. In the upper chamber of the Beauchamp Tower are some other inscriptions on the walls.

THE DEVEREUX TOWER was named after Devereux, Earl of Essex, who was imprisoned herein by Queen Elizabeth, see p. 111. In the BOWYER TOWER (named from being the residence of the King's Bowyer), the Duke of Clarence, brother of Edward IV., having been permitted to choose his mode of death, is said to have been drowned in a butt of Malmsey, 1474. In the JEWEL or MARTIN TOWER the crown jewels were formerly kept. In the SALT TOWER is a curious device on the wall, of a sphere, the signs of the Zodiac, &c., said to have been drawn by Hugh Draper, of Bristol, 1561, imprisoned here on suspicion of sorcery.

The HORSE ARMOURY contains a line of twenty-two equestrian and other figures, in the armour of several reigns, from Henry VI., 1422, to James II., 1685. The *First Compartment* contains helmets of 12th, 13th and 14th centuries; also a portion of chain armour and Guisarmes—weapons used at the Battle of Hastings. The adjoining stand of arms is formed of battle and pole-axes, " morning stars," &c. The *End Compartment* shows the arms and accoutrements of the time of Agincourt down to that of the Wars of the Roses. Under the wall (painted white and green to denote the colours of the Tudor liveries), is the *Third Compartment*, containing suits of armour of the period of Henry VIII. and Elizabeth, and including the figure of Henry VIII. himself in the King's own armour on horseback. In the *Fourth Compartment* (under the red and yellow colours of the Stuarts), are figures in the armour of the period from James I. to Charles II., including a figure in the armour of General Monk, and another in the armour which belonged to James II. In the reign of William III., defensive armour was abandoned, and the old suits were sent to the Tower. The last stand of arms shows the halberds and other weapons used at the Battle of Sedgemoor.

In the *Eastern Vestibule* are weapons from Indian battlefields, and at the side are helmets, shields, &c., and some masks, one of which is an executioner's. Upon leaving the Vestibule, visitors will see on their right some specimens of Toledo swords, then the Military Trophy at the east end of the Armoury, and on the wall some suits worn by the pikemen early in the 17th century. In the Room above are two compartments, one containing Oriental Arms and Armour, the other, Cannon captured at Waterloo, and kettledrums taken at Blenheim. In the *Centre of the Room* is a Model of the Tower; along the east side is the cloak upon which General Wolfe died at the capture of Quebec, 1759, also some blunderbusses, &c. In the other parts of the room, are interesting specimens of Burmese, Chinese, Saracenic, and Indian and Turkish armour.

The REGALIA or CROWN JEWELS, now kept in the Record or Wakefield Tower (named after the Yorkists imprisoned there after Queen Margaret's victory at Wakefield), consist of the following—all the regalia up to the time of Charles I. having been sold and melted down in 1625-6, "for the king's purposes"*:—(1.) The *Crown of Queen Victoria*, made for Her Majesty's coronation. The cap of purple velvet is enclosed in hoops of silver surmounted by a ball and cross, all resplendent with diamonds. In the centre of the cross is the "inestimable" sapphire, and in front the heart-shaped ruby said to have been worn by the Black Prince. (2.) *St. Edward's Crown*, made for Charles II., and used at every coronation since, is of gold embellished with diamonds, rubies, emeralds, pearls, and sapphires. This is the crown which Colonel Blood stole from the Tower. He was forthwith captured, and the Regalia restored. Blood was said to have escaped punishment for this and other serious offences, in consequence of his services to the Government as a spy and informer, and these eventually earned for him a pension of £500 per annum. (3.) The *Prince of Wales's Crown* made of pure gold, and without jewels, is placed before his Royal Highness's seat in the House of Lords. (4.) The ancient *Queen's Crown* worn at coronations by the Queen Consort. (5.) The *Queen's Diadem*,

* A *MS.* in the British Museum, No. 19,027, pp. 37, *et seq.*, shows what the old regalia consisted of, and the sum realised for each item, "delivered to Sir John Wollaston, &c., by order of the Council of State to be coyned":—The Imperial Crown of gold (7 lb. 6 oz.), with many pearls and precious stones, £10,001 10s. 6d.; the Queen's Crown of gold (3 lb. 10¼ oz.), £337; the Queen's small Crown, with diamond, £200; the Globe (1 lb. 5¼ oz.), at £3 6s. per oz., £57 10s.; Queen Edith's Crown, silver-gilt (50½ oz.); King Alfred's Crown, gold wire-work, set with stones and two little bells (79½ oz.), £248; a Dove of gold, set with pearls, &c., £26; two Sceptres, set with pearls, &c., £65 19s. 7d.; and divers other jewels and articles of gold.

adorned with pearls and large diamonds, made for the Queen of James II. (6.) *St. Edward's Staff*, 4 feet 7 inches long, of beaten gold, surmounted by an orb said to contain a portion of the true cross, is carried before the king or queen at the coronation. (7.) The *Royal Sceptre* of gold, the pommel and cross adorned with jewels, is placed in the right hand of the sovereign by the Archbishop of Canterbury at the coronation. (8.) The *Rod or Sceptre with the Dove*, is placed in the sovereign's left hand at the coronation. (9.) A smaller *Sceptre* adorned with jewels. (10.) The *Ivory Sceptre* made for the Queen of James II. (11.) The *Golden Sceptre* made, as is supposed, for Mary, Queen of William III. (12.) The *Curtana, or Pointless Sword of Mercy*. (13 and 14.) The *Swords of Justice* (temporal and ecclesiastical), borne before the sovereign at coronation. (15.) The *Coronation Bracelets*. (16.) The *Coronation Spurs*, used in the coronation ceremony whether the sovereign be king or queen. (17.) The *Anointing Vessel and Spoon*, (sole relic of the ancient regalia). (18.) The *Golden Salt Cellar*. (19.) The *Royal Baptismal Font*, dishes, spoons, and plate, used at royal christenings. (20.) An elegant *Silver Wine Fountain*, presented by the Corporation at Plymouth to Charles II. on his restoration.

The WELLINGTON BARRACKS in the Tower, named in honour of the Iron Duke, were built since 1845, on the site of a former building which had been burnt down. They are occupied by the troops.

In the three or four Towers of minor interest, the CRADLE TOWER and WELL TOWER, (of which only a portion remains,) the DEVELIN or IRONGATE TOWER, (the site of which is now occupied by a modern building,) the BRICK TOWER, the CONSTABLE TOWER, and the BROAD ARROW TOWER, the ordinary visitor need take little interest, and particulars about them are unnecessary here.

The CHAPEL OF ST. PETER'S AD VINCULA in the inner ward of the Tower at the north-west corner of the parade, dates from 1305-6, and consists of a nave and chancel and a north aisle; it is 66 feet long by 54 wide. Its name, indicating that it was dedicated to the memory of St. Peter in bonds, reminds one of a similarly named church in Rome, S. Pietro in Vincoli. St. Peter's was the Chapel for the prisoners of the Tower, St. John's for the court. St. Peter's has been so often renovated, that little is left of the earliest structure; what remains is chiefly of the reign of Henry VIII. The great historical interest which attaches to a spot where so many remarkable persons have been buried, far exceeds that which the building possesses on the score of antiquity. "There is no sadder spot on earth," says Macaulay, "than this little cemetery. Hither have been carried through successive ages by the rude hands of gaolers, without one mourner following, the bleeding relics of men who had been the captains of armies, the leaders of parties, the oracles of senates, and the ornaments of courts." The memorial tablet at the entrance contains the names of thirty-four persons of historical note who were buried in this chapel; of these we may mention the most prominent. 1. *John Fisher*, Bishop of Rochester, beheaded 1535, by Henry VIII., for refusing to take the new oath of succession to the crown; and (2) the body of *Sir Thomas More*, who was beheaded for the same cause a month afterwards. Sir Thomas More's head was set upon a pole on London Bridge, and was obtained by Mrs. Roper, one of his daughters, by bribing the executioner. She had it embalmed, and it was buried with her in 1544, in a vault at St. Dunstan's Church, Canterbury, where it was found in 1835, " in a niche in the wall in a leaden box." 3. *George Boleyn*, Viscount Rochford (brother of Anne Boleyn), beheaded 1536. 4. *Queen Anne Boleyn*, executed 1536 on the green outside this chapel. "The queen was beheaded with a sword, according to the French manner, by an executioner brought specially from Calais. With her own hands she took the coifs from her head and gave them to her ladies, then putting on a little cap of linen to cover her hair withal, she said, 'Alas, poor head, in a very brief space thou wilt roll in the dust on the scaffold.'" She addressed a few words to the people and to her ladies, then knelt down on both knees. "And thus without more to say or do, was her head stricken off; she making no confession of her fault, and only saying, 'O Lord God, have pity on my soul.' Suddenly the hangman of Calais smote off her head at one stroke with a sword; her body, with the head, was buried (in a common chest of elm made to put arrows in) in the quire of the chapel in the Tower." Froude thus describes the execution: "A little before noon on the 19th of May, Anne Boleyn, Queen of England, was led down to the green where the young grass and the white daisies of summer were freshly bursting in the sunshine. A little cannon stood loaded on the battlements, the motionless cannoneer was ready with smoking linstock at his side, and when the crawling hand upon the dial of the great Tower clock touched the midday hour, that cannon would tell to London that all was over. The yeomen of the guard were there and a crowd of citizens, the Lord Mayor too, and the deputies of the guilds and the sheriffs, and the aldermen; they were come to see a spectacle which England had never seen before, a head which had worn the crown falling under the sword of the executioner." The site is marked by a railing and a stone, with the words, "Site of the ancient scaffold. On this spot Queen Anne Boleyn was beheaded May 19, 1536." 5. *Thomas Cromwell*, Earl of Essex, the son of a blacksmith of Putney, whom Wolsey raised from the forge to eminent good fortune, and who, after "having cared for no man's displeasure to serve His Majesty," fell in his turn under Henry VIII.'s displeasure, and suffered the same death as Fisher and More. 6. *Margaret Plantagenet*, the aged Countess of Salisbury, niece of Edward IV., who had been governess to the Princess Mary, and who was accused of wishing to marry her son Reginald Pole to the princess, and of other plots. 7. *Queen Katharine Howard*, Henry VIII.'s wife, beheaded with (8.) *Jane Lady Rochford*, her attendant, and buried within the choir of this chapel. 9. *Lord Thomas Seymour*, brother of Lady Jane Seymour, and of the Protector Somerset. This nobleman married Katharine Parr, the widow of Henry VIII., and was subsequently charged with a design to marry the Princess Elizabeth and thus to reach the throne; beheaded 1548. 10. The *Lord Protector Somerset*, beheaded 1552, and buried in the church on the north side of the choir. 11. *John Dudley*, Duke of Northumberland, the powerful rival of the Protector Somerset, who was in his turn overthrown, his crime being the proclaiming, upon the death of Edward VI., his own daughter-in-law, Lady Jane Grey, Queen. The Duke repented, but too late; he turned Catholic to propitiate Mary, but without avail, he was beheaded, and his body, with the head, was buried by the body of Edward, late Duke of Somerset; "so that there lieth before the high altar two dukes between two queens, to wit, Somerset and Northumberland between Queen Anne and Queen Katharine." 12. *Lady Jane Grey*, beheaded outside this chapel on the 12th of February 1553-4, the same day that her husband suffered on Tower Hill. "She had the birth of a princess, the learning of a clerk, the life of a saint, yet the death of a malefactor." 13. *Henry Grey*, Duke of Suffolk, father of Lady Jane Grey; beheaded 1553, and said to have been buried here. 14. *Thomas Howard*, Duke of Norfolk, beheaded 1572, for having evinced a disposition to take as his third wife, Mary Queen of Scots, an arrangement which Queen Elizabeth forbad. "When the warrant for his committal to the Tower was brought, the first peer in the land, the head of the proud House of Howard, and the aspirant for the hand of England's expectant Queen, fell upon his knees and cried for mercy like a poltroon." 15. *Sir John Perrott*—"the first man of quality," says Swift, "I find upon record, to have sworn by 'God's wounds'"—a phrase which was vulgarly reduced to "zounds"! Sir John was said to have been a natural son of Henry VIII. by Mary, wife of Sir Thomas Perrott of Haroldston, Pembrokeshire,—"his qualities, gesture, and voice, were that of the King." He had been sent as Lord-Deputy to Ireland, in 1583, but was recalled in 1588. His haughty manner and severity of rule were complained of, and he was sent to the Tower for some "incautious and treasonable utterances," which his enemy, Sir Christopher Hatton, made the most of. "What!" said Sir John, "will the Queen (Elizabeth) suffer her brother to be offered up as a sacrifice to the envy of strutting adversaries?" The queen heard of this speech, relented, and respited his execution, but left him in prison, where he died suddenly, it was said of a broken heart, September 1592. The burial register records "Sir John P'rott, 1592," condemned for high treason. 16. *Philip, Earl of Arundel*, who also died, 1595, a prisoner in the Tower, on suspicion of assisting in Catholic intrigues on behalf of Mary, Queen of Scots. He was imprisoned for about ten years, of which he spent nine in the Beauchamp Tower, and carved the inscription still to be seen on the wall of the staircase— "*Sicut peccati causa vincire opprobrium est, ita e contra pro Cristo custodiæ vincula sustinere maxima gloria est.* Arundell 26 May, 1587." "Even as it is an infamy to be imprisoned on account of crime, so on the contrary it is the greatest glory to endure prison chains for Christ's sake." Over the fireplace in the room is the inscription: "*Quanto plus afflictionis pro Christo in hoc sæculo, tanto plus gloriæ cum Christo in futuro.* Arundell, June 22, 1587." "*Gloriâ et honore eum coronâsti Domine, in memoriâ æterna erit justus.*"—"The greater the affliction endured here for Christ, the greater will be the glory enjoyed with Christ hereafter." "O Lord, Thou hast crowned him with glory and honour. The righteous is held in everlasting remembrance."

His body was buried in the chancel of this chapel, but was removed, 1624, to the family vault at Arundel. 17. *Robert Devereux*, Earl of Essex, beheaded outside the chapel, February 25, 1600. This favourite of Queen Elizabeth (whose career and end savoured rather of romance than fact), gave his royal mistress much anxiety, he even dared to attempt by seizing her person to dictate to her the dismissal of his rivals from her counsels. When his plans were discovered, he barricaded himself in Essex House, Strand, and refused to surrender. He was forced to succumb, however, and was taken to the Tower, and imprisoned in what was till then called Robert the Devil's Tower, but ever since, Devereux Tower, now occupied by the commanding officer of artillery. It is said that the queen would have been glad to have pardoned Essex, had he sought forgiveness, and that his death is attributable to his own obstinacy; on the other hand, there is a story of Essex having entrusted a ring to Lady Nottingham, who promised to carry it to the queen with every expression of Essex's contrition. Lady Nottingham was induced by an enemy to break her promise, and to say nothing to the queen; Essex's execution consequently took place. Years after, Lady Nottingham on her death-bed confessed to the queen what she had withheld from her, and asked for forgiveness before she died. Whereupon Queen Bess, with characteristic indignation, replied, "May God forgive you, for I never can!" 18. *Sir Thomas Overbury* died of poison whilst in prison in the Tower, 15th September, 1613. He was a favourite of Robert Carr, Earl of Somerset, King James's favourite, and fell a victim to the enmity of Carr's wife, the notorious Countess of Essex, who got herself a divorce in order to be married to Carr. The Earl and Countess of Somerset were convicted of the murder of Overbury, but escaped punishment. Overbury is said to have been buried in the choir. 19. *Thomas Grey*, Lord Grey of Wilton, died a prisoner in 1614, having been sent here for his part in what was called the Raleigh conspiracy. 20. *Sir John Eliot*, died in the Tower (whither he had been sent by Charles I.), his imprisonment having broke down his health and brought on consumption. He was buried in this chapel. No stone marks the spot where he lies, but as long as freedom continues in England he will not be without a memorial. 21. *William Howard*, Lord Stafford, beheaded December 29, 1680, a victim of the Titus Oates conspiracy, and to the then mad condition of public opinion. Oates was convicted of perjury, and condemned to stand in the pillory five times a year so long as he lived, and to be whipped from Aldgate to Tyburn. William III. pardoned him, however, and gave him a pension. 22. *Arthur Capel*, Earl of Essex, who killed himself, while prisoner in the Tower for his share in the Rye House Plot. 23. *James, Duke of Monmouth*, beheaded 15th July, 1685, for rebellion against James II. This petted and spoiled son of Charles II. was encouraged by Whig statesmen, who wished at any hazard and by whatsoever means to drive James from the throne, and to set up Protestantism in the place of Popery. Monmouth's short history and many disasters culminated in his defeat in the battle of Sedgemoor. A heavy price was set upon his head, and he was pursued and captured in a wood at Cranbourne Chase, where this handsomely dressed man of fashion, the idol of the people and of the court, was found in most wretched plight, alone in a ditch, hidden under fern and brambles. In his pockets were only a few peas for subsistence, his watch and the decoration of the "George," together with a few papers in his own handwriting, containing charms and spells to open the doors of prisons, to keep him safe in battle, &c. Monmouth's execution was a cause of great grief to the populace, and the executioner did his part so badly, that he was in danger of being torn in pieces by the crowd. Monmouth was buried under the communion table in the chancel. 24. *George Lord Jeffreys*, the notorious judge who dealt so unmercifully with the unfortunate people who took part in Monmouth's rebellion, and who otherwise made himself the most evil reputation ever borne by a judge in this country, died in the Tower 18th April, 1689. When James II. fled from Whitehall, Jeffreys, the ex-chancellor, thought it time also to fly. He made arrangements to take boat for Hamburg, and had got down the Thames below London Bridge, but found that the boat did not start till next day. He went ashore at Wapping to indulge in his favourite vice of drinking, entered a public-house called 'The Red Cow' in Anchor and Hope Alley, and having drank off a pot of ale happened to look out of window. His face was immediately recognised by a man whom Jeffreys had once so abused in court, that the browbeaten man had often vowed " he should never forget the terrors of that face so long as he lived." Jeffreys turned away. It was too late; the alarm was given, a mob collected howling for "Vengeance," and would have torn him to pieces on the spot had not an armed force interfered. Jeffreys was taken to the Tower, where he became ill, and wasted from being a corpulent person into a mere skeleton, and died within a short time. He was buried in this chapel, but his body was disinterred in 1693, and removed to a vault under the Communion table in the church of St. Mary, Aldermary. 25. *John Roettier*, the medalist of Antwerp, whose father, a banker, assisted Charles II., when in exile, with money. He was appointed engraver to the Mint, and had quarters in the Tower, where he at length died, 1703. It is said that being an admirer of the charming Miss Stewart, afterwards Duchess of Richmond, he made a miniature of her face—" as well done," says Pepys, " as ever I saw anything in my whole life, I think, and a pretty thing it is that he should choose her face to represent Britannia." This figure Walpole also mentions as " Britannia, seated on the sea-shore, holding a shield and a sloping spear ; ships are

I

in the distance, and above is the sun in meridian." The same design slightly altered is still continued on our copper coinage. 26, *William, Earl of Kilmarnock*, and 27, *Arthur, Lord Balmerino*, both beheaded August 18, 1746, for their share in the rebellion on behalf of Prince Charles Edward, the Pretender. They were taken prisoners at the battle of Culloden. Their bodies were buried at the west end of the chapel, in the same grave where that of 28, *Simon Lord Lovat*, another of the chiefs of this rebellion, who was beheaded 7th of April, 1747, was also placed. The coffin-plates, with inscriptions (discovered in some excavations a little while ago), were placed against the west wall of the church. Lord Lovat was the last malefactor beheaded in this country. An altar tomb bears the figures of Sir R. Cholmondeley, Lieutenant of the Tower (*temp.* Henry VII.), also of his wife.

In the ROYAL MINT on Tower Hill, the coinage for the United Kingdom is produced. No coin is allowed to be issued until a portion has been tested by Her Majesty's assayer; he afterwards preserves one piece of each kind of coin in a pyx (Greek name for *box*) or casket, and these coins are compared by a jury with the standard plates kept in the cloisters of Westminster Abbey—a test called the *Trial of the Pyx*. The various processes of coining may be seen by visitors who have previously obtained a written order from the Master of the Mint—available but for one day marked thereon, and for a small number of persons, not exceeding six, the number to be stated when the application is made.

The TRINITY HOUSE on Tower Hill was built by Samuel Wyatt for a corporation, founded *temp.* Henry VIII., having for its object the increase and encouragement of navigation, the regulation of lighthouses and sea-marks, &c., and incorporated as " The Masters, Wardens, and Assistants of the Guild or Fraternity or Brotherhood of the most Glorious and Undividable Trinity, and of St. Clement in the parish of Deptford." There are here many pictures and busts of celebrated persons, and a large painting by Gainsborough of the "Elder Brethren of the Trinity House." The Museum contains some interesting naval relics and curiosities. Applications for admission should be made to the secretary.

LOWER THAMES STREET is that part of Thames Street below London Bridge, the above-bridge portion being known as Upper Thames Street. We have already traversed the former. The south side of UPPER THAMES STREET, now occupied by wharves, was once the site of riverside palaces, and in the lanes upon the north side were once to be seen merchants' mansions, which, if not equal to the edifices of stately Venice, might at least vie with many of the Hotels of Old Paris.

The Church of *St. Magnus*, destroyed in the Great Fire, was rebuilt by Sir C. Wren, 1676. In it is a monument to Miles Coverdale, once rector of this church, who was buried here. The footway under the tower was made in 1760, without interfering with the structure.

The *Weigh-house Chapel*, on Fish Street Hill, is of historical note, dating from the Act of Uniformity. Its chief recent pastor was the Rev. Thomas Binney.

OLD SWAN STAIRS, leading to the landing-stages for river steamboats, was a noted "stairs" of the fifteenth century. On LAWRENCE POUNTNEY HILL lived Dr. William Harvey, who here discovered the circulation of the blood. DOWGATE (the Dowr or Water Gate) was the way from Watling Street to the river. QUEENHITHE, so-called from being the hithe or landing-place of Eleanor, queen of Henry II., who possessed the adjoining property, was in Stowe's time the chief water-gate of the city. On ADDLE HILL stood the palace of the Anglo-Saxon king Adelstan of Athelstan, after whom it was named.

PALL MALL EAST, PALL MALL, ST. JAMES'S AND BUCKINGHAM PALACES, AND PIMLICO.

PALL MALL, one-third of a mile long, derives its name from the French game of *Paille Maille*, see p. 124. The tricornered block of houses, which stands upon the west side of Trafalgar Square, occupies the space between *Cockspur Street* and *Pall Mall East*, one of the most prominent positions in London. If we take the upper line of road called *Pall Mall East*, we shall pass upon our right *Whitcomb Street*, formerly *Hedge Lane*, before mentioned, and just beyond it the entrance to the *Gallery of the Society of Painters in Water Colours*, of which Sir John Gilbert is the president. Opposite is Messrs. *Colnaghi's* well-known print and picture shop. A few paces farther is *Suffolk Street*, in which is the entrance to the *United University Club-house*, built in 1824, by Wilkes & Deering, for 500 members of Oxford and 500 of Cambridge Universities.

Suffolk Street is chiefly noted for having been the scene of a political brawl. On January 30, 1735, some young gentlemen belonging to the Puritan Calves' Head Club, met at a tavern in this street to celebrate the anniversary of the death of Charles I. It is said that a bleeding calf's head was thrown out of the window of the tavern into the street, where some boys had lit up a bonfire, and that the members of the club then drank the toast of "Confusion to the race of Stuart." Stones were flung, the tavern windows broken, and a riot ensued which required a body of soldiers to suppress. In the upper part of Suffolk Street was the *Gallery of British Artists*, now removed to Conduit Street, a society founded in 1823, in consequence of the limited space for exhibition at Somerset House. *Richard*

PLATE V.

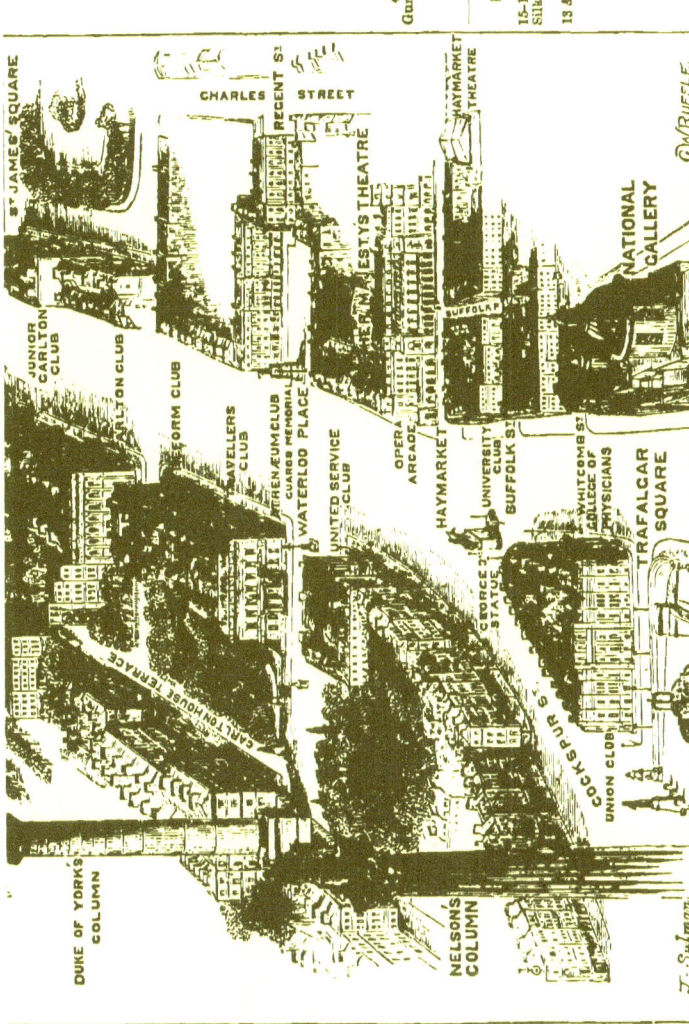

FROM CHARING CROSS THROUGH PALL MALL TO PIMLICO.

COCKSPUR STREET.
Hedling, Pearce, & Stone, 1-4.
Silk Mercers, Drapers, & Hosiers

4. T. W. Watson,
Gunmaker & Optician.

PALL MALL EAST.
15-18, Hedling, Pearce & Stone,
Silk Mercers, Drapers & Hosiers
13 & 14, Lombardi & Co.,
Photographers.

Cobden used, in his later days, to lodge in this street. The statue erected to his memory is set up in Camden Town.

Of *Cockspur Street* and its vicinity much might be said did space allow. *Spring Gardens* was a bowling-green in the time of Charles I., and in the second Charles's reign, a noted rendezvous for the gallants of the period. The celebrated tavern, mentioned by Pepys and others, called *Locket's Ordinary*, was upon this site. "Locket's stands where gardens once did spring." *Mrs. Centlivre* lived in Spring Gardens, and died there in the house of her third husband, Joseph Centlivre, chief cook to Queen Anne. *Colley Cibber* lived near the Bull's Head Tavern, in Old Spring Garden, and *John Milton* (when Latin Secretary to Cromwell) lodged in a house opening to Spring Gardens. An equestrian *Statue of George III.*, by M. C. Wyatt, occupies the ground where Cockspur Street and Pall Mall East join together, in front of the handsome general drapery establishment of Messrs. Halling, Pearce, & Stone, called *Waterloo House.*

We now arrive at the bottom of the Haymarket, under the Piazza of *Her Majesty's Theatre.* This edifice has been but recently rebuilt, after destruction by fire—the usual fate of theatres. The first Italian Opera-house in England was built by Sir John Vanbrugh on this site, and opened 1705; it was burnt down in 1789, and rebuilt next year. Nash & Repton designed the exterior, in 1820, in the Roman Doric style, and built the colonnade and the *Royal Opera Arcade.* The Haymarket front of Her Majesty's is decorated with a *basso-relievo* by Bubb, illustrating the progress of Music. It was at Her Majesty's Theatre that Jenny Lind obtained her wonderful success. The nightly expenses of this house have ranged from £700 to £1000 during the season.

A few yards higher up, and upon the east side of the Haymarket, is the *Haymarket Theatre*, long noted for its comedies. It was originally built in 1720, and opened as the "New French Theatre." English plays, operas, &c., afterwards

were performed; among which may be mentioned the
'Beggars' Opera,' produced here in 1727. Fielding wrote
his *Pasquin* for this theatre during his lesseeship, and by
his satire on the Ministry provoked the passing of the
Licensing Act. Samuel Foote was manager here for
thirty years, and then sold the theatre to George Colman,
who was succeeded by his son, Colman the younger. In
1820 the " Little Theatre " was taken down, and the present
edifice was built on its site, by Nash, and opened in 1821.
For many years, the Haymarket was noted for its good
management by Mr. B. Webster, and subsequently by Mr.
Buckstone. It has now passed into the hands of Mr. and
Mrs. Bancroft, the lessees of the Prince of Wales's Theatre.

Passing onwards through Pall Mall, we observe Messrs.
Graves's noted print-shop, and nearly opposite to it the
club-house of the *United Service Club*, sometimes called the
Senior United Service Club, to distinguish it from the
Junior United Service Club, close by, at the corner of Charles
Street. The first-named club-house was built in 1829,
after a design by Nash, who was the great planner and
designer of all the neighbouring Crown property in
Waterloo Place and Regent Street. At this club-house
the great Duke of Wellington at one time might often
be seen dining off the joint, and it is said that on one
occasion, when he was charged 15*d.* instead of 1*s.* for it,
he headed an attack upon the newly-increased tariff, and
came off victorious, of course, in the struggle for the odd
threepence. There are some handsome portraits of naval
and military heroes to be seen in this club-house, and a
few paintings, among which may be mentioned Stanfield's
Battle of Trafalgar.

Upon the open space between the United Service Club-
house and the Athenæum Club-house, east and west, and
between the bottom of Regent Street (where stands the
Guards' Crimean Memorial, designed by Bell, and cast
from cannon taken at Sebastopol), and the Duke of York's

Column (see p. 124) stood the once celebrated *Carlton House*, built by Lord Carlton, and occupied as a residence by George, Prince Regent. Carlton House was taken down in 1827, but its name survives in the present Carlton House Terrace and the Carlton Club. There are three memorial statues in the space between Carlton House Terrace and the club-houses above-named; one, by Marochetti, to *Colin Campbell, Lord Clyde* (d. 1863), the reliever of Lucknow; one, by Noble, to *Sir John Franklin*, the lost Arctic navigator; and one, by Boehm, to *Sir John Fox Burgoyne* (d. 1871).

The ATHENÆUM CLUB-HOUSE was erected by Decimus Burton in 1829; the Club itself dates from 1823, and consists of gentlemen eminent in literature, science, and art, and distinguished members of the learned professions. The architecture of the club-house is Grecian, with a frieze copied from that of the Parthenon.

Upon the north side of Pall Mall, at the corner opposite the *Athenæum*, is a new club-house, the *Wanderer's Club*. Adjoining the Athenæum is the *Traveller's Club*, which was instituted in 1814, for gentlemen who shall have travelled out of the British Islands, to a distance of at least 500 miles from London, in a direct line—a feat not difficult or uncommon in these days of railways and steamships, but otherwise in 1814. The *Traveller's Club-house* was designed by Barry, and built in 1832. Next door are the Reform Club Chambers, and then the *Reform Clubhouse*, built also by Barry, 1838–9. The Reform Club was established in 1830 to promote the passing of the first Reform Bill. It consists of 1000 members of Parliament and others of the Liberal party.

We are now in the very heart, so to speak, of clubland. Eight palatial-looking edifices are ranged upon the south side of Pall Mall, and upon the north, besides the one already mentioned and the *Marlborough Club-house* at No. 52, are the *Army and Navy Club-house* and the *Junior*

Carlton Club-house, each of which is as large, if not larger, than either of its opposite neighbours. With such luxurious buildings surrounding us, we can readily realise the humour of Captain Morris, in the lines :—

> "In town let me live then, in town let me die,
> For in truth I can't relish the country, not I;
> If one must have a villa in summer to dwell,
> Oh, give me the sweet shady side of Pall Mall."

The *Carlton Club-house*, the rendezvous of the chiefs of the Conservative party, is next door to its rival, the Reform. The Carlton is, however, the grander-looking edifice, its polished granite columns being a great contrast to the simplicity of the style of its neighbour. This house was built by Sir Robert Smirke, and improved by his brother, Mr. Sydney Smirke. Its façade is of the Italian school of architecture.

At 86 is the WAR OFFICE, in front of which is a Statue in memory of the late Right Hon. Sidney Herbert, Earl of Pembroke.

On the opposite, or north side of Pall Mall, is the *Army and Navy Club-house*, already mentioned, the entrance to which is in a short street leading from Pall Mall into *St. James's Square*. At No. 14 St. James's Square is the *East India U.S. Club-house*, at 11, the *Windham Club-house*, and in the corner, between the two, the *London Library*. In the centre of *St. James's Square* (which dates from 1674-76) is a Statue of William III. At No. 21, George III. was born.

Turning back into Pall Mall, we shall proceed, as before, westwards. At Nos. 81 and 82 is *Schomberg House*, the residence of the Duke of Schomberg, killed at the battle of the Boyne, 1690. It was subsequently divided into three houses. In the west wing Gainsborough the painter lived, from 1777 to 1788, and died there. Next door, that is to say, at No. 79 (but the house is now rebuilt, and is the office of the Eagle Insurance Company), lived Nell

Gwynne, from 1670 to 1687, when she died. It was from the garden of this house, then abutting upon St. James's Park, that Evelyn "saw and heard a familiar discourse between the King (Charles II.) and Mrs. Nellie, as they called an impudent comedian; she looking out of her garden on a terrace at the top of the wall, and the King standing on the green walk under it."

The *Oxford and Cambridge Club-house*, occupying from 71 to 76 Pall Mall, was built in 1838 by Sydney Smirke, for 1000 members of the two Universities, 500 from each. Above the principal windows are bas-reliefs from designs by Sir R. Smirke, representing Minerva and Apollo presiding on Parnassus; Homer singing to a warrior, a female, and a youth; Virgil reciting his Georgics to a group of peasants; Milton and his daughter; Shakespeare, attended by Tragedy and Comedy; Newton explaining his system; Bacon, his philosophy. Opposite, at 52, is the *Marlborough Club-house*, and at 53, the *Institute of Painters in Water Colours*. The *Guards' Club-house* is at No. 70, built in 1848–50, by Harrison. The members of this Club are limited to the officers of Her Majesty's three regiments of Foot Guards. The *Beaconsfield Club-house*, just beyond, has but recently been erected upon a precious bit of ground lying between Marlborough House and Pall Mall. The space was small, so the architect had to provide room by rearing an unusually lofty structure.

MARLBOROUGH HOUSE, St. James's, the residence of H.R.H. the Prince of Wales, was built, 1709–10, by Sir Christopher Wren, for the first Duke of Marlborough. The Great Duke died here in 1722. Here the first Duchess loved to speak of the King as "neighbour George," he being at St. James's Palace. In 1817 the house was purchased by the Crown for Princess Charlotte and Prince Leopold, and it was the Prince's house for many years. Queen Adelaide lived in it after the death of William IV. This building was used for the Exhibition of the Vernon Collection of

Pictures, after it was settled upon the Prince of Wales, down to 1859; and here commenced in the upper rooms a *School of Design*, which, with those pictures, was afterwards removed to the galleries of South Kensington Museum.

ST. JAMES'S PALACE, at the bottom of St. James's Street and the south-west corner of Pall Mall, was built on the site of a hospital dating from before the Conquest and dedicated to St. James. Henry VIII. obtained possession of the hospital, turned out the inmates, pulled down the buildings, and bought the surrounding meadows, and there built what was called the 'Manor House,' said to have been planned by Holbein—" a faire mansion and a parke for his greater commoditie and pleasure." Holbein's Gatehouse still faces St. James's Street. King Edward and Queen Elizabeth seldom came to St. James's; but Mary retired hither during the absence of her husband in Spain, and died here, as also did Henry, eldest son of James I. Charles I. enlarged the palace and lived in it; his son, Charles II., was born here, as also his other children. From St. James's Palace, where he slept the night before his execution, Charles I. walked, guarded by soldiers, through St. James's Park to Whitehall, where he was beheaded. James II. escaped hence on his abdication, and in female disguise reached Gravesend. Here Monk stopped while planning the Restoration; and in the old bedchamber next the levée-room was born (the old Pretender) James, the son of James II., by Mary of Modena; the baby having been, as was alleged by the Whigs of the period, conveyed in a warming-pan into the Queen's bed. The Court of St. James's dates from the time of William III., for it was not till the burning of Whitehall that this palace became the place for State ceremonies; William and Mary did not reside in it, but at Kensington Palace. The fourth plate of Hogarth's 'Rake's Progress' shows the Palace gateway in 1735. George III. celebrated his marriage, and George IV. was born here, and as Prince of Wales he was married in St. James's Chapel Royal; so was also Queen Victoria. William IV. and Queen Adelaide resided at St. James's. In the outer or east court the Guard is relieved every morning at a quarter to eleven, and the Band plays for a quarter of an hour; the visitor to London should make a point of attending. *The Chapel Royal, St. James's*, is well worth seeing, though of little interest architecturally, beyond its Holbein ceiling. Admission is occasionally to be obtained to Divine Services at 10, 12, and half-past 5 on Sundays, by ticket from the Lord Chamberlain or the Bishop of London.

CLARENCE HOUSE, adjoining St. James's Palace, and built for the Duke of Clarence, afterwards William IV., was fitted up and renovated for H.R.H. the Duke of Edinburgh upon his marriage with the Princess Marie of Russia.

Bridgewater House, on the east side of the Green Park, with entrance in Cleveland Row, contains a fine collection of pictures principally from the Duke of Orleans' collection. Among the chief are Guido's 'Assumption of the Virgin'; Raphael's 'Viérge au Palmier,' Poussin's 'Seven Sacraments,' 'Moses striking the Rock,' Turner's 'Gale at Sea,' and the 'Chandos Portrait of Shakespeare,' bought at the Stowe sale in 1848 for 355 guineas.

Stafford House in St. James's Park, close to St. James's Palace, was built for the Duke of York, second son of George III., and sold to the Duke of Sutherland. It is said to be the finest private mansion in London. The Sutherland Gallery of Pictures, though not large, is valuable and interesting; it includes three fine paintings from the Soult collection, and Delaroche's picture of 'Strafford on his way to the Scaffold.'

ST. JAMES'S PARK contains ninety-one acres, enclosed by Henry VIII. and improved by Charles II. and George IV. It has the Horse Guards on the east, Pall Mall and St. James's Palace on the north, Buckingham Palace and the Green Park on the west, and, upon the south, Birdcage

Walk, Queen's Square, and Westminster; but it is of very unequal proportions. In the open space in front of the Horse Guards, now called the *Parade* and formerly the *Tilt-yard* (see p. 25), is a Mortar left behind by the French in their retreat from Salamanca, which was presented to the Prince Regent by the Spanish Government. Here also, on the opposite side of the Parade, is a Turkish gun, taken from the French in Egypt. At a northern corner of the Parade is a gate leading into *Spring Gardens*, past the Office of the *Metropolitan Board of Works*. Westwards is the *Duke of York's Column* erected in 1833, of Scotch granite, 124 feet high, designed by Wyatt, surmounted by a statue by Westmacott. Admission 6d. to the top of this column, between 12 and 4, from May to September inclusive. The *Mall* extends from this point to Buckingham Palace, i.e. about half a mile. Here Charles II. and his courtiers often played at *paille-maille*, an ancient game in which mallets and balls were used, the latter being driven through an iron hoop suspended from the arm of a high pole. It is said that when Queen Caroline, the wife of George II., who occupied St. James's Palace, talked of shutting out the public from St. James's Park and converting it into a palace garden, she asked Walpole what it would cost, and he replied, "Only three crowns." The *Wellington Barracks*, built near the site of *Rosamond's Pond*, once famous for assignations and love suicides, were first occupied by troops in 1814. The *Ornamental Water* in the centre of St. James's Park is provided with a few boats for hire; the aquatic birds upon this water are extremely varied in character and plumage. Across the lake is an ornamental Bridge connecting the Mall with Westminster.

BUCKINGHAM PALACE was built by Nash and Blore (1825–37), upon the site of *Buckingham House*, which had been erected by Sheffield, Duke of Buckingham, in 1703, and purchased by George III. in 1761. In 1775 Buckingham

House was settled on Queen Charlotte, in exchange for Somerset House, and it was here that the King's Library was collected by George III., "the finest and most complete ever formed by a single individual," 80,000 volumes, exclusive of pamphlets, which was presented by George IV. to the British Museum in 1823. William IV. and Queen Adelaide did not occupy Buckingham Palace, but Queen Victoria took up her residence here in 1837. In 1846 the erection of the east side commenced, and a spacious ball-room has since been added. The State Apartments are the Green Drawing-room, in the centre of the east front; the Ball-room, on the south side; the Grand Saloon for concerts; and the Throne Room, 64 feet long, hung in crimson satin. In this room Privy Councils used to be held, and here Her Majesty holds her Court. The Picture Gallery contains some fine examples of Dutch and Flemish art, and Sir Joshua Reynolds' 'Death of Dido' and 'Cymon and Iphigenia,' also his own portrait in spectacles; Wilkie's 'Penny Wedding' and 'Blindman's Buff'; some works by Gainsborough; Sir Peter Lely's 'Anne Hyde, Duchess of York;' Zoffany's 'Florentine Gallery' and the 'Royal Academy, 1773,' &c. In the *Garden* is the *Palace Chapel*, also a lake of five acres, and a pavilion or gardenhouse; the whole grounds of Buckingham Palace comprise about forty-three acres. The *Queen's Stables* or *Mews*, in Buckingham Palace Road at the rear of the Palace, were built in 1824, and consist of two quadrangles, entered by a Doric archway beneath a clock-tower. In the first quadrangle are Her Majesty's State-coach (which cost £6,661), and the carriages; in the second quadrangle the horses. In the harness-room is the red-morocco State-harness for eight horses, with massive silver-gilt furniture; each set of harness weighing 1 cwt. Admission to the Buckingham Palace Stables may be obtained by an order from the Master of the Horse.

In *Buckingham Palace Road* we are in Pimlico, once

noted for its Gardens for public entertainment, of which the chief was known as 'Jenny's Whim.' The *District Post-office*, and *Buckingham Palace Hotel*, one of the largest hotels in London, face the garden wall of Buckingham Palace. Farther west *Arabella Row* turns off a little to the north, and the road is continued past *Grosvenor Place* to Hyde Park Corner. If, however, we pursue our way through Buckingham Palace Road but a little farther, we shall cross a main thoroughfare, the left or southern side of which almost immediately becomes *Victoria Street, Westminster*—a modern street of mansions divided into suites of chambers or flats, which has been recently constructed upon the site of *Old Tothill Fields*. The Stores of the *Army and Navy Co-operative Society* are in Victoria Street. *Victoria Station*, at the western end of the street, is a double terminus serving for two railways—the London, Brighton, and South Coast Railway; and the London, Chatham, and Dover Railway; and connected with those, by subterranean passages, is the *Victoria Station of the Underground* or Metropolitan District Railway. Abutting on Victoria Station is the *Grosvenor Hotel*, one of the handsomest and most extensive of railway hotels in London. Beyond is *Pimlico Road* leading to Queen's Road, Chelsea; or the pedestrian may, by turning more immediately to the left of *Pimlico Road*, pass over the Chelsea Bridge to *Battersea Park* (see p. 252). South of Victoria Station runs the *Vauxhall Bridge Road* to Vauxhall Bridge (see p. 253); Tram-cars carry passengers down this road (see p. 314) at frequent intervals.

PLATE VI.

REGENT STREET.

REGENT STREET

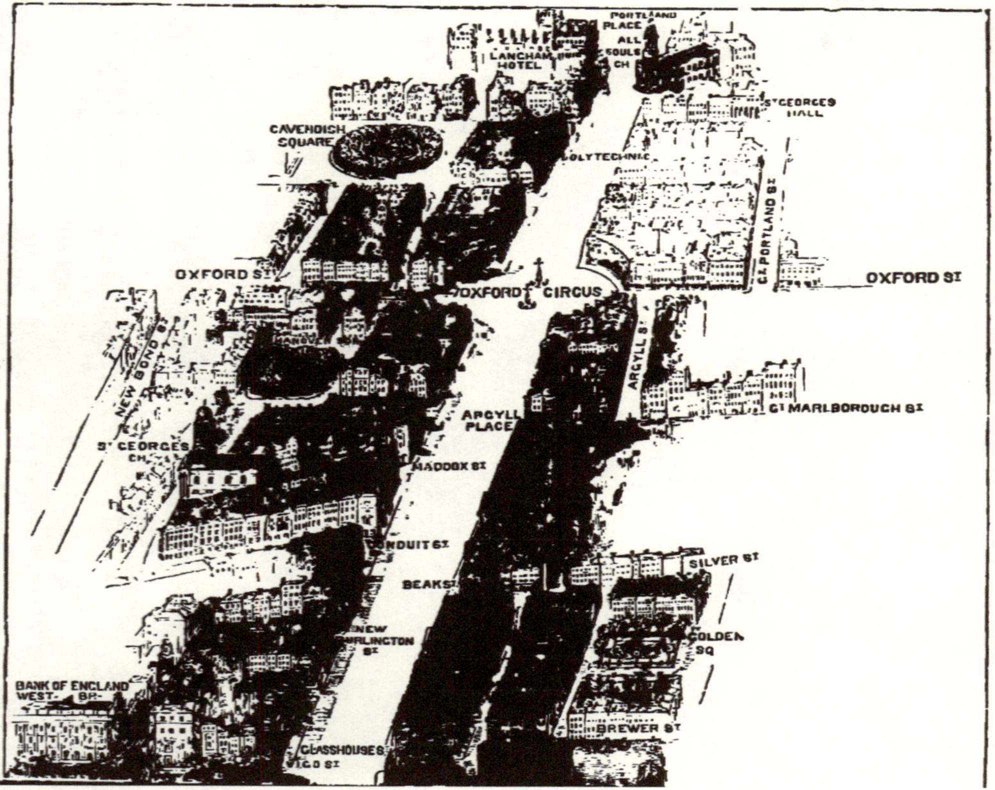

REGENT STREET.

138, *Barclay & Son,*
Lamp Makers & Wax Chandl

J. & J. Hopkinson, 235,
Pianoforte Manufacturers.

CONDUIT STREET.
1, *Kewell & Co.,*
Fishing Tackle Manufacturer.

REGENT STREET.
Edwards & Jones, 161, 167,
Stationery & Fancy Goods,
Ivory & China Depôt.

Willcox & Gibbs, 135,
Automatic Silent Sewing
Machine.

REGENT STREET,

FROM WATERLOO PLACE TO PORTLAND PLACE.

CAFÉ MONICO RESTAURANT,
REGENT CIRCUS, PICCADILLY.
(Nearly opposite Messrs. Swan & Edgar's Drapery Establishment.)

THE PROPRIETORS respectfully invite the attention of Ladies and Gentlemen to the SPECIALITIES offered at this Magnificent Establishment, recently erected at great cost.

DINNERS À LA CARTE.

TABLE D'HÔTE,
SERVED DAILY IN
THE GRAND SALOON on the FIRST FLOOR,
From 6 to 9 p.m.

COFFEE, TEA, &c., always ready in the
GRAND CAFÉ SALOON.
The Wines, Spirits, and Liqueurs only of First Quality.

This is considered one of the handsomest and most comfortable Restaurants in England.

Patronised by Royalty and the most Fashionable Classes.

THE PALL MALL RESTAURANT,
14, REGENT STREET, WATERLOO PLACE, S.W.

THIS ESTABLISHMENT, situated in the most Attractive and Fashionable Part of London, has recently been so Remodelled and Decorated, as to render it in every way one of the most agreeable for both Ladies and Gentlemen requiring

BREAKFAST, LUNCHEON, OR DINNER.

THE BEST CUISINE AND BEST WINES.
THE SERVICE PROMPT AND PERFECT.

TABLE D'HÔTE DINNERS DAILY,
AT SEPARATE TABLES.

From 12.30 to 3 . . . . . . 2s. 6d.
From 5.0 to 8 . . . . . . 5s. 0d. and upwards.

Private Rooms for Large or Small Parties.

LUNCHEONS and DINNERS, Hot or Cold, from the Daily Bill of Fare, with prices affixed; also TEA, COFFEE, &c., always ready at

THE BUFFET,
To which the Entrance is at the back of the Restaurant, in
ST. ALBAN'S PLACE.

REGENT STREET, THROUGH PORTLAND PLACE TO REGENT'S PARK.

REGENT STREET, the handsomest street of shops in London, was built from about 1813, by Nash, the architect, as a speculation; and it proved to him an unprofitable one. It commences from the line of Waterloo Place, Pall Mall, and traverses the ground formerly occupied by *St. James's Market* and *Swallow Street*. At its southern extremity, *Waterloo Place*, is the monumental group, by Bell, to the memory of the soldiers of the Foot Guards who fell in the Crimea. The first house upon the right or east side, where the Place begins to narrow, is the *Pall Mall Club*, founded, 1870, upon a non-political basis, by the Marquis Townshend, assisted by Mr. Herbert Fry. At the north-east corner of *Charles Street* is the *Junior United Service Club-house*, built by Sir R. Smirke, R.A., in 1824. Charles Street leads into St. James's Square. Howell and James's fashionable jewellery and mercery establishment is at Nos. 5, 7, 9. *Regent Street Chapel*, built by Repton, is on the same side of the street. Opposite is the building erected by Nash for his own residence, and which obtained some reputation as a place of entertainment when occupied by Mr. and Mrs. German Reed, as the *Gallery of Illustration*, but which is now converted into the *Pall Mall Restaurant*. The *Raleigh Club* is next door, and opposite are the *Junior Army and Navy Co-operative Stores*, but just established. A little above this point, Regent Street is intersected by Jermyn Street (see p. 134), and a few paces farther by Piccadilly (see p. 138), where is formed *Regent Circus*,

Piccadilly. Facing us northwards is the County Fire Office, and there in the bend westerly begins *Regent's Quadrant*, originally provided with two Doric colonnades, which had a peculiarly handsome architectural effect, but these being found to darken the shops, and to encourage loungers of questionable character, were removed in November, 1848, considerably to the advantage of the shopkeepers and their business. On the right, before entering the Quadrant, is *Tichborne Street*, in which, facing southward, under an archway, is the entrance to the *Café Monico Restaurant*, a large and handsome building, recently erected to comprise all the appointments of the best of these vast modern establishments. On the eastern side of the Quadrant is the *Café Royal Nicols Restaurant*, and nearly facing it, on the western side, is the chief entrance to *St. James's Hall and Restaurant* (see p. 140). *Vigo Street* leads between the top of the Albany and the end of *Savile Row*, where are the offices of the *Royal Geographical Society* (see p. 145); also the *Stafford Club*, the *Burlington Fine Arts Club*, and the *Scientific Club*. At No. 12 Savile Row lived George Grote, the historian; opposite is Mr. Poole's, the fashionable tailor. At 169 Regent Street is *Blanchard's Restaurant*, and at 229, *Verrey's Café Restaurant*.

Glasshouse Street, on the north of Regent Street, communicates by way of *Brewer Street* with *Golden Square*, which was inhabited by lords and ministers of state, and that not so very long since; for the whole of this part of London was open country in the time of Charles II. Macaulay tells us that at the period of the Restoration, a rambler, in what is now the gayest and most crowded part of *Regent Street*, " found himself in a solitude, and was sometimes so fortunate as to have a shot at a woodcock. On the north the Oxford Road ran between hedges. Three or four hundred yards to the south were the garden walls of a few great houses which were considered as quite out of town. On the west was a meadow renowned for a spring, from which long afterwards *Conduit Street* was named. On the east was a field (the *Pest Field*), not to be passed without a shudder by any Londoner of that age. There, as in a place far from the haunts of men, had been dug, when the *Great Plague* was raging, a pit into which the dead-carts had nightly shot corpses by scores. It was popularly believed that the place was deeply tainted." . . . . No foundations were laid there before the time of George the Second. The *Great Plague of London* began in December, 1664, and continued to November, 1666. Deaths occurred at the rate of 1000 to 7000 a week, amongst a population comparatively small; 4000 once died in one night; there died in the whole kingdom of the plague (1664-5) no less than 68,596. De Foe's account of it is admittedly the most wonderful piece of writing of the kind ever produced. He describes it as if he had been an eye-witness of all the portents and the horrors, as if he "actually saw the blazing star which portended the calamity; beheld the grass growing in the streets, read the inscriptions on the house-doors, heard the bellman cry, 'Bring out your dead,' saw the dead-carts pass, and the pits dug for the unfortunate victims."

Archbishop Tenison's Chapel, between 172 and 174 Regent Street, was built in 1702, and shares in the proceeds of the archbishop's estate left for the purposes of this chapel, and for the endowment of his *Grammar School*, now in Leicester Square (see p. 18). *Hanover Chapel* was built by Cockerell, 1823-5, it stands between *Princes Street* and *Hanover Street*. *Argyll Street* leads into *Great Marlborough Street*, wherein is the Gallery of the *Society of Lady Artists*, also *Marlborough Street Police Court*. Just beyond Argyll Street is *Regent Circus, Oxford Street*, at the intersection of the two streets, one of the busiest parts of London.

THE CHURCH OF ALL SAINTS, *Margaret Street*, Regent Street, is considered one of the handsomest of modern Gothic churches. Its painted windows, marble decorations;

polished granite piers, with carved alabaster capitals; its frescoes, and low choir screen of alabaster, are the accessories to a High-church service, which attracts many of the upper classes.

THE POLYTECHNIC INSTITUTION, a cheap place of instructive amusement, erected in 1838, is a little farther north. Opposite is the *German Gallery* for Toys, &c. Farther north still is *Langham Place*, named after Sir James Langham, and built upon the site of *Foley House*. Here stands the *Langham Hotel*, a magnificent structure upon the scale of the largest railway hotels of recent date, and chiefly noted as being a great resort of travelling Americans.

All Souls Church, Langham Place, was built by Nash, in 1822-5; and though not in the most attractive of ecclesiastical styles, it is not ill-adapted to the surrounding houses, so far as general effect is concerned. Nash was the great introducer of stucco. He taught how good or bad bricks might be slobbered over with cement and made to imitate Bath stone. The age of stucco and sham initiated by Nash has not yet entirely ceased. The following epigram on Nash is worth remembering, whilst we look at his best work in Regent Street:—

> "Augustus at Rome was for building renowned,
> And of marble he left what of brick he had found;
> But is not our Nash too a very great master,
> Who found us all brick and who left us all plaster?"

There is a well-known *School for Artists* in *Langham Place*, and at 4 Langham Place is *St. George's Hall*, wherein is given *Mr. and Mrs. German Reed's Entertainment*. *Portland Place* is a wide and noble street of mansions, built by the Brothers Adam (1778), and named after the Duke of Portland, the owner of the land about this quarter. It is continued to *Park Crescent*, across which runs *Marylebone Road*, and beyond the Crescent, a broad walk or avenue, in a line with Portland Place, is carried straight through Regent's Park and alongside of the Royal Zoological Gardens.

The Zoological Gardens.

REGENT'S PARK (named after the Prince Regent) of 472 acres, containing part of what was known as *Marylebone Park* or *Fields*, lies between the south foot of *Primrose Hill* and the *New Road*, and was formed in 1812 by Nash the architect, who also built most of the terraces which surround it, nearly all of which are Crown property. In the south-west portion is a lake with three forks crossed by suspension bridges. In the south part of the Park are two circles, the inner of which is the *Garden of the Royal Botanical Society*, open every week-day from nine till sunset, and on Sundays after two o'clock to persons presenting orders from Fellows of the Society. The *Garden of the Toxophilite Society* adjoins these grounds.

At the north end of the Park, near *Primrose Hill*, are the *Zoological Gardens*. Admission from nine till dusk; Mondays 6d., other days 1s., except Sundays, when admission is only by Member's order. The Zoological Collection includes 1000 birds, 500 quadrupeds, 100 reptiles, and is one of the sights of London. The great hippopotamus, the monkey house, the snakes, the fishes, the seals, the elephant calf, the bears, are well worth a visit. The lions, &c., are fed at 4 P.M. A promenade at the 'Zoo,' on a fine Sunday afternoon in the London season, is a pleasant opportunity for seeing fashionable life in London.

On the east side of Regent's Park is *St. Katherine's Hospital*, an ancient foundation for charitable uses, now serving as a retreat for old servants of the Crown. The *Marquis of Hertford's Villa* is in the outer road, its portico is an adaptation of the Temple of the Winds, at Athens; in a recess near the entrance are the clock and two gigantic statues, with clubs and bells from old St. Dunstan's Church, Fleet Street. From the top of Primrose Hill is to be had upon a fine morning one of the most extensive views of London. The *Shakespeare Oak* on the summit was planted April 23, 1864, to commemorate the tercentenary of the poet's birth.

ST. JAMES'S STREET AND BOND STREET.

ST. JAMES'S PALACE (see p. 122) stands at the bottom of St. James's Street. *Cleveland Row*, upon our left as we look up St. James's Street, derived its name from Barbara, Duchess of Cleveland, one of Charles the Second's mistresses, who at one time resided on this site. The first club-house which we pass on our way up St. James's Street is the *Thatched House Club*, No. 86, built in 1865 (and first known as the Civil Service Club), near the site of the once celebrated Thatched House Tavern, long noted for the eminence of its frequenters and for the number of its public and club dinners. At No. 87 is a new institution, the *Egerton Club*. Over the way, at the corner of Pall Mall, is Sams's Opera Ticket Office and bookshop, and at No. 8 the lodgings of Lord Byron in 1811. At 74 is the Conservative Club-house, erected from designs by Messrs. Bassevi and Sydney Smirke, upon the site of a house in which Gibbon the historian died. The *Conservative Club* extends to the corner of Little St. James's Street. It was established in 1840, to receive Conservatives, then too numerous for the Carlton. At 69, on the same side of the street, is *Arthur's Club*, so named from its founder, a keeper of White's Chocolate-house, who died in 1761. In *St. James's Place* is the entrance to the house of the late Samuel Rogers, the author of 'The Pleasures of Memory.' The house overlooks the Green Park, and was the pleasant scene of many re-unions of the literary celebrities of the last half century.

In *King Street*, opposite, is the *St. James's Theatre*, built by Beazley, for the celebrated John Braham, the singer, and opened in 1835. One of the earliest pieces played here was the *Strange Gentleman*, a dramatic effort by Charles

NEW BOND STREET.

The Blenheim Restaurant, 94,
Walter Thurn J.-Christ.

Grosvenor Gallery.

W. P. & G. Phillips, 155,
China & Glass Manufacturers.

NEW BOND STREET.

76, W. Lockwood & Co.,
Stationers & Engravers.

72, Perry & Co.,
Chandeliers, Pedestals, and
Brackets in all styles of Art.

44, J. T. Mackley,
Heraldic Stationer.

13 & 14, H. P. Truefitt.

ST. JAMES'S STREET, AND OLD AND NEW BOND STREETS.

Dickens in his younger days, which was followed by the same writer with an operatic burletta, *The Village Coquettes*, with music by John Hullah. Braham did not find, however, his enterprise at this theatre a successful one. It is a house which has never been very remunerative to any of its numerous lessees—British or foreign. Neither German nor English Opera have taken root here, although attempts to establish them were made under the most favourable auspices. Near the St. James's Theatre are *Willis's Rooms*, a noted house for public dinners, balls, and meetings, originally known as *Almack's*, the most fashionable and exclusive assembly in the metropolis. Admission to the society of Almack's was regarded as a high distinction. Ordinary mortals can scarcely conceive the importance of getting admission to Almack's—described by Captain Gronow as "the seventh heaven of fashion," the gates of which were guarded by seven lady patronesses, "whose smiles or frowns consigned men or women to happiness or despair, as the case might be." Opposite Willis's Rooms are the well-known auction-rooms of Messrs. *Christie & Manson*, wherein, during the London season, are disposed of week by week the finest pictures and other works of art which thus change hands in this country. Many a connoisseur would tell you that the exhibitions which take place at Christie & Manson's are generally better worth seeing than those of any shilling Gallery in London. At *No. 3 King Street*, a small tablet in the front of the house testifies that *Louis Napoleon Bonaparte* (afterwards Napoleon III.) lived here in 1847, and also in 1848, when he was sworn in as one of the 150,000 special constables to suppress the Chartist gatherings. The Prince was cheated out of £2000 one night at Crockford's gaming-house, near by, but fortunately got his money back again.

At 64 *St. James's Street* is the *Cocoa-tree Club*, named after the Cocoa-tree Chocolate-house, which stood here in Queen Anne's time, and was then specially a Tory resort. "A Whig," wrote De Foe, "will no more go to the Cocoa-tree than a Tory will be seen at the Coffee-house of St. James's." From the window of No. 29 St. James's Street, over a printseller's shop, Gillray, the caricaturist, threw and killed himself in 1815. At No 60 is *Brooks's Club*, opened in 1778, and ever since then the headquarters of the Whig aristocracy. It was named after its first proprietor, and became famous for its deep gaming, and from being the rendezvous of Charles James Fox and his Whig confrères. At 28 St. James's Street, is *Boodle's Club-house*, of which Fox, Gibbon, and others, were the earliest members. It was earlier known as the *Savoir Vivre*. The *New University Club* was founded in 1864, in a house just below Bennet Street. No. 24 is the *Junior St. James's Club-house*, and next door is the *Devonshire Club-house*, an offshoot of the Reform Club, established in 1874 in the building formerly known as *Crockford's* gaming-house. Crockford died in 1844, and Raikes, in his journal of that date, says of him, "That arch-gambler Crockford is dead, and has left an immense fortune. He was originally a low fishmonger in Fish Street Hill, near the Monument; then a 'leg' at Newmarket, and keeper of 'hells' in London. He finally set up the Club in St. James's Street, opposite to White's, with a hazard bank, by which he won all the disposable money of the men of fashion in London, which was supposed to be two millions."

In *Jermyn Street* and the small streets connected with it are several excellent hotels for families, and lodging-houses, much in request by country gentlemen belonging to the neighbouring clubs. It was named after Henry Jermyn, Earl of St. Albans, who was said to have married Henrietta Maria the Queen Mother of Charles II. Pennant said, "She ruled her first husband, King Charles I., but her second husband, a subject, ruled her." The Turkish

Baths, called the *Hammam*, in Jermyn Street, are the best of their kind in London, and are resorted to by persons of the higher ranks of society. The poet Tom Moore once lodged at 27, Crabbe at 37, and Daniel O'Connell at 29, *Bury Street*. Sir Richard Steele and Swift also lived in that street.

White's Club-house occupies 36 and 37 St. James's Street. This club was originally founded at White's Chocolate-house, towards the bottom of St. James's Street, in 1698. The house was restored and re-arranged by J. Wyatt in 1851. The club was, up to 1830, noted as *the* Tory club-house, as Brooks's was that of the Whigs; and it certainly rivalled Brooks's at one time in its reputation for gambling. Horace Walpole wrote, in 1750, of White's: "A man dropped down dead at the door, and was carried in. The Club immediately made bets whether he was dead or not, and when they were going to bleed him, the wagerers for his death interposed, and said it would affect the fairness of the bet."

At the top of St. James's Street we cross Piccadilly, and, bearing a little to the right, we shall arrive at the corner of *Old Bond Street*, built by Sir Thomas Bond in 1686. Passing through it we shall note, at 39B, *Messrs. Agnew's New Art Gallery*, in red brick.

Lawrence Sterne died at his lodgings, 41 Bond Street (now a tailor's), in 1768. On the 18th of March there was a gay party in Clifford Street close by—Garrick and David Hume being of the company—and from it a footman was despatched to Sterne's lodgings to inquire after his health, which had of late been failing. The man was directed by the landlady to the sick room and found his way to the bedside. Sterne was dying—" Yorick's last breath was hanging upon his trembling lips ready to depart"—and no friend was present to receive that last squeeze of the hand, and that last glance, which "cut Eugenius to the heart." The footman alone heard the last words of Sterne:

"Now it is come," said the dying man, and raised his hand as if to ward off the mortal blow, then dropt his arm and expired. For his burial-place, see p. 167.

Mr. *Mitchell, the publisher's* shop at the corner of Stafford Street, has a small brass-plate let into the doorpost to commemorate a personal visit from Her Majesty. We now enter upon that portion of this street which has long been noted for handsome shops for jewelry, clocks, plate, &c. Here also we find ourselves in the midst of the most fashionable court tradesmen, as perfumers, hairdressers, dressing-case makers, lacemen, and tobacconists. At each of the two corners of Burlington Gardens is a perfumer's shop. In *Cork Street*, is a noted house for steaks and simple dinners, known as the *Blue Posts*.

In *New Bond Street* we come upon more pictures. The *Exhibition of the Society of French Artists* is at 168, next door to Lacon & Ollier's Opera and Theatre Agency. At the end of *Grafton Street* is *Long's Hotel*, a noted house where Byron once dined with Walter Scott. At No. 4 *Grafton Street*, the first Lord Brougham resided. At No. 10 is the *Grafton Club;* at 12 and 13, the *Junior Army and Navy Club*. In *Clifford Street* are *Fischer's Hotel* and the *Queen's Hotel*. Farther on up New Bond Street are the great Court jewellers, Messrs. Hunt & Roskell, and Messrs. Hancocks. At 9 *Conduit Street*, are the offices and rooms of the *Royal Institute of British Architects;* the *Architectural Association;* the *Society of Biblical Archæology;* the *Photographic Society*, and the *Society for the Encouragement of the Fine Arts*. *Limmer's Hotel* is at the corner of George Street and Conduit Street. *Bruton Street* leads into Berkeley Square. At 35 New Bond Street, is a popular resort—the *Doré Gallery of Pictures*, chiefly of Scriptural subjects, and upon the grandest scale in point of size.

At 136 is the *Grosvenor Gallery*, recently founded by Sir Coutts Lindsay; it is a handsome edifice, and contains an excellent collection of pictures, old and new, but ever changing and ever interesting. The plan of the galleries is novel and striking, and the style of decoration elegant and effective. The doorway at the entrance is said to have been designed by Palladio.

There is a label on the house, 141 New Bond Street, to indicate that Lord Nelson lived there in 1797. Sir Thomas Picton resided at 146. In *Upper Grosvenor Street* is the House and Collection of Pictures of the Duke of Westminster. *Maddox Street* leads directly to St. George's Church, Hanover Square. *Brook Street* (named after the stream which used to flow from the north side of Oxford Street) crosses the north side of Grosvenor Square, and is continued by Upper Brook Street to Park Lane. It is a direct way also into Hanover Square. New Bond Street has for many years enjoyed the highest reputation as a fashionable street, replete with shops of every variety, stored with the best of such goods as they profess to vend. If a man may so cultivate his taste by continually frequenting galleries of the pictures of the greatest masters, that his eye will eventually reject unworthy works, and become critical by a process which may be defined as natural selection, it may reasonably be believed that the jewels exhibited in the windows of Bond Street, being generally of the finest water, would educate the regular Bond-street lounger to a true appreciation of colour, character, and brilliancy in gems of all descriptions.

PICCADILLY

EXTENDS from the top of the Haymarket to Hyde Park Corner,—only 110 yards less than a mile. Before setting out to traverse this route it will be well to make a brief survey of the streets which are within view from our starting-point. Looking down the HAYMARKET (so-named from its having been the place for selling hay, before the market was transferred in 1830 to Cumberland Market, Regent's Park), we have upon our left COVENTRY STREET, leading to Leicester Square; behind us GREAT WINDMILL STREET (named from a windmill that once stood in a field on the west side), which is the shortest way from this point into Oxford Street; and upon our right are Tichborne Street and Piccadilly, the latter a little lower, crossed by Regent Street. The name of Piccadilly has never been satisfactorily traced to its origin; some have ascribed it to *Piccadilly Hall*, a place of entertainment, which stood at the corner of Great Windmill Street. A gaming-house, at the corner of the Haymarket and Coventry Street, was called *Shavers' Hall*, because of its having been established by the Lord Chamberlain's barber, and perhaps also because of the money lost there in gambling. Some have derived Piccadilly from frills or ruffs, named Piccadillies, which were much in fashion early in the 17th century, when the old "way to Reading" became first known as Piccadilly. Higgins, a tailor who made most of his money by Piccadillies, is said to have built the street. Whether the fashionable Piccadilly Hall, then upon the frill or skirt of the western suburbs, took the name in whimsical fashion

ST. JAMES'S HALL, PICCADILLY.

ALL THE YEAR ROUND.

EVERY NIGHT AT EIGHT.

MONDAYS, WEDNESDAYS, and SATURDAYS, } 3 & 8

THE

MOORE & BURGESS

MINSTRELS,

The Oldest Established and the most Popular Entertainment in the World,

The source whence all imitators derive the salient features of the Musical Performances, brought to such a degree of perfection by MESSRS. MOORE AND BURGESS.

THE COMPANY NOW CONSISTS OF

FORTY ARTISTS OF KNOWN EMINENCE,

Comprising the most accomplished Singers and the Finest body of Instrumentalists ever brought together in a singular organisation.

As instance of the Sterling and Enduring Popularity of the MOORE AND BURGESS MINSTRELS, the following facts are submitted :—The Present Season at the St. James's Hall commenced in September, 1865, from which date, down to the present time, the Company has performed EIGHT, TEN, and frequently TWELVE TIMES IN EACH WEEK throughout the entire term IN ONE CONTINUOUS SEASON, without the break of a single lawful day; the present being the FIFTEENTH CONSECUTIVE YEAR AT ST. JAMES'S HALL, a fact altogether unparalleled in the history of amusements.

Fauteuils, 5s.; Sofa Stalls, 3s.; Area, Raised and Cushioned Seats, 2s.; Gallery, the best and most comfortable in London, 1s.
Private Boxes, £2 12s. 6d. and £1 11s. 6d.

NO FEES.

No Charge for Programmes.   No Charge for Booking Reserved Seats.

LADIES CAN RETAIN THEIR BONNETS IN ALL PARTS OF THE HALL.

OMNIBUSES run direct to the doors of the St. James's Hall from every Railway Station, and also from every other part of London.

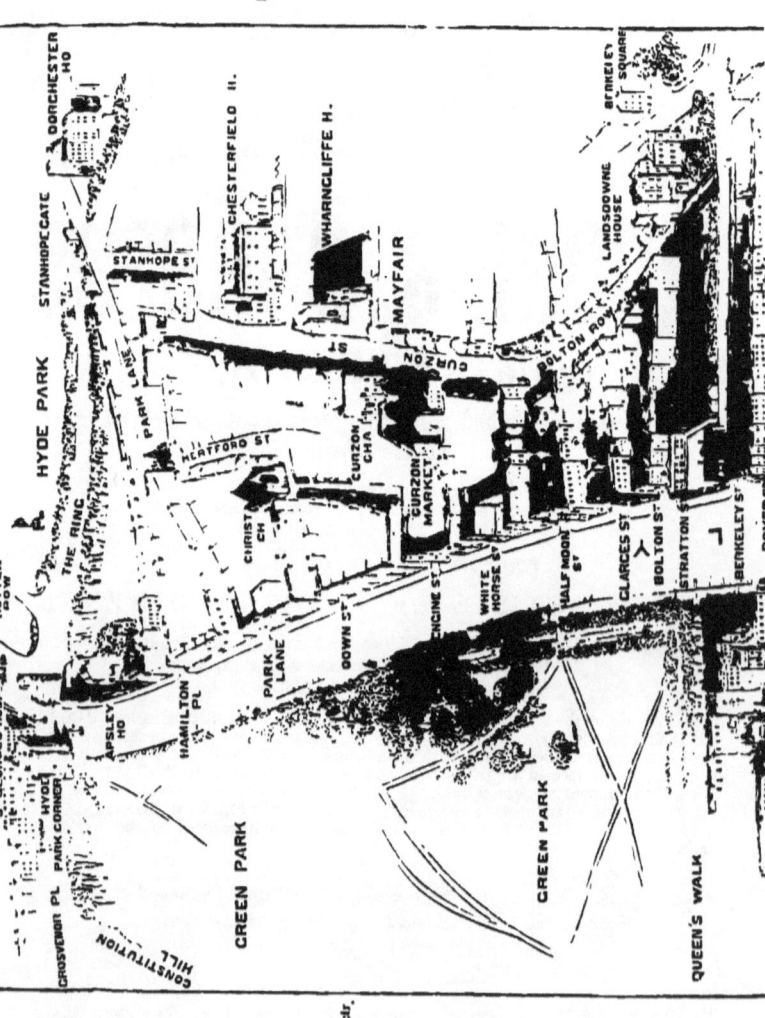

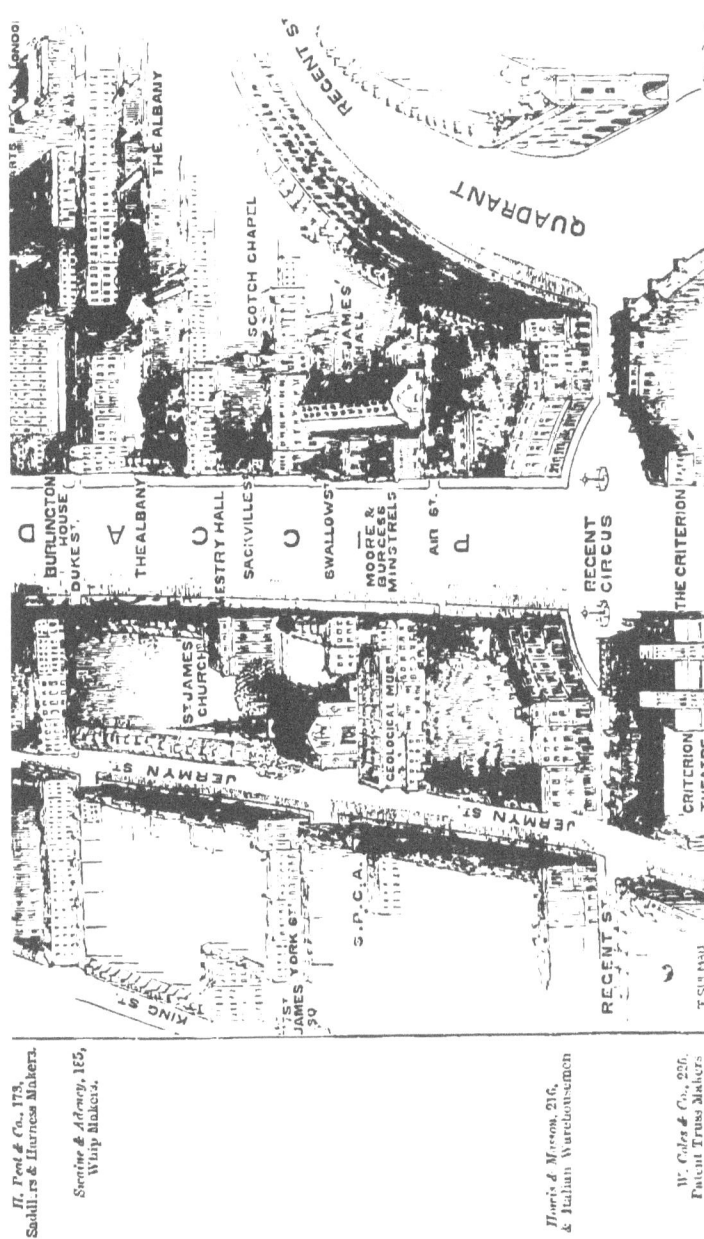

PICCADILLY,
FROM THE HAYMARKET TO HYDE PARK CORNER.

from the collar, or the latter from it, cannot now be known. Anyhow, the name became popular, and Piccadilly, which at first only extended to Sackville Street—whence ran Portugal Street to Albemarle Street—has long since George I.'s time become the name of the whole great thoroughfare. *Great Windmill Street*, not long since noted for the excellent Anatomical School, established by Dr. William Hunter, maintained until 1878 the less enviable reputation earned for the neighbourhood by Piccadilly Hall in years gone by. The Argyll Dancing Rooms are now converted into a restaurant.

In Tichborne Street are the *Pavilion Music Hall* and the *Café Monico*, and at No. 28 Haymarket is the Store of the Civil Service Co-operative Society. Proceeding through Piccadilly westwards, upon the south side of the way, is an extremely handsome and commanding edifice—the *Criterion Theatre* and *Restaurant*, built by Messrs. Spiers and Pond, and opened in 1873, at a cost of about £80,000. It stands on the site of a once-noted inn, the 'White Bear,' adjacent to which was a notorious nighthouse known as the *Piccadilly Saloon*. The Criterion Theatre, built entirely below the level of the roadway, is a beautiful structure, capable of holding about eight hundred persons. Nothing, approaching to the style and magnificence of this edifice had been, up to the year of its erection, seen in London, and it is even yet, after many endeavours to equal it, unsurpassed in the architectural beauty of its façade and entrance-halls.

Just beyond is *Regent Circus, Piccadilly*, where Regent Street intersects Piccadilly, and from which a beautiful view may be had upon a fine day of Westminster, in the distance beyond St. James's Park. We will, however, pursue our course up Piccadilly, observing as we pass through this Circus, so centrally and conveniently placed, that numerous Railway and Steamboat booking-offices are here to be found.

Swan and Edgar's large establishment presents one of its three fronts to the Circus, the others being in Regent Street and Piccadilly. Upon the south side of Piccadilly we note one or two fashionable shops of another character, such as Morel's, and Howis and Masson's, the Italian warehousemen, and a Branch Bank of the National Provincial Bank of England.

The *Government School of Mines and Museum of Practical Geology*, the entrance of which is in Jermyn Street, extends to Piccadilly. It was established in 1835, but the present edifice, constructed from the designs of Mr. Pennethorne, was not opened till 1851. In the School of Mines, pupils receive instruction in metallurgy, chemistry, natural history, applied mechanics, geology, mineralogy and mining, on payment of a fee of 30*l*. The Museum contains a valuable collection of the mineral products of the United Kingdom, with complete series of ores and fossils. Evening lectures are delivered in the Lecture Theatre (which holds four hundred and fifty persons) to working-men. Admission to the Museum is to be obtained gratis, from 10 A.M. to 10 P.M. on Mondays and Saturdays, and on Tuesdays, Wednesdays, and Thursdays, from 10 A.M. to 4 P.M., from November to February, and from 10 A.M. to 5 P.M. during the rest of the year, except during the autumn vacation, which extends from the 10th August to the 10th September.

AIR STREET, formerly Ayr Street, was, in 1659, the most westerly street in Piccadilly. Just at its south-west end is a passage continued to Jermyn Street, and next beyond, at No. 20, the establishment where Mr. J. L. Denman first introduced Greek wines. At No. 28 is the south, or Piccadilly entrance to St. James's Hall and the *St. James's Restaurant*—the latter, a highly-decorated edifice, rivalling even the magnificence of its neighbour, the Criterion. *St. James's Hall* was erected in 1857 from the designs of Mr. Owen Jones. The building contains one large room,

St. James's, Piccadilly.

139 feet long and 60 feet high, and two smaller ones. The former can contain a vast number of persons, and is used for great public meetings, popular concerts, &c.; Dickens gave his Readings in one of the smaller rooms; and here have flourished for many years the popular musical entertainers known first as Christy's and afterwards as the Moore and Burgess Minstrels.

SWALLOW STREET, now so unimportant, once extended through great part of the present line of Regent Street, northward to Oxford Street. In Swallow Street is the oldest *Scotch Episcopal Church* in London. *Vine Street Police Station* is near by, and at the corner of Swallow Street is the handsome and extensive book emporium of Messrs. Sotheran and Co.

St. James's Church, known as St. James's, Westminster, was built by Sir Christopher Wren for Henry Jermyn, Earl of St. Albans, after whose family Jermyn Street was named. Externally, the structure is of little architectural interest, but its interior is considered a masterpiece of skill, specially adapted for the use of large congregations and a Protestant Church Service. It is divided by Corinthian columns into a nave and aisles. " There are no walls of a second order, nor lanterns nor buttresses, but the whole rests upon the pillars, as do also the galleries, and I think," wrote Sir Christopher, " it may be found beautiful and convenient; it is the cheapest form of any I could invent." The organ was built for James II.'s Catholic Chapel in Whitehall, but was given by Queen Mary in 1691 to this church. The white marble font at the western end nearly five feet in height and six in circumference at the basin, was carved by Grinling Gibbons. The figures represent Adam and Eve, and the shaft, the Tree of Life, round which the Serpent is seen entwined while tempting Eve with the forbidden fruit. On the basin or bowl are bas-reliefs descriptive of the baptism of Christ; the baptism by St. Philip the deacon; and Noah's Ark, to which the dove is flying with the olive-branch. The cover of this font, also elegantly carved, was stolen a good many years ago, and served, it is said, for a time, as the sign of a neighbouring tavern. In this church are buried some noted persons, including Cotton the collaborateur of Isaak Walton, Dr. Sydenham, Hayman the painter, both Vanderveldes, Dr. Arbuthnot, Akenside the poet, Dodsley the publisher, and Tom d'Urfey the dramatist. There are portraits in the vestry of the many rectors of St. James's—several of whom became bishops and archbishops.

SACKVILLE STREET has the reputation, how acquired I know not, of being the longest street in London without a turning. It is noted for its fashionable tailors. At the corner are the well-known hatters, Lincoln, Bennett and Co. Next to *St. James's Vestry Hall*, on the south side of Piccadilly, is No. 177, the publishing house of Messrs. Pickering, who issued the once famous Aldine edition of the poets. Upon the opposite side of the way, between No. 46 and 47, is the *Albany*, planned and built as suites of chambers for the residence of single gentlemen, and named after the Duke of York and Albany, to whom it once belonged. The centre was designed by Sir W. Chambers. Many celebrated men have resided here, including Lord Byron, George Canning, Bulwer Lytton, and Lord Macaulay, who wrote, in these chambers, a large part of his 'History of England.' Nearly opposite the Albany are Messrs. Hatchard, the publishers, and next door, at the northern corner of *Duke Street*, is Messrs. Fortnum and Mason's, the great Italian warehousemen, known over the world for their excellent and varied stores of luxuries and delicacies.

A little farther west we shall see the handsome gateway to BURLINGTON HOUSE, erected upon the site of the once famous edifice which stood here but a few years since, and whose fine portico elicited the most extravagant encomiums of

Horace Walpole and other art-writers. It was, however, bought in 1854 from the Cavendish family; the famous gateway and colonnade (praised by Sir W. Chambers, who built Somerset House, as "one of the finest pieces of architecture in Europe") were pulled down, and, instead, have been since set up the present buildings by Banks and Barry. In the courtyard are to be seen, as you enter the new gateway from Piccadilly, on the right, the entrances to the rooms of the Royal Society, the Royal Geological Society, and the Chemical Society; on the left, those of the Royal Society of Antiquaries, the Royal Astronomical Society, and the Linnæan Society. Facing the visitor is the entrance to the Royal Academy of Arts, removed here in 1868 from some of the rooms now used by the National Gallery in Trafalgar Square.

The *Royal Society* was incorporated by Charles II. in 1663, and the Society's first meetings were held in the house in Crane Court, Fleet Street, recently burnt down, belonging to the Royal Scottish Corporation. They removed to Somerset House in 1780, and to Burlington House in 1857. The Royal Society, recognised throughout the world as the principal scientific authority extant, holds weekly meetings from November to June at 8·30 P.M., to which visitors are admitted on the order of a Fellow of the Society. There is here an interesting and valuable scientific library, and there are also to be seen some excellent busts, portraits, and autographs of the most prominent members of the Society, at present consisting of 510 Fellows, exclusive of foreigners. Fellows are elected in June each year from among the numerous candidates for the honour of F.R.S., and four medals are annually awarded—the Copley Medal being the highest distinction; the Davy Medal, for discoveries in chemistry; and two Royal Medals bestowed by the Queen. The Rumford Medals, for discoveries in light and heat, are awarded biennially. The 'Philosophical Transactions' of this Society are published regularly and are issued to the general public as freely as to its members.

The *Royal Geological Society*, numbering about 900 members, was established in 1807, and incorporated in 1826. Its fine museum and library are open every day from 11 A.M. to 5 P.M. to members and visitors introduced by them. Meetings for discussion and for the reading of papers are held upon alternate Wednesdays from November to June inclusive, commencing at 8·30 P.M. Members pay six guineas entrance fee and three guineas annual subscription. The Society's Journal is published quarterly.

The *Chemical Society* was founded in 1841, and incorporated in 1848, "for the promotion of chemistry and of those branches of science connected with it." The Society holds meetings fortnightly, from November to June inclusive, for the reading of papers and discussion, and publishes its transactions in its monthly periodical.

The *Royal Society of Antiquaries* was founded in 1572, but was not incorporated till 1751. It had rooms in Somerset House from 1776 until it removed here in 1871. Members are elected by ballot after being nominated by at least three Fellows of the Society, and these append F.S.A. to their names. The Society meets at 8 P.M. every Thursday, from November to June. Their transactions are recorded in the 'Archæologia,' which was commenced in 1770, and they possess an interesting library and museum. Entrance fee, five guineas; annual subscription, two guineas.

Royal Astronomical Society, founded in 1820 for the encouragement and promotion of Astronomy, consists of about 500 members, and publishes a series of memoirs and a monthly periodical. The initials F.R.A.S. indicate a Fellow of this Society.

Linnæan Society, founded in 1788 for the study of Natural History, has a good museum and library. It was named in honour of Linnæus, the great Swedish naturalist.

Its museum and library, very comprehensive and valuable, were removed hither from Soho Square in 1856. This Society publishes its 'Transactions' and a monthly periodical, circulated among its Fellows, who append F.L.S. to their names.

The *Royal Geographical Society*, founded in 1830 for the improvement of geographical knowledge, and having offices at the corner of Savile Row, holds its meetings in the theatre of the University of London, Burlington Gardens, every alternate Monday, from November to June inclusive, at 8·30 P.M. Members are elected by ballot, and pay an annual subscription of £2, and an entrance fee of £3. This Society has a good geographical library and a large collection of maps.

The ROYAL ACADEMY OF ARTS occupies a grand suite of rooms serving for the public exhibition of pictures and statuary, which opens annually on the first Monday in May and continues until the end of July. Admission from 8 A.M. till dusk 1s., catalogue 1s., except on the last week of July, when the rooms are open till 11 P.M. and the price of admission is 6d., and that of the catalogue 6d. Students are admitted to the Academy for seven years, after having satisfied the Council of their ability and respectability. Besides the exhibition galleries, there are in this building (which was designed by Sydney Smirke, R.A., and cost £120,000) a theatre for lectures, &c., schools of art for male and female students, and a fine library. There are forty-two R.A.'s, twenty A.R.A.'s, or Associate Royal Academicians, and two Associate Engravers.

The UNIVERSITY OF LONDON has established itself in a handsome edifice at the back of the Royal Academy of Arts, in *Burlington Gardens*, near Bond Street, with an entrance and grand façade in the Palladian style, which was built from designs by Pennethorne, 1869. The University of London was founded in 1837, not for the purposes of education, but merely for examining and con-

L

ferring degrees on graduates in Arts, Law, and Medicine. Examinations take place periodically by a Board of Examiners paid by the Government. The building contains a theatre for 700 persons, examination and council rooms, a library and offices. Externally it is decorated by a number of statues of famous men.

The sedent figures on the porch in Burlington Gardens, beginning from the east are—

Newton	Milton
Bentham	Harvey

The figures on the building, in the centre—

Galen	Plato
Cicero	Archimedes
Aristotle	Justinian

The three figures in the niches of the eastern wing—

Leibnitz	Linnæus
Cuvier	

The figures on the piers of the eastern wing—

Galileo (on the prominent angle-pier)	Goethe
	Laplace

The figures in the niches of the western wing—

Adam Smith	Bacon
Locke	

The figures on the piers of the western wing—

Hunter	Davy
Hume	(on the angle-pier).

BURLINGTON ARCADE was built (by S. Ware) in 1819 upon part of the grounds of old Burlington House.

The *Egyptian Hall*, next to 170 Piccadilly, was built in 1812, for a museum of Natural History, collected by Mr. Bullock in Central America, which was exhibited here until 1819, and was then dispersed by auction. The hall was built and decorated in the Egyptian style of architecture by G. F. Robinson; its entablature is supported by colossal figures of Isis and Osiris. Among the numerous exhibitions which have taken place at the Egyptian Hall may be mentioned the *Siamese Twins* (1829), Haydon's *Pictures of Xenophon*, &c. (1832), Siborne's *Model of the Battle of Waterloo* (1838 and 1846), with 190,000 figures now in the museum of the United Service Institution, Whitehall; *Tom Thumb*, the American Dwarf (1844), who in one room drew crowds to see him, and made over £100 a day, while in the adjoining apartment poor Haydon's grand pictures scarcely attracted as many shillings in a week. The result was the suicide of the painter. In 1852 Albert Smith gave his *Ascent of Mont Blanc* here for the first time. The *Dudley Gallery of Pictures* has worthily occupied for some years one of the chief exhibition rooms in this Hall; the other room being used for other popular entertainments. For Bond Street and St. James's Street, see pp. 132-7.

ALBEMARLE STREET was built, as well as Bond Street and Stafford Street, upon the site of *Clarendon House* (the residence of the great Chancellor Clarendon), which was sold to the young Duke of Albemarle after Clarendon's death. The entrance to Clarendon House was in Piccadilly, directly opposite the top of St. James's Street. In Albemarle Street is the *Royal Institution*, founded in 1799, to "diffuse the knowledge of useful mechanical inventions." It includes a Library, Reading Room, Lectures weekly during the season on Chemical Science, Philosophy, Physiology, Literature, Art, &c. Members are elected by ballot, after being proposed by four members, and pay an entrance fee of five guineas, and a subscription annually of five guineas. Subscriptions to the lectures are two guineas, either for the courses of the theatre lectures, or the laboratory lectures, or, for both, three guineas. Non-subscribers are admitted to the Friday evening lectures by tickets signed by members. In this laboratory, Davy and Faraday made their great experiments and discoveries, and here are delivered most admirable addresses on various important scientific questions by the first men of the day. In Albemarle Street is the publishing house of Mr. John Murray, also the *Royal Thames Yacht Club*, and the *Westminster Club*.

The *Royal Asiatic Society*, 22 Albemarle Street, was founded in 1823 for the advancement of the knowledge of Asiatic literature, &c. It has a valuable library and collection of MSS. The meetings of the Society are held on alternate Saturdays from November to June. Members pay an entrance fee of five guineas; annual subscription, two guineas.

ARLINGTON STREET was built upon the property of Henry Bennet, Earl of Arlington, from whom the name of Bennett Street is also derived. In Arlington Street have lived some notable persons, including Lady Mary Wortley Montague, and Sir Robert Walpole, on the site of No. 17 (where Horace Walpole was born). The houses on the west side have their best frontage towards the Green Park. The *Bath Hotel* at the corner of Arlington Street has an excellent reputation. The New *White Horse Cellar* in Piccadilly is nearly opposite Arlington Street, and worthily sustains the name made famous by the Old White Horse Cellar, before which, in the old mail coaching times, was to be seen, writes Hazlitt, "the finest sight in the metropolis, the setting off of the mail-coaches in Piccadilly." From the New White Horse Cellar, during the finer seasons of the year, may still be witnessed the departure and arrival of many handsomely provided four-horse mail-coaches, which convey passengers at moderate charges to numerous pleasant places within a few hours' journey of London, and which in several instances are driven by gentlemen who are themselves the proprietors of their team. The following are a few of the places to which these coaches run, generally starting about 10 or 11 A.M. :—

To Windsor, through Kew, Richmond, Twickenham, Hampton Court, &c. Fare, 5s.

To Guildford and back, 6s. or 10s., arriving at Guildford at 2 P.M., returning at 4 P.M. and reaching London at 7 P.M.

To Kingston-on-Thames on alternate days, in about an hour and a half from London, at 5.30 P.M., returning next morning by 10.15 A.M. Fare, 3s. 6d. On Saturdays from London at 3.30 P.M.

To St. Albans at 11 A.M., through Finchley, Barnet, &c., arriving at St. Albans at 1.30, returning at 4 P.M., and reaching Piccadilly at 6.30 P.M. Fares, 6s. or 10s.

The New White Horse Cellar is also a booking-office and a receiving house for coaches from Oxford to Cambridge through London, and for the principal railways of the metropolis; and is connected with *Hatchett's Hotel and Tavern*, at 67 & 68 Piccadilly.

DOVER STREET, named after Lord Dover, who was the owner of the property, was built in 1685. It is chiefly noted as having been the street in which John Evelyn lived "about nine doors up the east side," and died in 1705-6; where the Duke of Wharton lived and died, 1715; Robert, Earl of Oxford, and others of the nobility; many of whom have still residences in this street. There are two or three excellent private hotels here.

ST. JAMES'S HOTEL, at the corner of BERKELEY STREET, obtained a high reputation under Francatelli's management. This street and Berkeley Square were named from *Berkeley House*, which belonged to the Berkeley family, and was burnt down in 1733. Upon the site was built *Devonshire House*, by W. Kent, for the third Duke of Devonshire. To the present Devonshire House little interest attaches, except during the brief period when Georgiana, the beautiful Duchess of Devonshire (whose portrait was recently sold and stolen) held her court within its walls. In the ball-room of Devonshire House, however, took place the first amateur performance of Lord (then Sir E. Bulwer) Lytton's comedy, 'Not so Bad as we Seem,' for the benefit of the Guild of Literature, which Dickens and Bulwer did their best to promote, but which proved a great failure. There is here said to be the richest collection of old English plays, play-bills, &c., in the kingdom; it was bought from the executors of John Philip Kemble for £2000. There is also to be seen here the valuable collection called *The Devonshire Gems*. *Lansdowne House* is situated between Devonshire House and Berkeley Square. It belongs to the Marquis of Lansdowne.

THE GREEN PARK, sometimes named Upper St. James's Park, contains about sixty acres, bounded on the north by Piccadilly, south by the Mall and Buckingham Palace, west by Grosvenor Place, and east by the houses of Arlington Street and St. James's. Along the dead wall of Buckingham Palace Gardens is the carriage road called *Constitution Hill*, where Her Majesty has been three times shot at by mad, would-be assassins; at the upper part of this hill, Sir Robert Peel was thrown from his horse and killed, 1850, when on his way to the House of Commons, Westminster.

At the corner of STRATTON STREET, Piccadilly, was the house of Sir Francis Burdett; now of the Baroness Burdett Coutts.

At No. 82 Piccadilly is *Bath House*, built by Lord Ashburton, noted for the Ashburton collection of pictures of the Dutch Flemish schools, formed by Talleyrand.

At the corner of CLARGES STREET, named after Sir Walter Clarges, is the *Turf Club House* formerly Grafton House, the residence of the Duke of Grafton. This Club removed hither from Grafton Street in 1875. Edmund Kean lived for several years in Clarges Street.

HALF-MOON STREET was named after an old inn called the 'Half Moon' which stood on this site.

At 94 Piccadilly is *Cambridge House*, named after the Duke of Cambridge, youngest son of George III., who died here in 1850. Lord Palmerston lived in Cambridge House during the period of his premiership, and here Lady Palmerston, the sister and wife of a premier, for some years received and led the world of fashion. Cambridge House, soon after Lord Palmerston's death, was purchased by the *Naval and Military Club*, the present tenants, who have considerably enlarged and altered the premises.

WHITEHORSE STREET derived its name from an old inn called the 'White Horse.'

Hertford House (105), at the corner of ENGINE STREET, was built by the Marquis of Hertford, but never occupied by him. It has recently been sold by Sir Richard Wallace to a member of the Goldsmid family.

The *St. James's Club* (106) occupies *Coventry House*, the ancient town residence of the Earls of Coventry. This mansion was, previous to passing into the hands of its present owners, the Coventry House Club (Ambassadors).

The *Junior Athenæum Club* (116) occupies *Hope House* at the corner of DOWN STREET. This edifice was built by Mr. H. T. Hope, M.P., of Deepdene, 1849, and, during his residence in it, contained a valuable collection of pictures, chiefly of the Dutch and Flemish schools.

At the corner of PARK LANE, a thoroughfare which connects Piccadilly with the west end of Oxford Street, and skirts the east side of Hyde Park, is *Gloucester House*, the residence of the Duke of Cambridge, and previously known as *Elgin House*, whilst occupied by the Earl of Elgin; who brought hither in the first instance the celebrated Elgin Marbles, now in the British Museum.

At 138 & 139, then one house, between Park Lane and Hamilton Place, lived the notorious Duke of Queensbury, known as "Old Q." At 139, Lord Byron resided, and wrote the 'Siege of Corinth,' and 'Parisina;' and from this house Lady Byron fled, carrying away with her the poet's infant daughter.

Near this spot stood the old inn called the *Hercules Pillars*, a noted house for west-country visitors to London, and as such described in 'Tom Jones,' as the inn at which Squire Western stopped, and protected the fair Sophia.

At 148 Piccadilly, Baron Lionel de Rothschild's, there are a few fine paintings including specimens by Cuyp, De Hoog, Greuze, and Wilkie; the collection of plate, ancient china, &c., is exceptionally fine.

Apsley House, at Hyde Park Corner, the residence of the Duke of Wellington, derived its name from Baron Apsley, Lord High Chancellor, who built it towards the close of the last century. Here resided, from 1820 till 1852, the great Duke whom the Laureate called the " great world victor's victor," and who, though perhaps the most popular man of his time, was yet obliged, by the fury of the mob during the Reform Bill agitation, to turn his own dwelling-house into a sort of fortress, and to protect himself and his property from them by bullet-proof iron blinds. Apsley House has no particular merits from an architectural point of view. In the picture Gallery in the western wing the *Waterloo Banquet* was held annually until 1852, the year of the great Duke's death. Among the pictures—which, as well as the house, can be seen by special permission—are the master-piece of Correggio, 'Christ on the Mount of Olives,' captured by the Duke in Spain in the carriage of Joseph Bonaparte, and restored to Ferdinand VII., but bestowed by him upon the captor; also Wilkie's ' Chelsea Pensioners,' and Burnet's ' Greenwich Pensioners,' Landseer's ' Van Amburg in the Lion's Den,' also Allan's picture of the ' Battle of Waterloo.' The Duke's bedroom was a narrow, bare-looking, ill-lighted chamber on the eastern side of the house, with a bedstead so small that some one observed that there was no room to turn in it. " When I want to turn in bed," replied the old Duke, "I know it is time to turn out." The Colossal Statue of the Duke of Wellington, by Wyatt, placed upon the top of the triumphal arch opposite Apsley House, represents the Duke upon his horse, ' Copenhagen,' at the Field of Waterloo. It was set up on the 28th of September, 1846. " On fine afternoons," said a writer in

Belgravia.

the *Quarterly*, "the sun casts the shadow of the Duke's Equestrian Statue (opposite) full upon Apsley House; and the sombre image may be seen gliding spirit-like over the front." The turnpike toll-gates at Hyde Park Corner were removed in 1825.

St. George's Hospital, at the corner of Grosvenor Place, one of the best of the medical schools of the metropolis, was founded in 1733, and is particularly noted as the place in which the great physician, John Hunter, practised and died (1793). Further west is the highly fashionable *Alexandra Hotel*. Down *Grosvenor Place* is the direct road from this part of town to the Victoria Railway Station at Pimlico, and thence by the Vauxhall Bridge Road to the south-western districts of Kennington, Brixton, Stockwell, Clapham, &c. At the back of St. George's Hospital used to be the famous stables and horse auction yard of *Tattersall's*, or 'Tat's'— of which Tom Hood wrote, "His horse is a tit for Tat to sell to a very low bidder"—now removed to KNIGHTSBRIDGE, about a quarter of a mile off, in the direct road west of Piccadilly which skirts Hyde Park and is continued through Kensington. From Knightsbridge south is Sloane Street to CHELSEA, or south-westerly, the *Brompton Road* and the *Fulham Road*. *Prince's Cricket Ground* is at Hans Place, *Sloane Street*. The *Court Theatre* is opposite the *Sloane Square Railway Station*. Between Grosvenor Place and Chelsea is the aristocratic district called BELGRAVIA, named from Belgrave in Leicestershire, a village belonging to the Duke of Westminster, who owns all the land in this quarter. The *Cancer Hospital* and the *Brompton Hospital for Consumption*, two most valuable institutions, are in the Fulham Road.

In *Brompton Cemetery*, in the Fulham Road, lie: G. Herbert Rodwell, the composer; Robert Keeley and T. P. Cooke, actors; Albert Smith; Robert Landells, war artist of the *Illustrated London News* during all the campaigns from the Crimea to the taking of Paris, 1871; Sir Roderick

Murchison, the great geologist, and many more well-known persons.

HYDE PARK, named from the Hyde, an ancient manor of Knightsbridge, consists of 388 acres. Its chief Gates are those at *Hyde Park Corner*, Piccadilly (built by Decimus Burton, and decorated with bas-reliefs from the Elgin Marbles); *Cumberland Gate*, west end of Oxford Street, where stands the *Marble Arch*, removed from Buckingham Palace in 1851; *Prince's Gate*, between Knightsbridge and Kensington—near to the site of the Great Exhibition of 1851, and to the Queen's splendid memorial to the Prince Consort; and *Victoria Gate*, leading out towards Hyde Park Gardens. Its chief roads are a bridle road from Hyde Park Corner to Kensington Gardens called *Rotten Row*, and the carriage road by the north bank of the Serpentine called the *Lady's Mile*. The *Serpentine* (formed 1730-3), a misnomer, is an artificial sheet of water, whereon boats may be hired by the hour. The *Statue of Achilles*, at Hyde Park Corner, was a testimonial presented by the women of England to the Duke of Wellington and his brave companions in arms. It was cast by Westmacott from the cannon taken in the Peninsular War and at Waterloo, and erected in 1822.

KENSINGTON GARDENS are a highly fashionable resort during the London season, when the band plays. They are only accessible to promenaders on foot. The grounds now consist of 210 acres. The bridge connecting Kensington Gardens with Hyde Park was built by Rennie, 1826. The *Statue of Dr. Jenner* is by Marshall.

KENSINGTON PALACE was bought by William III. of the second Earl of Nottingham. Wren and Hawksmoor rebuilt portions of it, and Queen Anne subsequently had the banqueting-house erected. George I. made other additions. William and Mary, Queen Anne and her consort, and George II. all died here. In the lower south-eastern apartments, occupied by the Duke of Kent, Queen Victoria was born, 1819; here she was christened, and here held her first council. Here the Duke of Sussex collected his *Bibliotheca Sussexiana*, and eventually died.

Holland House, Kensington, the great resort of the Whig politicians during the life of the late Lord Holland, was built in 1607, about two miles west of Hyde Park Corner. It was in this house that Addison, who had married the widow of the Earl of Holland and Warwick, summoned his stepson, the Earl of Warwick, a youth of very irregular habits, to his deathbed. "I have sent for you," said Addison, "that you may see how a Christian can die." Of this old mansion, standing in its own grounds, in the midst and within view of the busy traffic of London, Sir Walter Scott wrote, "It will be a great pity when this ancient house must come down and give way to rows and crescents. It is not that Holland House is fine as a building—on the contrary, it has a tumble-down look; and although decorated with the bastard Gothic of James I.'s time, the front is heavy. But it resembles many respectable matrons, who, having been absolutely ugly during youth, acquire by age an air of dignity. But one is chiefly affected by the air of deep seclusion which is spread around the domain."

SOUTH KENSINGTON MUSEUM,

SITUATE at the corner of the Brompton Road and Exhibition Road, about a mile from Hyde Park Corner, is to be reached thence easily by omnibuses, or from other parts of town by the Metropolitan District Railway, which has a station at South Kensington. Admission, Monday, Tuesday, and Saturday, free, from 10 A.M. to 10 P.M. (the rooms being lighted at night), and Wednesday, Thursday, Friday, students' days, 6*d.* from 10 A.M. till 4 or 6 P.M., according to the season of the year. Tickets of admission to the museum, including the Art,

Library, and Educational Reading Room, are issued as follows: weekly 6d., monthly, 1s. 6d., quarterly, 3s., half-yearly, 6s., yearly, 18s., and to any school at £1 for all its pupils. This institution was begun in 1852 in rooms in Marlborough House, before the Prince of Wales took up his residence there; and it was established here by means of a surplus of £150,000 derived from the first Great Exhibition of 1851, to which various grants from Parliament, far in excess of that sum, have since been added. It will be admitted, we think, by all who visit this Museum, that the money spent upon it has been well bestowed, that the Institution has been well arranged, is liberally conducted, and admirably filled with collections of Art and Art Manufacture, mediæval and modern, of all kinds. The original edifice which contained the earliest collections, and which from its ungainly appearance obtained the name of the "Brompton Boilers," has for some time been removed to Bethnal Green, there to be known as the Bethnal Green Museum. The present permanent structure is a rather handsome building of red brick and terra-cotta, erected 1869-74, with spacious courts and galleries decorated in tasteful style. The Art collections are chiefly contained in three large courts and the corridors upon the ground floor. The *Architectural Court* is the first into which a visitor enters from the Cromwell Road entrance. This is the largest of the three principal courts, and is divided by a Central Gallery. Here are to be seen a large number of highly-interesting objects, and copies from original art-masterpieces, all of which are carefully labelled with briefly-stated particulars, which render reference to a catalogue almost unnecessary. A large diagram covers the north wall of this court, representing, to scale, the comparative dimensions of the Principal Churches, &c., of the world, executed by Professor Cockerell, R.A., in 1849. A copy of the *Bayeux Tapestry* is hung on the east wall. In the Central Passage are examples of Mosaics, ancient and modern, and a series of reproductions in electrotype, copies of which may be bought by visitors at prices stated upon the labels which are placed upon each. Descending the steps at the end of the central passage, we enter the *South Court*, embellished chiefly from the designs of the late Godfrey Sykes—the upper portion of the side walls divided into alcoves, eighteen on each side, to receive portraits in mosaic of eminent sculptors, painters, architects, and others specially noted as workers in bronze, marble, or pottery. The South Court is divided by a broad passage, and by the *Prince Consort's Gallery of Mosaics* already mentioned. Upon the west side of the South Court are the Loan Collections of Ecclesiastical Utensils—crosses, clocks, carvings, enamels, English and foreign plate, Russian and Albanian metal work, the gold crown and chalice of the Abima of Abyssinia. Here are Loan Collections of English, French, German and Oriental pottery and porcelain, including rare specimens of Bow, Bristol, and Plymouth; Collections of ancient Egyptian, Roman, Venetian, German, and other ancient and modern glass vessels. The east side of the South Court contains under the Arcade wall, cases in which are placed Oriental and other woven fabrics, Chinese and Japanese Bronzes, enamels, porcelain, lacquer-work, &c. The *Oriental Courts*, decorated by Mr. Owen Jones, are to be found east of the South Court, and in them will be seen specimens of the art-workmanship of the East Indies, China, Japan, Persia, &c.; as well as the royal treasures from Abyssinia. At the south end of the Arcade is arranged a complete Parisian boudoir, *temp*. Louis XVI. In the *South Arcade* are electrotype reproductions of the famous chair of Dagobert in the Louvre, salvers, &c. A large collection of examples of Metal-Work occupies the central passages. There is a handsome French Clock near the doorway to the Architectural Court, in the form of a large gilt globe supported by a bronze group of three boys.

The *North Court* is used for the exhibition of sculpture and large casts of different objects—chief among which are the marble Singing Gallery, from Florence, the Biga, or two-horse chariot from the museum of the Vatican, and two Pulpits from the cathedral at Pisa.

The *East Arcade* exhibits a number of finely-sculptured chimney-pieces, as also numerous textile and woven fabrics in the form of ecclesiastical vestments, and fragments of embroidery; also a set of costumed figures representing Icelanders and Laplanders.

The *North Arcade* contains a collection of sculptures in terra-cotta, both plain and enamelled. Of the latter, known as the Della Robbia Ware, there are here some excellent examples.

The *Reading Room* of the Art Library is in the West Arcade of the North Court. The *Library* consists at present of 42,000 volumes on all subjects connected with art, 15,000 drawings, 50,000 engravings, chiefly of ornamental art, and 40,000 photographs illustrative of architecture, &c. The Library is open during the same hours as the Museum. There is an interesting collection of Musical Instruments in the West Arcade, from which is a doorway leading into the Refreshment Room Corridor.

The *Refreshment Rooms*, Lavatories, and Waiting-Rooms, are comfortably and artistically planned, and the central Refreshment-Room has been handsomely decorated from the designs of artists connected with the department. There is also a grill-room or Dutch kitchen, and a dining-room. The viands are good, and are nicely served at most reasonable rates. From this point we will proceed to the left and enter the *West Corridor* containing a collection of Ancient Furniture and Tapestry; at the end of this corridor is the *Educational Reading-room*, open on students' days to all visitors; on free days to clergymen, school-teachers, or holders of tickets. In the *West School Corridor* are some examples of Modern Furniture, State carriages, and Sedan chairs, wood carvings, and casts of architectural details. From this Corridor is an exit leading to the Exhibition Galleries in Exhibition Road. The *North School Corridor*, at right angles with the other corridors, forms the Persian Court, wherein is arranged the collection of Persian earthenware, metal work, carpets, &c. At the end of this Corridor is a staircase leading to the PICTURE GALLERIES, and in the Hall at the foot of the staircase is a collection of Anglo-Saxon and other antiquities discovered near Faversham, in Kent, and including glass and bronze vessels, weapons, ornaments, and pottery. The staircase leading to the Picture Galleries is lighted by a large stained glass window, of which the design is descriptive of various kinds of handicraft.

The *Keramic or Pottery Gallery* is to be entered after passing through two rooms at the bend of the staircase, and then turning to the right. Here is the Museum Collection of earthenware, stoneware, porcelain, and Wedgewood ware; also examples of Bow, Chelsea, Bristol, Plymouth, Worcester, and Derby porcelain. Here are to be seen also modern reproductions and imitations of Majolica, Palissy, and other wares; numerous samples of Minton's art-manufactures, and choice specimens of continental work, including Sevres, Dresden, &c. After retracing his steps through the Keramic Gallery, the visitor will reach the *Picture Galleries* and will enter the rooms containing the Loan Collection of Pictures, and the water-colour paintings bequeathed to the museum by Mr. William Smith; thence he will enter the *Prince Consort Gallery*, which exhibits, in a double row of cases, many of the most costly possessions of the Museum; specimens of ancient enamelling, damascened work. At the west end of the Gallery are some fine specimens of carvings in ivory. At the south end of the Gallery is a Collection of ornamental ironwork, Italian, French, German, and English, window-grilles, balconies, cressets, or lamps, signs, &c.; also a set of drawings of Roman wall and floor mosaics. In five rooms at the south end of the western galleries, are placed the libraries, paintings, &c., bequeathed to the museum by the late Rev. W. Dyce, and Mr. John Forster.

The *Dyce Collection* consists of oil paintings, minerals, drawings, engravings, a few MSS., and a most valuable library of printed books, numbering over 11,000 volumes. The *Forster Collection* comprises oil and water-colour paintings, drawings, MSS., autographs, and 18,000 volumes. Amongst the MSS. are many of the original MSS. of Charles Dickens, and among the books is Grainger's biographical 'History of England,' illustrated with more than 5,000 portraits. *Oliver Goldsmith's Chair*, Desk, and Walking-Cane, bequeathed by Goldsmith to his friend Dr. Hawes, are exhibited in this gallery. A special reading-room for the Dyce and Forster collection has been recently opened for the accommodation of visitors.

The *Picture Gallery* above the arcade of the north and south courts may be reached by either of the three staircases. In the North Gallery are now placed the *Raphael Cartoons*, which have been recently removed hither from Hampton Court. These celebrated works of art, drawn with chalk upon strong paper, and coloured in distemper, were executed by Raphael and his scholars in 1513 as designs for tapestry work for Pope Leo X. The tapestries are still at the Vatican, but three of the original cartoons are now lost. Rubens having seen these cartoons in the warehouse of a manufacturer at Arras, advised Charles I. to purchase them, and he did so, for the use of a tapestry manufactory then being established at Mortlake. Cromwell, after Charles's death, bought them for 300*l*., and they were kept at Whitehall, till, by order of William III., Sir Christopher Wren built a room for them at Hampton Court, where they have remained until lately Her Majesty gave permission for their removal. The subjects are as follows:—

1. Christ's charge to Peter.
2. Death of Ananias.
3. Peter and John healing the Lame Man.
4. Paul and Barnabas at Lystra.
5. Elymas, the Sorcerer, struck blind.
6. Paul preaching at Athens.
7. The Miraculous Draught of Fishes.

The missing Cartoons are,

The Stoning of Stephen.
The Conversion of St. Paul.
St. Paul in his Dungeon at Philippi.

There is here a copy in black chalk by Casanova of the Transfiguration by Raphael, also now at the Vatican; also several other copies of examples by the same great master. At the east end of the Raphael Gallery, upon turning to the right, the visitors will find the gallery contain 247 pictures known as the *Sheepshanks' Collection*, besides pictures presented by other donors whose names, as well as the titles of the pictures, are very properly inscribed upon each frame. Here, also, is a collection of many hundreds of Mulready's drawings, and sketches placed in frames about the middle of the rooms; also cases containing enamels, miniatures, &c., by Essex, Bone, &c. The Sheepshanks' Collection comprises works by the following masters, the figures attached to their names indicate the numbers in the catalogue:—

Bird, 246.
Brooks, 241.
Burnet, J., 6.
Callcott, 8–15.
Carpenter, M., 17, 18.
Chalon, 234, 235.
Clint, 21.
Collins, 25, 27–32.
Constable, 33–38.

Cooke, 39–41, 43, 45, 47.
Cooper, 50.
Cope, 52, 55–60.
Creswick, 61, 62.
Crome, 64.
Danby, 65–7.
Duncan, 69.
Eastlake, 70, 71,
Etty, 72, 73.

Frith, 74.
Gauermann, 78.
Gilpin, 238.
Horsley, 81–83.
Howard, 242, 245.
Ibbetson, 247.
Jackson, 84, 85.
Lance, 86.
Landseer, Sir E., 87–102.
Landseer, C., 103–5.
Lee, F. R., 107, 108.
Leslie, C. R., 109–119, 121–128, 131, 132.
Linnell, 133, 134.
Morland, 237.
Mulready, 135–49, 151–9, 162, 163
Mulready, jun., 163, 164.

Nasmyth, 165.
Newton, 166.
Redgrave, 167, 170–172.
Rippingille, 173.
Roberts, 174–176.
Rothwell, 178, 179.
Simson, 180.
Smith, G., 186, 187.
Stanfield, 188–190.
Stark, 195, 196.
Stothard, 197, 201–203.
Turner, 207–211.
Uwins, 212, 213.
Ward, J., 216–218.
Webster, 219–224.
Wilkie, 225, 226.
Wetherington, 233.

The *Gallery of Water-colour Paintings* is also made up of a series of noble gifts to the nation, and forms a unique collection by means of which the history of water-colour painting in this country may be fairly traced. The specimens are hung in chronological sequence, but Mr. William Smith's collection is, very properly, separately placed. There are, in this gallery, cases containing Collections of Ancient and Modern Jewelry ; at the north end of the Long Room is a fine Collection of rare and Precious Stones.

In the *Exhibition Galleries*, which are reached by a doorway leading from the Museum to the Exhibition Road, are temporarily deposited various collections for which space cannot be found in the museum.

The NATIONAL PORTRAIT GALLERY, removed from Great George Street, Westminster, consists of a large and most interesting collection of portraits and busts of famous Englishmen and women. There is no catalogue, but the names are all given upon the picture-frames.

The *Educational Museum* contains models of school buildings, fittings, apparatus, &c., used in elementary instruction, and scientific apparatus, models of machinery, &c., used in technical education. There are also the *Munitions of War Collection* lent by the War Department, a *Collection of Building Materials*, and a *Fish-Hatching Apparatus*.

The *Loan Collection of Pictures* in the western picture galleries being frequently changed, need not be specially described here.

The NATIONAL ART TRAINING SCHOOLS, at South Kensington Museum, are maintained by the State as the centre of a national system for the promotion of Art and Science Schools, which are established in all parts of the kingdom, and of which public examinations are regularly made preliminary to awards of prizes to the most successful pupils. The institution of these Schools took place in 1852, and they are controlled and regulated by the Lord President and Committee of Council on Education. Art-pupils of both sexes are here trained to become teachers, and they receive grants in aid of their maintenance, in proportion to their attainments, as tested from time to time by the official examiners.

In the buildings which surround the Gardens of the Horticultural Society, and which were built for the International Exhibitions of 1871-4, is a gallery containing the *National School of Cookery*, entered from the Exhibition Road, for teaching practically the best methods of preparing food economically.

The NATURAL HISTORY MUSEUM, a very handsome edifice almost completed, fronting Cromwell Road, is intended for the reception of the Zoological Collection now at the British Museum. The latter institution will thus obtain more room for the Exhibition of the Antiquities, which are far too numerous for the rooms at present allotted to them at the British Museum.

The *Gardens of the Royal Horticultural Society* adjoin the grounds of the South Kensington Museum, and have been laid out with great care and expense. There is a fine hall for meetings of the Society, Exhibitions, &c., and a large glass Winter Garden with conservatories, also a Colonnade and Cloister surrounding the whole, built 1861. The gardens occupy twenty-two acres; they are open daily from nine till dusk, Sundays from two. Each Fellow has the privilege of introducing personally two friends, except on exhibition days.

The ROYAL ALBERT HALL, erected 1868-71, is an immense structure, circular in form, and covered by a glass dome. It will hold 10,000 persons, of which the area will take 1,000. It was built by a company at a cost of 200,000*l.* and is used for concerts, balls, and exhibitions.

The ALBERT MEMORIAL, erected near the site of the Great Exhibition of 1851, and near the Royal Horticultural Gardens and the Albert Hall, is one of the most magnificent monuments in the world. It was designed by Sir Gilbert Scott, and consists of a Gothic cross and canopy, with a spire reaching to the height of 175 feet; under the canopy is a colossal gilt sedent statue of the Prince, fifteen feet high, by Foley. It is approached by four flights of steps 130 feet wide. At each angle is a group of statues—Europe, by Macdowell; Asia, by Foley; Africa, by Theed; America, by J. Bell; above which are other groups upon a smaller scale: Agriculture, by Calder Marshall; Manufactures, by Weekes; Commerce, by Thorneycroft; Engineering, by Lawlor. Round the base of the Memorial is a series of 200 life-sized figures and portraits of the great men of all ages, sculptured by J. P. Philip and H. Armistead. The cost of the whole was £150,000., including a large sum from Her Majesty, and £50,000 from Parliament.

Mr G. H. JONES

SURGEON-DENTIST,
57, Great Russell Street, London

(*Immediately Opposite the British Museum*),

WILL BE GLAD TO FORWARD HIS

NEW PAMPHLET GRATIS & POST FREE.

It explains the only perfectly painless system of adapting Artificial Teeth which have obtained the Prize Medals of London, Paris, Berlin, Vienna, Philadelphia, and New York. These Teeth are adjusted on Celluloid, Thionite, Gold, Platina, &c., by Mr. G. H. Jones, on his perfected system, which is protected by

HER MAJESTY'S ROYAL LETTERS PATENT.

The "DAILY TELEGRAPH," Aug. 23, 1878, says,—"Celluloid is the most life-like imitation of the natural gums, and, with Prize Medal Teeth, is incomparable."

Nitrous Oxide, Ether Spray, and all the most recent improvements in Dental Surgery are in daily use. Consultation Free.

TESTIMONIAL.

January 27th, 1877.

MY DEAR SIR,—Allow me to express my sincere thanks for the skill and attention displayed in the construction of my Artificial Teeth, which render my mastication and articulation excellent. I am glad to hear that you have obtained Her Majesty's Royal Letters Patent to protect what I consider the perfection of Painless Dentistry. In recognition of your valuable services, you are at liberty to use my name.

S. G. HUTCHINS,

G. H. JONES, Esq.   *By Appointment Surgeon Dentist to the Queen.*

THE GUINEA CABINET
OF
DENTAL PREPARATIONS,

For Cleansing and Preserving the Teeth and Gums,

In Cut Glass Stoppered Bottles and handsome Gilt Mounted Leather Toilet Case, with Lock and Key.

Forwarded direct on receipt of Post Office Order, or may be ordered through any Chemist or Perfumer.

Wholesale, **BARCLAY & SONS**, Farringdon Street, London.

PLATE 19.

OXFORD STREET.
431 & 433, S. Webb & Co.,
Upholsterers.

422A, H. Heure,
Brush & Turnery Manufacto

393, Henry Heath,
Hat Manufacturer.

357-359, W. P. & G. Phillips
China & Earthenware Manu

357, J. J. Powers,
Antique China & Decorative A

315, Smith & Brodie,
Partnership & Finance Agen

GT. RUSSELL STREET.
Mr. G. H. Jones, 57,
Surgeon Dentist.

OXFORD STREET.
W. H. Bailey & Son, 16,
Trusses & Surgical Appliances.

RATHBONE PLACE.
Delain & Co., 41,
Pianoforte Makers, &c.

OXFORD STREET.
W. T. Cooper, 26,
Patentee of Effervescing Lozenges.

Hyam & Co. (Limited), 65 & 67,
Tailors & Outfitters.

Lipscombe & Co., 69,
Filter Manufacturers.

Thomas Aldred, 126,
Archery Manufacturer

Sampson & Co., 130-139,
Hosiers & Shirt Makers.

OXFORD STREET,
FROM THE MARBLE ARCH TO TOTTENHAM COURT ROAD.

263. *National Co-operative Supply Association (Limited),*
J. Dillon Garland, Secretary.

259. *S. Blackwell,*
Patent Saddlery, Harness,

PARK STREET.
118. *Mrs. Godfrey,*
Servants' Registry.

MARBLE ARCH.

Alfred Young, 174 B,
Fishing Tackle & Umbrellas.

C. G. Usher, 185,
Brush & Comb Maker. Sponges.

Samaritan Free Hospital for Women & Children,
13, Lower Seymour Street.

EDGWARE ROAD.

BLACKWELL
Patent Saddlery & Harness Manufacturer,
To Her Majesty and the Prince of Wales,
259, OXFORD STREET,
Near the Marble Arch, London, W.

Colts and Young Untractable Horses Broken by Kind and Gentle Treatment, Temperate and Easy Mouthed, by using Blackwell's Patent Whalebone and Gutta-percha Jockeys, Rubber Spring Reins, 70s.; Hire, 2s. per week, with option of Purchase.

Breaking Tackle of all kinds; Cavessons, Lunge Reins, Improved Straight Mouth Slide Cheek Breaking Bits, with Players, from 1 to 4 lbs.

Rubber Springs for Straps, Rollers, &c., 2s.

Metal Springs to Chains, Whips, Reins, &c.

VARIOUS SPECIAL APPLIANCES FOR HORSES.

Rubber Patent Springs to Driving and Riding Reins, very safe for Ladies, 12s a pair. Springs to Gag and Bearing Reins, &c.

Crib Strap, 21s., and various **Muzzles** to prevent Crib Biting, Wind Sucking Bits, &c.

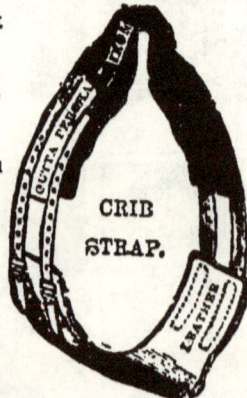

Web Fetlock, Speedy Leg, Knee, Hock, and Ring Boots to buckle on, **Sandal Hunting Shoes,** &c.

Patent Apparatus of **Perforated Tubes** for Legs of Horses, producing jets of cold water (or hot for fomentations), 15s.

TO BE HAD OF ALL SADDLERS.

OXFORD STREET, FROM THE MARBLE ARCH TO TOTTENHAM COURT ROAD.

IF we take our stand at the Oxford Street end of the Edgware Road, facing down Oxford Street, we shall have at our back Bayswater and Kensington Gardens, and on our right Hyde Park, with just the turn of the 'Ring' or Drive visible beyond the Park palings. Beyond the eastern limits of the Park is *Park Lane*, now the most aristocratic of addresses, formerly known as *Tyburn Lane*. It led immediately to the *Tyburn Gallows*, which stood, as nearly as can be ascertained, upon the site of 49 Connaught Place, Edgware Road. Here were executed the numerous malefactors, convicted in the County of Middlesex (of whom history, down to 1783, when Newgate gallows supplanted that of Tyburn, has much to say), upon that *Tyburn Tree*, of which perhaps the best representation is the last plate of Hogarth's 'Idle and Industrious Apprentices.' Here were hung the bodies of Oliver Cromwell, Ireton, and Bradshaw (torn from their graves in Henry VII.'s Chapel in Westminster Abbey, and still wearing their swords), from sunrise to sunset on the first anniversary of the death of Charles I. after the Restoration. The bodies were then taken down and beheaded, the heads stuck upon poles at the top of Westminster Hall, and the corpses buried beneath the gallows-tree. The list of all who were executed at Tyburn is too long to be given here; it will suffice to say that it includes the names of Perkin Warbeck (1449); the Holy Maid of Kent; Robert Southwell, the poet, for high treason; Mrs. Turner, in a yellow ruff, for the murder of Sir Thomas Overbury; John Felton, for the assassination of the Duke of Buckingham; Jack Sheppard

(1724); Jonathan Wild (1725); Catharine Hayes, for the murder of her husband—she was burnt alive by the mob, who would not in their indignation wait for the hangman; Earl Ferrers (1760), for the murder of his steward: he was drawn in his own coach-and-six from the Tower, wearing his wedding clothes, hanged by a silken rope, and the 'drop' was first used for his lordship instead of a cart; Mrs. Brownrigg (1767), for the murder of her two female apprentices; John Rann, the highwayman (otherwise Sixteen-string Jack, from the number of ribbons he was decorated with), (1774); Rev. Dr. Dodd, for forgery (1777).

The Marble Arch, at the corner of Hyde Park, facing Cumberland Street, was built by Nash, of Carrara marble —soon discoloured in our climate—and was set up originally before Buckingham Palace, and called *Buckingham Palace Arch*. The sculptures are by Flaxman, Westmacott, and Rossi, the gates by S. Parker. The arch cost £80,000, and its removal hither in 1851 cost £11,000 more. From the Marble Arch down Park Lane, towards Piccadilly, we may note *Holderness House* (the Marquis of Londonderry), *Dorchester House* (R. S. Holford, Esq.), *Dudley House* (Earl of Dudley), and *Gloucester House* (H.R.H. the Duke of Cambridge) at the extreme south end, see p. 151.

The *Edgware Road* runs past the end of *Marylebone Road* on the right or east side, and the end of *Harrow Road* on the left farther on; near to the latter is Paddington Green and the *Paddington Terminus* of the Great Western Railway. The Edgware Road (the *Marylebone Theatre* is in New Church Street, Edgware Road) is continued to the north of Paddington and eventually merges into *Maida Vale*, the great thoroughfare of a rapidly increasing London suburb, and proceeds to *Kilburn*. By St. John's Wood Road from the Edgware Road is the nearest way from this point to *Lord's Cricket Ground*, where the great *Cricket Matches* of the season take place. From a more easterly point Lord's is best reached by way of *Baker Street* and thence by Park Road, Regent's Park. *Swiss Cottage* is at St. John's Wood.

The road which is a continuation west of Oxford Street is the Uxbridge Road, skirting Hyde Park and Kensington Gardens on one side and *Bayswater* on the other, and leading to *Notting Hill* and *Shepherd's Bush*, all continually increasing London suburbs. *Bayswater* is a large district of fine handsome houses, long noted for its springs and conduits, by which it supplied streets as far as Bond Street with water. At Bayswater is the parish *Burial-ground of St. George's, Hanover Square*, founded in 1764, and in it were buried, near the west wall, Lawrence Sterne, the immortal author of 'Tristram Shandy'; and Sir Thomas Picton, one of the heroes of Waterloo, whose body was subsequently removed to St. Paul's Cathedral. *Notting Hill* is supposed to be a corruption of *Nutting Hill*. From Bayswater, up *Ladbroke Grove Road*, is one of the most convenient ways to the *Kensal Green Cemetery*—another being by the Harrow Road and Edgware Road omnibuses. This burial-ground is one of the most important of modern London. It extends over eighteen acres, and contains the remains of many of the worthies of modern art, science, and literature—as the Rev. Sydney Smith; Tom Hood, to whom there is a loving memorial, with the simple epitaph, "He sang the 'Song of the Shirt'"; Balfe, the musical composer; and Eastlake, the painter and P.R.A.; Liston, the actor; and Brunel, the engineer; Molesworth, the statesman and historian; and Birkbeck, the founder of Mechanics' Institutions; Allan Cunningham, and W. C. Macready; Barnes, of the *Times*; Shirley Brooks, of *Punch*; and many more—not forgetting those Royal personages, the Duke of Sussex and his sister, the Princess Sophia; or the inventor of Morrison's Pills; or Ducrow, the great equestrian; or George Robins, the flowery auctioneer; or Dr. John Long, the quack doctor; to the merits of all of whom the largest monuments of Kensal

Green do bear testimony. A visit to Kensal Green is well worth the stranger's making.

As we proceed from the Marble Arch down Oxford Street we shall observe on the left *Great Cumberland Street*, named after the Duke of Cumberland, hero of Culloden; *Quebec Street*, named in honour of the taking of Quebec by General Wolfe; *Portman Street*, leading into *Portman Square* west side, and *Park Street* opposite to Portman Street. Proceeding farther, we come on the left upon *Orchard Street*—the direct way from Oxford Street, along the east side of *Portman Square*, through *Baker Street* and York Place to the *Marylebone Road*, at which point there is a Station of the Underground line of Railway. In Portman Square, so named after a Mr. Portman, owner of the estate, is *Montague House*, at the north-west angle, built for Mrs. Elizabeth Montague, of literary celebrity.

In *Baker Street* is the well-known emporium called the *Panklibanon*, next to the still more celebrated *Wax-work Exhibition of Madame Tussaud*, open daily, admission 1s., Chamber of Horrors 6d. extra. This Exhibition (commenced in Paris in 1780, and removed to London, at the Lyceum, in the Strand, in 1802) now consists of a very large number of wax figures, dressed in various costumes, many of which are the dresses actually worn by the persons represented. Madame Tussaud taught drawing and modelling to many of the French *noblesse* before the Great Revolution of 1789, and during the Reign of Terror she was enabled, it is said, to model the faces of numerous Revolutionary leaders from the heads which had been severed upon the scaffold. She made an interesting Collection of Relics of the First Napoleon, which forms part of her Exhibition. The Model of the Guillotine is preserved here, with its lunette and decapitating knife. The heroes and the desperadoes of history, the follies, the vices, and the virtues of mankind, are all represented; the grandeur of the throne-room at a coronation; the groups at royal weddings and christenings are ably counterfeited; and the visages of the most atrocious of mankind have been also preserved in wax; in many instances the veritable costumes of both kings and culprits deck out their effigies. Madame Tussaud died in 1850, at the age of ninety; but her Exhibition has maintained its reputation, and continues deservedly to attract the sight-seers of London.

Duke Street leads from Oxford Street to *Grosvenor Square*, for a long time a place of the highest fashion. At Lord Harrowby's, 39 Grosvenor Square, Thistlewood and others of the *Cato Street Conspiracy* (Cato Street was in John Street, Edgware Road) purposed assassinating the whole Ministry, February 23rd, 1820, as they sat together at dinner. The plot was discovered to the Ministry by a man named Edwards, who had joined the conspirators purposely. The dinner preparations at Lord Harrowby's were allowed to proceed, but the Ministers stopped away. The Bow Street officers entered the stable in Cato Street and found the Thistlewood party arming themselves. The officers attempted to seize Thistlewood, but he ran the first of them (Smithers) through the body, then extinguished the lights within and escaped in the darkness. Nine of the conspirators were at once captured; a reward of £1000 was offered for the capture of Thistlewood, and he also was caught early next day in bed at the house of a friend in Little Moorfields. Thistlewood had been an officer in a regiment of the line stationed in the West Indies, and for some reason entertained the deepest personal animosity against Lords Sidmouth and Castlereagh. He and his four chief accomplices, Ings, Brunt, Tidd, and Davison, were hanged at the Old Bailey, May 1st, 1820. The name of *Cato Street* was then changed to *Homer Street*.

The thoroughfare called *Duke Street* is continued across Oxford Street into *Manchester Square*, begun in 1776. At *Hertford House*, Manchester Square, the residence of Sir

Richard Wallace, is the finest private collection of pictures in London; it was formed by the late Marquis of Hertford. From this Square runs *Manchester Street*, wherein resided the notorious Joanna Southcote. She died there in 1814, after having persuaded many hundreds of credulous persons that she was about to give birth to the true 'Shiloh.' *James Street* leads into *Wigmore Street*, *Davies Street* leads directly to *Berkeley Square*. *Stratford Place* was named after Edward Stratford, Earl of Aldborough, who built Aldborough House, at its north end, upon the site of *Old Conduit Mead*. *Marylebone Lane* is a narrow thoroughfare, which reminds us, however, of the immense parish and populous Parliamentary borough called *Marylebone*. The *Old Church of St. Mary-le-bone*, at the end of the High Street, was built in 1741, on the site of an older edifice—noteworthy as the church in which Hogarth depicted the Marriage of the Rake in his '*Rake's Progress*,' and as the burial-place of many remarkable persons, including the Rev. Samuel Wesley, brother of John Wesley; Allan Ramsay, author of the 'Gentle Shepherd,' &c. The *New Church of St. Mary-le-bone*, opposite York Gate, Regent's Park, built by Hardwick, consecrated 1817, has a handsome altar-piece, presented to it by the painter Benjamin West, P.R.A. The name of *Mary-le-bone* signifies St. Mary by or on the bourn, the Tybourn stream, hard by.

In *Vere Street* is *St. Peter's Chapel*, built from designs by Gibbs, with a Doric portico and a three-storied steeple, in 1724, and then considered a very handsome edifice. Opposite the end of Vere Street is *New Bond Street*, see p. 136. *Holles Street* (Lord Byron was born at No. 24) leads into *Cavendish Square;* it was named after Lady Henrietta Cavendish Holles, wife of Harley, Earl of Oxford, who planned it. There is an Equestrian Statue of the Duke of Cumberland, as well as a Statue of Lord George Bentinck, in Cavendish Square.

Immediately opposite Holles Street is *Harewood Place*,

leading to *Hanover Square*, built (1718) in honour of George I. *Harewood House* is at the south-east corner of Harewood Place. In *Tenterden Street*, Hanover Square, is the entrance to the *Oriental Club-house*, which occupies the north-west angle of the square, and which was established in 1824 for noblemen and gentlemen associated with the administration of our Eastern Empire. In Tenterden Street are also the *Arts Club-house*, for artists, literati, and connoisseurs, and the *Royal Academy of Music*, founded in 1822 by the Earl of Westmoreland, for teaching all kinds of music to advanced pupils, who are charged £10 per term, or £30 per annum, with an entrance fee of £5. The Hanover Square Concert Rooms, at the south-east corner of Hanover Square, have been abolished, and upon the site has been erected the *Hanover Square Club-house*. In George Street is the fashionable church for marriages, in which the great Duke of Wellington gave away so many brides—*St. George's, Hanover Square*, built by James, and consecrated 1724. It has three fine ancient windows, brought over from Mechlin and dating from the early part of the 16th century. Hanover Square is embellished with a *Statue of William Pitt*, by Chantrey. The view of this square from George Street has been considered to comprise one of the best bits of architectural effect in London.

REGENT CIRCUS, OXFORD STREET—to distinguish it from Regent Circus, Piccadilly—here intersects Oxford Street. Eastwards is *Argyll Street* on the right, wherein is *Hengler's Circus and Amphitheatre;* on the left or north side of Oxford Street is *Great Portland Street*, a direct thoroughfare to the *Euston Road* and the *Portland Street Railway Station* of the Underground Railway. *Oxford Market*, built for the Earl of Oxford, dates from 1731. On the south side of Oxford Street was the *Pantheon*, a fashionable resort, once known as the Winter Ranelagh, now converted into the central depot for Messrs. Gilbey's wine business.

At 73 Oxford Street is the *Princess's Theatre*, built originally as a Bazaar, the Queen's Bazaar, opened as a Theatre in 1841. This house obtained its highest popularity under the management of Mr. Charles Kean, who here produced his magnificently-mounted dramas, and illustrated with scenery and properties, in a manner never previously realised, the great plays of Shakespeare and others.

Middlesex Hospital, facing *Berners Street*, was founded 1745, and incorporated 1836. It contains 305 beds, and receives annually about 25,000 out-door patients and 2,500 in-patients. Its income is nearly £16,000 per annum.

Newman Street is noted for its numerous shops for articles required by artists. At 414 Oxford Street is a tavern called *The Mischief*, originally *The Man Loaded with Mischief*, which had a signboard said to have been painted by Hogarth, representing a man carrying a woman holding a glass in her hand, and attended by a monkey and a magpie. Underneath were the lines—

"A monkey, a magpie, and a wife,
Is (*sic*) the true emblem of strife."

In *Dean Street* is a small Theatre which has had its seasons of success and difficulty, and has occasionally changed its name. It was built in 1840, as a school for acting, by Mrs. F. Kelly. Its present name is the *Royalty Theatre*. In *St. Anne's Church*, Dean Street, was buried King Theodore of Corsica, who died a pauper in this parish 1686, and was interred at the cost of John Wright, an oilman in Compton Street, who declared that he for once would pay the expenses of a king's funeral. Horace Walpole's epitaph and tablet were set up in the church to the king's memory:—

"Fate poured its lesson on his living head,
Bestowed a kingdom and denied him bread."

Soho Square, built in the time of Charles II., was known as King Square, while the fortunes of the Duke of Monmouth flourished. On the southern side then stood the

Monmouth House (upon the site of the present *Hospital for Women*), every trace of which has long since disappeared. In the centre was a statue of King Charles II. The fields about this part were called *Soho Fields*, from perhaps some sporting associations, long before the neighbourhood was built upon, and the Duke of Monmouth chose "Soho" as his battle-cry on the field of Sedgemoor. In the northwest corner of Soho Square is an entrance to the *Soho Bazaar*, established by Mr. Trotter, after the great continental wars of 1815, to give employment to the orphans and widows, &c., of those who had been slain. The whole square still bears evidence of its earliest inhabitants—the nobility of two hundred years ago—the houses, so lofty and well built, denote their original purpose. The Catholic Chapel in Sutton Street and the mansion now occupied by Crosse and Blackwell's pickles were, about a hundred years since, the scene of the most fashionable assemblies in London. Here Mrs. Cornelys received the fine ladies of the period and their princely and noble admirers, who, in some of their masquerades carried affairs sometimes to extremes. We are told of a peer's daughter, who once exhibited herself here as an Indian princess—three black girls bearing her train, negro boys bearing the canopy over her head, and her dress covered with £100,000 worth of jewels. A "noble swell" of that period appeared as Adam, in flesh-coloured tights and an apron of fig-leaves; and a grand dame, the Duchess of Bolton, scarcely better clothed, figured as Diana.

Carlisle House, in Carlisle Street, near by, dates from the time of James II., and was the mansion of the Earl of Carlisle up to 1756.

Greek Street was named after the Greek church in *Crown Street*. *Wardour Street* is the most noted street in London for old curiosity shops. *Gerard Street*, named after Gerard, Earl of Macclesfield, the owner of the land, is to be remembered as containing the residence (No. 43) of John Dryden—the front parlour was the poet's study. At the

Turk's Head in Gerard Street, the *Literary Club*, founded by Dr. Johnson, Burke, Sir Joshua Reynolds, &c., was held; the same tavern had been previously the rendezvous of the Society of Artists, and from it was presented by West, Wilson, and other artists, the petition to George III. for patronage, which resulted in the founding of the Royal Academy of Art.

We will return now to Oxford Street, and proceeding as before, eastwards, we come upon *The Oxford Music Hall*, perhaps one of the most popular of those large metropolitan houses of entertainment where music and acrobatism, comic songs, grotesque dancing, tumbling, &c., are all combined with the accompaniments of drinking, smoking, and conversational interludes on the part of the spectators. *Hanway Street* is a short cut west, noted more than a century for its cheap jewelry, old China, and second-hand ornaments.

At the extreme north-eastern end of Oxford Street is *Tottenham Court Road*, the old thoroughfare from St. Giles's to Hampstead, past the mansion of William de Totenhall or Tottenhall, which stood on the site of the *Adam and Eve* tavern, near the Tottenham Court turnpike, shown in Hogarth's 'March to Finchley.' Tottenham Court Road is a broad and long street; of late years famed for its numerous good and economical shops for upholstery, &c. *Meux's Brewery*—one of the most celebrated in London for stout—stands at the south-east corner next to Oxford Street. A few paces north is *Great Russell Street, Bloomsbury*, the street of the British Museum. At the point where *Rathbone Place* runs northwards into Tottenham Court Road, stands *Percy Chapel*, made popular and fashionable by the Rev. Robert Montgomery (d. 1855), known from his poem of 'Satan,' as Satan Montgomery, and thus distinguished from his contemporary, James Montgomery—a sacred poet of a much higher order. *Charlotte Street* leads from Rathbone Place to *Fitzroy Square*, the headquarters for London artists. Here dwells Dick Tinto, and sets up his sitter's throne—" a gentle creature, loving his friends, his cups, feasts, merrymakings, and all good things." His club, the 'Hogarth,' founded in 1870, is at 84 Charlotte Street. About a quarter of a mile from the end of Oxford Street is the *Prince of Wales's Theatre*, built first as a concert-room, then transformed into a theatre, and known as such under various names—the Tottenham Street, the Regency, the Royal, the West London, &c. Towards the northern end of Tottenham Court Road is one of the most famous of dissenting chapels, *Whitfield's Tabernacle*, begun in 1756, and since considerably enlarged and improved. Whitfield here attracted such large congregations, that it is said Queen Caroline, consort of George II., seeing so many persons unable to obtain admission, sent him a large sum of money to enlarge his meeting-house. John Wesley here preached Whitfield's funeral sermon. Between Bloomsbury and the Euston Road (which runs past the end of Tottenham Court Road) were the *Southampton Fields*, one of which was called the *Field of the Forty Footsteps*. It was so named from a legend of a mortal fight between two brothers, which took place here on account of a lady whom both admired. She sat by and witnessed the deadly struggle for her hand. Both combatants were killed, and the indentations left in the ground by their footsteps whilst they were engaged in this deadly encounter were so deep and peculiar, that, as the story ran, no grass ever grew thereon afterwards. The legend has been dramatised more than once successfully. The *Hampstead Road* runs north in continuation, as we have said, of Tottenham Court Road, on to the High Street, Camden Town, where the thoroughfare divides into three ways, of which the eastern is *Camden Road*, the middle is *Kentish Town Road*, and the left or western is the *Chalk Farm Road* to *Haverstock Hill*. The broad open country of *Hampstead Heath* may be reached by railway or omnibus. Its most noted inns are 'Jack Straw's Castle' and the 'Spaniards.'

NEW OXFORD STREET, THROUGH HOLBORN, TO SMITHFIELD, AND CHEAPSIDE.

*S*T. *Giles's Church*, still described as in the Fields, was built in 1734 by Flitcroft, upon the site of an ancient chapel of a Hospital for Lepers, founded in 1117. The entrance gateway is decorated with an old bas-relief from the former edifice. Here were buried some very notable persons—Lord Herbert, of Cherbury; Chapman, the translator of Homer; Sir Roger l'Estrange; Andrew Marvell; Richard Penderell, who assisted the escape of Charles II. (his tomb is in the churchyard); and the Duchess Dudley.

NEW OXFORD STREET, a short street in continuation of Oxford Street and High Holborn, runs through part of the notorious old "rookery of St. Giles." It was opened in 1847. A portion of the old buildings may still be seen in a dirty slum leading from George Street (formerly Dyot Street), but which, bad as it is, must be infinitely better than the *Gin Lane* and *Beer Street* which Hogarth drew from this neighbourhood, even as he pourtrayed the *Idle Apprentice* apprehended for murder in a *St. Giles's* night-cellar, and the St. Giles's charity-boy as the Tom Nero of his *Four Stages of Cruelty.* The gallows was removed from the Elms at Smithfield to *St. Giles's*—then a wayside village, noted chiefly for its early inns and houses of entertainment. Sir John Oldcastle, after being drawn from the Tower hither, was here hanged and burnt. From the *Seven Dials*, St. Giles's, issued the yards of songs for one penny which Pitts and Catnach published and made fortunes by. The *Seven Dials* were planned and built for wealthy tenants by a noted architect in the time

THE HOLBORN RESTAURANT,
218, HIGH HOLBORN,
ONE OF THE SIGHTS AND ONE OF THE COMFORTS OF LONDON.

Attractions of the Chief Parisian Establishments, with the Quiet and Order essential to English Customs.

DINNERS AND LUNCHEONS FROM DAILY BILL OF FARE.

THE FAMOUS
TABLE D'HOTE DINNER
EVERY EVENING.

At Separate Tables, in the Grand Salon, the Prince's Salon, and the Duke's Salon.

From 5.30 to 8.30, 3s. 6d.

INCLUDING

TWO SOUPS, TWO KINDS of FISH, TWO ENTRÉES, JOINTS, SWEETS, CHEESE (in variety), SALAD, &c., with ICES and DESSERT.

THIS FAVOURITE DINNER IS ACCOMPANIED BY A SELECTION OF HIGH-CLASS INSTRUMENTAL MUSIC, PERFORMED BY AN ORCHESTRA OF WELL-KNOWN ARTISTS.

LADIES SHOPPING,
OR VISITING WEST-END EXHIBITIONS,

Find at the Holborn Restaurant QUIET ATTENTION and COMFORT.

A varied and economical Menu of Hot and Cold Luncheons.
SPECIAL SERVICE OF TEA AND COFFEE.
Entrance for Ladies by Cloak Room Corridor on Left of Vestibule.

Aux Étrangers.
THE HOLBORN RESTAURANT,
218, HIGH HOLBORN.

Cet établissement célèbre est au nombre des plus beaux spectacles et des plus grands agréments de Londres ; et réunit les avantages des meilleurs Restaurants Parisiens avec la quiétude et l'ordre de rigueur en Angleterre. Dîners et déjeuners tous les jours à la carte. Table d'Hôte, à tables séparées, chaque soir, entre six heures et huit heures et demie, dans le Grand Salon, le Salon du Prince, et le Salon Ducal. Le Menu contient deux Soupes, deux espèces de Poisson, deux Entrées, Relevés, Pâtisseries, Fromages divers, Salade, Glaces, et Dessert. Les attractions de ce dîner recherché sont rehaussées par une selection de la musique des auteurs les plus renommés, jouée par un bon orchestre.

PLATE X.

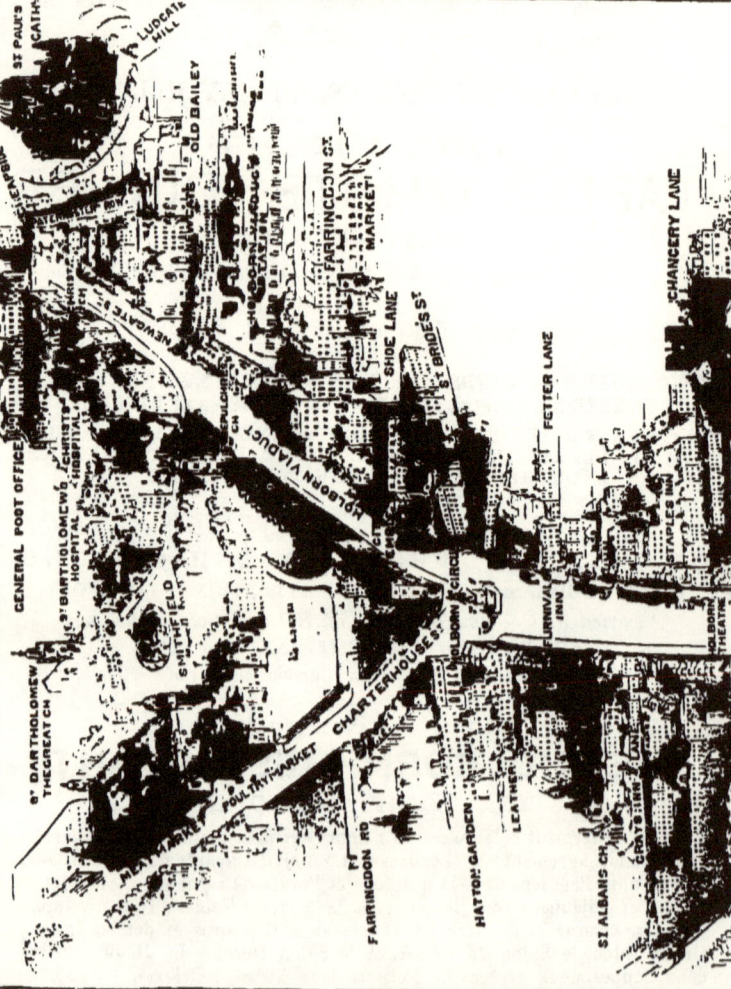

NEWGATE STREET.

Cromwell & Co.,
10, Paternoster Buildings,
Turkey Carpet Depôt.

11, *John Toms*,
Fire & Burglar Resisting Safes

HOLBORN VIADUCT.

1, The Patent Thorncliffe Range
Newton, Chambers, & Co.

FARRINGDON STREET.

73, *James Hoss & Co.*,
Scientific Instrument Maker

HOLBORN VIADUCT.

26, *"Our Boys"*
Clothing Company.

HOLBORN.

HIGH HOLBORN.

32½, *Barrow*,
Maker of the Knockabout Bag

LINCOLN'S INN.

NEWGATE STREET.

Mayo & Kilford, 116,
Paper Collars, Cuffs, & Fronts.

HOLBORN VIADUCT.

Jenks & Holt, 65,
Upholsterers & Decorators.

43-44,
Clarke, Bulleni, M'Council & Co.
American Doors, Mouldings, &c.

HOLBORN.

H. Lamplough, Chemist, 113,
Maker of Pyretic Saline.

Albion Lamp Co., 118,
Filippuzillo's Patent Oil Stoves.

George Wright & Co., 143,
Sewing Machine Manufacturers

HIGH HOLBORN.

199, 200, 201, *George Kent*,
Knife Cleaning Machines, &c.

NEW OXFORD STREET.

480, *Hugo Proskauer*,
Conjuring Depôt, Fretwork
Tools & Materials.

416 & 447, *Guy & Co.*,
Outfitters & Linendrapers.

NEW OXFORD STREET

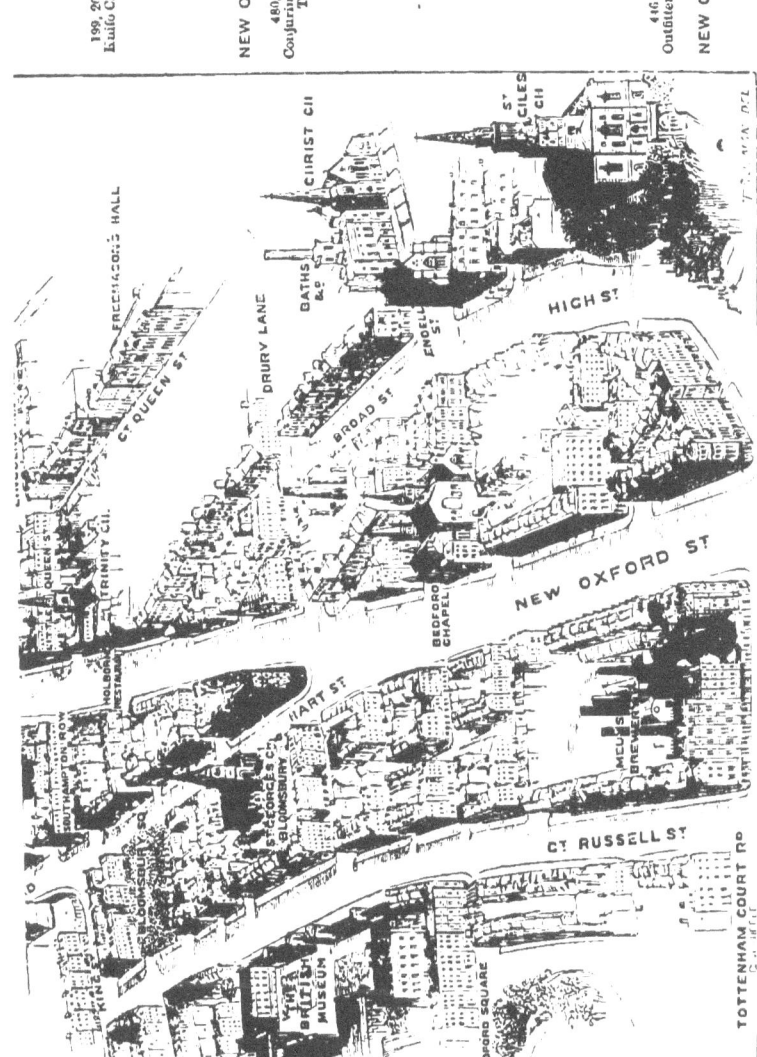

NEW OXFORD STREET AND HOLBORN.
TO SMITHFIELD AND CHEAPSIDE.

KENT'S
PATENT VENTILATED
ICE SAFES
AND
REFRIGERATORS,

In numerous Designs, kept in Stock.

Equally adapted for the smallest Family or largest Hotel, Tavern, Restaurant, &c., at

Prices from 50s.

Also Ice Making Machines, and Cream Freezers, and every article connected with cooling and freezing, combining all the real improvements of recent date.

KNIFE CLEANING MACHINES,
The Real and the Imitation.

Purchasers of Knife Cleaners are told by those who (on account of larger profits) are interested in the sale of machines made in imitation of Kent's that they are identically the same, Kent's patent having expired, and thus truth is employed to aid misrepresentation; the fact being that two old patents did expire some years since, but **Kent's Improved Knife Cleaners**, made in nine different sizes, from £2 2s. to £14 14s., are protected by two existing patents, and any infringement would subject the persons to proceedings in Chancery. Kent's original Knife Cleaners are, however, still supplied, and to meet the convenience of those with whom price is an important consideration, **Kent's Original Knife Cleaners**, made in nine different sizes, from £1 12s. to £10 10s., are quite as low in price as are the imitations, and are greatly superior to them in efficiency and durability.

Kent's Carpet Sweeper.
This Sweeper raises no Dust, takes up all Dirt as it moves, and Sweeps cleaner than any other Broom.

Kent's Potato Masher and
BREAD GRATER, 12s. 6d. Potatoes, by a few turns of the handle, Mashed to Perfection. Bread Grated with equal rapidity.

Kent's Marmalade Cutter.
Rapidly cuts Orange Peel or Vegetables to any degree of thinness.

Kent's Six-Minute Churns,
10s. 6d. to 27s. 6d. The Churn will make Butter from Milk in Six Minutes, and from Cream in about half that time, extracting every atom of Butter which the Milk or Cream contains.

Kent's Patent Mincer and
SAUSAGE MACHINE, the best and cheapest yet invented. Price 8s. 6d.

Kent's Bread and Meat
SLICER, will cut Bread or Meat as thin as paper, or as thick as required.

ILLUSTRATED CATALOGUES GRATIS,
Giving Full Description and Prices of numerous other Domestic Labour-saving Appliances, which insure the better performance of Household Work.

GEORGE KENT,
199, 200, & 201, HIGH HOLBORN, LONDON

of Charles II. Gay described the intricacies of the district which so many tired pedestrians have since verified—

> "Here to seven streets seven dials count their day,
> And from each other catch the circling ray;
> Here oft the peasant with inquiring face
> Bewildered trudges on from place to place,
> Tries every winding court and street in vain,
> And doubles o'er his weary steps again."

Monmouth Street, named after the hero of Sedgemoor, whose mansion was in Soho Square, has long been famous for its shops for old clothes, second-hand boots, and underground cellars. Monmouth Street is now called *Dudley Street*, but it has not changed its character with its name.

We will now return to *New Oxford Street*. *Bloomsbury Street* leads through Charlotte Street into *Bedford Square* and beyond into Gower Street.

University College, London (sometimes mistaken for the University of London, an entirely different institution, see p. 145), is situated on the east side of Gower Street. It was founded by Lord Brougham and others (1826) to afford at a moderate cost the means of a high educational training—fitting students for taking their degrees at the University of London. *University College School* is for lads up to the age of sixteen—hours, 9·30 A.M. to 3·45 P.M.—at a charge of £24 per annum. The *College* provides instruction, by means of a staff of forty professors, to students who chiefly reside in lodgings near by. *The Flaxman Gallery* of sculptures by our great English sculptor in the Hall of this College, and the *Marmor Homericum*, are well-worth seeing. *University College Hospital*, also in Gower Street, serves as a school of instruction in medicine, surgery, &c. It was founded in 1833 as a general hospital, with separate departments for diseases of women, children, the skin, the eye, the ear, the throat, and the teeth. It contains 154 beds, and treats over 2000 in-patients annually, besides 5000 out-patients. The income is about £12,000 per annum.

At the Holborn end of *Museum Street* is Mudie's well-known and extensive Circulating Library. *Great Russell Street*, at the north end, was once a fashionable street inhabited by the nobility and gentry, especially on its north side, which had gardens at the back. *Montagu House*, the seat of the Duke of Montagu, occupied its centre, upon which site now stands the

BRITISH MUSEUM.

It originated in 1753 under an Act of Parliament for the purchase of Sir Hans Sloane's Collection and the Harleian and Cottonian Collections of Manuscripts, and was opened to the public in 1759. At first it comprised but three departments, Printed Books, Manuscripts, and Natural History, and to these were subsequently added Antiquities and Art, including Prints and Drawings, Medals and Coins. In 1823, upon the presentation to the Museum by George IV. of the library collected by George III., it was found necessary to erect a new edifice. Montagu House gradually disappeared, and when Sir R. Smirke's building was completed in 1845 nothing of the old structure remained. Since then Mr. Sydney Smirke erected (1857) in the inner quadrangle a fine building which contains the Reading Room and accommodation for new books. In 1827 a fifth department, Botany, was added, in consequence of a bequest by Sir Joseph Banks of his collection and library of 16,000 volumes. The Museum at present comprises twelve departments, viz., Printed Books, Maps, &c., MSS., Prints and Drawings, Oriental Antiquities, Greek and Roman Antiquities, British and Mediæval Antiquities and Ethnography, Coins and Medals, Zoology, Geology, Mineralogy, and Botany; each department being under the care of an under librarian or keeper. Upon the western side of the

Entrance Hall, decorated by Roubilliac's *Shakespeare* and *Sir J. Banks* by Chantrey, is the principal staircase to the upper floor, which contains the Zoological, the Mineral and Fossil, and the Botanical collections. Opposite the foot of the staircase is the entrance to the *Grenville Library*, bequeathed to the nation in 1847 by the Rt. Hon. Thomas Grenville; from the Grenville Library the visitor proceeds to the *Manuscript Saloon*, where MSS., Charters, Autographs, &c., are arranged for inspection, and thence he passes to the *Royal Library*, containing some fine examples of prints and drawings. The entrance to the *Reading Room* is immediately in front of the visitor as he enters the building. Upon the left of the entrance hall is the way to the *Antiquities Department*. Catalogues of the collections are to be had at the Museum at prices from 1d. to 6d. each.

The *Zoological Collection* occupies three galleries and is arranged in two series. The beasts, birds, reptiles, and fishes are shown in the cases fixed against the walls; the shells, corals, sea-eggs, starfish, crustacea, and the eggs of birds are seen in the cases upon the tables. The *Mammalia*, or creatures which suckle their young, occupy three rooms; the *Ungulata*, or hoofed beasts, are in the central saloon, and Southern Zoological Gallery; and the *Unguiculata*, or beasts with claws, are in the Mammalia Saloon. The wall-cases in the 1, *Eastern Zoological Gallery*, contain the collection of birds, and the table-cases, the shells of molluscous animals; over the wall-cases is a series of deer and rhinoceros' horns. In the 2, *Northern Zoological Gallery*, first room, is a collection of nests of wasps and bees; in the second room the wall-cases contain stuffed exotic reptiles and batrachia; the table-cases, sea-eggs, sea-stars, &c. In the third room is the *British Zoological Collection*, the wall-cases holding the vertebrate animals except the larger species, which are suspended above, such as the whale, shark, sturgeon, &c.; the table-cases contain British birds' eggs, British insects, spiders, crabs and shells, and skeletons of British molluscs and radiata. In the fourth room is a stuffed collection of bony fishes and a selected series of insects, beetles, ladybirds, crickets, dragon-flies, ants, wasps and bees, butterflies, moths, gnats, flies, spiders, scorpions, centipedes, &c., also crustacea. In the fifth room are specimens of the ganoid or cartilaginous fishes.

The *Geological Collection* is to be seen in the North Gallery, in the upper story of the building; the table-cases in rooms 1 to 4 in this gallery are occupied by the collection of Minerals, and in rooms 5 and 6 by the Fossil remains of Vertebrate Animals.

The *Botanical Collection* is placed upon the upper floor of the Museum near the Central Zoological Saloon. The portion exhibited consists chiefly of fruits, stems, and such vegetable structures as cannot from their size and texture be incorporated with the herbarium or collection of dried and mounted specimens. The cases A to D contain the cryptogams or flowerless plants, the fungi, the algæ or seaweed, lichens, mosses, riverworts, ferns, club-mosses and horse-tails; and E to H, the flowering plants. The main series is arranged in order along the wall-cases. There is here also a fine collection of fossil plants, &c.

The *Antiquities Collections* are divided into two series, of which one consists of Sculpture, including inscriptions and architectural remains, and occupies the ground floor of the south-western and western parts of the Museum, as well as some floors in the basement; and the other, placed in a suite of rooms on the upper floor, comprehends all the smaller remains, such as Vases, Medals, Coins, Bronzes, and articles of personal use or adornment. The series of sculptures may be seen to the left of the entrance hall, immediately upon entering the building. Here is the *Roman Gallery*, in which are to be found the *Roman and Anglo-Roman Antiquities.* Along the north side are Roman portraits in chronological sequence. Beyond are the Græco-Roman rooms 1, 2, 3, and the staircase leading to the Græco-Roman basement room. In the *Lycian Room*, adjoining the head of the staircase, is a collection of architectural and sculptured remains from ancient cities in Lycia, in Asia Minor. In the *Mausoleum Room* are the remains of the Mausoleum at Halicarnassus, erected by Artemisia B.C. 352. The *Elgin Room* contains the Elgin Marbles, so called from the Earl of Elgin, who, when ambassador at Constantinople in 1801-3, obtained these sculptures by virtue of a firman of the Sublime Porte, and sold them to our Government in 1816 for £35,000. These works of ancient art comprise remains from the Parthenon at Athens, a portion of the frieze of the Temple of Victory at Athens, some architectural remains from the Erechtheum, and a number of casts and fragments. In the *Hellenic Room* are marbles brought at different times from Greece and its colonies, but chiefly from the ruins of the Temple of Apollo Epicurius in Arcadia. The *Assyrian Galleries* contain the Sculptures excavated chiefly by Sir A. H. Layard, 1847-50, on the site of Nineveh; the collections made under the direction of Sir H. C. Rawlinson, 1853, and by the late Mr. G. Smith. The *Kouyunjik Gallery* exhibits the collection of Bas-reliefs from an ancient Assyrian edifice at Kouyunjik, supposed to have been the palace of Sennacherib, B.C. 700. The *Nimroud Central Saloon*, the *Nimroud Gallery*, the *Assyrian Side-room*, the *Assyrian Basement Room*, and the *Assyrian Transept*, contain the other antiquities of Assyria. The *Egyptian Galleries* are upon the north of the Assyrian transept, and contain many antiquities dating at least 2,000 years before the Christian era. On the *North-west Staircase* are placed examples of Egyptian papyri, i. e., documents on rolls formed of slices of the papyrus. At the top of the staircase is the *Egyptian Ante-Room*, and, farther on, the *Egyptian Rooms*. The *Glass Collections*, comprising ancient and more recent glass of all countries, are upon the west side of the Egyptian rooms, and are highly interesting. The *Vase Rooms* exhibit a collection of painted fictile vases, discovered in tombs in Italy, Greece, &c. The *Bronze Room* contains the Greek, Etruscan, and Roman bronzes. The *British and Mediæval Room* exhibits all remains of the Middle Ages, English and Foreign, and includes examples of British antiquities relating to periods before the Roman invasion. The *Collection of Gold Ornaments and Gems* is arranged in cases round the east and south side of a room between the British and Mediæval Room and the Ethnographical Room. In the *Ethnographical Room* are placed both the antiquities and the objects in modern use belonging to all nations not of European race. The *Prehistoric Antiquities*, formed by the late Henry Christy, Esq., will probably soon find a place at the British Museum, to which they were presented in 1866.

The use of the READING ROOM is restricted to the purposes of study, reference, or research; and it is kept open on every day of the week except Sunday, Ash-Wednesday, Good Friday, Christmas Day, and any Fast or Thanksgiving Day appointed by authority; except also from the 1st to the 7th of February, the 1st to the 7th of May, and the 1st to the 7th of October, inclusive. The hours are from nine till four in the months of November, December, January, and February; from nine till five in the months of September, October, March, and April; and from nine till six in the months of May, June, July, and August. No person under twenty-one years of age is admissible, except under a special order from the trustees. Persons desiring to be admitted to the Reading Room must apply in writing to the Principal Librarian, specifying their profession or business, their place of abode, and, if required, the purpose for which they seek admission. Every such application must be made two days, at least,

British Museum. 183

before admission is required, and must be accompanied by a written recommendation from a householder or a person of known position, mentioning in full his, or her, name and address, and stating that he, or she, possesses a personal knowledge of the applicant, and of his or her intention to make proper use of the Reading Room. If such application and recommendation be satisfactory to the Principal Librarian, he will grant a ticket of admission without limit of term, and not requiring to be renewed periodically, as heretofore, but which may be withdrawn at the discretion of the Principal Librarian, and is not transferable.

The public are admitted to view the collections in the British Museum on every week-day from Monday till Friday, from 10 o'clock, and on Saturday from 12 o'clock till the time of closure, as follows:

From 10 *till* 4.	*From* 10 *till* 5.	*From* 10 *till* 6.
January.	March.	May.
February.	April.	June.
November.	September.	July.
December.	October.	August.

The arrangements for the admission of Students are as follows:

Students of Natural History, Tuesdays and Thursdays.
Students of Archæology, Wednesdays and Fridays.

The entire Collections are open to the public on Mondays and Saturdays; but, upon Students' days, as above, the Collections named are reserved for Students only.

The Museum is closed—February 1 to 7, May 1 to 7, October 1 to 7, inclusive; and on Sundays, Ash-Wednesday, Good Friday, and Christmas Day.

At the east corner of Museum Street is *Hart Street* which runs nearly in a parallel line with High Holborn and leads into *Theobald's Road* and, without interruption, through a new thoroughfare, across Gray's Inn Road and the Metropolitan Railway, to Clerkenwell and eastern districts. In *Hart Street* is the principal entrance to *St. George's Church, Bloomsbury*, built by a pupil of Sir Christopher Wren — Nicholas Hawksmoor, 1731. The portico of eight Corinthian columns has been much admired, but the tower, with a series of steps guarded by lions and unicorns, and having a statue of George I. in Roman costume for its apex, has been severely criticised by Horace Walpole and others. It gave rise to this epigram:—

> "When Harry the Eighth left the Pope in the lurch,
> The people of England made him head of the Church;
> But George's good subjects, the Bloomsbury people,
> Instead of the Church made him head of the Steeple."

This church stands in the unusual position of north and south; but, despite all objections, it must be admitted to be a picturesque edifice. In *Bloomsbury Square* is a statue of Charles James Fox. The continuation of Museum Street southwards, across Holborn, leads to *Drury Lane*, and through it direct to the *Strand*. *High Holborn* begins at the top of Drury Lane and is continued to *Holborn Bars*, near Brook Street, see p. 193.

In High Holborn, eastwards beyond Museum Street, a few doors before coming to *Little Queen Street* on the south side, nearly opposite to *Southampton Street* and *Southampton Row*, is the *Holborn Restaurant*, noted for the gorgeous appearance of its salon, galleried and bedecked with mirrors, and for the cultivated cuisine of its table d'hôte dinners, enlivened by choice instrumental music. On this site formerly stood the *Holborn Casino*, one of the chief dancing saloons of London. At the south end of Little Queen Street is *Great Queen Street*, in which is the *Freemasons' Tavern*—the headquarters of Freemasonry, and a noted house for public dinners. *Southampton Row* leads past *Queen's Square* through *Russell Square* (where is a statue of the Duke of Bedford) and *Tavistock Square*, to the

Terminus of the London and North Western Railway, Euston Square. Nearly opposite to *Kingsgate Street*, which, in the time of Charles II., was the Royal road to Newmarket, is the *Royal Music Hall*, for many years called *Weston's Music Hall*, after the name of its first proprietor. *Red Lion Square*, reached through *Dean Street, Holborn*, was named after the once celebrated *Red Lion Inn*, in Holborn, nearly opposite the *George and Blue Boar*. To the *Red Lion Inn* the bodies of Cromwell, Ireton, and Bradshaw were carried from Westminster Abbey, and next day dragged on sledges to Tyburn. The *George and Blue Boar*, 285 Holborn, was used by criminals, on their way to Tyburn, as their last "house of call." Swift wrote:—

"As clever Tom Clinch, when the rabble was bawling,
Rode stately through Holborn to die of his calling,
He stopt at the *George* for a bottle of sack,
And promised to pay for it when he came back."

But the *George and Blue Boar* is of much greater historical importance; for it is said that here was discovered a messenger carrying a letter from Charles I., by which Ireton ascertained that it was the King's purpose to execute Cromwell and himself—a piece of information which decided them to bring Charles himself to the block.

Red Lion Street leads through *Lamb's Conduit Street*, to the front of the *Foundling Hospital*, in Guilford Street, one of the most interesting places in London. It was founded in 1739 by Thomas Coram, a retired sea-captain, who, pitying the infants whom he had seen exposed and deserted in some of the public thoroughfares near his residence at Rotherhithe, established, after some labour and expense, the first Foundling Hospital in Hatton Garden—opened March 1740-1. The present Hospital was built in 1754 to receive 600 children, and country branch-hospitals were formed. Parliament voted £10,000. All that was then necessary for the admission of an infant was to ring a bell at the gate and to deposit the child in the basket placed there for the purpose; 117 were brought the first day, and 3727 during the first year. Before long, i.e., in less than four years, 14,934 children were received, having been conveyed by carriers and others from all parts of the country, and of those over 10,000 died; a far larger mortality than Captain Coram had been so shocked at. Parliament again intervened, undertook the support of the survivors, and stopped indiscriminate admission. In 1760 the basis of the Institution had so changed that none but the illegitimate infants of mothers whose circumstances were known to the Board, were admitted; and this continues to be the rule of the Hospital. If the mother of a first child can show previous good character, and that she has been deserted by the father; the Committee, who meet on Saturdays, would consider her case upon its merits; but application must be made to them personally by the mother. Two country houses connected with this Hospital receive the youngest children; they are transferred to London as they grow a little older. Captain Coram spent all his property upon this and similar philanthropical endeavours, and before he died was glad to accept assistance from a public subscription for his benefit. The architect of the Hospital was T. Jacobson, who died in 1772. The *Hospital Chapel* is open to the public every Sunday for morning service at 11, and for afternoon service at 3. After the former, visitors are admitted to see at dinner the children, whom they have just heard taking part in the musical service, which is led by professional singers, and accompanied by Handel's Organ. There is no fee for admission to the Chapel, but visitors on their admission are expected to contribute to the plate held at the doors. The Chapel is certainly one of the handsomest examples of the edifices of the Georgian era—simple, roomy, light, and comfortable, with stained-glass windows showing the arms of numerous donors and benefactors. Handel and

Lincoln's Inn Fields. 187

Hogarth were the two greatest of the latter. Handel gave the organ and frequently performed his oratorio, the *Messiah*, upon it, raising as much as £1000 by a single performance for the Hospital Fund. Hogarth painted the full-length portrait of Captain Coram, which now figures as but one of a very interesting though small collection of pictures to be seen here. Benjamin West's altar-piece, 'Christ Blessing Little Children,' is in the chapel. In the Committee-room, &c., are Hogarth's 'March to Finchley,' and Hogarth's 'Moses brought to Pharaoh's Daughter;' Sir Joshua Reynolds' portrait of Lord Dartmouth; Richard Wilson's 'Foundling Hospital' and 'St. George's Hospital;' Gainsborough's 'The Charter House;' Hartley's 'Chelsea and Bethlehem Hospitals;' portraits of Handel, by Kneller, &c., &c. In the vaults lie the remains of Captain Coram, Lord Chief Justice Tenterden, and others. The preacher at the Foundling is always a clergyman of note. The Rev. Sydney Smith was once a preacher here. The income of the Hospital, chiefly derived from old benefactions, and the increased value of its London property, is over £11,000 per annum. The children (no longer foundlings) number over 500, half of each sex. Of the earlier recipients of this charity there are some interesting relics, consisting of the small articles found upon the infants left in the admission basket. These are preserved in glass cases for the inspection of visitors.

Returning now to Holborn and proceeding as before, eastwards, we shall observe upon our right the *Inns of Court Hotel*, one of the most extensive and best situated hotels in London. On our left is *Brownlow Street*, leading to *Bedford Row* well known for its numerous solicitors' offices. On the opposite side of Holborn is *Great Turnstile*, leading to *Lincoln's Inn Fields*, now a large square tract of ground, enclosed since 1735 within palings, formerly an open space used for popular assemblies, fairs, and executions. Lord William Russell was here beheaded. " As he observed the great crowd of people, he said, 'I hope I shall soon see a much better assembly.' When he came to the scaffold he walked about it four or five times. Then he turned to the sheriffs and delivered his paper . . . . He prayed by himself, then Tillotson prayed with him. He undressed himself, laid his head upon the block without the least change of countenance, and it was cut off at two strokes." Lincoln's Inn Fields bore an evil name in Gay's time ; he writes :—

> " Where Lincoln's Inn's wide space is railed around,
> Cross not with venturous step ; there oft is found
> The lurking thief."

The Pillory was often set up here. Inigo Jones built many of the houses on the western side. *Sir John Soane's Museum*, is at No. 13, Lincoln's Inn Fields, on the north or Holborn side, and contains an interesting collection of pictures, books, MSS., and antiquities, open free from 10 to 4 on Wednesdays, Thursdays, and Fridays, in April, May, and June, and on Wednesdays and Thursdays in February, March, July, and August inclusive. On Saturdays, parties from schools are admitted by special order of the Curator, to be obtained previously. Sir John Soane, the founder, was an architect of some note in the early part of this century; he built the Bank of England and several other public edifices. He made this collection himself, endowed it, and left it to the nation at his death in 1837. The house is full of pictures and various objects of antiquity. Amongst the former are Hogarth's 'Rake's Progress' and the 'Election;' Sir J. Reynolds' 'Snake in the Grass;' Turner's 'Van Tromp entering the Texel;' Eastlake's 'Cave of Despair;' Ostade's 'Scene in a Village;' Views in Venice by Canaletti, and Hilton's 'Mark Antony;' amongst the Sculptures are several examples by Flaxman, Westmacott, Banks, and others; amongst the Books, the first four folio editions of Shakespeare ; amongst the MSS., the original of the 'Gerusalemma Liberata,' by Tasso; amongst the Antiquities, the Egyptian Sarcophagus or cenotaph discovered by Belzoni in 1816, formed of one block of alabaster, 9 feet 4 inches long, 3 feet 8 inches wide, and 2 feet 8 inches deep; 2½ inches thick, and yet so transparent that a lamp placed within it sends a light through. Inside is a carved full-length figure of Isis, the Egyptian guardian of the dead.

Upon the south side of Lincoln's Inn Fields is the *Museum of the Royal College of Surgeons*. John Hunter, the great anatomist, made (see p. 18) the collection which formed the basis and is still the chief portion of the contents of this Museum. The Government, upon the decease of Hunter in 1793, bought his collection for £15,000, and gave it to the College of Surgeons, who have since added to and improved it. Admission is to be obtained by order of a Member of the College, between 12 and 5 from March to August; and 12 to 4 during the winter months, on Monday, Tuesday, Wednesday, and Thursday. The Museum is closed in September. It is divided into three sections, called the Western, Middle, and Eastern Museums. The *Western* contains, on the ground floor, pathological preparations showing diseases and injuries of bone, wax anatomical models, mummies, illustrations of normal human osteology; and, in the galleries, collections of calculi and other concretions; Toynbee's specimens of diseased ear, and examples of skin disease. In the centre is a skeleton of a whale, and at the end of the room the skeleton of O'Brien, the Irish giant, eight feet high, who died, aged 22, in 1783. The *Middle Apartment* exhibits the fossil remains of extinct vertebrated animals, and, in the galleries, examples of parasitic or entozoic animals. The *Eastern Apartment* contains examples of the osteology of vertebrate animals, and the galleries, specimens of the various modifications of different organisms. From the middle of the ceiling is hung the skeleton of a sperm whale, and on the ground floor are the skeleton of the elephant of old Exeter Change, &c. The fashionable theatre of Charles II.'s time, called the *Duke's Theatre*, made famous by Betterton, Nell Gwynne, and others, mentioned by Pepys, stood upon the site of this Hall. The College possesses a fine library of over 30,000 volumes, relating to medical and surgical science, and a highly interesting collection of portraits of eminent surgeons, including Sir Joshua Reynolds' portrait of the founder, John Hunter.

Lincoln's Inn occupies the site of an ancient monastery of Black Friars, who having removed to the quarter since known by their name, the land was granted to Henry de Lacy, Earl of Lincoln, for his town house. At his death, in 1312, it became an Inn of Court, retaining the Earl's name. The older part of Lincoln's Inn dates from the time of James I. It is said that Ben Jonson helped in the building of a part of Lincoln's Inn, with trowel in hand and a Horace in his pocket. The *Chapel*, built by Inigo Jones, 1623, in a style of modernised Gothic, contains some fine stained glass windows. The *Hall or Library* is a fine edifice of red brick in the Tudor style, in keeping with the Old Tudor gateway (see p. 78). It was built by P. Hardwicke in 1843-5. The interior is decorated by a magnificent fresco by G. F. Watts, R.A., of the 'Lawgivers of the World,' and there are a few portraits in the Drawing-room. The Library is considered to be singularly excellent, and rich in ancient volumes and MSS. In Lincoln's Inn *Old Hall*, where the Lord Chancellor, &c., sit, is to be seen Hogarth's 'Paul before Felix,' painted by the artist, at the suggestion of Lord Mansfield, for the Benchers of the Inn. In the left-hand chambers, on the ground floor of No. 24 *Old Buildings*, lived Cromwell's secretary, Thurloe, and here in the reign of William III. were discovered the *Thurloe State Papers*, which had been concealed behind a false ceiling.

Gray's-Inn. 191

The *New Court*, LINCOLN'S INN, just built on the north side of Carey Street, will occupy an area of 5500 yards, extending to Portugal Street, and with Serle Street on the east. In the quadrangle there will be a garden, and surrounding it will be twelve distinct houses with staircases leading from the interior of the quadrangle to the several sets of chambers.

At 84–5, Holborn, is the *Holborn Amphitheatre*, a modern structure for equestrian performances. At 43 is the *Duke's Theatre*, a modern edifice of little note.

Chancery Lane (see p. 79) has been recently much widened and improved at its junction with Holborn. On the opposite side of Holborn is *Fulwood's Rents*, formerly a short cut from Holborn into Gray's Inn. The *Napier Tavern* (then the *Castle*), between Gray's Inn Gateway and Fulwood's Rents, was kept for many years by Tom Spring, the noted prize-fighter, whose real name was Tom Winter.

A few paces farther east bring us to the Gateway of *Gray's Inn*, an Inn of Court named after a Lord Gray de Wilton of Henry VII.'s reign. Jacob Tonson first kept shop in this gateway. The *Hall* of Gray's Inn was built in 1560; its interior is wainscoted, its windows richly dight with armorial bearings. Hard by is *Gray's Inn Chapel*. The Garden was first laid out in 1600, when Mr. afterwards Lord Bacon was Treasurer. *Verulam Buildings* still serve as a memorial of this the most famous of Gray's Inn students. Here died that greatest of all Lord Chancellors; he had retired from York House to his old chambers after his disgrace. He is still the *genius loci*, and we may say with the poet, Dr. Charles Mackay—

> "Whene'er through Gray's Inn porch I stray,
> I meet a spirit by the way;
> I roam beneath the ancient trees,
> And talk with him of mysteries;
> He tells me truly what I am—
> I walk with mighty Verulam."

Gray's Inn Lane, now *Gray's Inn Road*, leads from Holborn most directly to *King's Cross*, where are the *Great Northern Railway Terminus*, the hotel connected therewith, and a station of the *Underground Railway*. In *Fox Court*, Gray's Inn Lane, was born Richard Savage the poet; his mother, the Countess of Macclesfield, wore a mask at the time. Half-way up Gray's Inn Road is the *Royal Free Hospital*, founded (1828) for the free admission of the sick poor. It receives about 1500 in-patients and 40,000 out-patients annually. Its income is but £7500. Past the Great Northern Station is *Old St. Pancras Church*, a burial place of Roman Catholics after the Reformation. Here also were buried Woollett, the engraver; J. Walker, lexicographer; O. Walker; Jeremy Collier; W. Godwin, the novelist, and his two wives; Ned Ward, Paoli, and the Chevalier d'Eon. *New St. Pancras Church* is in the Euston Road. Between the *St. Pancras Terminus* of the *Midland Railway*, St. Pancras Road and the Hampstead Road, lies the poor district of *Somers Town*, named after Lord Somers, the owner of the land here.

Bagnigge Wells Road, near King's Cross, was once noted for its mineral spring, and for tea-gardens opened to the public in 1758, and finally closed in June 1841. *Cold Bath Fields Prison* is at its southern end.

Returning down Gray's Inn Road to Holborn, we shall at this point find *Staple Inn*, one of the old Inns of Chancery. It derived its name from the woolstaplers, who once owned it. The present structure is of the time of James I., and the Memorial Window-glass is still earlier. *Barnard's Inn*, another Inn of Chancery, named after an ancient owner, is the smallest of the Inns of Court. The gabled houses in Holborn near Staple Inn are among the oldest and most picturesque in London. Right in the middle of the present thoroughfare, and just at the end of Gray's Inn Lane, stood the old row of buildings known as *Middle Row, Holborn*, pulled down in 1867.

At a point nearly opposite *Brook Street* stood old *Holborn Bars*, the City boundary, destroyed in 1867. *Furnival's Inn* (now occupied as chambers, and by *Furnival's Hotel*) derives its name from the Lords Furnival, whose mansion was converted into an Inn of Chancery *temp.* Henry IV. No part of the ancient Hall remains. The present building is rendered interesting by the fact that Charles Dickens began 'Pickwick' in his chambers in Furnival's Inn. "I can remember," said Thackeray, "when Mr. Dickens was a very young man, and had commenced delighting the world with some charming humorous works in covers, which were coloured light green, and came out once a month, that this young man wanted an artist to illustrate his writings; and I recollect walking up to his chambers in Furnival's Inn with two or three drawings in my hand, which, strange to say, he did not find suitable."

The Church of St. Albans—rendered prominent by the extreme ritual and the sacerdotal claims of its incumbent, the Rev. Mr. Maconochie, is placed in a court leading out of Brook Street, Holborn. It is visited by many travellers from the country and abroad, who are curious to see to what extent ceremonial may be practised by a minister of the Church of England. This church was built by Butterfield.

LEATHER LANE, on the same side of Holborn, is chiefly noteworthy for its Italian colonists. Here live nearly all those organ-grinders, who are to be found roaming over the metropolis, discoursing to the discomfort of some, and to the delight of many, the latest popular musical compositions; and here also are their compatriots, the makers of plaster-of-Paris casts. Leather Lane is one of the tolerated markets for costermongers' wares, and is worth seeing on a Saturday night, by persons curious to know how their poorest neighbours live, what they buy and sell, and eat and drink, and amuse themselves withal. If one wanted to learn how much a penny can buy, an hour spent in such a market might afford the desired information.

Thavie's Inn, on the south side of Holborn, is named after John Thavie, its owner, in the time of Edward III. He let out his premises to students at law, and the property eventually became an Inn of Chancery, in connexion with Lincoln's Inn.

Ely Place occupies the site of the ancient palace of the bishops of Ely, and has many historic associations. *Ely Chapel*, the sole relic of the old pile, was sold in 1874, and is now a Roman Catholic chapel. It was of the church lands and gardens here—required by Queen Elizabeth to be demised by the Bishop to her till certain sums were repaid—that the Queen, finding the Bishop disposed to demur, wrote, " Proud prelate, know that if you do not immediately fulfil your engagement, I, who made you what you are, will immediately unfrock you." The Bishop had to make over the property to the crown, and Sir Christopher Hatton (the Queen's handsome Chancellor) entered into possession. *Hatton Garden* preserves the memory of Sir Christopher, whose widow held possession of it against all comers, and even against her second husband, Sir Edward Coke, whom she quarrelled with and kept at a distance. The Bishops of Ely, in consideration of being granted their house in Dover Street, Piccadilly, transferred in 1772 to the crown all claim to this property. In Ely Palace died John O'Gaunt, " time-honoured Lancaster," and of the then adjoining garden Shakespeare speaks in ' Richard III.,' "My lord of Ely, when I was last in Holborn, I saw good strawberries in your garden there; I do beseech you send for them." *Fetter Lane*, see p. 79.

Bleeding Heart Yard, described by Dickens "as inhabitated by poor people who set up their rest among its faded glories, as Arabs of the desert pitch their tents among the fallen stones of the pyramids," has been improved out of existence. It stood north of Ely Place. Its name was derived " from the heraldic cognisance of an old family to which it had once belonged," or from "a legend of a young lady closely imprisoned by her cruel father, who behind the bars of her prison window used to sing a pitiful song, with the burden, 'Bleeding heart, bleeding heart, bleeding away.'"

St. Andrew's Church, which used to stand considerably above the roadway, now appears much beneath its level, for the Viaduct spans the road far beyond it, to the top of what used to be Holborn Hill. This is one of Wren's churches, but is noted chiefly for its associations with the histories of a few remarkable men. John Webster, the Elizabethan dramatist, is said to have been its parish clerk. Savage the poet was christened here. Bishops Hacket, and Stillingfleet, and Dr. Sacheverell, were among its rectors; the last-named was buried here in the chancel. It is narrated, in connection with the Great Plague of London, that a blind Highland piper who fell asleep on the steps of this church was carried off in the dead-cart, and would have been buried in his trance, but for the howling of his dog, which at the last moment awoke him. Cibber the sculptor made a group from this incident for the Duke of Argyll.

Immediately upon the north side of and at the bottom of old Holborn Hill, ran *Field Lane* and *Saffron Hill*, notorious places for thieves and their receiving-houses, depicted by Boz as the home of Fagin and his school of pickpockets. It used to be asserted of this quarter of London, that if a gentleman in the Strand or the West-end lost his pocket-handkerchief and wished to recover it, he need but take a walk to Field Lane or Saffron Hill and there, about an hour or so after it had been picked from his pocket, he would be pretty sure to find it already washed and ironed, with his name erased, hanging with a hundred others of divers qualities and colours, outside one of the twenty shops for the sale of such articles then to be found here. The whole neighbourhood has been reformed. Field Lane scarcely exists but as a name upon the Night Refuges near by, and Saffron Hill has lately had enough fresh air and light let in upon the site of its old and wretched tenements to enable it if necessary to grow saffron once more.

At *Holborn Circus* is an Equestrian Statue of the late *Prince Consort*, near the new thoroughfare to Smithfield named Charterhouse Street, and here also is the Nonconformist chapel named the *City Temple*. Holborn Viaduct was built in 1867, by Mr. W. Haywood, for the City of London, and a wonderfully useful and ornamental improvement it is. Omnibuses and other heavy vehicles no longer crawl up Holborn Hill or Snow Hill, but run on level road from Newgate Street to Holborn. The old coaching-house, the *Saracen's Head*, on Snow Hill, which was rendered memorable by Dickens as the headquarters of Squeers, in London—whence the north country coach carried him, Nicholas, Smike, and the small boys off to Dotheboys Hall, has been taken down and rebuilt. Upon the Viaduct is the *Holborn Viaduct Terminus* of the London, Chatham, and Dover Railway; also the *Imperial Hotel*, and a large *Railway Terminus Hotel* adjoining.

St. Sepulchre's Church, injured by the Great Fire of London, was repaired by Wren. St. Sepulchre's tower, one of the most ancient in London, has four pinnacles with vanes—which have given rise to many observations, "Unreasonable people are as hard to reconcile as the vanes of St. Sepulchre's tower, which never looked all four upon one point of the heavens." The interior of the church is heavy and uninteresting, excepting the south-west porch, which is an example of the Perpendicular style, and has a roof of fan-tracery. From the steps of St. Sepulchre's, it was the custom, provided for by an old benefaction, to present the criminals, who would pass by in a cart on their way to be hanged at Tyburn (that being the more ancient place of execution), each with a nosegay. In St. Sepulchre's Church was buried, on the south side of the choir, the famous Captain

John Smith (d. 1631), sometime Governor of Virginia, to whom is an epitaph beginning—

"Here lies one conquered that hath conquer'd kings."

At the south-western corner of *Newgate Street* is the grim old building known as *Newgate Prison*, which has a frontage of considerable length to the open space called the *Old Bailey*. Well may a visitor pause to look at these prison walls, whose dinginess has passed into a sort of proverb—"black as Newgate." Here are the gigantic symbols, over the doors, of those iron fetters which await the felon within. Here is the spot whereon was reared the Newgate gallows, and here, within the limited space of a few hundred square yards, the ground upon which the crowd, packed so densely that the street seemed paved with heads, would wait through the long hours of night and darkness for the dawn which should bring the sensational sight of a "hanging." Opposite are the houses from whose windows the Lord Tom Noddies of the period beheld the sickening spectacle, after paying, as for a private box at a theatre, for the use of the room and window upon such occasions. All down the Old Bailey to the utmost point from which a sight of the gallows could be had, and far up into Giltspur Street, did that crowd extend—and it may be truly averred of it that perhaps no such collection of rascality could be found elsewhere in the world; for it is known that a "hanging" had a singular fascination and attraction for London thieves—and hither turned, as a needle to a magnet, all the numerous villains of this most densely-populated metropolis. When old St. Sepulchre's clock, hard by, struck eight, on a hanging morning, the upturned faces of that multitude, begrimed by the night of watching, and all directed gallows-ward, were a sight that once seen could never be forgotten. The bell of St. Sepulchre's Church, which tolled throughout the dismal ceremony, was one of its most depressing features.

Newgate.

The history of the *Prison of Newgate* would require many volumes. The first prison was founded, as all other similar City prisons were, in the tower connected with the City gate. Old Newgate was burned down in the Lord George Gordon Riots, in 1780, before the present prison, then in process of building by George Dance (the Architect of the Mansion House), was ready. The whole structure was completed soon afterwards; Tyburn-tree was abolished in 1783, and the first execution in front of Newgate took place, December 9, 1783; the last in 1868, when public executions were prohibited. Old Newgate was the prison in which Titus Oates, Jack Sheppard, and others were confined, and Howard the philanthropist laboured. In the present edifice Mrs. Fry performed her kindly offices for the female prisoners. Adjoining Newgate (to which admission may be obtained under an order from the Lord Mayor or the Sheriffs) is the *Central Criminal Court*, or *Old Bailey Sessions House*, to which admission can also be obtained by means of a fee to the official in charge. Opposite the place of execution at Newgate was a house, 89, said to have been occupied by Jonathan Wild, the thief-taker. Hogarth's father kept a school at the corner of Ship Court, Old Bailey; William Hone lived at No. 67. In *Green Arbour Court*, Old Bailey, near to where *Break-Neck Steps* mark the relics of Old London Wall, Oliver Goldsmith, at an early part of his career, lived in the deepest poverty, and wrote his 'Enquiry into the Present State of Polite Literature.' Whilst here he was called upon by a visitor, who, as there was but one chair in the room, was invited to sit in it while Goldsmith removed to the window-seat. A gentle tap was heard at the door of the room, and a ragged child came in, dropped a curtsey, and said, "Mamma sends her compliments, and would you do her the favour to lend her a chamber-pot full of coals?"

At the corner of *Giltspur Street* (so called from the knights, who wore gilt spurs, riding that way to the jousts

The Cock Lane Ghost. 199

in Smithfield) and Newgate Street stood *Giltspur Street Compter*, a debtors' prison and house of correction, built by Dance, in 1791, and pulled down in 1855. A hundred yards or so from the Old Bailey, up Giltspur Street, is *Pye Corner*, with a little figure and inscription testifying that the Great Fire of London, 1666, which began in Pudding Lane, near London Bridge, stopped at this point (see p. 237). Just beyond Pye Corner is *Cock Lane*, the scene of the imposture, known as the *Cock Lane Ghost*, which in 1762 set all London, high and low, a-talking. Dr. Johnson did not think it beneath his dignity to make inquiry into this deception, any more than Faraday did in our own time into the mystery of spirit-rapping, and with of course the same result, namely,—to convince every person of common sense that such communications are imaginary. The Cock Lane Ghost story amounted to this, that a girl, twelve years old, the daughter of the clerk of St. Sepulchre's Church, living in Cock Lane, had been communicated with by the ghost of a lady, whose husband had poisoned her, and she had been informed by certain scratchings—equivalent we may suppose to the spirit-rappings of a later time—that this ghost had particulars to communicate, which would bring the charge home to the criminal. The ghost promised to give the information in the vault of the church of St. John, Clerkenwell, where the murdered woman had been buried. All London was on the *qui vive* to follow up the matter, and avenge the murder. The Duke of York and Horace Walpole, amongst other persons of quality, visited the house in Cock Lane; Dr. Johnson and other gentlemen solemnly took up the inquiry, went to the vault of St. John on the night named by the supposed ghost, waited there, and adjured it solemnly to give the promised information. None was forthcoming. The worthy Doctor published his statement. The imposture came to an end. Parsons, the father of the girl, was condemned to the pillory for having promoted it, but the mob were not convinced; their faith in ghosts protected Parsons, they collected money for him, and they did not pelt him. *Populus vult decipi, et decipiatur.*

SMITHFIELD lies immediately north of *Giltspur Street*, and to the back of Christ's Hospital. In ancient times Smithfield being just beyond the city walls was the scene of all public amusements, fairs, and recreations. It was the place for tournaments, for ordeal fights, for quintain matches, and other such tough encounters as to earn for it the name of 'Ruffian's Hall.' It had its green and its clump of elm-trees, which afterwards became the site of executions, and the place whereon William Fitzosbert and Mortimer, and Sir William Wallace were executed. In Smithfield, Walworth, mayor of London, slew Wat Tyler, at the head of the rebels, near the priory of St. Bartholomew. In Smithfield were burnt the religious martyrs of the time of Queen Mary, in whose reign no less than 277 so suffered for 'heresy'; and there stands in the centre of the space, which still remains of old Smithfield, a memorial of these martyrs, also a memorial church close by. It is pretty certainly ascertained that the Protestant martyrs were burnt just opposite the entrance to the gate of St. Bartholomew's priory, the prior of which was generally the chief ecclesiastical personage present. The stake was fixed so that the martyr's face was turned towards the east, and to the priory gate. Human bones charred, and stones blackened by fire, were dug up at this spot during some excavations in March 1849. In the time of the Great Fire of London, the houseless people built themselves huts in Smithfield. Here *Bartlemy Fair* was held, from the reign of Henry I. to 1853, when it was finally abolished. The sights included shows of wild beasts, dwarfs, and monstrosities; operas, tight-rope, and saraband dancing; morrice-dancing by dogs, the hare beating the tabor, a tiger pulling feathers from live fowls,

Punchinello, &c. An ox roasted whole, and roast-pig, were the chief attractions of the great fair, which at one time used to last for a fortnight, but was afterwards restricted to three days. The name of Bartlemy was a corruption of *St. Bartholomew*, whose priory certainly enjoyed in early times some privileges connected therewith. There are two churches dedicated to this saint in Smithfield—one being known as *St. Bartholomew-the-Less*, and standing within the precinct of the present St. Bartholomew's Hospital, is a very small building; the other, *St. Bartholomew-the-Great*, is part of the ancient priory of St. Bartholomew, founded 1102, by Rahere, the king's minstrel (companion of Hereward, the last of the Saxons, who fought against William the Conqueror), who became the first prior, and to whom a monument still remains. This edifice is considered to be the oldest and one of the most remarkable of the churches of London. Its gate is Early English, and the church of Norman Gothic with Perpendicular additions. Amongst the remaining monuments may be named one to Sir W. Mildmay, founder of Emmanuel College, Cambridge. The name of William Hogarth appears upon the parish register. *Bartholomew Close* indicates the extent of this most ancient priory.

St. Bartholomew's Hospital originally formed a portion of Bartholomew's Priory, but, after the dissolution of monasteries, under Henry VIII., it was refounded in 1546 by the king, at the instance of Sir Richard Gresham, then Lord Mayor, father of Sir Thomas—the city agreeing to contribute 500 marks annually for its support; a sum equivalent to that derived from its royal endowment. The Hospital was spared by the Great Fire. It was rebuilt by Gibbs in 1730. A statue of Henry VIII. is still preserved over the entrance. St. Bartholomew's Hospital has always ranked amongst the first of our schools of medicine and surgery. Harvey, who discovered the circulation of the blood, was for thirty-four years physician to this Hospital. Abernethy was one of its famous lecturers, and reared many worthy disciples; but none more famous than Richard Owen, pronounced by Cuvier "the greatest anatomist of his age." Here are 676 beds, of which about 400 are for surgical cases; there are 100 nurses, and 27 different wards. About 6000 in-patients and 100,000 out-patients are treated annually. The income is about £45,000 per annum. There is a *Convalescent Home* at Highgate for the reception of convalescents from this Institution.

SMITHFIELD MARKET is now no longer used for the sale of cattle in the open pens, which once covered the whole of the space known as Smithfield. It is a large red-brick building in the *renaissance* style, erected for the City of London by Mr. Horace Jones, and opened in 1868, extending over three and a half acres of ground, roofed in with glass, and including a market for poultry as well as meat. Below it are cellars planned for the storage of such provisions, and a railway depot adjoins it. The great *Metropolitan Cattle Market* is held at Copenhagen Fields, between Camden Town and Islington, opened in June 1855, covering thirty acres (half enclosed), in which four millions of cattle, sheep, and pigs are sold annually. In the centre of the market is a clock-tower, also a telegraph-office and offices of different banks. Near by are eight slaughter-houses. Tolls are levied by the City of London upon the animals sold in this market.

Long Lane, Smithfield, leading into Aldersgate Street, has been well known for its shops for new and second-hand clothing and for the numerous small courts and alleys which lie between it and the *Barbican*. Upon the north side of Smithfield Market is the new street called *Charterhouse Street*, out of which runs, in a northerly direction, *St. John Street*, continued on to *St. John Street Road*, a direct way to the *Angel* Inn, Islington. If we proceed a short distance up St. John Street we shall see the place where the once-noted Sessions House (called after its founder, *Hicks's Hall*) formerly stood, and where Lord William Russell was condemned to death; and, if we bear a little to the left from that point, we shall come upon one of the most interesting relics of ancient London, namely, *St. John's Gate, Clerkenwell*—all that remains of the great monastery of the Knights of St. John of Jerusalem, founded in 1100. Wat Tyler's rebels destroyed, in 1382, the whole commandery, and beheaded the grand prior, in what is now called *St. John's Square.* Docwra, grand-prior from 1502 to 1520, commenced to rebuild the monastery and completed the gateway, now standing, about 1504. The monastery was suppressed in 1540, and the building which then stood here was given over to secular purposes, but chiefly " for the king's stores." In Edward VI.'s reign the Lord Protector Somerset undermined and blew up the edifice and removed a large portion of the materials wherewith to construct Somerset House. The Gate remained untouched. In 1731 it had become the printing-office of Edward Cave, and in that year he published in it the first number of the *Gentleman's Magazine.* Here Dr. Johnson was engaged in the editorial work of that periodical—" shut up in a room which he would suffer none to approach save the printer or the printer's boy for matter, which, as fast as he composed, he tumbled out at the door." Here he ate his food behind the screen, his dress being too shabby for him to show himself. In the great room over the archway, Garrick made his first essay as an actor in London—the journeymen printers read the subordinate parts, and Garrick represented the chief personage in Fielding's farce of 'The Mock Doctor'—Dr. Johnson and Cave being nearly the entire audience. Externally the Gateway is decorated on the north front with the arms of the priory and of Docwra, and on the south the arms of France and England. In the low doorway of the west tower was the entrance to Cave's printing-office. In the east tower is now a tavern-bar, from which Elizabethan stairs are carried to the rooms over the gateway. Among the relics treasured in these premises is an old-fashioned chair said to have been used by Dr. Johnson. The visitor will be much interested in this ancient place:—

> "Here Johnson and St. John's brave knights,
> Our wandering glances share:—
> The badge won in Jerusalem,
> The Doctor's elbow-chair.
> Such are the shreds which History
> Alone has cared to save;
> St. John leaves but his Gateway,
> Johnson, the seat of Cave."

CLERKENWELL GREEN is upon the north-west of St. John's Square, and is to be reached through *Jerusalem Passage*. It is noted as having been a great political rendezvous for many years, but the Vestry have failed to enclose it. At one end stands the *Sessions House* for *Middlesex*, removed here from Hicks's Hall, and near it is the *Clerkenwell House of Correction*, under the wall of which a barrel of gunpowder was exploded by some Fenian conspirators, December 1867, with a view to the escape of two prisoners, Burke and Casey. Forty innocent persons were injured and one killed by the explosion. The prisoners could not escape, but were afterwards punished with penal servitude. Barrett, who fired the powder-barrel, was hanged; he was the last malefactor who was publicly executed at Newgate. The parish *Church of St. James*, Clerkenwell, overlooks Clerkenwell Green. The name of *Clerkenwell*, derived from Clerk's Well in *Ray Street*, applies to a large district, which of late years has been chiefly noted for its numerous watchmaking and jewelry industries. The Marquis of Northampton being the owner of the land of this quarter, many of the streets have been named after his family—Compton, Perceval, Spencer, &c. At the *Red Bull Theatre*, in *Woodbridge Street*, women are said to have first appeared on a London

The Blue-Coat School.

stage. CLERKENWELL CLOSE is noted for *Newcastle House*, wherein the eccentric Duchess of Albemarle lived in state, and vowed she would never re-marry except to a sovereign prince. Lord Montague won the lady by courting her as Emperor of China, and used her as a barbarian. We will now (passing by the side of Farringdon station, one of the depots of the London, Chatham, and Dover line) return to the main thoroughfare from which we branched off at the corner of Giltspur Street, and will proceed eastwards.

On the north side of NEWGATE STREET we shall pass in front of *Christ's Hospital*, which recedes from the main thoroughfare, fenced in by tall iron gates and palings; and in the courtyard we shall probably see many a Blue-coat boy taking his diversion. This magnificent charity dates from the time of Edward VI.; the costume, still worn by the scholars, is the same as was generally adopted when the School was founded, and gives the name "*Blue-coat School*" to the Institution. Christ's Hospital occupies the site of the old convent of Grey Friars, and it was originally intended for the reception of young and helpless children. The cloisters and buttery are the only remains of the ancient priory. Charles II. founded the Mathematical School and endowed it; and many benefactions succeeded those of the king. Christ's Hospital is maintained by these bounties, administered by the Corporation of London, and its revenues are about £55,000 per annum. With this sum about 1100 boys are supported and educated, of whom about 200 are usually being reared at the Preparatory School at Hertford. Admission for scholars (age eight to eleven) to this School is obtained on presentation of the governors of the School. A list of those governors who have presentations during the year is published annually at the office of the School in March, price one shilling, and a general list of all the governors (who present once in three years), also their years of presentation can be had for half-a crown. Boys remain in the School until they are fifteen, or, if they become King's Scholars or Grecians, for some time longer, in order to qualify for the Universities. The public are admitted to the Lenten Suppers on every Thursday in Lent in the great Hall, by tickets issued by the governors. The tables are laid with bowls, bread-baskets, platters, &c. The official company then enter; the Lord Mayor takes the state chair at the end of the hall, a hymn is sung, accompanied by the organ in the gallery; a Grecian in the pulpit reads the evening service. After prayers the boys begin their meal, whilst the visitors walk up and down the alleys formed between the tables. When the meal is done the visitors return to their seats, the boys take up the baskets, bowls, bread-platters, and candlesticks, fold up the table-cloths, and then pass in regular procession before the Lord Mayor, bowing every two of them to his lordship, and then retiring in due order with their matrons until the whole eight hundred boys have performed this singular ceremony. There are several portraits of interest preserved in this Hospital, including those of the founder, Edward VI., of Charles II., James II., Queen Victoria, and the Prince Consort. The Edifice was almost entirely rebuilt in 1825–29, by J. Shaw. It is extremely probable that this great School, like that of the Charterhouse, will, before long, be removed to the country. Among the chief of the celebrated persons educated here may be mentioned the poet Samuel T. Coleridge, Charles Lamb, Leigh Hunt, in the present century; and, in former times, Camden, Stillingfleet, and Samuel Richardson, the novelist.

In *Christ Church*, adjoining the Hospital, are preached the Spital Sermons; and here was buried Samuel Baxter, the author of the 'Saints' Everlasting Rest.' *Warwick Lane* was named after Warwick, the great king-maker, whose house was in this locality, and of whom a *bas-relief* is still to be seen. Here was the *Old College of Physicians*, built by Sir Christopher Wren, after the Fire of

London, and pulled down in 1866, see p. 10. The old *Bell Inn* and the *Oxford Arms*, two noted hostels, were in this lane. In the Bell Inn died Archbishop Leighton, 1684, who is reported by Bishop Burnet to have often said, " that if he were to choose a place to die in, it should be an inn; it looked so like a pilgrim's going home, to whom this world was all a pilgrimage."

Upon the north side of Newgate Street we find *King Edward Street* (named after the founder of the neighbouring Blue-coat School), but formerly known as *Butcher Hall Lane*, and noted for its numerous butchers' shops. Like its neighbour, Butcher Hall Lane, *Newgate Market* is now a thing of the past; the carcases and the carcase-butchers have taken their departure hence to Smithfield Market, hard by, and Newgate Market, having been metamorphosed into comparative cleanliness, quiet, and decency, has taken the title of *Paternoster Square*.

LITTLE BRITAIN (named from the mansion of the Duke of Bretagne, *temp.* Edward II.), no longer known for its bookshops, but abandoned to city warehousemen, lies out of King Edward Street, from which there is a short cut into *Smithfield*. In *Bull-head Court* was a *bas-relief* of William Evans, a giant of 7 feet 6 inches, and Sir Geoffrey Hudson, King Charles's dwarf, of 3 feet 9 inches. Opposite is *Queen's Head Passage*, in which is a noted literary rendezvous, *Dolly's Chop-house*, wherein, over a pint of wine and a chop or steak, has been ratified many a publisher's bargain with his author. We next pass BATH STREET, the name of which still preserves the memory of the Turkish baths first introduced into London in the time of Charles II., and called Bagnios;—this thoroughfare was then called *Pincock* or *Pentecost Lane*, another of the religious names belonging to the locality.

At the north-east corner of Newgate Street is the new *Government Telegraph Offices*, connected with the General Post Office at St. Martin's-le-Grand (see p. 210); at the south-eastern end of Newgate Street, and at the point where a colossal *Statue of Sir Robert Peel* faces Cheapside, is a narrow opening to one of the best-known, but smallest streets in London, namely, *Paternoster Row*—long famous throughout the civilised world as the centre and fountain of English Literature. The names over the shops are all " familiar in our mouths as household words." Here are Bagster, and the Religious Tract Society, Blackwood, and Longmans, and Nelson, and Chambers, and Kent, and fifty more, and, when we get to *Stationers' Hall Court*, at the western end, we find the busily thronged warehouse of Simpkin and Marshall, supplying its clamorous customers under, as it were, the approving eye of *Stationers' Hall* itself (see p. 86), over the way.

The *Chapter Coffee-house*, at the corner of Chapter House Court, Paternoster Row, was long a famous resort for literary men, booksellers, publishers, &c., Oliver Goldsmith being of the company. No wonder that to such a place should come country parsons and others who visited London, for here they could listen to the latest news about books and newspapers, and could learn something of public opinion to carry home with them. The chiefs of the neighbouring publishing trade held their business meetings regularly in the long low dark room of the Chapter Coffee-house, and in the coffee-room met many of the popular critics of a hundred years ago. Chatterton boasted in his letters to Bristol, " I am quite familiar at the Chapter Coffee-house, and know the geniuses there." The house is now no longer a coffee-house but a tavern.

ST. MARTIN'S-LE-GRAND, CHEAPSIDE, CORN-HILL, ALDGATE, WHITECHAPEL, &c.

ST. MARTIN'S-LE-GRAND was anciently a Collegiate Church and Sanctuary within the walls of London, claiming to be a liberty of itself. Henry VII. having added his magnificent chapel to Westminster Abbey, bestowed the advowsons of this church upon the Abbey of Westminster, by way of providing for its support. Like all other sanctuaries, St. Martin's attracted the vicious and dissolute part of the population, and obtained through them an evil name. It was even reckoned one of the chances of escape by a criminal on his way to punishment, that he might be able to dash off from the constables in charge of him, and get into St. Martin's liberty, where they could not lay hold of him. The privilege of sanctuary at length became such a nuisance that it was abolished by James I.

The present *General Post Office* stands upon the site of the old church of St. Martin's. It was built by Sir R. Smirke, 1825-9. Here, and in the adjoining buildings but recently erected, is conducted under the Postmaster-General not merely the business of the *Letter*, *Newspaper*, and *Book* posts—all largely increased of late years—but that of the *Money Order*, *Savings Bank*, and *Postal Telegraph* systems. The reduction of the Postage to a uniform rate of a penny was made in 1840, after a long and persevering struggle by Sir Rowland Hill, in opposition to the Post Office authorities. Upon the Postal service, carried on at a cost of two millions per annum, a considerable profit accrues to the State. The hours at which letters are posted and received in the different parts of London and its suburbs may be seen on each pillar letter-box (coloured red), now very numerous in every district. Letters addressed Post-office, London, are to be inquired for at St. Martin's-le-Grand, from 10 A.M. to 4 P.M. A foreigner so applying must produce his passport, or send a letter with it, and a written order. Letters which lie unclaimed two months are sent to the *Dead Letter Office*, whither also unclaimed letters from country post-offices are sent after one month. The *General Telegraph Office* is opposite the General Post Office, at the corner of Newgate Street. When the Government bought, for seven millions in 1870, the electric telegraphs throughout the kingdom, it had to arrange for connecting them with the General Post Office, and these offices were built by J. Williams, and finally opened in 1873. The *Central Money Order Offices*, by means of which money may now be transmitted to the colonies and to France, are in the same building. See also Postage and Telegrams, p. 299.

Opposite to the west front of the General Post Office is the *Queen's Hotel*, once named the *Bull and Mouth*, and as such known far and wide at one time from being the starting-point for mail coaches. A device of the Bull and Mouth is still to be seen in front of this hotel, with the legend:—

"Milo the Crotonian an ox killed with his fist,
And eat him up at one meal, ye gods what a twist."

The name of Bull and Mouth has generally been derived from Boulogne Mouth, or the entrance to Boulogne Harbour. The old inn gave its name to Bull and Mouth Street close by.

In *Foster Lane*, at the back of the Post Office, is the *Hall of the Goldsmiths' Company*, built by P. Hardwick, R.A., in 1835, a handsome edifice containing portraits of

The Charterhouse. 211

Her Majesty and several of the royal family, also of Sir Hugh Myddelton, by Jansen, &c. The Goldsmiths' Company have the privilege of assaying and stamping with their Hall-mark all articles of gold, so as to indicate the proportion of gold and alloy in each, according to Goldsmiths' Hall standard. The *Church of St. Vedast*, in Foster Lane, was rebuilt by Sir Christopher Wren. Over the west door of this church may be seen a curious old allegorical bas-relief representing 'Religion and Charity.'

Beyond St. Martin's-le-Grand, a little west of Aldersgate Street, is Charterhouse Square, upon the north side of which is the CHARTERHOUSE, a Collegiate Asylum for the maintenance of 80 aged gentlemen; a School (removed to Godalming in 1872) for the young, and a Chapel, the whole occupying more than 13 acres of land, and founded upon the site of a monastery of Carthusians (an order instituted at Chartreux, in France) by Thomas Sutton, in 1611. The monastery was one of those dissolved by Henry VIII., who hung its last prior at Tyburn, for denying his supremacy, and set his head on London Bridge, and one of his limbs over his own monastery gate. Sutton, who was born of humble parentage, at Knayth, in Lincolnshire, 1532, amassed great wealth as head of the commissariat of the army in the North (which put down the Rebellion in 1573), and subsequently as chief victualler for the navy and commissioner of prizes. Being childless, he determined upon founding this hospital, and obtained a patent from King James I. for the purpose, but died 1611, before the completion of his work, which Stowe pronounced to be "the greatest gift in England, either in Protestant or Catholic times, ever bestowed by any individual." The buildings as they now stand, although considerably changed since Sutton's time, are highly interesting, particularly the *Hospital Chapel*—wherein lie buried

Thomas Sutton and many recipients of his bounty, who have been more or less famous; the *Master's Lodge*, where there is a gallery of portraits; and the *Old Court-room*, where, on December 12, the anniversary of the founder's death, used to be sung the old Carthusian song, with the chorus :—

> "Then blessed be the memory
> Of good old Thomas Sutton,
> Who gave us lodging, learning,
> As well as beef and mutton."

The scholars of the *Charterhouse School* have, as we have said, been removed to Godalming, but the School-house and buildings have nevertheless been rebuilt, and are now tenanted by the *School of Merchant Taylors' Company*. The eighty old brethren of the Charterhouse have, however, not been dispersed : they still "live together in collegiate style, provided with handsome apartments and all necessaries except apparel, in lieu of which they receive £14 a year and a gown each." Thackeray, who was a Carthusian scholar himself, has given in his picture of noble old Colonel Newcome, the *beau ideal* of a Brother of the Charterhouse. Never was written anything more pathetic than the Colonel's death in Grey Friars, as Thackeray called the Charterhouse : "At the usual evening hour the chapel bell began to toll, and Thomas Newcome's hands outside the bed feebly beat a time. And just as the last bell struck, a peculiar sweet smile shone over his face, and he lifted up his head a little, and quickly said '*Adsum*,' and fell back. It was the word he had used at school when names were called; and lo! he whose heart was as that of a little child had answered to his name, and stood in the presence of the Master." Besides the eighty old Brothers, the Charterhouse provides for sixty scholarships on the foundation of the School at Godalming, open by competitive examination to boys entering between twelve and sixteen. If the foundationer passes a satisfactory examination at the age of eighteen he is entitled to an Exhibition of £80 per annum for four years at Oxford or Cambridge. The Poor Brothers are admitted to the Charterhouse upon the presentation of a Governor—a list of governors may be had from the Registrar on the premises in Charterhouse Square. The income of the charity is £29,000 per annum. Admission is granted to visitors to the Great Hall any day but Sunday, except during the Poor Brothers' dinner-hour, which is from 3 to 4 o'clock. On Sunday, visitors may attend service in the Chapel at 11 and at 4 o'clock. Among the eminent men educated at Charterhouse School, may be named Addison, Blackstone, Steele, Ellenborough, Liverpool, Grote, Thirlwall, John Wesley, and Thackeray.

ALDERSGATE STREET leads into *Goswell* (God's Well) *Road*, and from the latter runs *Old Street*, "the oldest way in or about London, and probably older than London itself, forming the road from the eastern to the western counties." John Milton went to live in *Jewin Street*, off Aldersgate Street, 1661, and here he married his third wife. He was buried in *St. Giles's, Cripplegate*, close by. It is said that 'Paradise Lost' obtained no notice from the public until the Earl of Dorset (himself a poet) accidentally happened to take up the book at the publisher's shop. Lord Dorset carried the book home, and afterwards showed it to Dryden, who forthwith pronounced upon its author, "This man cuts us all out and the ancients too." *St. Giles's, Cripplegate*, is perhaps the most famous of the old London churches. In it Oliver Cromwell was married to Elizabeth Bourchier, August 20, 1620. Many an antiquarian pilgrim visits St. Giles's to see the bust of Speed, the historian, and the tomb of Foxe, the author of the 'Book of Martyrs.' *Sion College* in *London Wall* is an ancient institution for aged persons, and provides a handsome library for the city, of which all London clergymen are fellows *ex-officio*. Near *Fore Street* is *Milton Street* (not named from the poet, but from the man who rebuilt it), formerly *Grub Street*, the abode of poor authors, in regard to which Pope wrote that,

"Mighty Dulness crowned,
Shall take through Grub Street her triumphant round."

CHEAPSIDE, one of the chief streets of the City of London, extends from the east end of Newgate Street to the Poultry. In olden time the north side of this street was not built upon, and the land beyond it was the scene of festivities, tournaments, jousts—notably in Edward III.'s reign. *Cheapside Cross*, which stood at the end of *Wood Street*, was the next finest to Charing Cross of all the nine Crosses erected to the memory of Queen Eleanor. It was demolished, to the sound of trumpet, by order of the Puritan Parliament, in 1643. The *Standard*, in Cheapside, opposite *Honey Lane*, was the place of execution for criminals. From the *Standard*, in 1439, Eleanor Cobham, wife of Humphrey, Duke of Gloucester, walked barefoot to St. Paul's, with a white sheet over her and a taper in her hand, to do penance for the crime of witchcraft. The *Conduit* which brought fresh water from Tybourne to Cheapside terminated in a leaden cistern cased with stone; it was burned down in the Great Fire and never rebuilt. Cheapside has been more than once remarkable for the riots and tumultuous assemblages therein raised. Here Wat Tyler's mob beheaded many people, and Jack Cade shed the blood of Lord Saye and Sele; here began a great riot of apprentices, *temp.* Henry VI. and Henry VIII. Cheapside has also long been famous for its shops and merchandise—its most popular "linen-draper bold" being, perhaps, that "train-band Captain," John Gilpin, who ineffectually endeavoured to combine business with pleasure, and whose wife drove off with her relatives to keep the wedding day at Edmonton, "all in a chaise and pair," while "the stones did rattle underneath as if Cheapside were mad." Upon the right hand of a pedestrian walking eastwards is *Old Change*, so called, says Stowe, "of the King's Exchange there kept." *Gutter Lane* is said to be derived from Guthrum, an ancient Dane; the Hall of the *Saddlers' Company* presents itself prominently at 141 Cheapside. *Friday Street* traces its name to a Friday market of fishmongers held here; the name belonged to it, as it seems, before Chaucer's time. In *Wood Street*, which connects Cheapside with London Wall, stood a prison called *Wood Street Compter*, burnt down in the Great Fire. The *Haberdashers' Company's Hall* is to the west of Wood Street. At the corner of Wood Street is the tree referred to by Wordsworth in his verses on Poor Susan, who, far away from her native home, has been, by the song of the thrush in this tree, reminded suddenly of the country:—

> "'Tis a note of enchantment; what ails her? she sees
> A mountain ascending, a vision of trees;
> Bright volumes of vapour through Lothbury glide,
> And a river flows on through the vale of Cheapside."

In Wood Street is *St. Alban's Church*, rebuilt by Wren 1684–5, upon the site, it is said, of a chapel of King Offa. An hour-glass, such as were once common in churches to remind the preachers of the flight of time, is here to be seen fitted in brass to the pillar over the pulpit. *Milk Street* is famous as the birthplace of Sir Thomas More, "the brightest star," says Fuller, "that ever shone in that *Via lactea*." *The City of London School* in this street is but of recent foundation (1834). The boys are all day scholars, each nominated by a member of the Corporation of London, and paying £9 per annum. In *Monkwell Street is Barber-Surgeons' Hall*, famous for its Theatre of Anatomy, built by Inigo Jones; and for Holbein's picture of Henry VIII. conferring the Company's Charter.

BREAD STREET was the birthplace of John Milton, whose father was a scrivener in this street. The poet was baptized at the *Church of Allhallows*, which was demolished in

1877. At the side of this church, in Watling Street, was a tablet containing Dryden's lines, and a memorial as follows :—

> "Three poets in three distant ages born,
> Greece, Italy, and England did adorn;
> The first in loftiness of thought surpassed,
> The next in majesty—in both the last.
> The force of nature could no further go,
> To make a third she joined the former two.

" John Milton was born in Bread Street, on Friday, the 9th day of December, 1608, and was baptized in the Parish Church of Allhallows, Bread Street, on Tuesday, the 28th day of December, 1608."

The *Mermaid Tavern*, famous for the club to which Shakespeare, Ben Jonson, Sir Walter Raleigh, Beaumont, and other great men belonged, stood south of Cheapside, between Friday Street and Bread Street. Beaumont reminds Ben Jonson of these re-unions, in words which stir the pulses of readers in this generation, at thought of the conversation which passed between such men. How much the world must have lost from the want of a Boswell at the *Mermaid* meetings :—

> "What things have we seen
> Done at the *Mermaid!* heard words that have been
> So nimble and so full of subtle flame,
> As if that every one, from whence they came,
> Had meant to put his whole wit in a jest,
> And had resolved to live a fool the rest
> Of his dull life."

In Cheapside, upon the south side of the way, stands *Bow Church*, or *St. Mary-le-Bow*, otherwise St. Mary de Arcubus, from being built on stone arches, wherefrom was named The *Court of Arches*, formerly held here. Bow Church is memorable for ever for those bells which stirred Dick Whittington's poetic fancy so that he could realise their voices as calling upon him to

> "Turn again, Whittington, Lord Mayor of London."

Whittington did turn and return—he was so good at turning he should have been Master of the Turners' as well as of the Mercers' Company; and his cat afterwards turned so well out of the bag that it enabled himself to turn Lord Mayor no less than four times to the music of Bow Bells— no doubt adopting the principle of the old maxim, that one good turn deserves another. In Hogarth's last engraving of the set of 'Industry and Idleness,' we see the summit of civic ambition fully attained—Industry, in the person of the new Lord Mayor, enters Cheapside in grand procession, the streets lined with balconies filled with spectators, even Royalty (in Hogarth's picture represented by Prince Frederick, father of George III.) not disdaining to take part in the display. Bow Church was built by Sir Christopher Wren, after the Great Fire, upon the site of earlier edifices; its bells, originally eight, were increased to ten in 1762. In 1472 two tenements in Hosier (now Bow) Lane were bequeathed "to the maintenance of Bow Bell"—to be born within the sound of which was to be a veritable Cockney. Bow Bell would, we are told, be occasionally rather late in his performance, much to the annoyance of certain 'prentices, who wished to shut up shop as early as possible. Those young men are said to have vented their indignation in the threatening rhyme:—

"Clerke of the Bow bell with the yellow lockes.
For thy late ringing thy head shall have knocks."

To which the Clerk amiably replied, also in rhyme:—

"Children of Chepe hold you all still,
You shall have Bow bell rung at your will."

Bow Church is one of Wren's finest works. The spire was repaired and in part rebuilt by Gwilt in 1820, but was not lowered, as is generally believed. Its height is 225 feet, and the dragon 10 feet long. Over the large Palladian doorway in Cheapside is a balcony for sight-seers, in lieu of the old Sildam built for the same purpose. The Bishops elect of the Province of Canterbury attend at this Church before their consecration to take the oaths of supremacy, &c.

Down KING STREET, we pass to the GUILDHALL, which immediately faces us, and which dates from 1411. The crypt and the old walls alone remain of the ancient structure, which was much injured in the Great Fire. The present front was erected in 1865-8, when the fine Gothic roof was built. The Guildhall interior is 153 feet long, 50 feet broad, and 55 feet high, and the city giants Gog and Magog,* carved in 1708, are still to be seen here, as well as many statues, monuments, busts, and portraits of more modern personages, as Lord Chatham, William Pitt, Lord Nelson, Duke of Wellington, George III., Sir Matthew Hale, &c. At each end of the Hall is a Gothic window occupying the entire width, the arches resting on columns and retaining perfect their rich tracery. In the Guildhall—which will contain between 6000 and 7000 persons—have been held the *Lord Mayors' Banquets* since 1501; of late invariably attended by the Cabinet Ministers. The Guildhall has been the scene of many historical events. Here, in 1483, Richard III., through Buckingham, strove to persuade the citizens to accept his usurpation; here Anne Askew (subsequently burnt at Smithfield) was tried

* These figures take the place of much older ones made of wickerwork, which used to be carried about the streets in City pageants, "to make the people wonder," and were then returned to their places in Guildhall. "The young one is supposed to represent *Corineus*, a famous chieftain of the earliest traditional period, who ruled in Cornwall — the hugest giants in rocks and caves were said to lurk there." The older giant represents *Gogmagog*, in height 12 cubits, who broke three of Corineus's ribs in a wrestle, whereupon Corineus enraged, "heaving up by main force, bore the giant to the next high rock, threw him headlong into the sea, but he left his name on the cliff, called ever since Langoemagog, which is to say, the giant's leap." See *Milton's History*.

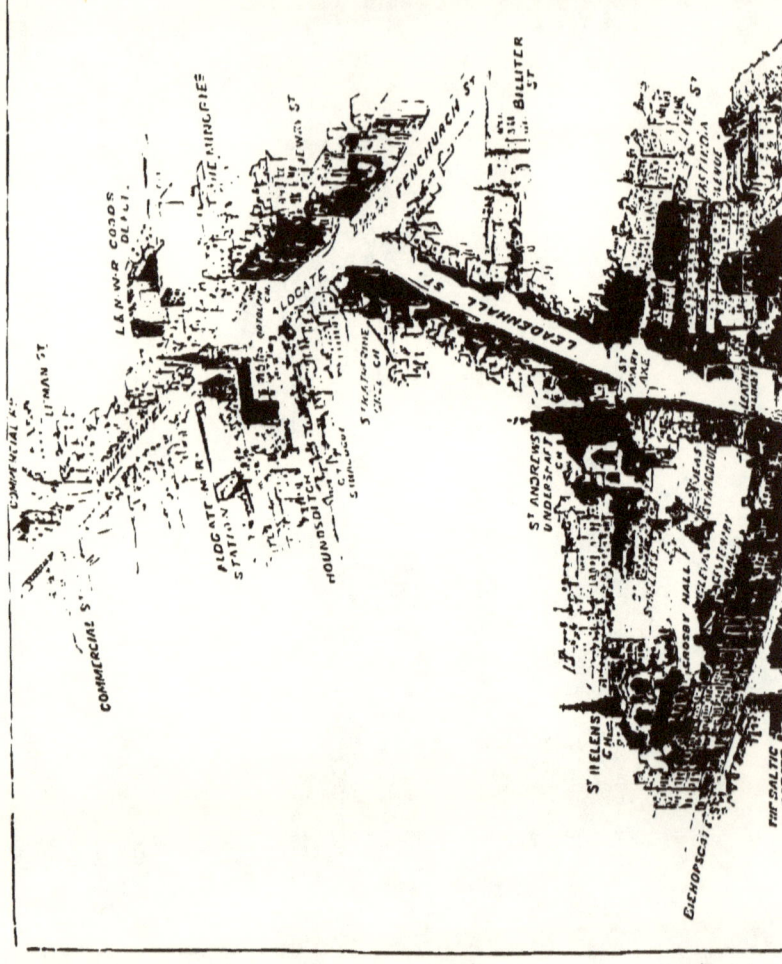

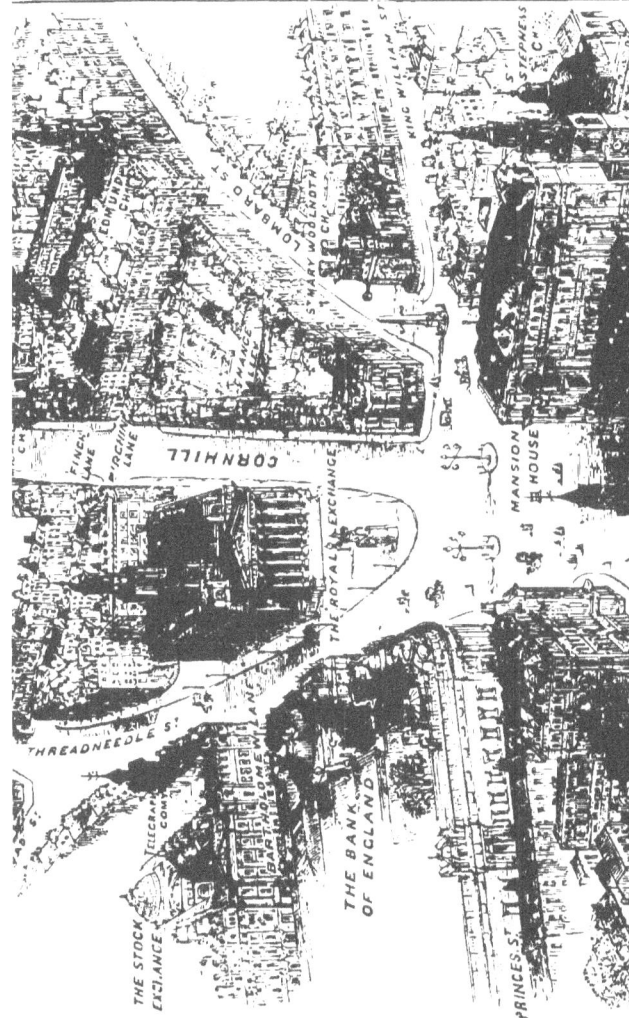

and condemned by Bishop Bonner for heresy; here the Earl of Surrey was tried and convicted of high treason, as were also, soon after, Lady Jane Grey and her husband. Here Sir Nicholas Throgmorton was tried and acquitted for his share of Sir Thomas Wyat's rebellion against Queen Mary; here the Jesuit Garnet was tried and convicted for participation in the Gunpowder Plot; here Charles I. attended a Common Council to ask assistance in apprehending Hampden and others, who had taken shelter from the Crown in the city to avoid arrest; here, after the Abdication of James II., the Lords of Parliament assembled, under the presidency of Sancroft, and declared for the Prince of Orange. The *Guildhall Library and Reading Room*, containing over 50,000 books, and many MSS., coins, medals, &c., is open daily, free to all comers, from ten to five. This very handsome and useful edifice was built in 1871-2, behind the Guildhall. The Courts of Law at Guildhall are not worthy of mention; they will soon be removed, it is hoped, to the new *Palace of Justice* in the Strand. Opposite the Cheapside end of King Street is *Queen Street*, leading to Southwark Bridge. *Mercers' Hall and Chapel*, belonging to the Mercers' Company, the oldest of the city guilds, is at 87 Cheapside, but the entrance to it is in Ironmonger Lane. Thomas à Becket was born in a house then standing on the site of Mercers' Hall. *Old Jewry* was named from the Jews dwelling there. They were first introduced by William Rufus, in whose reign, it is said, the parishes of St. Martin, St. Edward, and St. Aldgate were denominated the New and Old Jewry.

THE POULTRY.—The east end of Cheapside was so named from the poulterers' stalls of the *Stocks-market*. The *Poultry Compter* was at one time a prison of some note. Tom Hood was born in the Poultry (1798); his father was one of the firm of Vernor and Hood, publishers of Bloomfield's Poems, &c., at No. 31. Robert Bloomfield, son of a tailor at Honington, in Suffolk, was himself a shoemaker, and worked in a garret in Great Bell Alley, Coleman Street. He composed his 'Farmer's Boy' while at work, and when he obtained time and writing materials, "had nothing to do," as he said, "but to write it down." "There was a dash of ink in my blood," wrote Tom Hood. "My father wrote two novels, and my brother was decidedly of a literary turn." In the Poultry were many old taverns of some note. The *Hall of the Armourers' Company* is in *Coleman Street*. *Grocers' Hall*, next 35 in the Poultry, belongs to the *Grocers' Company* (originally Pepperers' and then united to the Apothecaries' Company), which is second on the list of the twelve great companies incorporated by Edward III. Grocers' Hall was used from 1694 to 1734 for the business of the Bank of England. At the end of the Poultry is the new street called *Queen Victoria Street*, leading from the Mansion House to Blackfriars Bridge.

BUCKLERSBURY, a short street, south of the Poultry, running into Walbrook, used to be noted for grocers and apothecaries' shops—referred to by Falstaff, who speaks of "many of those lisping hawthorn buds, that come like women in men's apparel, and smell like Bucklersbury in simple-time."

The MANSION HOUSE, the residence of the Lord Mayor during his year of office, was built 1739–41, by Dance, the then city surveyor, at a cost of over £70,000. The principal part of the building is the *Egyptian Hall* (named so after the Egyptian Hall described by Vitruvius with which it is said exactly to correspond), decorated with numerous statues by modern artists. The *City Police Court* is held in one of the rooms of the Mansion House, and here the Lord Mayor, or one of the Aldermen, sits daily. The *Lord Mayor's Show*, as it is called, is a procession which takes place every 9th of November (Lord Mayor's Day), when the new Lord Mayor succeeds to the dignity, and goes, attended by the Aldermen, Sheriffs and Common Councilmen, with bands of music and with banners flying of all the city guilds, to the Exchequer Court at Westminster to be sworn in. The official income of the Lord Mayor is £8000—considerably less than the sum which each Lord Mayor has to spend in order to maintain the credit of the Mansion House for hospitality.

St. Stephen's, Walbrook, at the back of the Mansion House, is considered to be one of the best works of Sir Christopher Wren, who rebuilt the edifice after the Great Fire. The interior has been specially admired for its well-proportioned cupola and roof, with a circle of light arches springing from column to column. "As you enter the dark vestibule a halo of dazzling light flashes upon the eye through the central aperture of the cupola." There is a fine painting here by West, of the Martyrdom of St. Stephen. Here lay buried, it is said, beneath the Church, when the repairs of 1850 took place, as many as 4000 coffins. John Lilburne and Sir John Vanbrugh have memorials here, where they were buried. Amongst the incumbents of St. Stephen's, were Pendleton, the celebrated Vicar of Bray, who stuck to his Vicarage through all the changes of the Revolution era, fitting himself to each fashion of theology as it arose, and who only gave up the Vicarage of Bray when he had been promoted to the Rectory of St. Stephen's, Walbrook.

Nearly opposite the Mansion House is the BANK OF ENGLAND, which occupies about three acres of ground, bounded by Prince's Street on the west, Bartholomew Lane on the east, Lothbury on the north, and Threadneedle Street (belonging to Merchant Tailors' Company), on the south, and was founded by Paterson in 1691 and incorporated by William III. 1694. The general architecture, chiefly by Sir John Soane, is Corinthian—"from the Temple of the Sybil at Tivoli," of which the south-west angle is a fac-simile. The entrance to the Bullion-yard is a copy of Constantine's Arch at Rome, and is decorated with allegorical figures of the Thames and the Ganges, by

T. Banks, R.A. The *Bullion-Office*, on the east side of the Bank, is inaccessible to visitors unless in the company of a Director of the Bank. The Directors, of whom there are twenty-four (eight of whom retire annually), have the management of the Bank, under the presidentship of a Governor and Deputy Governor—the qualification being for a Governor, £4000 Bank Stock; Deputy Governor, £3000; and Director, £2000; and these meet weekly, on Thursday, at half-past eleven, in the room called the Bank Parlour. Close by hangs a portrait of Abraham Newland, the noted chief-clerk whose signature to the Bank of England Notes gave rise to the lines in the old song :—

> "For the lawyers they say,
> Sham Abraham you may,
> But you must not sham Abraham Newland."

In the *Weighing Office* are the ingenious instruments invented by Mr. Cotton, a Deputy-governor of the Bank, which are so contrived that when one hundred sovereigns are placed in a round tube, as they descend on the machines the coins of a full weight are carefully separated into one box, while those of light weight are passed into another, where they are defaced at the rate of 60,000 or 70,000 a day. The *Bank-Note Machinery* invented by the Oldhams, father and son, is just as accurate and unerring in numbering and registering each note, so as to secure against fraud in every possible form. There are Bank notes in circulation to the value of eighteen millions sterling, but every note is cancelled immediately upon its being paid in. The Bank is the agent of the Government, on behalf of which it receives the taxes, pays the interest of the National Debt—about twenty-five millions in dividends to 284,000 holders of Stock, and, in return for work done, the Bank receives a percentage equivalent to about £120,000, with more than the same sum, usually, profit derived from the discounting of mercantile bills with the floating balance, never less than four millions sterling, of public money, left in the Bank. Since the riots of 1780, a military force has been stationed nightly within the Bank, and the officer on guard is provided with a dinner for himself and two friends. The accountant, secretary, and the cashier, reside on the premises; and, as well as the military guard, a certain number of clerks sit up nightly to watch and patrol the building. Visitors to the Bank are admitted to view the premises, on the introduction of one of the Directors, a list of whom is always readily obtainable.

St. Mary, Woolnoth, at the east corner of Lombard Street, was designed by Hawksmoor, assistant of Christopher Wren, and erected (1716) upon the site of a church of the same name—" the reason of which name," says Stowe, " I have not yet learnt." The church exterior has been much admired. There is a tablet here to the memory of Cowper's friend, the Rev. John Newton (rector of this church for 28 years, who died 1807), as follows:—" John Newton, clerk, once an infidel and libertine, a servant of slaves in Africa, was, by the rich mercy of our Lord and Saviour Jesus Christ, preserved, restored, pardoned, and appointed to preach the faith he had long laboured to destroy."

LOMBARD STREET, extending from the Mansion House to Gracechurch Street, has long been noted as the street for Bankers. It derived its name from the Longobards, a rich race of Bankers who settled here in the reign of Edward II., whose badge, the "three golden pills" of the Medici family, continues to be the sign of all pawnbrokers. Sir Thomas Gresham, who founded the Royal Exchange, kept a shop on the site of the bank, No. 68, in Lombard Street. Pope was born in Lombard Street, where his father, a Roman Catholic, was a linen-draper. The churches of *All Hallows* and *St. Edmund, Lombard Street*, were both built by Sir C. Wren. *Pope's Head Alley* derived its name from the *Pope's Head Tavern*, which existed here in Pepys' time.

The name was a reminiscence of the age when the Popish merchants sold wafer cakes and pardons here.

The ROYAL EXCHANGE, facing Cheapside and north-west of Cornhill, the third building of the kind upon this site, was built by Sir W. Tite, and opened 1844. It consists of an open quadrangle, with a statue of Queen Victoria in the centre, by Lough, surrounded by a colonnade, and having shops externally upon the ground-floor; upon the sides which face towards Cornhill, and Threadneedle Street; and at the rear of the building; in the upper floors are Lloyd's Subscription Rooms, or, more commonly, *Lloyd's*. The Exchange, a handsome edifice, is said to have cost £180,000. Its busiest time is from half-past three to half-past four, about which hour may be seen here the foremost Bankers in London—the Rothschilds, near to a pillar on the south side of the quadrangle. The first Exchange—Gresham's—was almost totally destroyed in the Great Fire of London; and the second Exchange was built upon the old foundations by Jerman, the City Surveyor, who, it is said, consulted Sir C. Wren in the projected rebuilding. This second edifice was opened in 1669, and was totally burnt down on the night of January 10, 1838. The fire—a memorable event—commenced in Lloyd's rooms soon after ten at night, and at three next morning the clock-tower alone remained unconsumed. It was remarked that the last air played by the chimes was 'There's nae luck aboot the house.' The west front of the present Exchange has a portico very superior, it has been said, to any in Great Britain. It is 96 feet wide and 74 feet high, and has eight columns, 4 feet 2 inches in diameter, and 41 feet high. On the frieze of the portico is an inscription to indicate that the Exchange, which was built in the thirteenth year of the reign of Elizabeth, was restored in the eighth year of Victoria. The tympanum of the pediment is filled with sculpture by Westmacott, consisting of seventeen figures, representing Commerce in the centre, holding the charter of the Exchange; on her right are the Lord Mayor and Aldermen and Common Councilmen, a Hindoo, a Mahommedan, a Greek bearing a jar, and a Turkish merchant; on the left are two British merchants and a Persian, a Chinese, a Levant sailor, a negro, a British sailor and a supercargo. Upon the pedestal of Commerce is, " The Earth is the Lord's and the fulness thereof."

Lloyd's Subscription Rooms were founded by Edward Lloyd, who kept a coffee-house in Tower Street, in the reign of Charles II., and who, noting the loss of time resulting from the underwriters being scattered over different parts of the city, brought them together first of all in the Tower ward; then (1692) at the corner of Lombard Street and Abchurch Lane, where he held periodical sales " by the candle," and started a weekly paper, ' Lloyd's News,' which was suppressed, upon the decision of the Judges that the liberty of printing did not extend to Gazettes. Lloyd's sales nevertheless increased, till, at the accession of George I., Lloyd's Coffee-house had become the centre of shipping business, including marine insurance. *Lloyd's List*, which continues to this day, was then first issued. The Underwriters who undertake insurances are about four hundred and fifty in number; it is said there is no one engaged in extensive shipping business who is not a member or a subscriber to Lloyd's. More than this, it may be asserted that there is not a port or maritime resort of any importance on the globe where Lloyd's is not in some form represented. Lloyd's classifies ships according to age, build, and sea-worthiness, and a ship can have no better reputation than to be A 1 at Lloyd's. The entrance to Lloyd's is in the area near the eastern gate of the Royal Exchange. Chantrey's equestrian Statue of the *Duke of Wellington* is in front of the Royal Exchange. The Statue of *Mr. Peabody*, an American merchant who lived in London, and gave half a million of money for dwellings for the industrious poor, is placed opposite the east end of the Royal Exchange.

The *Stock Exchange*, in Capel Court, Bartholomew Lane, facing the east end of the Bank of England, had its origin from Jonathan's Coffee-house in Change Alley, was opened in 1802, and in 1822 the business in the foreign funds was removed to it from the Royal Exchange. There are about 2000 members of the Stock Exchange, at an entrance fee of £100, annual subscription 20 guineas, unless they have served previously as clerks to members, in which case the entrance fee is £60, the annual subscription, 12 guineas. Members are either brokers or dealers; the former buy or sell for outside clients, the latter are the wholesale merchants. The dealer must "make a price," i.e. he is bound to state when asked by the broker the price at which he will sell or buy a given stock. Strangers who stray into the Stock Exchange are sometimes roughly hustled out. Among the Exchange cries are—" Borrow money?" "What are Exchequers?" "Five with me;" "Ten with me;" "A thousand consols at $96\frac{1}{2}$;" "Take 'em at $96\frac{1}{4}$;" "Egyptians" at so and so; "Turks" so and so, &c. The phrases *Bull* and *Bear* are among the slang of the Stock Exchange—a Bull means one who speculates for a rise; a Bear one who speculates for a fall of prices. If consols fall, the Bull finds himself on the wrong side of the hedge; if they rise, the poor Bear is compelled to buy back his stock at a sacrifice. "Consols" is the business name for Consolidated Government Stock.

CORNHILL, so called from a corn-market, "time out of mind there holden," extends from the eastern side of the Mansion House to Leadenhall Street. The noted "Standard at Cornhill" (still mentioned on suburban mile-stones as the point of measurement—so many miles from the Standard at Cornhill), stood at the east end of the street where it joins Gracechurch Street, Bishopsgate, and Leadenhall Street, and consisted of a sort of conduit with four spouts of water conveyed in lead pipes from the Thames, and chiefly used for cleansing the adjoining thoroughfares. At a corner house between Lombard Street and Cornhill lived Thomas Guy, the stationer, who founded Guy's Hospital; the poet Gray was born at a house upon the site of No. 41, and De Foe lived in a house which then stood nearly opposite to the Cornhill entrance to CHANGE ALLEY. Pope charged Curll with having gone to Change Alley and turned Jew for the sake of lucre; Gay wrote a remonstrance to his friend Snow—

> " Why did Change Alley waste thy precious hours,
> Among the fools who gaped for golden showers?"

St. Michael's and *St. Peter's Churches*, Cornhill, are two of the edifices rebuilt by Wren after the Great Fire. *St. Michael's Alley* is noted for having been the place wherein was set up the first coffee-house in London; in reference to which the elder D'Israeli mentions a hand-bill which he had discovered, setting forth " The Virtue of the Coffee Drink first publiquely made and sold in England by Pasqua Rosee, in St. Michael's Alley, Cornhill, at the sign of his own head." Hard by is *Lothbury*, out of which are *Founders' Court*, named from its brass founders, and *Tokenhouse Yard*, from the " Tokens," or copper coins made here in the seventeenth century. From *Old Broad Street*, running out of Threadneedle Street, we may turn into *Austin Friars*, the site of an old monastery of Augustine Friars, founded 1243; after the Dissolution the church was given by Edward VI. " to the Dutch in London to have their service in." The remains of a great number of eminent persons were buried here. The monastery was granted by Henry VIII. to the Marquis of Winchester, who built his mansion, *Winchester House*, where *Great Winchester Street* now stands.

Leadenhall Street was chiefly noted for the East India House, the Museum and Antiquities of which have been transferred to the South Kensington Museum; here is *Leadenhall Market*, famous for its poultry, game, bacon, leather, hides, &c. The house of *Dirty Dick* stood on the south side of Leadenhall Street. He is said to have been an ironmonger, young and handsome, who had made all preparations to be married; the wedding feast was ready laid, when news was brought of the sudden death of his bride. He thereupon locked up the rooms, and abandoned himself to neglect and dirt—all remained so for forty years, in darkness and accumulating dust. The old church of *St. Andrew Undershaft*, named from the Shaft or Maypole which stood before it, contains an interesting monument to John Stow, the city historian.

St. Catherine Cree, or *Christ Church*, is historically remarkable as having been consecrated by Laud with such ceremonies as laid him open to the charges upon which he was afterwards tried; as also for its rector, Nicholas Brady, the associate of Tate in the production of Tate and Brady's Psalms. Sir Nicholas Throgmorton (from whom *Throgmorton Street* was named) lies buried here (1570). The name of *Bevis Marks* is said to be a corruption of Burie's Marks, this being the site of a mansion belonging to the Abbots of Bury. *St. Mary Axe*, locally pronounced *Simmery Axe*, is named from the church of St. Mary at the Axe—of the sign of the Axe, which has been for some time removed. This being a quarter of the City where busy Jews used to be numerous, suggested the lines :—

"Jews from St. Mary Axe, for jobs so wary,
That for old clothes they'd even axe St. Mary."

ALDGATE, or Old Gate, so called from its antiquity, was the east gate of the City. The ancient *City Wall* began at a fort near the Tower of London, passed through the Minories* to Aldgate, thence bore to the north-east by *Bishopsgate* to *Cripplegate*, thence to *Aldersgate*, where it

* So named from a convent of nuns of St. Clare, called *Sorores Minores*, which stood here in the thirteenth century. There is a Catholic charity even now in London similarly named—the *Little Sisters of the Poor*.

curved south-west to *Newgate* and *Ludgate*. From Ludgate it skirted the Fleet brook to the Thames, where it was completed by another fort. The circuit of the whole line was a little over a mile. Along the banks of the Thames was another wall connecting the two forts, east and west. A "draft on *Aldgate Pump*" was, according to Fielding, a mercantile phrase for a bad note. In *Fenchurch Street* is the Hall of the *Ironmongers' Company*, as also the railway *Terminus* of the *Blackwall Railway*, by means of which railway communication with the districts lying upon the north bank of the Thames and the Essex coast is obtained.

Houndsditch and *Rag Fair*, in Rosemary Lane, Wellclose Square, Whitechapel, have long been noted for the sale of old linen and cast-off clothes; the latter is particularly worth seeing by any visitor who can keep his pockets buttoned and can walk on regardless of any invitation to stop and make purchases. *Whitechapel*, a long, spacious street, which used to be the high road to Essex, and contained a large number of Inns with old galleried yards, of which few relics still remain, is now of small interest to visitors. The *East London Theatre* is at 235 Whitechapel Road. *Petticoat Lane*, Whitechapel, long famous for its Sunday morning traffic, has been named *Middlesex Street*. The *London Hospital* in Whitechapel Road contains 790 beds, and its expenses are £44,000 per annum. It dates from 1740, and relies almost entirely upon voluntary contributions.

If, passing back through Leadenhall Street, we pursue our way down *Bishopsgate*, we shall see some interesting relics of old London. *Crosby Hall*, a fine example of 15th century architecture, was built by Sir John Crosby, an alderman and M.P. for London, in 1461. Here lodged Richard of Gloucester (afterwards Richard III.), and " drew the Court to him ;" here he schemed the deposition and death of his nephew, and here Lady Anne awaited his return from Henry VI.'s funeral, as described in Shakespeare's play of 'Richard III.' Sir Thomas More, it is said, wrote his Life of Richard III. while residing here. Crosby Palace was subsequently owned by Sir John Spencer, the wealthy lord mayor, whose daughter, married to the Earl of Northampton, was one of the greatest heiresses in the kingdom, and lived here in the most expensive style. The Countess of Pembroke, " Sidney's sister," resided here for some time. The Palace subsequently became a Presbyterian conventicle, then a warehouse, and at length has been converted into one of the restaurants of Messrs. Gordon, who have embellished it at great expense.

The *Church of Great St. Helen's*, Bishopsgate Street, is the remaining portion of the priory of the Nuns of St. Helen's, founded 1216. This church, famous for its numerous monuments, consists of two aisles separated by arches, with chapels attached on the south-east. Among the monuments may be named those of Sir John Spencer and his wife and daughter; Francis Bancroft, founder of the almshouses at Mile End; Sir Thomas Gresham, founder of the Royal Exchange; Sir Andrew Judde, founder of the Tunbridge Grammar School; Sir William Pickering, a favourite of Queen Bess; Alberico Gentili, the great jurist and author of 'De Jure Belli;' Sir John Crosby and his wife. In the Chapel of the Virgin is the tomb of John de Oteswich and Mary his wife, *temp.* Henry IV., founders of the lately demolished church of St. Martin's Outwich. In the Chapel of the Holy Ghost is the tomb of Sir Julius Cæsar, Chancellor of the Exchequer, &c., in 1606, sculptured by *Nicholas Stone*.

In St. Helen's Place is the *Hall of the Leathersellers' Company*; rebuilt 1815. The crypt of the old priory of St. Helen's extends beneath the Hall of the Company. In the Hall yard is Cibber's sculpture of a Mermaid as a design for a pump.

Spitalfields, Shoreditch, &c. 231

Towards Broad Street from this point stood *Gresham College*, founded in memory of Sir Thomas Gresham, as the condition of his gift to the City, of the Royal Exchange. The Gresham Lectures on Divinity, Civil Law, &c. (which are now delivered free to all comers at 6 P.M. in April, May, and June), gave rise to the *Royal Society*, whose first meetings were held here in Gresham College.

The *House of Sir Paul Pindar* is one of the most remarkable in Bishopsgate. Sir Paul frequently lent large sums of money to James I., Charles I., and Charles II. The last-named king seems to have exhausted Sir Paul's funds; but the great merchant had been able to give as much as £10,000 towards the rebuilding of St. Paul's after the Great Fire. Sir Paul was buried in *St. Botolph's*, hard by.

Beyond BISHOPSGATE WITHOUT is SPITALFIELDS, a district which once belonged to the priory of St. Mary Spital, 1197, and which, at the period of the Revocation of the Edict of Nantes, received many thousands of silk-weavers, who were then driven out of France; "whereby," says Stowe, "God's blessing is surely not only brought upon the parish, by receiving poor strangers, but also a great advantage hath accrued to the whole nation, by the rich manufactures of weaving silks and stuffs and camlet, which art they brought with them." Bethnal Green lies east of Spitalfields, see p. 272.

SHOREDITCH derives its name not from Jane Shore, as is generally alleged, but from Sir John Soerdich, lord of the manor, *temp.* Edward III. The church of *St. Leonard* was connected with the Holywell nunnery, the name of which still survives in *Holywell Lane* (one of the streets of Shoreditch), the site of the *Old Curtain Theatre*. The *National Standard Theatre* is at 204 High Street, Shoreditch. It was rebuilt in 1867. In a direct line with Shoreditch is the Kingsland Road, continued by Stoke Newington Road, see p. 291.

Hoxton is a populous suburb connected with Shoreditch by the New North Road and by railway from Moorgate Street. The *Britannia Theatre* (holds 3400) is in Hoxton.

FROM FINSBURY TO ISLINGTON AND HIGHGATE.

THE *Museum* of the London Missionary Society, in Bloomfield Street, Moorfields, is open from ten to three in winter, and to four in summer. *The London Institution*, in Finsbury Circus, Moorfields, established 1806, has a fine library of sixty thousand volumes. In FINSBURY (named after Sir John Fines, or Fiennes) are the *Barracks of the Hon. Artillery Company*—representatives of the old "Trained Bands" of London, so prominent in the Parliamentary Army during the Civil Wars. Near to these barracks is the noted burial-place of the Nonconformists, named *Bunhill* (Bone-hill) *Fields*, open daily from nine to seven in summer, and till four in winter, and on Sundays after one o'clock. Here lie the remains of *John Bunyan*, for ever celebrated as the author of 'The Pilgrim's Progress.' "The spot where Bunyan lies," wrote Macaulay, "is regarded by Nonconformists with a feeling which seems scarcely in harmony with the stern spirit of their theology. Many Puritans, to whom the respect paid by Roman Catholics to the reliques and tombs of their saints seemed childish and sinful, are said to have begged with their dying breath that their coffins might be placed as near as possible to the coffin of the author of 'The Pilgrim's Progress.' John Bunyan's grave is almost in the centre of the burial-ground—a white marble figure upon a high tomb. "There were many clever men in England during the latter half of the seventeenth century, but only two great creative minds. One of these produced the 'Paradise Lost,' the other 'The Pilgrim's Progress.'" Near to Bunyan lie three members of the *Cromwell* family, and just beyond is buried the *Mother of John and Charles Wesley*—Susannah, daughter of an ejected vicar of St. Giles's, Cripplegate, and widow of a clergyman. Her last request was, "Children, as soon as I am released, sing a psalm of praise to God." Many hundreds of celebrated Nonconformist divines lie in this ground, now no longer used for burial, but serving as a quiet wayside place for meditation, out of the noise and bustle of the great metropolis. We may mention the following as among the chief of those who here "rest in hope": *Daniel de Foe*, son of a butcher in Cripplegate, one of the ablest of English writers, renowned for his 'Robinson Crusoe;' *Dr. Isaac Watts*, the author of so many well-known psalms and hymns; *Dr. John Owen*, "the great Dissenter," who was Dean of Christchurch, and Vice-Chancellor of Oxford, in Cromwell's time; *Dr. Daniel Williams*, founder of the Williams' Library, 1716; *Daniel Neal*, author of 'The History of the Puritans;' *Dr. J. Conder*; *Dr. N. Lardner*, author of 'Credibility of Gospel History'; *Joseph Hughes*, founder of the Bible Society; *Abraham Rees*, Editor of 'Rees's Cyclopædia;' *William Blake*, the painter; *Ritson*, the antiquary, and *John Horne Tooke*, the reformer. Near to Bunhill Fields is the *Friends' Burial-ground*, where lies *George Fox*, founder of the society called Quakers. Opposite the entrance to Bunhill Fields, in the City Road, is a Wesleyan Chapel, wherein is a tablet to the memory of the Rev. *Samuel Wesley*, and behind the chapel is the grave of *John Wesley*, the founder of Methodism.

Farther north up the City Road is the *Eagle*, or *Royal Grecian Theatre*, which originated from some tea-garden entertainments. The *Eagle* was built by Mr. T. Rouse, and derived its early popularity from allowing the audience to indulge in their favourite beverages whilst the performances were going on. Mr. Conquest considerably enlarged and improved upon the edifice of his predecessor.

At the top of the City Road is the *Angel Inn*, at Islington, and beyond it *Pentonville* and the *New Road*, which joins the *Euston Road* at *King's Cross*, and thus becomes one of the chief London thoroughfares.

ISLINGTON, one of the ancient village suburbs of London, was at one time as famous for its dairies and cheese-cakes as Chelsea was for buns. The *Angel Inn* and the *Peacock Inn*, at Islington, were noted houses of call for the old mail coaches travelling the Great North Road. These inns still remain, but they have altered their appearance and character, and, instead of low, old-fashioned wainscoted parlours, filled with country guests and northern graziers, we have the usual characteristics of a London tavern—plate-glass, and spacious bars with the smart fittings of a gin-palace, and customers to match. The last fashion is all in favour of what is called "counter business;" the inn is no longer an inn, but a dram-shop; the licensed victualler of to-day sells drink rather than victuals; and, in modern coffee-rooms, scarcely a cup of coffee is served from year's end to year's end; tavern coffee-rooms are indeed becoming out of date; the publican hastes to grow rich whilst providing a minimum of accommodation with a maximum of drink. The *Belvidere Tavern*, on *Pentonville Hill* (named after Mr. Penton, who built upon it), hard by, was for many years famous for its Debating Society, wherein many a prominent counsel and statesman won his early triumphs; but the politician, like the traveller, has had to make way for the dram-drinker, and here also the tavern has been displaced by the gin-palace.

The *Philharmonic Theatre*, in the *Islington High Street*, is a comparatively recent institution, grown out of a music hall. Farther up the High Street, upon the left-hand side going north, is the *Agricultural Hall*, an enormous structure covering three acres, built by Peck, in 1861, and having a main hall of 384 feet by 217 feet, roofed with glass. Herein are held many public meetings—

the chief exhibition being the *Annual Christmas Cattle Show*, and in the summer the *Horse Show*. The old *Church of St. Mary, Islington*, is just beyond Islington Green. The Statue of *Sir Hugh Myddelton* (the great benefactor by means of whom the New River was made, and a large part of the metropolis was, and is supplied, with its purest water) stands at the southern entrance to Islington Green. The *New River* property is now estimated to be worth over eleven millions sterling; its shares readily sell from three hundred to four hundred per cent. over their nominal value. It is indeed a rare thing to hear of more than a small fraction of a share being in the market.

Sadler's Wells Theatre, said to be the oldest theatre at present in London, is situate near the upper part of St. John Street Road, which leads to Islington from Smithfield. The *Favourite* omnibuses pass the gate. The name of the theatre was derived from Sadler, who kept a music-house here, in the time of Charles II., and who re-discovered in the garden a well of excellent tonic water, which years previously had been dispensed with much solemnity by the monks of the Priory of St. John of Jerusalem. For a time, Sadler's entertainment and the medicinal spring became highly fashionable and successful; but, in 1764, the well was covered over, the house demolished, and the present theatre was built by Rosoman—whose name still exists in *Rosoman Street*, Clerkenwell. The most prominent of its subsequent proprietors were King of Drury Lane, Charles Dibdin and his sons Thomas and Charles, then Messrs. Phelps and Greenwood, who for some years maintained it in the honourable position of home for the legitimate drama. Amongst the performers who appeared here may be mentioned, Belzoni the traveller, before his wanderings in the East, and the Grimaldis of three generations, after whom the neighbouring tavern, the *Clown*, was named. Amongst the *corps dramatique* under Mr. Phelps, were Mrs. Warner, Miss Glyn,

Miss Cooper, Mrs. Charles Young, and Messrs. Henry Marston, G. Barrett, L. Ball, J. W. Ray, and W. Belford.

The *Upper Street*, Islington, leads to *Highbury* and *Hornsey*; from the former runs a road to *Holloway* and *Highgate*, and easterly towards *Canonbury* and the City. *Pentonville Prison* is at Holloway.

CANONBURY TOWER was built on the site of the country retreat of the Prior of the Canons of St. Bartholomew, Smithfield. It is of red brick, seventeen feet square and nearly sixty feet high, contains twenty-three rooms, and dates from the latter part of the sixteenth century. It has a literary interest of considerable extent. In it lived Ephraim Chambers (the compiler of the first English Encyclopædia, and the predecessor of Rees), who died here in 1740. Newbery, the bookseller of St. Paul's Churchyard, had rooms in this tower, in which Oliver Goldsmith took refuge from his creditors, and it was here, under the pressure of pecuniary difficulty, Goldsmith wrote 'The Vicar of Wakefield.' *Canonbury Tea Gardens*, a favourite resort some seventy or eighty years ago, occupied the site of the old priory mansion and grounds—now built over and known as *Canonbury Place*, &c. Goldsmith, in his 'Elegy on the Death of a Mad Dog,' lays the scene in Islington:

> "In Islington there was a man,
> Of whom the world might say,
> That still a godly race he ran,
> Whene'er he went to pray."

On HIGHGATE HILL are the Almshouses of Sir Richard Whittington, who is said from this distance to have heard Bow Bells telling him to return to London. *Highgate* is also noted for its beautiful Cemetery. To be "sworn in at Highgate" was an ancient custom; the vow being, "Never to drink small beer, when you can get ale; never to walk when you can ride; never to kiss the maid when you can kiss the mistress, unless you like her, or either of the commoner articles, better."

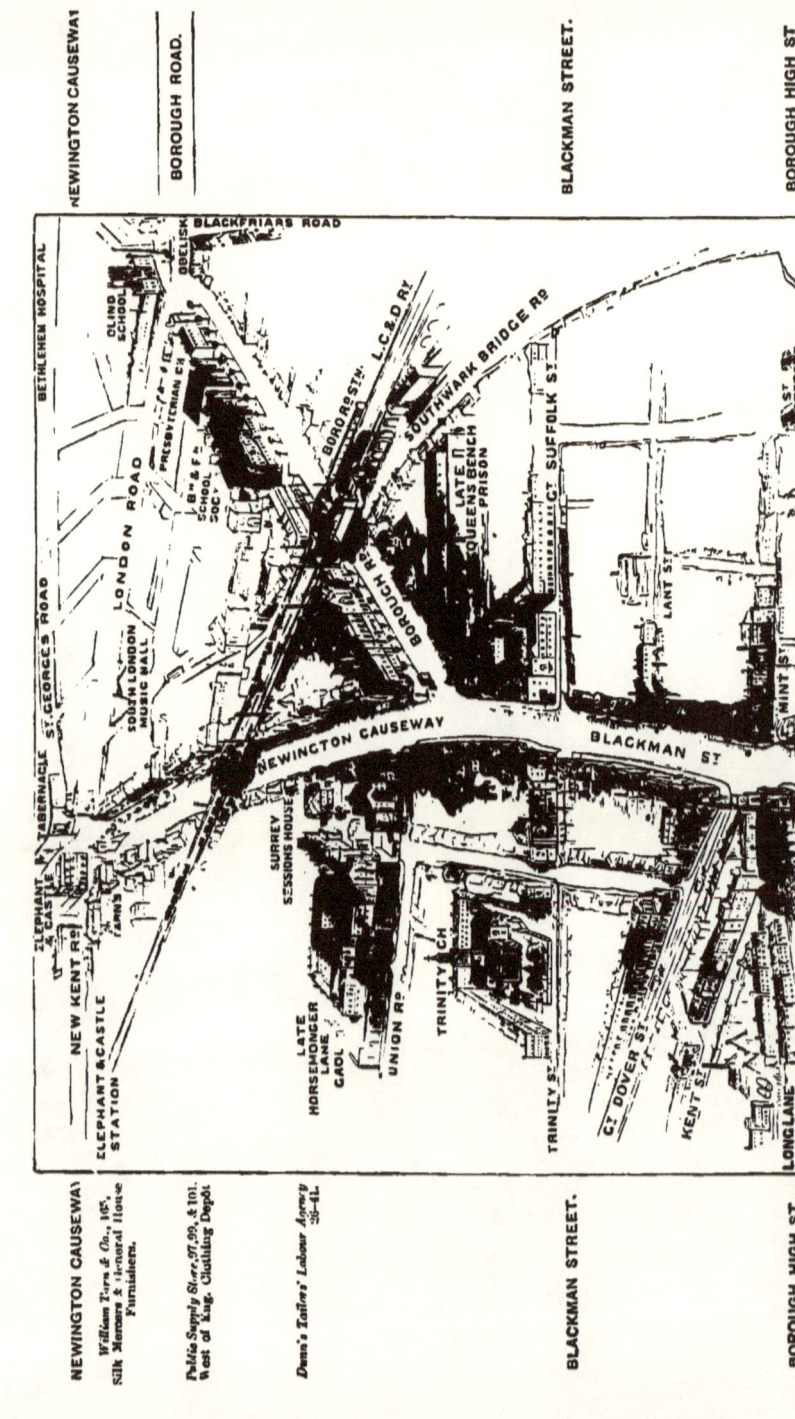

SOUTHWARK STREET

LONDON BRIDGE.

DUKE STREET.
Benjamin Edgington, 2,
Flag & Rickcloth Maker.

LONDON BRIDGE.

FROM LONDON BRIDGE THROUGH THE BOROUGH, TO NEWINGTON BUTTS AND ST. GEORGE'S FIELDS.

LONDON BRIDGE, SOUTHWARK, NEWINGTON, ELEPHANT AND CASTLE, ST. GEORGE'S CIRCUS, AND KENNINGTON.

THE MONUMENT, on Fish Street Hill, the work of Sir Christopher Wren, was erected on the site of St. Margaret's Church, to commemorate the Great Fire of London in 1666, which commenced at the house of a baker named Farryner, in *Pudding Lane*, hard by, and extended to *Pye Corner*, near Smithfield. The Monument is of Portland stone, 202 feet high, and has a pedestal of about 21 feet square. On the *abacus* is a balcony, surrounding a moulded cylinder of gilt bronze, made to resemble flame. From the top of the Monument, reached by a staircase inside, consisting of 345 steps, is to be had a fine view of the great metropolis. The charge for admittance, 3d., is made for each visitor—entrance from 9 A.M. till dusk. The bas-relief on the pediment was by C. G. Cibber, father of Colley Cibber; the four dragons by E. Pierce. The Latin inscriptions record the destruction of London by fire, and how it was rebuilt and improved. There used also to be inscribed upon the pediment the statement that the fire of London had been caused by a conspiracy of Papists, " in order to the carrying out of their horrid plot for extirpating the Protestant religion." This allegation has never been substantiated. It was based upon the fact that a young man of weak intellect, named Hubert, a French Papist, accused himself of having begun the fire, " suborned at Paris to do this action," and he was hanged for it, but Clarendon states that " neither the judges nor any present at the trial did believe him guilty, but that he was a poor distracted wretch weary of his life, and chose to part with it in this way." Pope, in reference to the charge against the Papists in the above inscription, wrote—

> "Where London's column pointing to the skies,
> Like a tall bully, lifts its head and lies."

It has often, as a matter of course, been remarked that if the Fire of London had occurred but a few years before, the Great Plague would never have visited the city; and that had not the Fire cleared away the close alleys and courts of Old London, and prepared the way for the rebuilding of the city upon a better and healthier plan, the Great Plague would probably have repeated its visitation. The extent of the calamity by the Fire may be estimated by the fact that there were consumed in it eighty-nine churches, four city gates, the Guildhall (all but the walls), and other public edifices; 13,200 houses, and 460 streets, and property in all worth nearly ten millions sterling, but only six lives were said to have been lost, one of these being that of a watchmaker, who could not be induced to leave his house and property, and who was burnt amidst the ruins. It is upon record that within a few days after the Great Fire, two separate plans, by Sir C. Wren and J. Evelyn, for the complete rebuilding of the city, were submitted to the King. The city merchants carried on their business abroad, as if no such disaster had happened, and within four years a city of brick was reared upon the site of the old wooden houses.

Fishmongers' Hall, on the north-west of London Bridge, belongs to the Ancient Company of Fishmongers, formed by the junction of the Stock and Salt Fishmongers' Company, and incorporated, 1536, by Henry VIII. Long before that time the Fishmongers were historically and socially important. Sir William Walworth, who slew Wat Tyler in Richard II.'s reign, was a Fishmonger, and Sir William's dagger is still preserved here (with other of his relics) and is to be seen in the hand of a statue of the knight which stands at the head of the grand staircase. Beneath the statue are the lines :—

> " Brave Walworth, knight, lord mayor that slew
> Rebellious Tyler in his alarmes,
> The king, therefore did give in lieu
> The dagger to the city armes.
> In the fourth year of Richard II. anno Domini 1381."

This verse was written in error, and it has given rise to a general and erroneous belief. The dagger in the City Arms was there long before Walworth's time ; it represents the sword of St. Paul, the patron saint of the Corporation of London. The following, culled from an early writer, seems to suggest that Walworth may have entertained a personal grudge against Wat Tyler, who certainly had just cause for complaint, and appeared at Smithfield quite disposed to submit to the King, when Walworth's dagger cut short the life of the poor blacksmith, who led the insurrection against serfdom, and an unjust poll-tax : " The Bordello, or stew-houses, on Bankside, were dwellings licensed by the Bishop of Winchester for the repair of incontinent men and women. In the fourth of Richard II. these stew-houses, then belonging to Sir William Walworth, Mayor of London, were farmed by Froes of Flanders, and were spoiled by Wat Tyler and other rebels of Kent, who expressed their longing for a right rule, for plain and simple justice ; their scorn of the immorality of the nobles and the infamy of the court." Did the blacksmith suffer at the hand of Walworth, because of his having destroyed what was certainly a source of some revenue to the knightly Fishmonger ? *Fishmongers' Hall* is the third of that name built on this site, and dates from 1830–33. It was erected by Roberts, and has a fine banqueting-hall, 73 feet long by 38 feet wide, and 33 feet high, with a music-gallery, upon the front of which are emblazoned the arms of the twelve Great City Companies.

The Borough of Southwark.

The City Companies number altogether eighty-two, of which forty are without halls of their own. The twelve Great Companies take precedence as follows :—

1. *The Mercers' Company*, Hall, 87 Cheapside.
2. *The Grocers' Company*, Hall, Poultry.
3. *The Drapers' Company*, Hall, Throgmorton Street.
4. *Fishmongers' Company*, Hall, London Bridge.
5. *Goldsmiths' Company*, Hall, Foster Lane, Cheapside.
6. *Skinners' Company*, Hall, Dowgate Hill.
7. *Merchant Tailor's Company*, Hall, Threadneedle Street.
8. *Haberdashers' Company*, Hall, 8 Gresham Street West.
9. *Salters' Company*, Hall, St. Swithin's Lane.
10. *Ironmongers' Company*, Hall, Fenchurch Street.
11. *Vintners' Company*, Hall, Upper Thames Street.
12. *Clothworkers' Company*, Hall, Mincing Lane.

Having traversed London Bridge (for particulars of which see p. 260), we enter the *Borough of Southwark*, generally spoken of as The Borough. The district which lies upon the right or west of the pedestrian is called *Bankside* (see p. 259). The *Clink* on *Bankside* still belongs to the Bishop of Winchester. At the south-eastern foot of London Bridge is *Tooley Street*, a name derived, or rather corrupted, from *St. Olave*, the neighbouring parish church. "The three tailors of Tooley Street," who began their political appeal with, "We the people of England," are now proverbially celebrated. Tooley Street was the scene, a few years ago, of an immense conflagration of storehouses, which lasted some days. Farther east lies *Bermondsey*, or Bermond's Eye, the seat of an ancient priory; but the district is now chiefly known for its trade and manufacture of leather. *Horselydown*, an ancient grazing ground for horses, lies beyond. Just at the top of Tooley Street is the entrance to the *London Bridge Railway Station* of

St. Saviour's, Southwark.

the London and Brighton, and South-Eastern Railways—the line of the latter crosses the top of the High Street. *Bridge House* is a relic of an ancient foundation to serve as a storehouse of grain, and for materials for keeping London Bridge in repair. The Bridge-masters are appointed by the City. There is a large *Railway Hotel* at London Bridge Station.

The Church of *St. Mary Overy*, or *St. Saviour's, Southwark*, is only second in interest to Westminster Abbey itself. It dates from before the Conquest, and was a religious house for women, having for revenue the profits from the Ferry which was here established previous to the building of London Bridge—St. Mary Overy meaning St. Mary's over the river. It subsequently became a priory. The church was rebuilt about 1400; and *John Gower*, the poet, who died in 1402, and was buried here (see a fine tomb and figure of the poet in the south transept), aided it with benefactions. In 1539, at the Dissolution, the priory was surrendered to Henry VIII., and the priory church was then made a parish church, under the name of *St. Saviour's*, and a chapel was added to it. It subsequently passed through many vicissitudes. In Stowe's time the Lady Chapel was converted into a bake-house; but it remained to the present century (1840) to destroy the ancient Nave and to spoil the most magnificent Early English Church on this side of the Thames. The chief parts remaining are the Choir, Transepts, and Lady Chapel, and there is a fine altar-screen erected by Fox, bishop of Winchester, who died in 1528. St. Saviour's Church was the scene, during the reign of Mary, of the Trial of Heretics by Bishop Gardiner. In it are now to be found, besides the Gower monument above named, memorials of *Bishop Lancelot Andrews; John Bingham*, saddler to Queen Elizabeth; *John Trehearne*, porter to James I.; and *Lockyer*, the quack pill-maker of Charles II.'s reign. Among the burials in this church may be named that of *Edmund Shakespeare*,

1607 (youngest brother of the poet); *John Fletcher*, 1625, of the literary partnership of Beaumont and Fletcher; *Philip Henslow*, 1615; and *Philip Massinger*, buried in the churchyard, 1638–9.

The Borough Market, adjacent to this church, is chiefly noted for its vegetable and fruit supply. On the opposite or east side of the Borough High Street is *St. Thomas's Street*, named from St. Thomas's Hospital, which once stood here, but is now removed to Lambeth (see p. 47).

Guy's Hospital, in St. Thomas's Street, was founded, 1721, by Thomas Guy, son of a lighterman at Horselydown, who became a bookseller in Lombard Street, and there made a large fortune by printing and selling Bibles, and by speculation in the South Sea Company. Guy gave a considerable sum to St. Thomas's Hospital, and eventually bought (at a rent of £30 a year) of the Governors of that Hospital a lease for 999 years of the land upon which he built Guy's Hospital, at a cost of nearly £20,000; and at his death he bequeathed to it £210,499. Guy's Hospital was endowed subsequently by Mr. Hunt of Petersham with nearly £200,000. Its income is £40,000 per annum, its beds 1,000. This is one of the largest of the London Medical Schools; its students number 350. A Statue of *Thomas Guy* by Scheemakers stands in the front court upon a pedestal bearing bas-reliefs, 'Christ Healing the Sick' and the 'Good Samaritan.' In the chapel is another statue of Guy, in marble, by Bacon the sculptor, who also produced the other statues in the front of the building. Sir Astley Cooper was buried in the Hospital chapel. At Guy's Hospital accidents and urgent cases are admitted at all hours; ordinary cases on Wednesdays, from 10 to 12 o'clock. Sickness and poverty combined require here no ticket of admission, they are admitted at once.

Returning to the High Street, and proceeding south, we shall find relics of some old hostelries. "In the Borough," wrote Dickens forty years ago, but he could not have said so now, for the tide of renovation and alteration has since swept away many of the antique structures of this quarter —" in the Borough there still remain some half dozen old inns which have preserved their external features unchanged. Great rambling queer old places, with galleries and passages and staircases wide enough and antiquated enough to furnish materials for a hundred ghost stories." It was in the yard of the *White Hart Inn* in the Borough that Sam Weller was first discovered by the world, officiating as Boots, "habited in a coarse striped waistcoat with black calico sleeves and blue glass buttons, drab breeches and leggings, a bright red neckerchief, and an old white hat carelessly thrown on one side of his head." But the glory of Southwark was the old *Tabard Inn*, which Chaucer immortalised as the *rendezvous* of his Canterbury Pilgrims on their way to the shrine of Thomas à Becket. Little more than a shadow now remains of

> "This gentil hostelrie
> That hight the Tabarde, fasté by the Bell."

The pilgrims described by Chaucer were representatives of every class of English society, from the noble to the ploughman. We see in the 'Canterbury Tales,' says Mr. Green, the "verray perfight gentil knight" in cassock and coat of mail with his curly-headed squire beside him; behind them the yeoman in green coat and hood carrying a yew-bow. Next a brawny monk, followed by a friar, first of wayside beggars; then the parson, poor, learned, and pious; then the summoner with fiery face, then the pardoner, with pardons hot from Rome; the prioress, with dainty face and manners acquired in courtly France; then the doctor and the serjeant-at-law, both busy men; then the learned, hollow-cheeked clerk of Oxford; the merchant venturer; the franklin well to do, in whose house it snowed of meat and drink; the sailor fresh from sea, the buxom wife of Bath, the burly miller, the haberdasher, carpenter, weaver, dyer, tapestry maker, each in the garb of his calling; and last, the simple ploughman. Each and all are living, breathing men and women, whose characters are distinctly marked and maintained throughout the stories with unmistakable individuality, both of sentiment and expression.

A few doors short of the church of *St. George* (wherein lies *Cocker*, the noted arithmetician), on the left-hand side of the way, going southwards, stood the *Marshalsea Prison*. " It is gone now, and the world is none the worse for it. It was an oblong pile of barrack buildings partitioned into squalid houses, standing back to back, so that there were no back rooms, and used as a prison for debtors and for defaulters under the Excise laws. In the adjoining skittle-ground the Marshalsea debtors bowled down their troubles." *Mint Street* was named from a *Mint* founded here in the reign of Henry VIII. on the site of a mansion of the Duke of Suffolk. In *Lant Street* lodged Mr. Bob Sawyer and Mr. Ben Allen, of Pickwick fame; the Crown revenues, Dickens said, were "seldom collected in this happy valley; the rents are dubious, and the water communication is frequently cut off." These were probably relics of the old privilege from arrest claimed by this ancient parish. The *Winchester Music Hall* is at the corner of Great Suffolk Street. At the south-east corner of *Blackman Street*, in *Horsemonger Lane*, stood the *Surrey County Gaol*, removed in 1879, and at the south-west corner was the *Queen's Bench Prison* for debtors, &c., abolished as such in 1860, now used by the Convict Department. It was at the execution of the Mannings, in front of *Horsemonger Lane Gaol*, that Dickens saw the hideous scene of riot which he depicted next day in a letter to the *Times*, and which led to the abolition of public hanging. We are now arrived at *St. George's Fields*, anciently a marshy tract, which extends to the boundary of Lambeth. At *St. George's Circus* is an *Obelisk* erected, 1771, which forms the centre of six roads, namely the *Borough Road* from London Bridge, the *Blackfriars Bridge Road*, the *Waterloo Road* leading to the Strand, the *Westminster Bridge Road*, and *Lambeth Road*. At the corner of London Road is the *School for the Indigent Blind*, established, 1799. The Blind are admitted (by election) between 10 and 20 years of age, for about six years, and are taught a trade, or music. There is also here a workshop for Adult Blind. At 92 London Road is the *South London Music Hall*.

BETHLEHEM or BETHLEM HOSPITAL, vulgarly Bedlam, at the corner of Lambeth Road, Southwark, derives its name from a priory of canons belonging to the Order of the Star of Bethlem, established in a monastery near Bethlehem, and having especial care for the sick and the insane—the badge of the order being a star, worn upon their mantles. This Hospital was founded at the Dissolution by Henry VIII., upon the endowments of a priory established by Simon Fitz-Mary, a Sheriff of London in 1246, who gave to it all his land in Bishopsgate Without, and there built the first Bethlem Hospital, in Liverpool Street. It was removed to Moorfields in 1675, and again removed in 1814 to the present site, in St. George's Fields, Southwark. Its cupola, resembling that of St. Paul's, was added by Smirke. In the entrance are Caius Cibber's two statues, restored by Bacon in 1814. Bethlem Hospital accommodates about 400 patients of both sexes, and receives *gratis* any poor lunatics likely to be cured within one year, and who are not fit subjects for a county lunatic asylum. Preference is given to patients of the educated classes, and all are treated with the greatest kindness and consideration. Instead of the ancient methods of chaining up lunatics in solitary cells, and letting in sight-seers to stare at them like so many wild animals in a cage, modern Bedlam treats its patients like ladies and gentlemen, and, while keeping them from harming themselves, provides them with various means of amusement; the women are provided with pianos, needle-work, embroidery, knitting; the men with bagatelle and billiard tables, newspapers, and periodicals; and the improved system produces good results. In the course of last year 225 patients were discharged as benefited and 113 as actually cured. Information as to this Hospital may be readily obtained upon application being made by letter to the Hospital Physician, or personally to the Steward, at the office in St. George's Road, Southwark. The last year's income of Bethlem Hospital was over £25,000.

St. George's Roman Catholic Cathedral is opposite Bethlem, at the corner of *St. George's Road*. It was built by Mr. A. W. Pugin, in 1848.

The *Surrey Theatre* stands at the end of *Great Surrey Street*, which is a continuation of Blackfriars Road, near the *Obelisk*, where five roads meet. The original theatre was built (1782) for C. Hughes and C. Dibdin, the well-known naval song-writer, and was first used for equestrian performances, and named the Royal Circus. It was burnt down and rebuilt in 1806. Elliston and Tom Dibdin were among its early lessees. Mr. J. B. Buckstone first appeared in London at this house in 1823. The Surrey Theatre, whilst under the direction of Messrs. Shepherd and Creswick, vied with Sadler's Wells, in its preference for the legitimate drama.

The *Surrey Gardens*, near Kennington Park Road, once so popular and famous for its Zoological Collection, for the Jullien Monstre Concerts, &c., were abandoned some time since to the suburban builder, who always seems to be the final annexer and holder of such places.

The *London Road* leads from the Obelisk to the *Elephant and Castle*, a noted rendezvous in the old coaching times for mail coaches and now for omnibuses. Near by is the *Elephant and Castle Station* of the Chatham and Dover Railway, as also *Mr. Spurgeon's Tabernacle*, capable of holding 5000 persons, which was built in 1860-1 at a cost of £31,000. Out of *Newington Butts*, and immediately from the Railway Station, the Walworth Road leads to *Camberwell*; by the Kennington Park Road we may reach *Kennington Park* (formerly Kennington Common, the place of meeting of the Chartists in 1848), and beyond it *Kennington Oval*, famous for its *Cricket-ground*. *St. Mark's Church, Kennington*, occupies the site where the gallows used to stand, for the execution of criminals for the County of Surrey; and at this point were the Turnpike Gates (abolished Oct. 31, 1865), on the *Clapham Road* leading to Stockwell and Clapham; the *Brixton Road*, to Brixton and Tulse Hill; and the *Camberwell New Road*, to Camberwell, Dulwich, or to Peckham and Peckham Rye.

The *Horns Tavern* at Kennington, having large assembly-rooms, has for many years been used for large political and other public meetings, and the name of the house is consequently widely known. The poet Shenstone has thrown over Kennington the only poetic grace associated with this district. His poem, ' Jemmy Dawson,' describes in simple language the execution, on Kennington Common, of one of the eight officers who fought and suffered for the Pretender, in 1745-6, the usual barbarous punishment inflicted for high treason. Dawson's sweetheart, despite all entreaty, insisted upon witnessing the fearful atrocities, and seemed to behold them without emotion, but when all was over she fell back in her coach, exclaiming " My dear, I follow thee!" and expired.

THE RIVER THAMES

Has its source in the Cotswold Hills, and flows between Gloucestershire and Wiltshire, then between Berkshire and Oxfordshire, and Berkshire and Buckinghamshire, then between Surrey and Middlesex, and last between Kent and Essex, reaching the sea at the Nore, 110 miles east from its source, or about twice that distance measured by its own windings. Its most remarkable feature is, perhaps, that of being navigable by large sea-going vessels nearly one-fourth of its entire length—from London Bridge to the Nore, being forty-five miles. Its breadth at London varies from 800 to 1,500 feet; at the Nore it is seven miles. The Tide rises about fifteen miles above London Bridge, i.e. to Teddington (Tide-end-town?), and, even at ebb-tide, there are 12 or 13 feet of water off Greenwich; at London Bridge the mean range of tide is about 17 feet, and of the highest spring-tides about 22 feet. Throughout its entire course, from its source to the sea, the Thames passes through so many picturesque and historically interesting places that it would need volumes to describe it justly; it must suffice here to indicate those objects of interest upon its banks which are in the immediate vicinity of the Metropolis. The small Steamers which ply every five minutes from Chelsea to London Bridge for 2*d*., and to Woolwich for 5*d*., touching at the various piers on either side of the river, will enable the visitor to London to make himself easily acquainted, at the smallest possible expense, with this "great silent highway." We propose, therefore, to accompany such a visitor in his brief trip upon the Thames—occupying indeed, but about an hour and a half, but so varied in character, so crowded with reminis-

PLATE XIII.

THE THAMES.
FROM THE TOWER TO WESTMINSTER.

cences, that it will require our best faculty to furnish of them the most sketchy outline.

Taking boat at the *Chelsea Pier*, a few yards from the site of the late Cremorne Gardens, we turn for a moment to note what remains of this old suburb of London—still exhibiting in some of its ancient houses, relics of that old-world time, when Chelsea was the abode of the noblest and the wisest. Here, in a mansion upon the site of *Beaufort Row* before us, lived the great Sir Thomas More, who there received his guests, the learned Erasmus, the great artist Holbein, and many more of his no less celebrated contemporaries, including Henry VIII., who, it is said, " after dinner, in this fair garden of his, walked with him by the space of an hour, holding his arm about his neck, and ascended with him to the house to observe the stars and discourse of astronomy." A few years later the king beheaded his friend and set up his head on London Bridge. Sir Thomas More's first wife was buried in *Old Chelsea Church* near by, which dates from the sixteenth century, and possesses an eastern chapel added by Sir Thomas; and in the chancel a black marble tablet inscribed to the memory of Lady More three years before his death. Sir Hans Sloane (to whom there is a gravestone in the churchyard), Cipriani, and other eminent persons, were buried in this church and churchyard. In the eastern end of *Cheyne Walk* was *Don Saltero's Museum and Coffee-house*, once noted for its collection of natural curiosities, and for having been the resort of Steele, Swift, and others, who endowed it with literary celebrity. Don Saltero was a barber named John Salter, whom Steele is said to have dignified with the Spanish title and termination to his name; he is mentioned in the 'Tatler,' and the house is also reported in connection with the swimming exploits of Dr. Franklin. *Old Chelsea Bun-house* in Cheyne Walk, once famous for its buns, had also a kind of museum in rivalry of Don Saltero's. Both collections have long since been dispersed, the Bun-house was taken down in 1839. At 5 *Great Cheyne Row*, leading from Cheyne Walk, has lived for many years—long may he continue to do so—one of the greatest literary men of this century, Thomas Carlyle; he is frequently spoken of as the Chelsea Philosopher. The eminent J. M. W. Turner died in a house between Chelsea Pier and Cremorne Gardens in 1851. "Rare Old Chelsea China" was manufactured in buildings (long since removed), near Church Street, and extending to the waterside. *Chelsea China* is marked with an anchor, red on the inferior, *gold* on the best specimens.

As the steamboat puts off from Chelsea Pier we may catch a glimpse of the site of the late *Cremorne Gardens* above referred to, popularly known for its entertainments after the style of old Vauxhall Gardens (also long since built over). Cremorne House was once noted as the elegant seat of Lord Cremorne, and for his fine collection of pictures.

The CHELSEA EMBANKMENT of the Thames, extending from the *Old Battersea Bridge* to *Grosvenor Road, Pimlico*, was completed in 1874. Moving down the river, a little past Cheyne Walk, we are within almost a stone's-throw of the *Botanic Garden* of the Apothecaries' Company (open daily from eight to eleven, to persons bringing an order of admission from a member of the Company). These gardens, consisting of about three acres, were given by Sir Hans Sloane to the Company.

THE ROYAL CHELSEA HOSPITAL is a handsome old edifice, of which the river view is certainly the finest. It was built by Sir Christopher Wren for Charles II., some say at the instigation of Nell Gwynne; but more certainly we know that Sir Stephen Fox, grandfather of the great statesman, Charles James Fox, was its first projector. The story as to Nell Gwynne was as follows: "One day when she was rolling about town in her coach, a poor man came to the coach door soliciting charity, who told her a story of his having been wounded in the civil wars in defence of the royal cause. This circumstance greatly affected the benevolent heart of Mrs. Gwynne .... she hurried to the king .... and to Nell Gwynne is now owing the comfortable provision which is made for decayed soldiers, and that pleasant retreat they find at Chelsea." The building is of red brick with stone quoins, cornices, &c., and consists of three courts, of which the central one faces the Thames. The In-Pensioners, of whom there are five hundred and forty, occupy the wings of the building, and dine in the hall in the left wing. There are 60,000 Out-Pensioners, receiving from $1\frac{1}{4}d.$ to $3s.$ $10d.$ each *per diem.* In the centre of the Great Quadrangle is Grinling Gibbon's statue of Charles II. There are several portraits in the Hospital of the royal family of the Stuarts, as also of William III., George III., and Queen Charlotte. The Hall and Chapel are hung with a large number of colours, eagles, &c., captured by the British Army. The ROYAL MILITARY ASYLUM, or DUKE OF YORK'S SCHOOL, for the maintenance and education of the sons of soldiers, is north of the Hospital, and contains five hundred boys. The Hospital and Asylum may be seen daily from ten to four. It is worth while remembering that the once fashionable RANELAGH GARDENS and Rotunda occupied the site a little to the east of Chelsea Hospital. Of Ranelagh it was said: "My Lord Chesterfield is so fond of it that he says he has ordered all his letters to be addressed thither." Dibdin's 'Jolly Young Waterman' was—

"Always 'first oars' when the fine city ladies
In parties to Ranelagh went or Vauxhall."

Opposite Chelsea Hospital and upon the south side of the Thames, which here flows, according to the old conundrum, between two seas (Chelsea and Battersea*), is BATTERSEA

* The terminations of Chelsea and Battersea seem to have been the same as Bermondsey, though now differently spelt. *Ey* or *Eyot* indicate Saxon origin, and mean a place by the water. Chelsea has been spelt Chelsey, and has been said to have been originally named Cealchyth, or pebble bank. Battersea has been derived from Patrick's Eye.

PARK, containing 180 acres of land formerly a marsh, and but recently (1852–8) drained, embanked, and laid out and planted with shrubs, trees, and flowers. Its chief attraction is the *Sub-Tropical Garden* of four acres, containing a number of semi-hardy plants, the culture of which has been promoted with the greatest horticultural science and skill. There are some fine walks here, including a riverside promenade, and there are grounds for cricket and other athletic sports. The Ornamental Lake adds considerably to the attractions of this popular resort. This Park may be reached by steamboats which continually ply up and down the river, or by road through Pimlico over the handsome ALBERT SUSPENSION BRIDGE, built by Mr. Page (1858). The BATTERSEA RAILWAY BRIDGE, under which the steamboat passes after leaving *Battersea Park Pier*, conveys the trains of the London and Brighton Railway Company, and the London, Chatham, and Dover Railways, to the termini of those lines at the Victoria Station, Pimlico. Upon the north bank of the Thames at this point is the entrance to the *Grosvenor Canal*, and a few yards farther east is the *Low Level Pumping House* (completed 1875) of the new system of Main Metropolitan Drainage. It is stated that there are now 1,300 miles of Sewers in London, and eighty-two miles of main intercepting Sewers. The Sewage on the north of the Thames amounts to about 10,000,000 cubic feet a day; on the south to 4,000,000, which with the rainfall, and the probably ever-increasing size of London, have all been allowed for in the construction of this main drainage system (at a cost of £4,000,000), which is capable of disposing of 63,000,000 cubic feet *per diem*, equal to a lake of 428 acres, 3 feet deep, or fifteen times as large as the Hyde Park Serpentine. Before this drainage, planned by Sir John Bazalgette, was made, the Thames was the great main sewer of London; all drains north and south poured into the river at dead low water, and, with the rising tide, "kept churning backwards and forwards" till the river became one of the foulest of open sewers. The present system consists of three great main lines of sewers running from west to east at right angles below the levels of previously existing sewers, and conveying their contents to an *Outfall at Barking*, fourteen miles beyond London Bridge, and discharging them there and at *Crossness, near Plumstead*, at high water, equivalent to a discharge at low water of twelve miles farther down the river. The *Low-Level Sewer*, besides intercepting the sewage from the low-level area of eleven square miles, is also the main outlet for a district of about fourteen and a half square miles, forming the western suburb of London, which lies so low that the sewage has to be pumped up here to a height of $17\frac{1}{2}$ feet into the upper end of the Low-Level Sewer, which passes hence to Westminster, where it runs under the Victoria Embankment, thence to Tower Hill, and on by Limehouse and Bow Common, under the river Lea to the *Abbey Mills Pumping-station*, where the low-level sewage has again to be raised 36 feet. On the south of the Thames the *High-Level Sewers*, beginning at Clapham, the *Low* at Putney, after uniting at Deptford, are discharged as above, at Crossness at high water.

VAUXHALL BRIDGE connects Vauxhall with Millbank. The origin of the name of Vauxhall has been traced to a family of the name of Vaux, who held an estate here in the reigns of Elizabeth and James I. The tradition of its having been the abode of Guy Vaux or Fawkes, of Gunpowder Plot notoriety, still lingers, but, as the antiquarians say, without being authenticated. The old song is but an echo and play upon words of the tradition—

> " He wished the state was undone.
> And, crossing over Vauxhall Bridge,
> That way came into London."

Vauxhall Bridge was completed in 1816 after long difficulties, arising from changes of plans, and disputes among four engineers. It was intended to have been built of stone, but it is made of cast iron. The river is here 900 feet wide. *Old Vauxhall Gardens*, closed in 1859, were situated a little to the south-east of Vauxhall Bridge. *Millbank Penitentiary* or Prison, on the north bank of the river, said to be one of the largest prisons in the kingdom, was commenced in 1812. Its ground is laid out in six sets of buildings, radiating like a wheel from the centre, where stands the Governor's house. The corridors are more than three miles in length, and there are 1,550 cells in this prison which is said to have cost half a million of money. *Doulton's large Pottery for Stoneware*, seen on the south bank opposite Millbank Prison, is rapidly becoming celebrated for its improved style of art manufacture.

LAMBETH IRON SUSPENSION BRIDGE, built by Mr. Barlow, 1862, at a cost of £40,000, connects Horseferry Road, Westminster, with Lambeth. From this point the *Albert Embankment* runs to the south foot of Westminster Bridge.

LAMBETH, one of the ancient suburbs of London, forms with Southwark one of the metropolitan boroughs, returning two members to Parliament. *St. Mary's Church, Lambeth*, adjoining Lambeth Palace, is the mother church of the parish, and dates from the fifteenth century. The Howard Chapel in the north aisle was built 1522. In this church (which has a perpendicular tower) were buried the following Archbishops of Canterbury: Bancroft, Parker, Tenison, Hutton, Secker, Cornwallis, Moore, as also the well-known antiquarians, Tradescant, father and son. At *Lambeth Ferry* and just below this church occurred the memorable scene so dramatically described by Macaulay of the landing of the Queen of James II. and her infant son on the first stage of their flight from Whitehall. " The King and Queen retired to rest as usual. When the palace had been some time profoundly quiet, James rose and called a servant. . . . The Count de Lauzun was ushered into the royal bed-chamber. 'I confide to you,' said James, 'my Queen and son; everything must be risked to carry them into France.' . . . Lauzun gave his hand to Mary ; Saint Victor wrapped up in his warm cloak the ill-fated heir of so many kings. The party stole down the back stairs, and embarked in an open skiff. It was a miserable voyage. The night was bleak, the rain fell, the wind roared, the water was rough ; at last the boat reached Lambeth, and the fugitives landed near an inn where a coach and horses were in waiting. Some time elapsed before the horses could be harnessed, Mary, afraid that her face might be known, would not enter the house ; she remained with her child, cowering for shelter from the storm under the tower of Lambeth Church, and distracted with terror when the ostler approached her with his lantern. Two of her women attended her, but . . . they could be of little use to their mistress, for both were foreigners, who could hardly speak the English language, and who shuddered at the rigour of the English climate. The only consolatory circumstance was that the little boy was well, and uttered not a single cry. At length the coach was ready. Saint Victor followed it on horseback. The fugitives reached Gravesend safely, and embarked in the yacht which waited for them. . . . The yacht proceeded down the river with a fair wind, and St. Victor, having seen her under sail, spurred back with the good news to Whitehall."

LAMBETH PALACE, the residence of the Archbishops of Canterbury for six centuries and a half, dates as far back as 1190, that being the year in which Archbishop Walter built the ancient manor house which is now the Palace, but the building as it stands is so varied in style, from Early English to late Perpendicular, that it by no means denotes the work of one age or one builder. The Gatehouse entrance built by Archbishop Morton, 1490, has an embellished centre, two large square towers of red brick with stone dressings, and a spacious Tudor archway. The towers are reached by a spiral staircase leading to the Record room, which contains many of the archives of the See of Canterbury. The dole to the poor has been given from time immemorial at this gate. The lower part of the gatehouse was used as a small prison. The *Chapel* dates from 1244–70, and is Early English, with lancet windows. In it every Archbishop has been consecrated since the latter date. Its original stained-glass windows were destroyed in the Civil Wars; the present windows were set up and the chapel re-decorated by the present Archbishop (Tait). The roof bears the arms of Laud, Juxon, and Cornwallis. The oak screen presented by Laud also bears his arms. In front of the altar Archbishop Parker was buried.

The *Lollards' Tower* on the left of the outer court was built (1434–5) by Archbishop Chichley, whose arms are sculptured on the river front, over a Gothic niche, wherein formerly appeared a statue of Thomas-à-Becket. Entrance to the Lollards' prison—a chamber about fifteen feet long, eleven feet wide, and eight feet high, with two narrow windows and open fireplace—is obtained by a spiral staircase. Eight large iron rings are here fixed in the walls about breast-high, and upon the oaken wainscoting are cut names, crosses, sentences, &c., as it would seem, by the captives who were kept here in bonds. Whether such captives were Lollards (or followers of Wycliffe) is disputed; if they were, and were merely sheltered here, as has been said, from the civil power, it seems hard to understand why they should have been chained as well as sheltered. The name Lollard was given by way of reproach by the priests, who thereby intimated that these Wycliffites who had dared to read and interpret the Bible for themselves, were lollards, i.e. spouters, talkative, uneducated men. The ceiling of the East Room has some fine carving. The *Library* or Hall and the Great Dining-room form the west side of the inner court. The former, containing some 30,000 volumes, many of great historical interest and value, is open to the public, throughout the year (except Easter week and the week after Christmas-day), from ten till three on Monday, Wednesday, and Friday. The Palace possesses also an historical line of portraits since 1633 of the Archbishops of Canterbury, now decorating the chief apartment, showing the changes in archiepiscopal costume during that lengthened period.

St. Thomas's Hospital and the *Houses of Parliament* upon the opposite embankment are described, the former at p. 47, the latter at p. 42. For *Westminster Bridge* see p. 46.

At the north end of Westminster Bridge is the *Westminster Station* of the Underground Metropolitan Railway, here carried beneath the Victoria Embankment, which begins at this point and is continued to Blackfriars Bridge. The VICTORIA EMBANKMENT forms part of a series of works for the improvement of the Thames and the thoroughfares of the metropolis, projected and carried out by Sir J. Bazalgette on behalf of the Metropolitan Board of Works. This Embankment, consisting of a solid granite wall, eight feet thick, forty feet high, and 7,000 feet long, provides a roadway one hundred feet wide, underneath which, besides the Underground Railway, are two tunnels, of which the lower is the great sewer, the upper contains water pipes, gas pipes, and telegraph wires, all accessible without disturbing the roadway. The land reclaimed from the river by means of this Embankment varies from 200 to 450 feet in width, and amounts to about thirty acres. The cost of the embankment and its approaches was about two millions, derived partly from rates, partly from wine and coal dues, and partly from the sale of the surplus land for building purposes. The Victoria Embankment was finished in 1870.

Upon leaving the *Steamboat Pier at Westminster* we shall observe *St. Stephen's Club-house*, recently erected for conservative politicians—an admirable situation; the

s

new *National Opera House*, still only partly erected, and *Montague House*, the town residence of the Duke of Buccleuch, in which are a few good pictures by Van Dyck and a fine collection of miniatures. A little later we pass the end of the new *Northumberland Avenue*, see p. 49. The *Charing Cross Steamboat Pier* is immediately in front of the *Charing Cross Station* of the Underground Railway, and below the Charing Cross Railway and Foot Bridge of the South Eastern Company, see p. 51. Near this point is the *Statue of Sir Francis Outram*, an Indian General. There is a large Public *Swimming Bath* moored west of this bridge, open from 7 A.M. to 8.30 P.M., possessing a continual flow of clear filtered water, regulated in temperature to the season. Admission, 1s. Upon leaving Charing Cross Pier we shall observe the *Water-Gate of York House*, see p. 51, and farther on the charmingly situated *Adelphi Terrace*, and the *Cleopatra Obelisk*, see p. 54. We afterwards pass the *Savoy*, see p. 61, and *Waterloo Bridge*, see p. 62, leading to the *South Western Railway Station* in Waterloo Road, then *Somerset House* and *King's College*, see p. 63-4, to the *Temple Pier*, in front of the Temple and Temple Gardens, see p. 74, thence past *Whitefriars* or *Alsatia*, see p. 80, to *Blackfriars Bridge*, see p. 83, where there is another Underground Railway Station. We now catch sight of the new *Victoria Street*, with some new buildings, including the offices of *The Times* newspaper, and of the British and Foreign Bible Society, and then get a near view of St. Paul's, see p. 87, and of the towers and spires of many of Wren's finest churches.

PAUL'S WHARF PIER is the nearest to St. Paul's Churchyard, and here passengers to the Surrey side of London Bridge usually have to change to the Surrey side boats.

Vintners' Hall, 68 Upper Thames Street, was rebuilt by Sir Christopher Wren, after the Great Fire. It contains some full-length portraits of Charles II., and James II., and a picture ascribed to Vandyke of 'St. Martin (the tutelar saint of the Company) dividing his cloak with a

Beggar.' The Vintners' Company is one of the most ancient of the London Companies.

SOUTHWARK BRIDGE, built by Sir John Rennie at a cost of £800,000, and opened in 1819, has an arch of a wider span (402 feet) than any bridge built previously to the invention of tubular bridges. It was bought in 1866 by the City from the private company for which it was built for £218,868; the toll of one penny was abolished in 1865. It is the most direct line of communication between Queen Street and other busy parts of the City with Southwark, and if its approaches were improved, would doubtless be much more generally used.

The CANNON STREET RAILWAY BRIDGE was built by the South Eastern Railway Company, and connects their Cannon Street Terminus with the lines which branch to London Bridge on the one hand, and Charing Cross upon the other, see p. 50.

BANKSIDE, Southwark, near the Cannon Street Bridge of the South Eastern Railway, was the site of the *Old Globe Theatre*. The ancient theatres on *Bankside, Southwark*, consisted of *Paris Garden Theatre*, dating from the time of Richard II. and continuing till James I., when Henslow and Alleyn (the endower of Dulwich College) kept it; the *Globe*, built about 1594 for Richard Burbage, and for which James I. granted a licence to Shakespeare and others. The Chorus to Henry V. refers to the shape of the Globe Theatre when he asks—

"May we cram
Within this wooden O the very casques
That did affright the air at Agincourt?"

Barclay's Brewery stands upon the site of the Globe Theatre. The *Hope Theatre* is chiefly remembered for its bull-baiting. The *Rose Theatre*, dating from about the middle of the sixteenth century, stood near where *Rose Alley* afterwards kept its name in memory. The *Swan Theatre* was cotemporary with the *Rose*. All were suppressed in 1648. To

Barclay's Brewery visitors are occasionally admitted upon previous written application to the Manager. This immense establishment is one of the most remarkable sights of London, and great personages from abroad make a point of seeing it. When Marshal Haynau, some years ago, visited Barclay's, the brewers'-men hustled him off the premises, in their indignation at the stories told of women spies whipped in Austria, by order of Haynau. The founder of Barclay's Brewery was Mr. H. Thrale, the friend of Dr. Johnson. Upon Mr. Thrale's death, Dr. Johnson, as one of his executors, had to dispose of the property, on behalf of Mrs. Thrale, and obtained for it no less than £135,000 at the auction, whereat he made this remarkably Johnsonian speech: "We are not here to sell a parcel of boilers and vats, but the potentiality of growing rich beyond the dreams of avarice."

LONDON BRIDGE. Little more than a hundred years ago, i.e. before 1750, the only bridge across the Thames was Old London Bridge, described as having originally "a stone platform, 926 feet long, 40 feet wide, standing 60 feet above the level of the water, and consisting of a drawbridge and nineteen broad-pointed arches, with massive piers raised upon strong oak and elm piles, covered by thick planks bolted together. It had a gate-house at each end, and towards the centre on the east side was built a beautiful Gothic chapel. In the reign of Elizabeth it was adorned with sumptuous buildings, and stately and beautiful houses on either side like one continuous street. Some of the houses had flat roofs with gardens and arbours, so that "As fine as London Bridge" passed into a proverb. Near the drawbridge was the famed *Nonsuch House*, constructed in Holland entirely of timber, four stories high, richly carved and gilt. The history of London Bridge, for nearly six centuries, would include many of the most stirring incidents of the History of England. De Montfort here repulsed Henry III. in 1264; Wat Tyler entered

London Bridge. 261

London by this bridge in 1381; Richard II. was here welcomed with great ceremonial in 1392; as was also Henry V. in 1415. In 1450 Jack Cade having "gotten London Bridge, the citizens fly and forsake their houses," but the Gate-House of London Bridge was soon after decorated by Jack Cade's head (it was pretty regularly garnished with heads), instead of the Bridge being set on fire according to Cade's order—*teste* Shakespeare. In 1477 the Bridge was attacked and fired by Falconbridge; in 1554 it witnessed some of the most daring incidents of Wyatt's rebellion; in 1666 the houses were burnt down in the Great Fire, but were rebuilt twenty years after; in 1757 the houses were removed and replaced by ordinary balustrades; in 1832 the old bridge was demolished altogether. Its narrow arches impeded navigation, and rendered possible what is now improbable, the freezing over of the Thames. The present bridge was built from the designs of Sir John Rennie, and was opened in great state in August 1831, by King William IV. and Queen Adelaide. It cost, with its approaches, no less than £1,458,311. It consists of five semi-elliptical arches, two of 130 feet, two of 140 feet, and the centre of 152 feet 6 inches span. The roadway is 52 feet wide. More than 20,000 carts, carriages and other vehicles have been reckoned whilst crossing over this bridge in 24 hours, and in the same time 107,000 foot passengers. A scheme has been submitted to Parliament to enable the Corporation of London to enlarge London Bridge to the extent of about 11 feet on each side, and thereby to widen both the carriageways and footways, but there is much opposition made to any additions to the present excellent structure.

The River Traffic above London Bridge is of course limited to vessels of comparatively small size. Below it the PORT OF LONDON may be said to begin. The *Upper Pool*, as it is called, is reckoned to the first reach in the river, i.e. to about the *Thames Tunnel, or Execution Dock*, where pirates used to be gibbeted. The *Lower Pool* to *Cuckold's Point*, where colliers usually lie, leaving a water-way of some 300 feet for the shipping to pass up and down. Nearly 50,000 vessels enter the Port of London annually.

The *Below Bridge Pier* for Margate, Ramsgate and other steamboats too large to pass under London Bridge, is immediately east of the bridge upon the Middlesex side.

BILLINGSGATE FISH MARKET (on the site of one of the old Water-gates of the City from which it derives its name), is the red brick building with stone dressing, just below London Bridge. In 1872 an Act of Parliament enabled the Corporation to rebuild the market upon a larger scale, and to annex some adjoining ground for the purpose, the result being, that in July 1877, when the new buildings were opened, there was an addition made to Billingsgate Market equivalent to nearly as much again as its previous area; the old building occupied 20,000 feet, the new one comprises 39,000 feet. The market, open daily, excepting Sundays, at 5 o'clock, summer and winter, is well worth a visit at that early hour; when, if there be much activity, noise and bustle, there is comparatively little of the violent language and abuse for which Billingsgate has been historically noted. Instead of the old miserable wooden sheds and pent-houses, we see a spacious building, well-provided with stone-slabbed benches, and kept clean by a good water supply and perfect drainage; instead of the old flaring oil-lamps " showing a crowd struggling amidst a Babel din of vulgar tongues," we shall find orderly business bustle, and a considerable traffic carried on in a rapid methodical style; no screaming, fighting, fish-fag abuse between the women; little gin, but plenty of tea and coffee-drinking; little haggling, but plenty of buying and selling, different kinds of fish being represented by their several wholesale dealers—the whiting dealer, the sole and flat-fish dealer, the oyster dealer, the cod-fish dealer, the cured-fish dealers, all being separate traders confining

The Custom House. 263

themselves to their several specialties in fish-selling. Oysters and shell-fish are sold by measure, and salmon by weight, but all other fish by tale or number, and the wholesale market is over, generally, by eight in the morning; after that time, the business is left to the retailers who supply the costermongers and the public in the vicinity, for the fishmongers of London have received their supplies from Billingsgate by about eight o'clock. A large quantity of fish now reaches London by railway. There are two large taverns, upon the river front, east and west of Billingsgate, in the upper rooms of which Fish Dinners are to be had daily, comprising every kind of fish in season, at a very small cost.

THE COAL EXCHANGE is in Lower Thames Street, nearly opposite Billingsgate; it is a fine building of its kind, built by Bunning in 1849, and is decorated by some curious examples of ferns, palms, &c., found fossilized in the coal formations. The London coal trade is said to employ 10,000 seamen.

THE CUSTOM HOUSE adjoins Billingsgate and faces the river. The business of this establishment has been of course considerably narrowed by the removal, of late years, of a large number of articles from the list chargeable to the Inland Revenue, but there is, nevertheless, an amazing sum levied at this port annually. The present building was designed by David Laing upon a portion of the site of the former Custom House, destroyed by fire, February 1814, but Laing's front was altered when the foundation gave way in 1852, and the present façade was erected by Sir Robert Smirke. The interior contains a great many warehouses, cellars and apartments, and the 'Long Room,' 190 feet by 66, is a fine room, but not equal to that which was taken down at the failure of the foundation. Articles seized at the Custom House are sold by auction, quarterly, in Mark Lane.

The *Thames Subway*, from Tower Hill to Tooley Street,

runs across the river. It is 1330 feet long, and was made by Mr. Barlow at a cost of only £16,000.

THE TOWER OF LONDON (see p. 99) is a prominent feature at this point of the river, from which is to be had the best view of 'Traitor's Gate'—the entrance for prisoners formerly brought hither by water, but now closed. Immediately behind the Gate is seen the Bloody Tower, where the infant princes were smothered by command of Richard III. Traitor's Gate was restored and rebuilt in 1866.

ST. KATHERINE'S DOCKS are the nearest to London Bridge of the eight docks (six on the north and two on the south side of the Thames) which receive the London shipping, and occupy altogether 900 acres, the whole of them having been constructed within the present century. St. Katherine's Docks, planned by Telford and opened in 1828, at a cost of about £2,000,000, cover 24 acres, nearly half being water, and occupy the site of the old HOSPITAL OF ST. KATHERINE, transferred to Regent's Park (see p. 131).

LONDON DOCKS, amalgamated with St. Katherine's in 1863 were planned by Rennie and opened 1805, and contain 90 acres, about a third being water, and cost £4,000,000. Here are the great warehouses for tobacco, rented by the Crown; in the north-east corner of which is the kiln where condemned tobacco and other articles are burnt, the smoke being carried off by a long chimney known as the 'Queen's Pipe.' "The huge mass of fire," wrote one not long since, "in the furnace is fed night and day with condemned goods; on one occasion 900 Australian mutton hams were burnt, on another 45,000 pairs of French gloves, and silks and satins, tobacco and cigars are here consumed in vast quantities, the ashes being sold by the ton or measure. Nails and other pieces of iron sifted from the ashes are prized for their toughness in making gun-barrels; gold and silver, the remains of plate, watches and jewelry thrown into the flames, are sometimes found among the ashes." Here also are the Wine Vaults, covering many acres of ground; the Mixing House, having one vat of over 23,000 gallons; the casks of wine for which "tasting orders" are obtained from the wine owners; the wool; spices, tea, drug, sugar, and other warehouses, seemingly innumerable. The public are admitted without ticket to the docks and shipping, but an order from the Secretary at the London Dock-House is necessary for admission to the vaults and warehouses. For "tasting orders" apply to your wine-merchant. The Docks, being one of the few public places where employment can be had without character or recommendation, attract many hundreds of persons out of work. "Here," wrote Mayhew, "at half-past seven in the morning, may be seen swarms of men of all grades, looks, and kinds, decayed and bankrupt butchers, bakers, publicans, grocers, old soldiers, old sailors, Polish refugees, broken-down gentlemen, discharged lawyer's clerks, suspended government clerks, almsmen, pensioners, servants, thieves, indeed every one who wants a loaf and is willing to earn it."

THE THAMES TUNNEL, formerly one of the sights of London, is now used by the East London Railway, to carry its lines from the north to the south side of the Thames; that is to say, between Wapping and Rotherhithe. The Tunnel consists of two arched ways, 1,200 feet long, 14 feet wide, 16½ feet high, and 16 feet below the river, and was opened in 1843, having been built by Brunel, at a cost of £468,000; the Railway Company bought it for £200,000, in 1865. It was never a profitable undertaking, but it was reckoned a wonderful and unprecedented example of skilled engineering.

WAPPING derives its name, as is supposed, from Wapp, a ship's rope, and it maintains its reputation as a place for shipping and seafaring people. Wapping will long be remembered as the birthplace of Arthur Orton of Tichborne notoriety; but yet longer for its landing-place, still in use, called 'Wapping Old Stairs,' for ever associated with the genius of Dibdin, and with his Molly—the most constant and affectionate of sweethearts, whose name is much more indelibly engraved upon the hearts of all true Jack Tars than it could possibly have been upon the 'baccy box,' which she presented to her Tom as a love token. Opposite Wapping is *Rotherhithe*, vulgarly *Redriff*, famous as the supposed birthplace of Lemuel Gulliver. Gay writes *apropos* of waterside constancy—

> "In five long years I took no second spouse,
> What Redriff wife so long hath kept her vows?"

In Rotherhithe churchyard was buried Prince Lee Boo of the Pellew Islands, who died during his visit to England.

THE THAMES STEAM FERRY, opened in 1877, connects Wapping with Rotherhithe, and crosses the line of the Thames Tunnel. Vehicles and passengers are transferred from the landing-stages to the boats, and *vice versâ*. The level of the boat's decks at low water is 24 feet below that of the river bank, and at such times the boats cannot approach within 170 feet of the Wapping Wharf, or 70 feet at Rotherhithe. From the jetty at Wapping, and the wharf at Rotherhithe, however, traffic is transferred to the boat's decks by means of hydraulic machinery. There is an elevated railed footpath for foot passengers upon each side of the lift platform, and thus, in a somewhat clumsy way perhaps, the great difficulty was overcome of providing means of transit across the Thames at this point, whilst leaving a passage for sea-going vessels. The tariff charges are one penny for a pedestrian or passenger, threepence per head for cattle, 1s. 9d. for a four-horse carriage or vehicle when it is empty, or 3s. 9d. when laden. The Steam Ferry is said to save in some instances six or seven miles in the double journey, besides the blocks and delays in the busy thoroughfares of both sides of the river.

The *Surrey Docks* and the *Commercial Docks*, spacious

and convenient both as basins and for storage of corn, &c., face the *Thames Tunnel Steamboat Pier.* SHADWELL lies a little farther down the river bank. *Stepney,* the parish to which all children born at sea were supposed to belong, lies next to it. DEPTFORD and LIMEHOUSE are opposite to one another, the former being upon the south, the latter on the north bank of the river. Deptford was a government dockyard till 1869; it has since passed into the hands of the Corporation of London, who use it as a market and slaughtering place for foreign cattle. The *Pool* ends at Limehouse Reach, at which is an entrance to the *West India Docks.* These extend over nearly 300 acres to Blackwall. They were built by Jessop, and opened 1802. The *East India Docks,* containing only 32 acres adjoin the above, and both are best reached by railway from Fenchurch Street. *Millwall Docks,* in the Isle of Dogs, are also near the West India Docks, and cover 200 acres. They were opened in 1868; the *Great Eastern* steamship was built at Millwall. *Victoria Docks* below Blackwall, occupy 200 acres; they were opened in 1856.

Opposite to the ISLE OF DOGS, a name said to be a corruption of Isle of Ducks, and upon the south bank of the Thames, we arrive at *Greenwich.* GREENWICH HOSPITAL faces the river, and has a highly commanding aspect. The *Greenwich Steamboat Pier* immediately adjoins the grounds of the Hospital. Perhaps the first object which presents itself to the visitor upon entering the pier-terrace, in front of the Hospital, is an Obelisk of red granite in memory of Lieutenant Bellot, the French Arctic Navigator. Greenwich Hospital was built by William III., at the request of his wife, for the reception of the sailors wounded in the battle of La Hogue. It stands upon the site of a palace, wherein Henry VIII., Queen Mary, and Queen Elizabeth were born, and consists of four parts: King Charles and Queen Anne's fronting the river, King William's containing the Painted Hall, and Queen Mary's containing the Chapel.

The Queen's house, now the Royal Naval College, was designed by Inigo Jones for Queen Henrietta Maria. The river front was by Webb, Jones's relative, the *Great Hall* and Colonnades, 106 feet by 56 feet wide and 50 feet high, by Sir Christopher Wren, the *Chapel* by Stuart. Sir James Thornhill painted the ceiling, &c., of the Great Hall. In the *Picture Gallery*, formed by George IV., are many valuable portraits of noted admirals, and some fine paintings of naval battles, including Lord Howe's victory, by Loutherburg, and J. M. W. Turner's 'Battle of Trafalgar.' In the *Upper Hall* are some peculiarly touching souvenirs of Nelson; the coat and waistcoat which he wore when he was killed in the Battle of Trafalgar, with numerous other relics. "The course of the fatal ball," says Sir H. Nicholas, "is shown by a hole over the left shoulder, and part of the epaulette is torn away. The coat and waistcoat are stained in several places with the hero's blood." Here also is the astrolabe presented by Queen Elizabeth to Sir Francis Drake; and here are the relics of the lamented Sir John Franklin's Arctic Expedition. In the *Chapel* is B. West's 'Shipwreck of St. Paul.' Greenwich Hospital is no longer used for the purpose for which it was built, namely the reception of naval pensioners. Since 1865, nearly all of these have taken extra out-pensions of 2s. a day, and, in preference to remaining in the Hospital, have gone to live with their friends. The *Royal Naval College* occupies their rooms in the building, and instructs sailors in the science of mathematics, navigation, and gunnery. The *Museum of Naval Architecture*, containing models of ships from the earliest period, was removed from South Kensington to Queen Anne's wing here; the Infirmary is now used as a *Merchant Seamen's Hospital* in lieu of the old *Dreadnought* line of battle ship, which for many years was moored off Greenwich, and served for the same purpose. The Museum is open daily from 10 to 4, the Hall and Chapel from 10 till dusk; free on Monday and Friday, and on other days upon payment of 3d. *Greenwich Park* immediately adjoins the Hospital, and is singularly beautiful. The view of the Thames from *Greenwich Observatory* (where the Astronomer Royal conducts his observations and gives "Greenwich time" to all the world) is "worth a day's journey, though every mile were taken on foot." In this Park, which extends to *Blackheath*, and contains 180 acres, King James rode a hunting as described in the 'Fortunes of Nigel.' Our limits will not permit of a lengthy notice of Greenwich, suffice it that we mention that it can easily be reached from London, either by the South Eastern Railway, from Charing Cross and Cannon Street; by omnibuses from Charing Cross; or by tramway from Westminster Bridge. *White-bait Dinners* at the *Ship* or the *Trafalgar*, Greenwich, are part of the joys of the London season. General Wolfe was buried in Greenwich Church 1759.

Blackwall is a little farther down the river, upon the north side. There is a terminus of the *Blackwall Railway*, close to the *East India Docks, Blackwall*, which are used by vessels of large tonnage.

The next bend of the Thames shows us the green heights of *Charlton*, and a few minutes more bring us to *Woolwich*, considered one of the chief of the royal dockyards. Here is also the Royal Arsenal. The covered slips, for building vessels, are seen by us as we pass down the river. Here are all the appliances by means of which Britannia continues to rule the waves—the armoured vessel, the "Woolwich infant"—the largest gun of the period—the steam-engine factory, all the ingenious scientific contrivances for improving military and naval warfare, as well as the workshops wherein thousands of artisans are engaged in preparing munitions of war. In front of Woolwich, the Thames is a mile wide, at its back rises *Shooter's Hill*, so named from the bandits who used to infest it. The *Artillery Barracks* at Woolwich face the Common.

The *Royal Military Repository*, at the west end of the barracks, contains some interesting specimens of ancient weapons and other curious relics. Opposite *Woolwich Pier*, is a large place of amusement called the *North Woolwich Gardens*. The visitor may return to London if he pleases by the railway upon the North Woolwich side, to which he may pass by means of a steam ferry-boat continually plying from one side of the river to the other.

If, however, he should desire to proceed farther down the Thames, as far as, shall we say, the mouth of the river, his wishes may be gratified at but small expense. By river steamboats he may be carried in a short time to *Gravesend*, an ancient town, which, before the days of railway travelling, the citizens of London regarded as a kind of seaside resort. Here are the *Rosherville Gardens*—"the place to spend a happy day"—containing a theatre, dancing platform, and restaurant. The return home may be made by railway. Farther down the Thames the visitor may proceed to *Sheerness*, and thence to *Rochester;* or he may cross to *Southend*, on the Essex coast, and thence come back to London by rail or steamboat. In the summer, steamers run daily from London Bridge to the above places, as well as to towns more remote, such as Margate and Ramsgate.

ENVIRONS AND SUBURBS.

ACTON, a village near Hanwell, is about five miles from London. It may be reached by railway from Paddington, Kensington, Victoria, or Broad Street, E.C.

Alexandra Park and Palace, Muswell Hill, may be reached in about 15 minutes by the Great Northern Railway from King's Cross to Wood Green, or from Moorgate Street Station. The entertainments include Concerts, Theatrical performances, Picture and other Exhibitions, &c., as at the Crystal Palace. The Palace (first opened 1863, but burnt down and immediately rebuilt) is a fine structure, commanding beautiful views over five counties; the Park consists of about 400 acres, beautifully laid out. Admission 1s., except on special days, and when otherwise advertised. Return Railway Tickets from King's Cross, including admission on shilling days, cost 2s. 6d., 2s.., or 1s. 6d., according to class.

Amwell, is a village in Hertfordshire, which is said to derive its name from Emma's Well. A spring issues here which supplies the New River, and gives its name to Amwell Street, &c., Pentonville—as Chadwell Street is derived from St. Chad's Well, a once noted spring at Battlebridge, King's Cross.

Anerley, a suburb on the South-Eastern line, near Sydenham and the Crystal Palace, is 7½ miles from London.

Ascot, famous for its June races, is 29 miles from London by the railway line from Waterloo Station.

Balham is a residential suburb, about 5 miles from Pimlico, on the London and Brighton line of railway.

Ball's Pond, named after John Ball, a licensed victualler, who lived here in the middle of the seventeenth century, and who kept a pond for duck-hunting and other such sports, is a hamlet connected with Islington, and is reached by the Essex Road, Islington; it abuts on the Stoke Newington Road.

Barking (see p. 97) was the seat of the oldest and richest Benedictine nunnery in England. It is 8 miles from London by the line from Fenchurch Street.

Barnes, a village on the Thames, reached by the South-Western Railway, from Waterloo, is 7 miles from London.

Barnet, sometimes *High Barnet*, so named from its being situated on a hill; sometimes *Chipping Barnet*, from its famous cattle market, is about 11 miles from London by the Railway from Ludgate Hill, King's Cross, or Broad Street. *East Barnet* is a neighbouring village. At *Hadley*, beyond Barnet, is a Memorial Pillar of the Battle fought (1471) between Edward IV. and the Earl of Warwick, who was defeated and slain, in this last but one Conflict of the Roses.

Barnsbury adjoins Islington, and may be reached by the line from Broad Street or by omnibus from the Bank, or elsewhere; see Omnibuses, p. 303.

Battersea, see p. 252.

Bayswater, see p. 167, also Omnibuses p. 303.

Bethnal Green, at the eastern end of London, is chiefly noted for its silk weavers, and for the Museum, which was removed hither from South Kensington, when the latter set up its permanent structure. *Bethnal Green Museum* is about five miles by omnibus from Charing Cross, and is situated in the Cambridge Road, Bethnal Green. It contains some excellent collections illustrative of food manufactures, &c., besides many pictures, which are being sent hither on loan. The Museum is open, free, from 10 A.M. to 10 P.M., except on Wednesdays, Thursdays, and Fridays, when the charge is 6d., and the closing takes place at 6 P.M. The legend of the *Blind Beggar of Bethnal*

Green is best preserved in the ballad to be found in Percy's 'Reliques.' The tradition is that the Blind Beggar was the son of Simon de Montfort, Earl of Leicester, and that he was found among the slain after the battle of Evesham by the daughter of a neighbouring baron, who married him. It being necessary to conceal himself from the vengeance of Henry III. against whom he had fought, he assumed the disguise of a blind beggar, and his wife shared his privations. Their child was the pretty Bessie of the ballad :—

> "My father shee sayde is soone to be seene,
> The seely blind beggar of Bednall-greene,
> That dayly sits begging there for charitie,
> He is the goode father of prettye Bessee."

The *Columbia Market*, at Bethnal Green, erected at the expense of the Baroness Burdett Coutts was intended for the benefit of the East-end poor, but hitherto it has not been so useful as was expected. *Victoria Park*, at Bethnal Green, contains 290 acres, pleasantly laid out and planted with trees and shrubs, and ornamented by two lakes. In the centre is a handsome drinking fountain, presented by Baroness Burdett Coutts, which cost £5000. This park was begun in 1842; the funds for the original expenditure were derived from the sale of the Crown lease of York House, St. James's, to the Duke of Sutherland, for £72,000, see p. 123.

Blackheath, see p. 269, is seven miles from Charing Cross Railway Terminus; may be reached by railway from Fenchurch Street, or by steamboat from any pier.

Blackwall, see p. 269.

Bow, or *Stratford-le-Bow*, is a populous suburb of London on the Great Essex Road. The name *Bow* is derived from the arched bridge which here crosses the River Lea. *Stratford* indicates a road or *street* and a *ford*, and there are several places so named in different parts of the

T

kingdom. *Stratford-atte-Bowe* is associated with Chaucer; Stratford-on-Avon with Shakespeare, but not for the same reason; for the 'Daystar of English Poetry' was not born here. He merely transmitted to posterity his opinion of the style of French spoken in this district, as being—

> "After the scole of Stratford-atté-Bowe,
> The French of Paris was to her unknowe."

Boxhill, near Dorking, a favourite holiday resort, is about 30 miles from London upon the South-Eastern, and also the Brighton Railway.

Brentford is an ancient town about seven miles from London, on the Middlesex side of the Thames, and is divided between the parishes of *Great Ealing*, *Hanwell*, and *Isleworth*. Old Brentford stands on rising ground, nearly opposite Kew Green. Canute was defeated by Edmund Ironside in a battle at Brentford, 1016, and Charles I. here ineffectually treated for peace with the Parliamentarians after the victory at Edgehill. Brentford may be reached from Waterloo Station.

Brentwood is in Essex on the road to Colchester, and is a little over 18 miles from London by railway from Liverpool Street.

Brixton lies south of the Thames, beyond Kennington, and adjoins Clapham, Stockwell, and Tulse Hill. It is easily reached by omnibus from Charing Cross, or by railway from Victoria or Blackfriars. Brixton Prison, noted as the first wherein a tread-mill was introduced, is now converted into a Female Convict Prison, and the tread-mill of course abolished.

Bromley is an ancient village near *Bow*, in Middlesex, said to date back to the Conqueror, in whose reign a nunnery was here founded. It is but a few miles from London by the line from Fenchurch Street. Bromley in Kent is over twelve miles from London by this line from Charing Cross.

Broxbourne is a favourite holiday resort for Londoners. It is upon the Great Eastern line of Railway. Near Broxbourne is Rye House, the locality of the *Rye House Plot*— a conspiracy for assassinating Charles II. and his brother (afterwards James II.) on their way to Newmarket Races.

Bushy Park adjoins Hampton Court Palace grounds, from which is to be had a magnificent view of a fine avenue of horse chestnut and lime trees more than a mile in length. A bronze figure of Diana decorates the fountain in the centre of the ornamental water in the south end of the Park.

Camden Town and *Kentish Town* lie to the north of London, the chief thoroughfares thither being the Hampstead Road and the St. Pancras Road, from King's Cross. The *Veterinary College*, at Camden Town, dates from 1791. The *Park* Theatre is in Park Street, Camden Town.

Cheshunt, twelve miles from London, is a large and ancient manor, with a fine old church, and a College for the education of young men for the Nonconformist ministry. It is about fourteen miles from Liverpool Street Railway Terminus.

Chigwell lies between Buckhurst Hill and Loughton, and is about thirteen miles from London by the lines from Liverpool Street or Fenchurch Street. Dickens, in 'Barnaby Rudge,' made Chigwell memorable for generations. Solomon Daisy, the chief spokesman at John Willett's fireside at the *Maypole*, was parish-clerk and bell-ringer of Chigwell, "hard by." The visitor to Chigwell will probably realise the truth of Dickens's prophecy as to the juvenile inhabitants, but he will scarcely find a fit representative of the old *Maypole* Inn; though he may, of old John Willett. "Go to Chigwell when you will, there will surely be seen either on the village street, or on the green, or frolicking in the farm-yard, more small Joes and Dolly Vardens than can easily be counted."

Chiswick is about five miles from London, beyond Hammersmith, and adjoining *Turnham Green*. In Chiswick Churchyard were buried, Ugo Foscolo, 1827, an Italian poet, for some time resident in England; Mary, third daughter of Oliver Cromwell; Barbara Villiers; De Loutherbourg, the artist; and William Hogarth, whose tomb bears an epitaph by Garrick. Hogarth's house is still standing near the grounds of *Chiswick House;* an historical mansion, belonging to the Duchess of Devonshire, in which Charles James Fox, and subsequently George Canning, died. Chiswick House has been used of late as a nursery for the children of the Prince of Wales, and occasionally, during the summer, the Prince and Princess have invited Garden-parties hither, which have been among the chief attractions of the London Season. Chiswick may be reached by omnibus (see p. 304) or by rail from Ludgate Hill or Waterloo.

Clapham is upon the Surrey side of the Thames, and may be reached by omnibus, or by rail to the *Clapham Road* on the London, Chatham, and Dover line. *Clapham Junction*, connected by numerous railways with London, is some distance from Clapham. Clapham is a busy and handsome suburb, considerably benefited by its proximity to Clapham Common, a beautiful and extensive piece of ground, whereon cricket and other sports are carried on without interference with the enjoyment of the pedestrian or the nursery-maid. The *Clapham Sect*, which represented the Evangelical School of the early part of this century, was an active religious party composed of both Churchmen and Nonconformists, and including Wilberforce, Lord Teignmouth, Zachary Macaulay, Henry Thornton, &c. Mr. Macaulay lived in the house, No. 5, near the *Plough Inn*, at Clapham, now a fishmonger's shop, and Lord Macaulay, as a boy, used to go regularly to the old church on Clapham Common. He indulged his early literary fancies by constructing out of the hillocks of the latter an imaginary range of

Alps and an ideal Mount Sinai. Of the church, he wrote many years after, " I love the church for the sake of the old times. I love even that absurd painted window, with the dove, the lamb, the urn, the two cornucopias, and the profusion of sunflowers, passion-flowers, and peonies;" but the High Church sermon he last listened to there was very different from those he heard as a boy. Tom Hood was at school, at Clapham, and thus described it:—

> "Ay, that's the very house! I know
> Its ugly windows, ten a row,
> Its chimneys in the rear;
> And there's the iron rod so high,
> That drew the thunder from the sky,
> And spoiled our table beer."

Clapton, see *Hackney*, may be reached by omnibus (see p. 306) or by railway from Liverpool Street.

Claremont, see *Esher*.

Colney Hatch, about 7 miles from London, may be reached by Southgate Station on the Great Northern line. There is a large lunatic asylum here.

Copenhagen Fields, beyond *Holloway*, is the site of the Great Cattle Market, removed from Smithfield, see p. 202.

THE CRYSTAL PALACE, at Sydenham, situated in extensive and beautiful grounds upon a height commanding magnificent views of the surrounding country for many miles round, is one of the most prominent, as it is also of the best and cheapest, places of amusement in London. Here, let the weather be what it may, there is ample space and comfort and amusement. On fine days nothing can be more delightful than a walk round the grounds, where landscape gardening is practised to perfection, and where out-door sports and athletic exercises are continually being carried on—archery, cricket, football, boating, lawn tennis, bicycling, &c., and merry-go-rounds and swings for the children—all having ample space and verge enough, with room for twice the number if the demand were made. It is, indeed, not unusual for this place of entertainment to receive and accommodate without difficulty or the slightest accident 60,000 or 70,000 people in a single day. The trains of the two lines of railway, the London and Brighton, from London Bridge and Victoria, and the Chatham and Dover, from Holborn and Victoria (on the High-level), run almost every quarter of an hour and bring and carry away thousands most easily and cheaply— namely, for return tickets 1s., 1s. 6d., and 2s. The price of admission is 1s.; on Saturday, 2s. 6d. (in August, September, and October, 1s. also on Saturdays); children under twelve half-price. Visitors may buy at the railway stations a railway ticket to include the price of admission on shilling days to the Palace for 1s. 6d. third class, 2s. second class, or 2s. 6d. first class. Good and cheap refreshments of all kinds are to be had in the Palace; from a cup of coffee or a bun, to a dinner of the most elaborate kind, public or private. This vast establishment was reared and fitted, 1853–54 (at a cost of nearly a million and a half sterling), by Sir Joseph Paxton, the builder of the Great Exhibition, 1851, many of the materials of which were used for the Crystal Palace, opened 1854. The present edifice comprises a magnificent Nave, 1608 feet long, with two Aisles and Transepts; the third Transept, at the north end, was destroyed by fire in 1866. The Central Transept is 390 feet long by 120 feet broad, and 175 feet high; the South Transept is 312 feet long by 72 feet broad, and 110 feet high. The Towers, at either end of the building (from the top of which is a wonderfully fine prospect well worth the slight fatigue of the ascent), are 282 feet high. It is impossible to furnish in a few lines an adequate account of the Crystal Palace; it must suffice, that its leading features are indicated. The building is entered from the London, Chatham, and Dover High-level Station, by the principal doorway in the Central Transept, or from the London and Brighton Station, through a long arcade adjoining the grounds. If we arrive by the latter, we shall enter the building by the *South Transept*, near to its largest Refreshment Rooms, and the Crystal Fountain. Close by is the *Pompeian Court*, representing a Roman house of the time of Titus. Passing down the building, we shall come to the *Central Transept*, where (upon our left) we shall find the *Handel Orchestra*, to hold 4000 persons. The Organ is a wonderfully grand and powerful instrument. Fronting this Orchestra is the *Stage*, for theatrical performances, and near by, on the south of it, an enclosed *Concert Hall*, to hold 4000 persons, wherein the Saturday and other Concerts are given. There is an *Opera House*, also to hold 4000 persons, north of the Concert Hall. Beyond the Central Transept, on either side of the Nave, are numerous Courts, exhibiting the styles of architecture and decoration of various nations. The *Egyptian Court* contains a model of the Temple of the Ptolemys, B.C. 300, with an Avenue of Lions in front of it; the Pillared Hall of Karnak, with Tomb; also the Rock of Beni Hassan. The *Greek Court* exhibits a model of the Acropolis, copies of the Venus of Milo, the Laocoon, the Discobulus, &c. In the Gallery beyond are casts of the Elgin Marbles. The *Roman Court* contains models of the Pantheon, the Colosseum, and the Forum ; copies of the Apollo Belvedere, Venuses, and busts of Roman Emperors. The *Alhambra Court* suffered in the fire of 1866, but is now restored. It is a copy of the Moorish Palace at Granada, containing *Court of the Lions*, *Hall of Justice*, and *Hall of the Abencerrages*, with other apartments. On the East side of the North Transept are the *Byzantine and Romanesque Court*, with various art specimens from the sixth to the thirteenth century ; *Mediæval Courts*, with examples of the Gothic period, twelfth to sixteenth century, showing the styles of German, English, and French Gothic of different periods. Adjoining are the *Renaissance Court*, the *Elizabethan Vestibule*, and the *Italian Court* which possesses copies of the Raphael Frescoes in the Vatican and a number of works by Michael Angelo. The *Industrial Courts*, containing articles for sale, lie on either side of the Central Transept. In the *Picture Gallery* is a large number of Paintings by English and Continental Artists, with prices affixed thereto; beyond are the stalls for toys, and the Camera-obscura. At the North-end of the Terrace are the Monkey-house and Aviaries, and immediately adjoining is the *Aquarium* (admission 6d.), with numerous tanks and specimens of fresh and salt-water fish. Besides all these items, which we have briefly mentioned, there are at the Crystal Palace a thousand and one subjects of interest, and exhibitions, continually being changed, which provide ample amusement for the most active and persistent sight-seer; for people of all ages, tastes, and predilections.

Dalston adjoins Kingsland Road, Hackney, and is accessible by tram and omnibus. *Shacklewell* is on the north side of Dalston. The *German Hospital*, for the reception of poor sick Germans, and others, dates from 1845. The income is nearly £10,000 per annum.

Dulwich is a populous suburb, of some reputation for beauty, situate about five miles from London, and to be easily reached by omnibus from Charing Cross, or by the London, Chatham, and Dover line of Railway, from Victoria, or Ludgate Hill Stations. The place is chiefly remarkable for its *School or College*, and for its *Gallery of Pictures* connected therewith. The *College of God's Gift*, at *Dulwich*, was founded (1619) by Edward Alleyn, a successful actor and theatre manager, in the reign of James I., and the endowments are worth £18,360 per annum, of which £4625 go to the School. Twenty-four old people are supported in the Almshouses, 16 as out-pensioners; 12 foundation scholars are clothed, fed, and educated. The *Upper School* has 500 boys, at from £12 to £18 per annum; the *Lower School*, 160 boys, paying £1 or £2 per annum.

Dulwich Gallery. 281

The charitable benefits are restricted to the parishes of St. Saviour (Southwark), St. Luke, St. Botolph, Bishopsgate-Without, and St. Giles's, Camberwell. Admission is to be obtained for pupils by written application to the Master or Clerk of the College. *Dulwich Gallery of Pictures*, open daily, except Sundays, from ten to four, or five in summer, was founded by Sir Francis Bourgeois, R.A. (1807), who obtained these masterpieces from M. Desenfans, a collector for Stanislaus Augustus, King of Poland. The King died before coming into possession of the pictures, and Desenfans, at his death, bequeathed them to his friend, who, in turn, left them to this College, together with £10,000 for a building to keep them in, and £2000 for a custodian. The Collection contains the finest examples of the Dutch School of Painting, and a few master-pieces of the French, Spanish, and Italian Schools. In no other Gallery is Cuyp (the Dutch Claude) to be seen to such advantage. Rembrandt is here represented by two of his finest works; Teniers, father and son, are also seen at their best. Wouverman's twelve pictures are fine examples; and there are excellent works by Ostade, Botti, Neiss, Van der Neer, Vandyck, Van de Velde, Berchem, Hobbema, and others. Poussin's masterpieces favourably represent the French School. The Murillos are numerous, and fine; and the Velasquez much admired. The Italian pictures are by Titian, and by the later School of A. Caracci. There are a few works of the English School: Gainsborough's picture of Mrs. Sheridan and Mrs. Tickell being the most worthy of note. In the private apartments of the College are some highly interesting portraits, chiefly of actors and poets, viz., Edward Alleyn, the founder; Richard Burbage; Cartwright; Michael Drayton; Lovelace himself and Lovelace's ' Althea,' &c.

Ealing is an ancient suburb of London, near the road to Uxbridge, and about six miles by railway from Paddington.

Edmonton is about ten miles by railway from Liverpool Street. The ' Bell at Edmonton,' rendered memorable as the rendezvous of John Gilpin upon his wedding-day, still exists, and flourishes upon its poetical fame. People from Cockneydom, and travellers from remote countries even, still repair unto the ' Bell at Edmonton,' where Mrs. Gilpin awaited her spouse so long, and where John " threw the wash about," but could not join his wife, although he felt that—

> " All the world would stare,
> If my wife should dine at Edmonton,
> And I should dine at Ware."

The ' Merry Devil at Edmonton ' was the name of an old drama played at the *Globe* at Bankside, and founded upon the story of one Peter Fabell, whose sleight of hand was so great that he " could deceive him who is deceyt itself." *Ware*, which is " ten miles off," is famous for its Great Bed, 12 feet square, of which the tradition was, " that it lodged twelve butchers and their wives, lying thus, two men and two women,—so that each man lay only next his own wife." Ware is upon the Great Eastern Railway, twenty-two miles from Liverpool Street.

Enfield is twelve miles from London by the Liverpool Street Railway, or nine from King's Cross. It was once the site of a Royal Palace.

Epping is an old market town, seventeen miles from London by the Fenchurch Street or Liverpool Street lines of railway. Epping Forest (now preserved from being built over by Act of Parliament) was a Royal chase, extending almost to London, and upon the south-east adjoining Hainault Forest. Tom Hood's poem of the ' Epping Hunt ' indicates the kind of sport which Cockneydom not long since enjoyed here.

Epsom, an ancient town in Surrey, eighteen miles by the London and Brighton, and London and South-Western

Eton College. 283

Railways. The *Derby* and *Oaks* Races are run on Epsom Downs annually, on or about the last week in May.

Erith is a pretty old-fashioned village on the Thames, below Barking, and about fifteen miles by railway from Charing Cross.

Esher is about fourteen miles by railway from Waterloo Railway Station. The *Sandown Park Races* take place in the vicinity. Her Majesty's house, *Claremont*, once the property of Lord Clive, and subsequently the residence of the Prince and Princess Christian, is near Esher.

Eton, famous for its College, is but half a mile from Windsor, with which it is connected by a bridge over the Thames. The College, Chapel, and playing fields are well worth seeing. Tickets of admission to the handsome Gothic Chapel are to be had of Mr. Burgess, High Street, Eton. *Eton College* was established in 1441, and consists of a Provost, a Head-Master, 7 Fellows; 70 scholars, called King's Scholars (on foundation, and who live in the College, and wear black gowns); 3 Chaplains, 10 Lay Clerks, 12 Choristers, and several Assistant-Masters. Its Endowments amount to £20,569 per annum. The 70 King's Scholars are admitted, between eight and fifteen years of age, after a competitive examination, and pay £25 per annum, inclusive, for washing and attendance. The other 700 scholars, called Oppidans, are admitted, from seven to fourteen years of age, into the Upper School, upon application to the College Tutor. The Oppidans are charged £150 to £210 per annum; they reside at the house of one of the Masters, or in one of the authorized Dames' houses. The King's Scholars are exclusively eligible to Scholarships at King's College, Cambridge, but there are sixteen other Scholarships, worth about £800 per annum. Eton College has forty benefices in its gift, worth from £100 to £1200 each.

Finchley, see *Hendon*.

Finsbury Park, between Stoke Newington and Hornsey,

and connected with London by the Great Northern Railway from King's Cross, contains 120 acres, tastefully laid out, and is intersected by the New River. It was opened in 1869.

Fulham is a pretty village, about four miles from London, on the banks of the Thames, which is here crossed by a bridge connecting it with *Putney*, on the opposite bank. The *Manor House* at Fulham has been the summer residence of the Bishops of London for a considerable length of time. *Hurlingham House*, Fulham, is noted for pigeon-shooting matches. See Omnibus Routes, p. 303.

Gravesend, see p. 270, is twenty-four miles by railway from Charing Cross. *Rosherville Gardens* immediately adjoin the town, which is also easily reached by steamboat at low fares.

Greenhithe, with villa residences, on the Thames, is about twenty miles from Charing Cross by railway.

Hackney is reached by omnibus (see p. 306) and by railway from Fenchurch Street and Broad Street. As a parish it includes *Upper and Lower Clapton*. Hackney is said to have been the first suburb provided with carriages for casual passengers, and consequently its name was given to Hackney coaches. *Homerton* is also in the parish of Hackney. At *Homerton* is an old-established Dissenters' Academy, which now affords unsectarian religious training at a fee of five guineas for two years, to young men and women who wish to become teachers in Government-aided Schools.

Haggerstone is an outlying hamlet of St. Leonard's, Shoreditch.

Hammersmith, beyond Kensington, connected by a Suspension Bridge over the Thames, with *Castelnau*. See Omnibus Routes and District Railway.

Hatcham is a new suburb near New Cross, on the South Eastern Railway.

Hampton Court Palace is easily reached by the South-Western Railway, from Waterloo Station, in less than an

Hampton Court Palace. 285

hour, at fares of 2s., 1s. 6d., and 1s. 3d. Return Tickets available for four days cost 2s. 9d., 2s., and 1s. 10d. Admission to the Palace and Gardens is to be had daily, excepting Friday, from ten to six in summer, and to four in winter; Sundays, from two to six, or in winter to four. Hampton Court Palace was built by Cardinal Wolsey, and was given by him to King Henry VIII. Edward VI. was born here, 1537. Oliver Cromwell took possession of it after the death of Charles I., who, as well as his father and his two sons, Charles and James, resided here. William III., Queen Anne, George I. and II., continued to use it as a royal residence, but since their time it has been tenanted only by pensioners of the Crown. After passing through the *Entrance Court*, we come into the *Clock Court*, so named from an Astronomical Clock placed over the gateway. Here also are the Arms of Cardinal Wolsey, with his motto, "*Dominus mihi adjutor*" (God is my helper), and on the small towers, busts in *terra-cotta* of Roman Emperors, presented by Leo X. to the Cardinal. Through a fine Colonnade, built by Sir Christopher Wren, in the Ionic style of architecture, we are admitted to the *King's Grand Staircase*, decorated by Verrio in the richest manner, and thence into the *Guard Chamber*, exhibiting portraits of famous naval and military men. The visitor will subsequently proceed through other apartments which contain over one thousand paintings, a list of which he may buy in the Palace. *Wolsey's Great Hall*, in the Gothic style, is 106 feet long, 40 feet wide, and 60 feet high, and is considered a remarkably handsome structure. It was used as a theatre during the reigns of Elizabeth and James I.; and it has been said that some of Shakespeare's plays were originally performed in it; it is on record that, in 1718, George I. commanded several performances, and that, among others, Shakespeare's *Henry VIII.* with the Fall of Wolsey was performed here in Wolsey's own building. The Gardens are handsomely laid out. The

Maze in the Wilderness, north of the Palace, should be seen; admittance 1*d*. To thread the Maze, keep (except the first turning) always to the left, and in returning keep to the right until you reach the first turning passed on entering.

Hanwell is a village of little note, except in connection with a large Institution, which has been of late years established here, for the treatment of lunatics. It is about seven miles by the Great Western Railway from Paddington.

Harrow-on-the-Hill is an ancient town, nearly twelve miles from London, by the London and North-Western Railway. It is chiefly noted for its great public school, wherein Byron, Sir R. Peel, Palmerston, and many other eminent men were educated. *Harrow School* was founded in 1571. Its endowments amount to about £1500 per annum. It instructs about 500 youths from 12 to 20 years of age, of whom about 30 are foundationers (admitted by the Governors, from residents in the parish), paying 17 guineas per annum; 10 are house boarders (not on foundation), paying £41 5*s*.; and the remainder, boarders in Master's house, at rates varying from £109 to £176 per annum, including schooling and entrance fees, &c. A separate day-school, at £5 per annum, is provided for the sons of Harrow tradesmen, &c. The Head Master practically enjoys entire control of and grants admission to this school, which awards numerous scholarships, exhibitions, and medals, to its most successful pupils. At Westbourne Green, Harrow Road, is the *Lock Hospital and Asylum*, connected with the Institution and Chapel, founded in 1747, in Grosvenor Place, by the Rev. Thomas Scott, the Biblical commentator, for the cure and reclamation of profligate persons. The name has been traced to different sources; the most probable being a Spital for Leprous persons, called the Lok, or Loke, in Southwark. *Lok* is Saxon for shut up or separated. Patients need no letter of recommendation

Kew Gardens. 287

The income of the Lock Asylum is about £2500, of the Female Hospital, £6000 per annum. In the latter were received more than 500 patients, in the former 78, last year.

Hendon, about seven miles from London, by rail from St. Pancras, and joining *Finchley*. Hogarth's 'March to Finchley' exhibits the Guards leaving London to suppress the Rebellion in Scotland, 1745.

The *Welsh Harp* at Hendon is a highly popular resort.

Henley-on-Thames, thirty-six miles from London, by Great Western Railway, is noted for its *Regatta*, held annually about the last week in June.

Herne Hill, a suburb four miles from Victoria Station, Pimlico, or Ludgate Hill, by the London, Chatham, and Dover Railway.

Homerton, see *Hackney*, p. 284.

Hounslow is a town about thirteen miles by rail from Waterloo Terminus. *Hounslow Heath* was the site of an encampment by the forces of James II. after Sedgemoor; and was once notorious for its numerous highwaymen and for its range of gibbets, which were at length removed, out of deference to the sensibilities of the Royal Family, whose road to Windsor lay this way.

Isleworth, pronounced Izleworth, twelve miles by rail from Waterloo Terminus, is noted for its fruit and market gardens, and for its villa residences.

Kew, a village five miles from Hyde Park Corner, is accessible from London by rail, river, or omnibus. *Kew Palace*, a royal residence, has been of late years the residence of the Duchess of Cambridge and the Duchess of Teck. *Kew Gardens* are Crown property, and comprise 270 acres, beautifully and scientifically cultivated under the able botanists, Sir William Hooker and his son, Dr. Hooker. The Gardens, open to the public, *gratis*, every day from 1 till dark, and on Sundays from 2 till 6, deserve more detailed description than can be given here. In the Hot-houses is the most perfect collection in the world of all manner of orchids, ferns, cactuses, and other tropical plants and trees. The palm trees grow to the roof of the Palm House, 64 feet high, as in a tropical forest, the banana and the cocoa-nut, the coffee plant, the cotton, ginger, nutmeg, and clove, all flourish here, and even the dreaded Upas Tree of Java. Out of doors are cultivated the hardier shrubs, and the intermediate climates are provided in the *Winter Garden* for plants and trees requiring certain temperatures. Overlooking the ornamental lake is the highly interesting Museum of Economic Botany. No wonder that visitors come in great numbers to these magnificent grounds, or that having come they frequently renew their visits.

Kingsland is partly in Hackney, partly in Islington parish, and lies between Hoxton and Clapton. It is on the road from London to Stamford Hill, and may be reached by omnibus.

Leyton and *Leytonstone*, in Essex, are small places on the Great Eastern line.

Lewisham is six miles by rail from Charing Cross.

Lillie Bridge, near West Brompton, reached by omnibus from Charing Cross, is noted for its Athletic Sports.

Mildmay Park is a new suburb of private dwellings, leading to Stoke Newington Green from the western end of Balls Pond. It derives its name from Sir Henry Mildmay, who owned it in Charles I.'s reign. The name of King Henry's Walk, given to a path from Balls Pond, is connected with a tradition that Henry VIII. had a private retreat here. This is the site of numerous Protestant Charities.

Mortlake, a river-side village on the South-Western line of Railway, not far from Hammersmith. The *Oxford and Cambridge Boat-race* takes place annually on the Thames, between Putney and Mortlake, on the second Saturday before Easter Sunday. The distance, $4\frac{1}{4}$ miles, is rowed in about twenty minutes.

Richmond. 289

Muswell Hill derived its name from the Mosel, a small stream, and from a famous Well here which belonged to the Knights of St. John of Jerusalem. Muswell Hill Railway Station is six miles from Ludgate Hill,—see Alexandra Park.

Norwood, a suburb on the London and Brighton Railway line, was a few years since but a small village, chiefly known to the world in connexion with a certain prophetess and fortune-teller styled the Norwood Gipsy. Norwood is now divided into sections known as *Upper and Lower Norwood*, each of which is a flourishing town; and *Gipsy Hill*, another division, preserves the memory of the Norwood Gipsy. There is a large *Cemetery* at Norwood, well laid out and kept, in which lie buried many persons of literary and artistic reputation, including Sir William Napier, Douglas Jerrold, Sir T. N. Talfourd, Laman Blanchard, &c.

Near *Peckham Rye* (i.e. a rivulet) which lies beyond *Camberwell*, on the Surrey side of the Thames, is *Nunhead Cemetery*, fifty acres in extent, consecrated in 1840.

Plumstead and *Common*, below Woolwich.

Purfleet is a village on the Thames, below Erith.

Putney, see Mortlake.

Richmond, originally West Sheen, is a populous town of considerable beauty on the right bank of the Thames, about 8 miles from London, and may be reached by railway (South Western), by omnibus, or (in the summer) by steamboat. Nothing remains of the old Royal Palace of Sheen—the scene of so many historical incidents, and particularly of Queen Elizabeth's death, dramatically described by Hume—but the gateway of the Wardrobe Court, now known as Old Palace Yard. Here it is said took place the interview between Queen Elizabeth and Lady Nottingham, then on her death-bed (see p. 111). The view from the terrace on the top of Richmond Hill is scarcely to be excelled in England. Well may

U

we say with Thomson (who lived for some time in Kew Foot Lane):

> "O vale of bliss! O softly swelling hills,
> Heavens! what a goodly prospect spreads around
> Of hills and dales and woods and lawns and spires
> And glittering towns and gilded streams."

The 'Lass of Richmond Hill,' celebrated in the pretty song of the last century, is not without worthy successors at the present day. *Richmond Park*, which may be entered by a gateway from Richmond Hill, is a royal demesne in which stands *Pembroke Lodge*, for some years the residence of the late Earl Russell; *White Lodge*, heretofore occupied by the Prince of Wales; the *Thatched Lodge*, and *Sheen Lodge* (Professor Owen). In Richmond Church are several interesting memorials. The *Star and Garter Hotel*, on Richmond Hill, is a fashionable resort of some celebrity. It commands the beautiful prospect already referred to.

Roehampton, beyond Putney, by railway from Waterloo Station.

St. Albans, twenty miles from London, by the London and North-Western, Midland, or Great Northern Railways, or by coach from Hatchett's, Piccadilly, in summer. The *Abbey of St. Albans* has been renovated, and was raised to the dignity of a bishopric in 1877.

Sandown Park, see Esher.

Snaresbrook, on the Great Eastern line of Railway, beyond Stratford.

Southall, on the Great Western line, next to Hanwell.

Southwark Park, near Rotherhithe New Road, contains 62 acres, and was opened in 1869. It was laid out by the Metropolitan Board of Works at a cost of £100,000.

Spitalfields, see p. 231.

Staines, an ancient and picturesque town on the South-Western Railway, about nineteen miles from London, is connected with *Egham* by a granite bridge. In the neighbourhood of Egham is *Runnimede*,—the meadow wherein King John signed the Great Charter, as certified in the document itself, "per manum nostram in prato quod vocatur Runingmede inter Windlesoram (Windsor) et Stanes." *Charter Island* was the exact site of the interview, according to Matthew of Paris. The modern proprietor of the island has set up a cottage on the spot, where refreshments are to be obtained, and a copy be seen of that Great Charter, which Hallam pronounced "the Keystone of English Liberty."

Stoke Newington is an ancient village bordering on Islington, and consisting principally of one long street on the high road from London to Cambridge, extending from Kingsland Road to Stamford Hill. General Fleetwood and his wife Bridget, the daughter of Oliver Cromwell, were buried in Stoke Newington Church. *Abney Park Cemetery*, Stoke Newington, has a monument to Dr. Isaac Watts, who lived at Sir Thomas Abney's, in this neighbourhood for thirty-six years, and died here.

Stoke Pogis, see Windsor.

Streatham, a healthily situated suburb, on the London and Brighton line, is noted as the site of *Thrale House*, Dr. Johnson's agreeable resort. Mrs. Thrale, afterwards Mrs. Piozzi, was a lady of some literary power, and drew round her a circle of notable persons. Streatham is now a large place, chiefly composed of villa residences, and *Streatham Common* is near thereto. The *Magdalen Hospital*, formerly in the Blackfriars Road, has for some time been removed to Streatham. This Hospital was founded in 1758, to receive, maintain, and employ after probation, repentant public women. Its annual income, derived chiefly from old endowments, is £5450, and it receives 200 women annually.

Surbiton is twelve miles from London, on the South-Western line of Railway.

Sydenham, see *Crystal Palace*, p. 277. There are three

railway stations here: Sydenham from London Bridge, Sydenham Hill from Victoria and Ludgate Hill, and Lower Sydenham, about nine miles from Charing Cross.

Teddington, see p. 248. *Teddington Lock* is the first lock on the Thames as you ascend the stream from London.

Thames Ditton, fourteen miles from Waterloo Railway Terminus.

Tilbury Fort, nearly opposite Gravesend, noted as the scene of Queen Elizabeth's warlike demonstration preparatory for the Armada.

Tottenham lies beyond Stoke Newington and *Stamford Hill*, on the old Cambridge road. *Tottenham Cross*—the present structure dates from 1600—stands near the centre of the village. The *Seven Sisters Road* was named from seven elms planted in a circle, with a walnut tree in the centre, which used to stand at the end of Page Green, and which have been replaced by younger trees.

Tooting, on the Epsom road, just beyond Balham, reached by London and Brighton Railway, and by omnibus from Gracechurch Street. *Upper Tooting* is the part nearest *Balham*.

Twickenham adjoins Richmond. *Orleans House* (now a Club-house), at Twickenham, was once the residence of King Louis Philippe. Pope lived and died at Twickenham, and was buried in the church. *Pope's Villa* has been replaced by a new structure. *Strawberry Hill*, Horace Walpole's villa, now belongs to the Countess of Waldegrave.

Uxbridge, on the Great Western line, now a London suburb, once the chief market-town in Middlesex, is noted in history for the Treaty negotiated here between Charles I. and the Parliamentarians, which was, however, never completed. *Gunnersbury*, *Pitshanger*, and *Coldhawe* are its subordinate manors.

Walham Green lies between West Brompton and Fulham.

Walthamstow is but a few miles from London by the Great Eastern line of railway from Liverpool Street.

Windsor Castle. 293

Walton-on-Thames and *Weybridge* are on the London and South-Western line.

Wimbledon, chiefly noted for its Common, upon which the contests for the Prizes of the Annual Volunteer Gatherings take place every summer. About seven miles by train from Waterloo, Victoria, London Bridge, and Ludgate Hill.

Walworth is a suburb on the Surrey side, easily reached by omnibus or by London, Chatham, and Dover Railway.

Wandsworth, an ancient suburb, originally *Wandlesworth*, from the stream Wandle, which flows through it, lies west of Battersea, and is reached by train from Waterloo. *Wandsworth Common* Railway Station is upon the London and Brighton line from Victoria or London Bridge. *Wandsworth Road* Station is upon the London, Chatham, and Dover line, from Victoria or Ludgate Hill. The *Surrey County Prison* is on *Wandsworth Common*.

Windsor, a large and ancient town, with a population of about 12,000, may be reached in about an hour either from the Paddington Terminus of the Great Western Railway, or from Waterloo Station of the South-Western Railway. Passengers by the former line change carriages at Slough, unless the train be marked "through." From Slough visitors may, if they please, visit *Stoke Pogis*, 2 miles off, the scene of 'Gray's Elegy,' or the famous *Burnham Beeches*, now unhappily the worse for time and storm, but reckoned the finest in the kingdom. *Beaconsfield* is within a short distance; the residence and place of burial of Edmund Waller and Edmund Burke, and the locality which gave Mr. Disraeli his title.

Windsor Castle was built by William of Wykeham, for Edward III. (upon the site of a more ancient castle erected by William the Conqueror), and enlarged by Henry I. and II. Nearly a million of money has been expended here in improvements during and since the reign of George IV. Visitors will find the Northern Terrace and Gardens always open; the Eastern Terrace (whereon the Guards' Band plays on

Sundays) is open during the Queen's absence, on Saturdays and Sundays, only, from 2 to 6 P.M. The State Apartments (not shown while Her Majesty is in residence) are open *gratis* to the public on Mondays, Tuesdays, Thursdays, and Fridays, from 11 to 4 in summer, or 11 to 3 in winter, by tickets available for a week; obtainable in London at Messrs. Colnaghi's, 14 Pall Mall East; or Mr. Mitchell's, 33 Old Bond Street; or Messrs. Keith, Prowse, and Co.'s, 48 Cheapside; or in Windsor, at Mr. Collier's, bookseller, on the Castle Hill. *St. George's Chapel* (open daily for divine service at 10.30 A.M. and 4.30 P.M., on Sundays at 11 A.M. and 5 P.M.) is to be seen any day, from 12.30 to 4. P.M. It is considered one of the most beautiful examples of Perpendicular Gothic ever known. The Choir is decorated with the banners, &c., of the Knights of the Garter, whose stalls are placed therein. The West Window, of old stained glass, exhibits subjects in connection with the Order of the Garter; the East window, designed by Sir G. Scott, is a fine Memorial of the Prince Consort. Observe the Reredos below it; the monument of Edward IV. on the left of it; also, the Duke of Kent's tomb, in the Beaufort Chapel; Henry VI.'s tomb; the monument to the Duchess of Gloucester; the vault in the Middle of the Choir, wherein Henry VIII., Jane Seymour, and Charles I. were buried. In the *Royal Tomb-house*, on the east of the Chapel, lie George III., George IV., William IV., and other personages. Above the Tomb-house is the *Albert Chapel*, erected by the Queen (on the site of an ancient edifice called Wolsey's Chapel), in memory of her Consort—and it is a magnificent and worthy memorial. The Ceiling is composed of devices in Venetian Mosaic; the West-end window is a fine specimen of workmanship; the walls are decorated with marble mosaic-work by Trinqueti. In the centre is the Sarcophagus, with the recumbent figure of the Prince Consort in white marble. This Chapel is open from 12 to 3 every Wednesday, Thursday, and Friday, without tickets. The *State Apartments of Windsor Castle* are:—(1) the *Queen's Audience Chamber*, hung with tapestry and decorated by Verrio, as is also (2) the *Queen's Presence Chamber;* (3) the *Guard Chamber*, containing the Shield by B. Cellini, and memorials of Nelson, Marlborough, and Wellington; (4) *St. George's Hall*, embellished with the armorial bearings of Knights of the Garter, since 1350, and portraits of Kings of England, from James I.; (5) the *Grand Reception Room*, hung with tapestry representing the Story of Jason and Medea; (6) the *Throne Room*, containing numerous portraits, also pictures by West, relating to the Order of the Garter; (7) the *Waterloo Chamber*, decorated by carvings of Grinling Gibbons, contains portraits of the Waterloo heroes; (8) the *Grand Vestibule* exhibits banners and other memorials, also Boehm's Statue of Her Majesty; (9) the *Grand Staircase* shows Chantrey's Statue of George IV.; and (10) the *State Ante-Room*, has carvings by Grinling Gibbons; (11) the *Small Vestibule*, (12) the *Rubens Room*, (13) the *Council Chamber*, (14) the *King's*, and (15) *Queen's* Closets, have not been shown of late; (16) the *Queen's State Drawing Room* contains some landscapes and portraits. The *Old Ball Room* is decorated entirely by Vandyke's portraits of the period of Charles I. and II.

The *Royal Stables*, on the south of the Castle, are open daily from 1 to 3 by tickets, to be had of the Clerk of the Mews.

The *Mausoleum*, erected by the Queen for Prince Albert, stands in the grounds of *Frogmore*.

The Long Walk from Windsor leads to *Virginia Water*. If perchance the visitor to Windsor should find time, after seeing the Castle, the Chapel, &c., to extend his interest further, he would derive much pleasure in a drive to *Virginia Water*—an artificial lake guarded by a miniature man-of-war. A carriage from Windsor and back should not be more than 10s. The avenue starting alongside of the Long Walk is named *Queen Anne's Ride*, and leads to *Ascot* and the course for Ascot Races. *Datchet* village is but a mile from Windsor through the *Home Park*, where, until 1863, stood *Herne's Oak*, immortalised in Shakespeare's 'Merry Wives of Windsor':—

> "Herne the Hunter,
> Sometime a keeper rare in Windsor Forest,
> Doth all the winter time at still midnight
> Walk round about an oak."

Queen Victoria's Oak is now the attraction of Windsor Park, *vice* Herne's, blown down, 1863.

At *Woking*, twenty-four miles from London, by the South-Western Railway line, is one of the largest of our Cemeteries. Here also was founded the *Royal Dramatic College*, which at one time promised to be a flourishing institution; but modern experience seems to show that the asylums, which were in former times the source of so much honourable pride and satisfaction, are not the best means for taking care of old and decayed people. The Greenwich Pensioners preferred removing themselves and their pensions away from the fine edifice with handsome grounds, known as Greenwich Hospital; and people have discovered that old actors and actresses are not best provided for within a sort of barracks, built in an uninhabited district and within too easy distance of a cemetery. A few shillings a week in their own lodgings, or in the house of a friend or relative, and within range of theatrical news, are likely to be much more beneficially spent.

Wormwood Scrubbs, a station near Notting Hill. Upon the Common—but recently a waste—used to be fought many of the fashionable duels which took place at the beginning of this century.

PRINCIPAL CHURCHES AND CHAPELS.

Some of the following are mentioned in the body of this book:

Bavarian (Roman Catholic).—12 Warwick Street, Regent Street.
Danish (Lutheran).—King Street, Poplar.
Dutch (Reformed Calvinist).—6 Austin Friars.
French (Protestant).—5 St. Martin's-le-Grand; Monmouth Road, Westbourne Grove, Bayswater; and 36 Bloomsbury Street, New Oxford Street.
Do. (Roman Catholic).—Little George Street, Portman Square.
German (Lutheran).—Marlborough Court Yard, St. James's Palace.
Do. (Evangelical) Church is in Walton Street, Islington.
Do. (Protestant Reformed), Hooper Square, Leman Street, Whitechapel.
Do. (Roman Catholic).—9 Union Street, Whitechapel.
Greek.—81-84 London Wall, E.C.
Do. (Russian).—32 Welbeck Street, Cavendish Square.
Italian (Roman Catholic).—28 Hatton Wall, Holborn.
Polish (Roman Catholic).—110 Gower Street.
Sardinian (Roman Catholic).—Duke Street, Lincoln's Inn Fields.
Spanish (Roman Catholic).—Spanish Place, Manchester Square.
Swedish (Protestant).—Prince's Square, Shadwell (where Swedenborg was buried).
Swiss (Protestant).—26 Endell Street, Bloomsbury.
Welsh (Calvinist).—Nassau Street, Soho; Bridgewater Square, Barbican, E.C.

The *Jews' Synagogues* are in several parts of London. The Central Synagogue is at 129 Great Portland Street. The City Synagogue is in Great St. Helen's, St. Mary Axe, E.C. The West London Synagogue is at 34 Upper Berkeley Street, Edgware Road, the Western Wall Synagogue in St. Petersburg Place, Bayswater, and the German Jews Synagogue is at Duke's Place, Aldgate. Service begins at sunset every Friday.

NONCONFORMISTS.

Baptists.—Mr. Spurgeon's Tabernacle, Newington Butts.
    Dr. Landells, Park Square Chapel, Regent's Park.
    Bloomsbury Chapel, Bloomsbury.

Congregationalists.—Rev. Dr. David Thomas, Augustine's Church, Clapham Road.
    Rev. Newman Hall, Christ Church, Westminster Bridge Road.
    Rev. Dr. Allon, Union Chapel, Islington.
    Whitfield's, Tottenham Court Road; and Tabernacle Row, Finsbury.
    Rev. Dr. Parker, City Temple, Holborn Viaduct.
    Rev. Dr. Raleigh, Allen Street, Kensington.
    Rev. W. Evans, Falcon Square, E.C.

Wesleyan Methodists.—Wesley Chapel, Warwick Gardens, Kensington.
    Brunswick Chapel (New Connexion), 156 Great Dover Street, Southwark.

Presbyterians.—Dr. Cumming, Crown Court, Covent Garden.
    Regent Square, Gray's Inn Road.
    Dr. D. Fraser, Little Queen Street, Bryanstone Square.

Unitarians.—Essex Street, Strand.
    Little Portland Street.
    11 South Place, Finsbury.

Rev. C. Voysey, Langham Hall, Langham Place, Regent Street.

Society of Friends, or Quakers.—The Meeting Houses are at 110 St. Martin's Lane, near Charing Cross; and at 12 Bishopsgate Street Without.

THE CATHOLIC APOSTOLIC CHURCH, founded by Irving, in Gordon Square, was designed by Brandon, in a style of Early Gothic. The service is of a ceremonial kind, with a full proportion of music, and the robes of the priests, or 'Elders,' are highly pictorial, and probably unique.

The ENGLISH ROMAN CATHOLIC CHURCHES are:

    St. George's Cathedral, Westminster Bridge Road.
    Pro-Cathedral, Newland Terrace, Kensington.
    The Oratory, Brompton Road.
    The Jesuits, Farm Street, Berkeley Square.
    St. Mary's Chapel, Moorfields.

POSTAGE AND TELEGRAMS.

Letters to any part of the United Kingdom, including all outlying British isles, are charged, when prepaid, as follows:

Not more than 1 ounce		1*d.*
Above 1 oz., but under 2 oz.		1½*d.*
,, 2 ,, ,, 4 ,,		2*d.*
,, 4 ,, ,, 6 ,,		2½*d.*
,, 6 ,, ,, 8 ,,		3*d.*
,, 8 ,, ,, 10 ,,		3½*d.*
,, 10 ,, ,, 12 ,,		4*d.*

Letters over 12 oz. are charged 1*d.* for every additional ounce or part thereof. Letters are not to be larger than 18 inches by 9 inches. Letters posted unpaid are charged double postage, and if posted with insufficient stamps, the deficiency is charged double.

Letters to any country in the Postal Union, *i.e.*, nearly every country in Europe, also the United States, are charged 2½*d.* each, under ½ oz.

Newspapers are charged ½*d.* each (prepaid) within the United Kingdom, or double to any country in the Postal Union.

Post Cards for the United Kingdom are sold at ¾*d.* each, or in packets of 7*d.* or 8*d.* per doz., according to thickness; for places within the Foreign Postal Union they cost 1¼*d.* each.

Books not exceeding 5 lbs. in weight, or the size stated above for largest letters, are charged at the rate of 2 oz. for ½*d.* They must be packed open at the ends, so as to be readily examined.

London Districts.

London and its environs are divided into Eight POSTAL DISTRICTS, each of which is treated, in many respects, as a separate Post Town. The following are the names of the Districts, with their abbreviations, viz.:

Eastern Central	E.C.	South Eastern	S.E.
Eastern	E.	South Western	S.W.
Northern	N.	Western	W.
North Western	N.W.	Western Central	W.C.

Town Deliveries.

The portion of each District within about three miles of the General Post Office is designated the Town Delivery, and the remainder the Suburban Delivery.

Within the limits of the Eastern Central District there are daily twelve deliveries, and within the Town limits of the other Districts eleven deliveries. The *first*, or General Post delivery, including all Inland, Colonial, and Foreign letters arriving in sufficient time, commences about 7.20 A.M., and, except on Mondays, or on other days when there are large arrivals of letters from abroad, is generally completed, throughout London, by 9 o'clock. In the Eastern Central District the *second* delivery begins at about 8.30 A.M., and includes the correspondence received by Night Mail from Ireland and by the North Mails arriving at 6.40 and 8.0 A.M.; and the third delivery in this District, corresponding with the second delivery in other districts, is made at about 10 A.M., and includes the letters collected in London generally at 8.45 A.M., and the correspondence by the Scotch Mail arriving about 9 A.M. The next nine deliveries are made in every District hourly.

Suburban Deliveries.

There are six despatches daily to the Suburban Districts. The first (at 6·30 A.M.) is to all places within the London District; and includes the correspondence by the Night Mails from the Provinces, and by any Colonial or Foreign Mails arriving in sufficient time. This delivery is generally completed in the nearer Suburbs by 9 A.M., and at the more distant between 9 and 10 A.M. The second despatch (at 9.30 A.M.) is to the nearer Suburban Districts only. The third despatch (at 11.30 A M.) comprises, with a few exceptions, every part of the London District. Except to isolated places, the fourth despatch (at 2.30 P.M.) is to most of the Suburban Districts. The fifth despatch (at 4.30 P.M.) extends to the whole of the Suburban Districts; and, except in the remoter rural places, the letters are delivered the same evening. The sixth despatch is at 7 P.M. Letters for this despatch posted at the Town Receiving Houses and Pillar Boxes by 6 P.M., *or at the Chief Office of the District to which they are addressed* by 7.30 P.M., are delivered the same evening; except at a few distant places, where the delivery is made early the following morning.

There is no delivery or collection of letters in London on Sundays.

Letters for the Evening Mails for the country and abroad should be posted in the branch post offices or the pillar boxes within the London district before 5.30 P.M., or may be posted at the branch offices with an extra stamp before 6 P.M.; at the General Post Office, St. Martin's-le-Grand, with one extra stamp before 6.45, or with two extra stamps till 7.30 P.M.

Letters for most European Mails are despatched morning and evening; for the United States, Tuesday, Thursday, and Saturday evenings: for India, every Thursday morning at 6d. per ½ oz., on Friday evening at 8d. per ½ oz.

Post Office Orders for sums not exceeding 10s., 2d.; £2, 3d.; £3, 4d.; and so on, up to £10 for 1s.

Foreign Post Office Orders payable in the United States, India, the Colonies, and to most of the countries of Europe, are charged 9d. for less than £2; 1s. 6d. under £5, and so on.

Telegrams.

Messages of not more than 20 words in the United Kingdom, 1s., and 3d. for each additional 5 words if delivered within one mile of the office they are sent to, but if beyond, then 6d. per mile for delivery. To New York, 4s. per word, including address and signature.

All London Telegraph Offices are open from 8 A.M. to 8 P.M., and the following five are open night and day:—1. St. Martin's-le-Grand; 2. Moorgate Street; 3. Paddington; 4. Victoria (London, Chatham, and Dover Station); 5. West Strand. Foreign Telegrams are not under the control of the English Government system.

PARCELS DELIVERY COMPANIES.

Parcels for London and suburbs are sent by the *London Parcels Delivery Co.*, which has 1,200 receiving offices, at a charge of—

Within 3 miles. Under 4 lbs., 3d.; 14 lbs., 6d.; 28 lbs., 8d., or 112 lbs. for 1s. 2d. Beyond 3 miles, charges from 4d. upwards.

Parcels for *Provincial Towns* are sent by Sutton & Co., 35 Aldersgate Street.

Parcels for *the Continent* are sent by Continental Parcels Express: offices, 34 Regent Circus; 33 St. Paul's Churchyard.

Globe Parcels Express to all parts of the World: offices, 53 Gracechurch Street; 156 Leadenhall Street; 23 Regent Street; 300 Oxford Street.

Parcels or *Messages* are carried by *Commissionaires*—office, 419a Strand, at the rate of 3d. per mile, or 6d. per hour; or extra for parcels over 14 lbs.

RAILWAY STATIONS AND TERMINI.

Great Eastern Railway Terminus Station, in Liverpool Street, E.C., opened in 1874, superseding the old Terminus in Shoreditch, is the Terminus of the line through the Eastern Counties (and formerly called the Eastern Counties Railway), connecting Cambridge, Colchester, Harwich, Ipswich, Norwich, Peterborough, &c., with London; and viâ Harwich and a line of steamboats to Antwerp, forming a cheap and direct route to Belgium and North of France, or to Rotterdam for Holland and the Rhine.

Great Northern Railway Terminus Station, at King's Cross, built in 1852, is the Terminus of the line which runs through Yorkshire to Edinburgh. There is a fine large Hotel connected with this line at King's Cross, called the Great Northern Hotel.

Great Western Railway Terminus Station, at Paddington, finished in 1856, is the Terminus of an extensive line running through the Western Counties to Exeter and Cornwall, or to South Wales, and thence to Waterford by mail steamers, or by Weymouth to Cherbourg, or the Channel Islands. The Great Western Hotel, at Paddington, adjoins the Terminus.

London, Brighton, and South Coast Railway has one Terminus at London Bridge, the other at Victoria Station, Pimlico, for the West-end of London. This line runs by way of Portsmouth to the Isle of Wight, and by the Newhaven and Dieppe line of steamers connects London and Paris by the cheapest and shortest route through Normandy. The London Bridge Hotel and the Grosvenor Hotel, Pimlico, are two vast edifices, specially adapted for the reception of railway travellers.

London, Chatham, and Dover Railway has two Termini, the one at the Holborn Viaduct for the City of London, the other at Victoria Station, Pimlico, for the West End. This line traverses Kent, and by way of Rochester and Chatham runs on to Dover, whence, by a line of mail steamers, it connects England with Belgium at Ostend, and by another set of mail steamers to Calais, with France, &c., and carries passengers and merchandise by the shortest passage across the English Channel. Hotels in connection with this line are to be found at each Terminus.

Midland Railway Terminus Station, in the Euston Road, is the noblest of all the structures of this kind in London, its roof being

700 feet long and of 240 feet span. This line runs through the Midland Counties to Scotland, and has a fine Hotel at the London Terminus.

South-Eastern Railway has a Terminus at Cannon Street, with a large Hotel for the City of London, and another Terminus at Charing Cross for the West End. The magnificent Charing Cross Hotel is connected with it. This line branches to Gravesend and Maidstone, but its chief way is through Surrey and Kent to Folkestone and Dover, whence mail steamers run to the Continent—from Dover to Calais or Ostend; from Folkestone, by way of Boulogne, to Paris.

London and South-Western Railway Terminus Station is in the Waterloo Road, on the Surrey side of London. This line runs through the Southern and Western Counties to Southampton, whence it despatches a line of steamers to Havre and the Channel Islands, and westerly to Devonshire.

London and North-Western Railway Terminus is in the Euston Road. This line passes through the Midland Counties to North and South Wales, and by way of Holyhead, its mail steamers connect London and Dublin; it is also the chief line to Liverpool and the North-Western Coast of England and Scotland.

OMNIBUSES.

Omnibuses from various quarters of London to other districts run daily from 8 A.M. till 12 at night, at fares, according to distance, from 1*d.* to 6*d.* each person. Each fare must appear distinctly painted upon some prominent part of the vehicle. After 8 P.M. on Sunday nights the fares are in some instances doubled. The following are the routes of the different omnibuses, now chiefly owned by the London General Omnibus Company; chief office, 6 Finsbury Square, E.C., whither all complaints should be sent, addressed to the Secretary, A. G. Church, Esq.

From Barnsbury to Kennington and back.—Every eight minutes— Through Caledonian Road, Offord Road, Liverpool Road, past the Angel Inn, Islington, down Goswell Road, by St. Paul's Churchyard, Ludgate Hill, Bridge Street, and over Blackfriars Bridge to Kennington Park Road.

From Bayswater to Victoria Station, Pimlico and back.—Red Bus; every ten minutes—Through Westbourne Park, Bishop's Road, Praed Street, Edgware Road, past the Marble Arch, down Park Lane to Hyde Park Corner, Piccadilly, then past the St. George's Hospital, through Grosvenor Place, Belgravia, to Pimlico.

Omnibuses.

From Bayswater to Whitechapel and back.—Dark Green Bus; every ten minutes—Through Westbourne Grove, Edgware Road, Marble Arch, Oxford Street, Holborn, Newgate Street, Cheapside, Bank, Cornhill, Leadenhall Street, Aldgate, to Whitechapel.

From Bermondsey to Gracechurch Street.—Frequently; the "John Bull" Bus—Through Blue Anchor Road, Grange Road, Star Corner, Bermondsey Street, Tooley Street, over London Bridge to Gracechurch Street.

From Bethnal Green to Chelsea and back.—Chocolate Bus; every fifteen minutes—Through Bethnal Green Road, Church Street, Bishopsgate, Cornhill, Cheapside, St. Paul's, Ludgate Hill, Fleet Street, Strand, Charing Cross, Haymarket, Piccadilly, Hyde Park Corner, Knightsbridge, Sloane Street, to King's Road, Chelsea.

From Blackwall to Regent Circus, Piccadilly.—Blue Bus; every twelve minutes—Through West India Docks, Poplar, Limehouse, Stepney, Commercial Road, Leadenhall Street, Cornhill, Bank, Cheapside, St. Paul's, Ludgate Hill, Fleet Street, Strand, Charing Cross, to Regent Circus.

From the Borough (Elephant and Castle) to the Bank.—Red Bus; frequently—Meeting the Brixton and Clapham Tram Cars, and conveying passengers down the Dover Road and over London Bridge.

From Bow and Stratford to Oxford Street.—Green Bus; every ten minutes—Through Bow, Whitechapel, Aldgate, Leadenhall Street, Cornhill, Bank, Cheapside, Ludgate Hill, Fleet Street, Strand, Charing Cross, Pall Mall East, Waterloo Place, Regent Street to Oxford Street.

From Brentford to St. Paul's Churchyard and back.—Red Bus; every hour—Through Kew Bridge, Chiswick, Turnham Green, Hammersmith, Kensington, Knightsbridge, Piccadilly, Regent Circus, Haymarket, Charing Cross, Strand, Fleet Street, to St. Paul's Churchyard.

From Brixton to Oxford Street.—Green Bus; every ten minutes—Through Brixton Road, Kennington Road, Westminster Road, over Westminster Bridge, through Parliament Street and Whitehall, Charing Cross, Regent Street, to Oxford Street.

From Brixton to Gracechurch Street.—Every ten minutes—Through Brixton, Kennington Park Road, Newington, the Borough, over London Bridge, to Gracechurch Street.

From Brompton to Islington and back.—Blue Bus; every eight minutes—From Queen's Elm, through Brompton, Knightsbridge, Hyde Park Corner, Piccadilly, up Regent Street to Regent Circus, Oxford Street, through Mortimer Street, Great Portland Street, Marylebone Road, Euston Road,—past London and North-Western, Midland, and Great Northern Railway Stations,—King's Cross, Pentonville Hill, to Islington.

Omnibuses. 305

From Brompton to Holloway and back.—Blue Bus, 'Favourite,' as preceding, to King's Cross, thence, by the Caledonian Road, to Holloway.

From Brompton to the Bank and back.—White Bus; every eight minutes—Through Brompton, Knightsbridge, Hyde Park Corner, Piccadilly, Regent Circus, Haymarket, Charing Cross, Strand, Fleet Street, Ludgate Hill, St. Paul's, Cheapside, Bank, to Broad Street Railway Station.

From Camberwell to Gracechurch Street and back.—Yellow Bus; every five minutes—Through Walworth Road, past Elephant and Castle, Newington Causeway, the Borough, over London Bridge, to Gracechurch Street.

From Camberwell Gate to Camden Town (Regent's Park) and back.— 'Waterloo,' Blue Bus; every eight minutes— Through Walworth Road, London Road, Waterloo Road, over Waterloo Bridge into the Strand, Charing Cross, Regent Street, to Regent Circus (Oxford Street) Great Portland Street, Albany Street, to the York and Albany.

From Camden Town to Westbourne Grove, Bayswater.—Claret Bus; every fifteen minutes—Through Park Street, Regent's Park, Grove Road, Church Street, and Bishop's Road, to Westbourne Grove.

From Camden Town to Westminster and Victoria Station, Pimlico, and back.—Yellow Bus; every five minutes—From the 'Mother Red Cap,' through High Street, Hampstead Road, Tottenham Court Road, St. Giles's, Seven Dials, St. Martin's Lane, Trafalgar Square, Charing Cross, Parliament Street, Westminster, Victoria Street, to Victoria Station, Pimlico. A few of these buses stop short at St. Martin's Church, Trafalgar Square.

From Camden Town Railway Station to Kennington Gate and back.— Green Bus; every seven minutes—Through Great College Street, St. Pancras Road, past the London and North-Western, Midland, and Great Northern Railways, King's Cross, Gray's Inn Road, down Holborn to Holborn Circus, New Bridge Street, Blackfriars Bridge, London Road, Elephant and Castle, Newington Butts, Kennington Park Road, to Kennington Gate.

From Charing Cross to Paddington, Westbourne Grove and back.— Red Bus; every ten minutes—Through Regent Street, Oxford Street, past Marble Arch, Edgware Road, Praed Street, and Great Western Railway, Paddington.

From Chelsea to Bethnal Green and back.—Chocolate Bus; every twelve minutes—Through King's Road, Sloane Square, Sloane Street, Knightsbridge, Hyde Park Corner, Piccadilly, Regent Street, Pall Mall East, Charing Cross, Strand, Cheapside, Bank, Cornhill, Bishopsgate Street, Shoreditch, Bethnal Green Road, to Bethnal Green.

x

From Chelsea to Hoxton and back.—Chocolate Bus; every twelve minutes—As preceding to the Bank, thence through Moorgate Street, Finsbury Square, Pitfield Street, to Hoxton.

From Clapham to Gracechurch Street and back.—Chocolate Bus; every eight minutes—From the 'Plough,' Clapham, by Stockwell, through Kennington Park Road, Newington, the Borough, over London Bridge, to Gracechurch Street.

From Clapham to Regent Circus, Oxford Street, and back.—Green Bus; every fifteen minutes—From the 'Plough,' Clapham by Stockwell, Kennington, Westminster Bridge Road, Westminster, Parliament Street, Whitehall, Charing Cross, Regent Street, to Regent Circus, Oxford Street.

From Clapton and Hackney, past the Bank, to Regent Circus, Oxford Street and back.—Dark Green Bus; every twenty minutes—Through Hackney Road, Shoreditch, Bishopsgate, Bank, Cheapside, Holborn, Oxford Street, to Regent Circus. On Sundays, Lea Bridge to the Bank only.

From Clapton to Oxford Street and back.—Dark Green Bus; five minutes after each hour—From the 'Swan,' Clapton, through Dalston Lane, Balls Pond Road, Lower Road Islington, New Road, Pentonville, King's Cross, Euston Road, Great Portland Street, Regent Circus, Oxford Street, to 'Green Man and Still,' Oxford Street.

From Deptford to Gracechurch Street and back.—Dark Green Bus; every thirty minutes—Through Rotherhithe, Lower Road, Tooley Street, over London Bridge, to Gracechurch Street.

From Farringdon Street Railway Station to Elephant and Castle, Newington.

From Fulham to London Bridge. White Bus; through Piccadilly, Strand, &c.

From Hackney to Oxford Street.—Dark Green Bus; every thirty minutes—Through Dalston, Kingsland, Balls Pond, Lower Road Islington, Euston Road, Great Portland Street, Regent Circus, Oxford Street.

From Hackney Road to Camberwell Gate.—Every five minutes—Through Hackney Road, Shoreditch, Bishopsgate, Cornhill, London Bridge, Borough, Elephant and Castle, to Red Lion.

From Hammersmith and Kensington to the Bank.—Red Bus; every six minutes—Through King Street, Broadway, Kensington, Knightsbridge, Piccadilly, Regent Circus, Haymarket, Charing Cross, Strand, Fleet Street, Cheapside, to the Bank.

From Hammersmith to Liverpool Street Railway Station.—Red Bus; every eight minutes—Same as above to Bank, and thence to Broad Street.

From Hampstead to Oxford Street.—Yellow Bus; every fifteen minutes—Through Haverstock Hill, Camden Town, Hampstead Road, Tottenham Court Road.

From Harrow Road to London Bridge.—Yellow Bus; every ten minutes—Through Bishop's Road, Edgware Road, Oxford Street, Holborn, Cheapside, over London Bridge.

From Haverstock Hill to Victoria.—Yellow Bus; every five minutes—Through Hampstead Road, Tottenham Court Road, Oxford Street, Charing Cross.

From Highgate and Kentish Town to Oxford Street.—Yellow Bus; every twelve minutes—Through Camden Town, Hampstead Road, Tottenham Court Road.

From Holloway to the General Post Office.—Red Bus; every morning and evening—Through Holloway Road, Islington, Goswell Road, Aldersgate Street.

Hornsey to Victoria Station.—'Favourite,' Green Bus; every ten minutes—Through Holloway Road, Highbury, Islington High Street, St. John Street Road (Sadler's Wells Theatre), Exmouth Street, Gray's Inn Lane, Chancery Lane, Fleet Street, Strand, Parliament Street, to Victoria Station.

From Highbury to the Bank.—Red Bus; every ten minutes—Through Canonbury Road, New North Road, City Road, Moorgate Street.

From Highbury to Victoria.—'Favourite,' Green Bus; every ten minutes—Through Highbury, Islington High Street, Angel, St. John Street Road, Gray's Inn Road, Chancery Lane, Strand, Charing Cross, Parliament Street, to Victoria Station.

From Holloway and Islington to Victoria Station.—'Favourite,' Green Bus; every fifteen minutes — Through Highbury Place, Islington High Street, Clerkenwell, Gray's Inn Lane, Strand, Parliament Street, to Victoria Station.

From Holloway to London Bridge.—Green Bus; every ten minutes—Through Grove Road, Holloway Road, Islington, City Road, Moorgate Street, over London Bridge.

From Hornsey Road, Highbury, and Islington to London Bridge Railway Station.—'Favourite,' Green Bus; every six minutes—Through Seven Sisters' Road, Holloway Road, Highbury, Islington High Street, City Road, Finsbury Circus, Moorgate Street, Bank, King William Street, over London Bridge.

From Hounslow to St. Paul's Churchyard.—Red Bus—Through Isleworth Gate, Brentford, Kew Bridge, Turnham Green, Hammersmith, Kensington, Hyde Park Corner, Haymarket, Strand, Fleet Street, and Ludgate Hill.

From Islington, Barnsbury Park, to Kennington Gate.—Chocolate Bus; every seven minutes—Through Barnsbury Road, Islington, Goswell Road, Aldersgate Street, St. Paul's Churchyard, Ludgate Hill, Blackfriars Bridge, London Road, Elephant and Castle, Kennington Park Road.

From Islington (Lower Road) to Old Kent Road (Southwark).— Green Bus; every eight minutes—Through Lower Road, New North Road, East Road, City Road, Moorgate Street, London Bridge, Borough, Old Kent Road.

From Kennington to Charing Cross.—Red Bus; every eight minutes —Through Kennington Park Road, Westminster Road and Bridge, Parliament Street, and Trafalgar Square.

From Kensington and Hammersmith to the Bank.—See Hammersmith.

From Kensal Green to the Bank and London Bridge.—Yellow Bus; every hour—From Royal Oak, through Edgware Road, Oxford Street, Holborn, and Cheapside.

From Kentish Town to Oxford Street.—Yellow Bus; every twelve minutes—Through Twains Lane, Highgate Hill, Kentish Town, Camden Town, Hampstead Road, Tottenham Court Road.

From Kentish Town to Kennington.—Green Bus; every ten minutes — Through Great College Street, King's Cross Railway Station, Gray's Inn Road, Chancery Lane, Fleet Street, Ludgate Circus, Blackfriars Bridge and Road, Elephant and Castle, Kennington Park Road.

Kew to the Bank.—Red Bus; every hour—Only those marked Kew Bridge go as far as the Bridge.

Kilburn to the London Docks.—Green Bus; every eight minutes— Through Edgware Road, Oxford Street, Holborn, Cheapside, Cornhill, Leadenhall Street, and Minories.

From Kilburn to Charing Cross.—Red Bus; every fifteen minutes —Through Edgware Road, Oxford Street, and Regent Street.

From Kilburn to Victoria. — Every fifteen minutes — Through Edgware Road, Park Lane, Grosvenor Place, and Victoria.

From Kilburn Gate to Whitechapel.—Sundays only; Dark Green Bus; every fifteen minutes—Through Maida Hill, Edgware Road, Oxford Street, Holborn, Cheapside, Leadenhall Street.

From Kingsland Gate to the Bank.—Every five minutes—Through Kingsland Road (Dalston), Shoreditch, Bishopsgate Street, Bank; returns from the end of Threadneedle Street.

From Kingsland Gate to the Elephant and Castle, Newington.—Green Bus; every six minutes—Through Kingsland Road, Shoreditch, Finsbury Square, London Bridge, and Borough.

From Mildmay Park to the Bank.—Green Bus—Through Albion

Road, Mildmay Park, by Stoke Newington Green, Southgate Road, and Finsbury Square to the Bank.

From Notting Hill and Bayswater to Whitechapel.—Green Bus; every eight minutes—Through Notting Hill, Harrow Road, Edgware Road, Oxford Street, Holborn, Cheapside, Bank, Cornhill, Aldgate, and Whitechapel.

From Notting Hill and Bayswater to Mile End.—Light Green Bus; every five minutes—Same as above, the route to Whitechapel.

From Notting Hill and Bayswater to London Bridge.—Dark Green Bus; every eight minutes—By St. John's Church, Royal Oak, Regent Circus, Oxford Street, Holborn, Cheapside, Bank to London Bridge.

From Notting Hill to Charing Cross.—Every ten minutes—Through Westbourne Grove, Bishop's Road, Harrow Road, Edgware Road, Oxford Street, Regent Street, Cockspur Street.

From Old Ford to the Bank.—Yellow Bus; every ten minutes—Through Victoria Park, Hackney Road, and Shoreditch.

From Paddington to London Bridge Railway Station.—Yellow Bus; every five minutes—Through Edgware Road, Oxford Street, Holborn, Newgate Street, Cheapside. Ditto by light Green Bus, through Euston Road; every seven minutes.

From Peckham to Gracechurch Street.—By King's Arms; every ten minutes—Through Camberwell, Walworth Road, Borough, over London Bridge to 'George and Gate,' Gracechurch Street.

From Peckham Rye to Gracechurch Street—By King's Arms, Peckham Rye, Rye Lane, Peckham Road, Camberwell Green; then same as above.

From Pimlico to the Bank—Chocolate Bus; every eight minutes—Through Warwick Street, Vauxhall Bridge Road, Westminster Abbey, Parliament Street, Charing Cross, Strand, Fleet Street, Ludgate Circus, St. Paul's Churchyard, Cheapside.

From Pimlico to Oxford Circus.—Blue Bus; every ten minutes—From Victoria Station, Grosvenor Place, Piccadilly, Bond Street, and Oxford Street.

From Putney Bridge to London Bridge Railway Station.—White Bus; every fifteen minutes—Through Fulham, Brompton, Knightsbridge, Piccadilly, Charing Cross, Strand, Fleet Street, St. Paul's Churchyard, Cannon Street, over London Bridge.

From Regent Circus to Peckham.—Every fifteen minutes—Through Regent Street, Charing Cross, Westminster Bridge, St. George's Road, Camberwell, to Rye Lane.

From Rotherhithe to Gracechurch Street.—Every fifteen minutes—By Red Lion, Lower Road, Southwark Park; from thence by the same route as Bermondsey.

From Royal Oak, Westbourne Grove, to London Bridge.—Green Bus; every ten minutes—By Royal Oak, Westbourne Grove, Bishop's Road, Harrow Road, Edgware Road, Marylebone Road, Euston Road, King's Cross, Islington, City Road, Finsbury Square, Moorgate Street, and King William Street.

From Royal Oak to London Bridge.—Yellow Bus; every five minutes—Same as above to Edgware Road, then by Oxford Street, Holborn, and Cheapside.

From Shepherd's Bush to the City.—Green Bus; every fifteen minutes—Through Shepherd's Bush Green, Uxbridge Road, Bayswater Road, Oxford Street, Holborn, Cheapside.

From St. John's Wood to Camberwell Gate and Old Kent Road.—'Atlas,' Green Bus; every eight minutes—Through Finchley Road, St. John's Wood, Baker Street, Portman Square, Orchard Street, Oxford Street, Regent Street, Charing Cross, Westminster Bridge Road, London Road, and Walworth Road.

From St. John's Wood to London Bridge Railway Station.—'City Atlas,' Green Bus; every eight minutes—By Swiss Cottage, Marlborough Road, Finchley Road, St. John's Wood Road, Park Road, Baker Street, Oxford Street, Holborn, Newgate Street, Cheapside, Bank, King William Street, to London Bridge.

From South Hackney to the Bank.—Red Bus; every thirty minutes—Through Victoria Park Road, Hackney Road, to Shoreditch.

From Starch Green to the City.—Green Bus; every thirty minutes—Through Goldhawk Road, Shepherd's Bush, Uxbridge Road, Bayswater Road, Oxford Street, Holborn, and Cheapside.

From Stoke Newington to Victoria.—Green Bus; every fifteen minutes—By Abney Park Cemetery, Church Street, Newington Green, Mildmay Park, Essex Road, Islington, St. John Street Road, Gray's Inn Road, Holborn, Chancery Lane, Strand, Charing Cross, and Victoria Street.

From Stoke Newington to Westminster Abbey.—Green Bus; every thirty minutes—Through Essex Road, Islington, Clerkenwell, Gray's Inn Road, Chancery Lane, Strand, to Whitehall.

From Tulse Hill to Gracechurch Street.—Every hour—Through Upper Tulse Hill, New Church Road, Brixton Road, Kennington Park Road, Elephant and Castle, Borough, and over London Bridge.

From Walham Green to the City, Broad Street Station.—White Bus; every twenty minutes—Through Brompton Road, Knightsbridge, Piccadilly, Charing Cross, Strand, Fleet Street, Ludgate Circus, to Cheapside.

From Wandsworth Road to Gracechurch Street.—Every fifteen minutes—By 'King William the Fourth,' Wandsworth Road, Albert

Embankment, York Road, Stamford Street, Southwark Street, over London Bridge.

From Westminster to the Bank.—Chocolate Bus; every six minutes—Through the Strand, Parliament Street, and by Westminster Abbey.

TRAMWAY OMNIBUSES.

From Aldersgate Street to Dalston Junction.—At 8.10 A.M. and every six minutes, to 11.15 P.M.; cars and lamps green—Through Goswell Road, Islington Green, Essex Road, and Balls Pond Road. From Dalston at 7.30 A.M., and every six minutes, to 11 P.M.

From Aldersgate Street to Lea Bridge Road.—At 8.30 A.M., and every six minutes to 11.30 P.M.; cars and lamp, blue—Through Goswell Road, Old Street, Old Street Road, Hackney Road, Mare Street, Hackney, to Clapton. From Lea Bridge at 8 A.M., and every six minutes, to 10.52 P.M.

From Aldgate to Stratford.—At 6.40 A.M., and every five minutes, to 12 P.M.; cars and lamp, blue—Through Whitechapel, Mile End Road, Bow, and Stratford New Town. Passengers for Leytonstone change cars at Stratford. From Stratford at 6 A.M., and every five minutes, to 11.5. P.M.

From Blackheath Road to Blackfriars Bridge.—At 7.55 A.M., and every twelve minutes, to 10.40 P.M.; lamps, amber—Through Blackheath Road, Broadway, New Cross Road, Hatcham, Old Kent Road, New Kent Road, London Road, Blackfriars Road, to Blackfriars Bridge (Surrey side). From Blackfriars Bridge at 8.45 A.M., and every twelve minutes, to 11.45 P.M.

From Brixton to Blackfriars Bridge.—At 8 A.M., and every twelve minutes to 11 P.M.—Through Brixton Road, Kennington Park, Kennington Road, Lambeth Road, to Blackfriars Bridge (Surrey side). From Blackfriars Bridge at 8.37 A.M., and every twelve minutes, to 11.37 P.M.

From Brixton and Lawson Street, Dover Road.—At 8.8 A.M., and every twelve minutes to 9.52 A.M., and every twelve minutes, to 9.25 P.M.; on Saturday extra, 2.39 P.M., and every twelve minutes to 4.50 P.M.; white lamps—Through Brixton Road, viâ St. George's Church, Kennington Park.

From Lawson Street.—At 7.27 A.M., and every twelve minutes, to 9.16 A.M. and 3.30 P.M., and every twelve minutes to 8.43 P.M.; Saturday extra, 1.54 P.M., and every twelve minutes, to 4.5 P.M.

From Brixton to Westminster Bridge.—At 8.4 A.M., and every twelve minutes, to 11.35 P.M.; cars, red; lamps, red and white—Through Brixton Road, Kennington Park, Kennington Road, Westminster Road, to Westminster Bridge (Surrey side). From Westminster at 8.35 A.M., and every twelve minutes, to 12 P.M.

From Clapham to Blackfriars.—At 8.6. A.M., and every twelve minutes to 10.55 P.M.; green cars; lamps, red and green—Through Clapham Road, Kennington Park, Kennington Road, Westminster Road, to Westminster Bridge (Surrey side). From Westminster at 8.41 A.M., and every twelve minutes, to 12.5 P.M.

From Clapham to Westminster Bridge.—At 8.10 A.M., and every twelve minutes, to 11.25 P.M.; cars and lamps, yellow—Through Clapham Road, Kennington Park, Kennington Road, Westminster Road, to Westminster Bridge (Surrey side). From Westminster at 8.41 A.M., and every twelve minutes, to 12.5 night.

From Clapham to St. George's Church, Borough.—At 8.2 A.M., and every 12 minutes, to 12 midday, and 3.25 P.M., and every twelve minutes, to 9.20 P.M.; Saturday, 1.54 P.M., and every twelve minutes, to 10.53 P.M.; cars and lamps, red—Through Clapham Road, Kennington Park Road, Newington. From Lawson Street, 7.20 A.M., and every twelve minutes to 11.25 P.M.; Saturday at 11.9 A.M., and every twelve minutes, to 10.6 P.M.

From Camberwell to Blackfriars.—At 7.38 A.M., and every twelve minutes, to 10.41 P.M. From Blackfriars at 8.3 A.M., and every twelve minutes, to 11.50 P.M.—Through Camberwell Road, Walworth Road, London Road, to Blackfriars Road.

From Camberwell to Vauxhall.—At 8.30 A.M., and every eight minutes, to 11 P.M.; cars, brown; lamps, red—Through Camberwell New Road, Kennington Oval, Harleyford Road, to Vauxhall Bridge (Surrey side). From Vauxhall at 8.54 A.M. and every eight minutes, to 11 P.M.

From East Greenwich to Blackfriars Bridge.—At 7.20 A.M., and every 12 minutes, to 10.20 P.M.; cars brown; lamps, yellow—Through Trafalgar Road, Nelson Street, London Street, Greenwich Road, Broadway, New Cross Road, Hatcham, Old Kent Road, New Kent Road, London Road, Blackfriars Road, to Blackfriars Bridge (Surrey side).

From East Greenwich to Westminster Bridge.—At 7.44 A.M. and every twelve minutes, to 10.30 P.M.; cars and lamps, dark blue—Through Trafalgar Road, Nelson Street, London Street, Greenwich Road, Broadway, New Cross Road, Hatcham, New Kent Road, London Road, Westminster Road, to Westminster Bridge (Surrey side). From Westminster at 8.36 A.M., and every twelve minutes, to 11.50 P.M.

From Highgate to Euston Road.—At 7.50 A.M., and every nine minutes, to 11.50 P.M. Sundays at 9.30 A.M. to 11 P.M.; cars and lamps, red—Through Highgate Archway, Junction Road, Kentish Town Road, High Street, Hampstead Road, and Euston Road. From Euston Road at 8.21 A.M., and every nine minutes, to 12.20 P.M. Sundays at 10.5 A.M. to 11.25 P.M.

From Holloway to Euston Road.—At 7.35 A.M., and every six minutes, to 11.30 P.M. Sundays at 9.30 A.M. to 11 P.M.; cars and lamps, green—Through Park Road, Camden Road, High Street, Hampstead Road, to Euston Road. From Euston Road at 8.7. A.M., and every six minutes, to 12 P.M. Sundays 10 A.M. to 11.55 P.M.

King's Cross to Kentish Town.—At 8.32 A.M., and every eight minutes, to 12 P.M.; lamps and cars, blue—Through Kentish Town Road, Great College Street, Old St. Pancras Road, to King's Cross. From Kentish Town at 8.8 A.M., and every eight minutes, to 11.45 P.M. Sundays at 9.45 A.M. to 11.5 P.M.

From Limehouse to Victoria Park.—From Limehouse at 7.25 A.M., and every few minutes, to 10.15 P.M.; cars and lamps, green—Through Burdett Road to Grove Road. From Victoria Park at 7 A.M., and every few minutes, to 10 P.M.

From Moorgate Street to Finsbury Park.—At 8.1 A.M., and every six minutes, to 11.45. P.M.; cars and lamps, yellow—Through City Road, Angel, Upper Street, Holloway Road, and Seven Sisters' Road. From Finsbury Park at 7.30 A.M., and every six minutes, to 11 P.M.

From Moorgate Street to Archway Tavern.—At 8.7 A.M., and every six minutes, to 11.45 P.M.; cars and lamps, blue—Through City Road, Angel, Liverpool Road, and Holloway Road. From Archway Tavern at 7.15 A.M., and every six minutes, to 11 P.M.

From Moorgate Street to Highbury New Park.—At 8.5 A.M., and every five minutes, to 11 P.M.; cars and lamps, green—Through City Road, East Road, Bridport Place, Southgate Road, Newington Green, and Green Lanes. From Highbury New Park at 7.30 A.M., and every five minutes, to 10.30 P.M.

From Moorgate Street to Stamford Hill.—At 8.30 A.M., and every six minutes, to 11.30 P.M.; cars and lamps, red—Through Old Street Road, Kingsland Road, and Stoke Newington. From Stamford Hill at 7.45 A.M., and every six minutes, to 10.30 P.M.

From Moorgate Street to Clapton.—At 8.30 A.M., and every twenty minutes, to 11 P.M.; cars and lamps, white—Through Old Street Road, Hackney Road, Mare Street, Hackney, and Lower and Upper Clapton. From Clapton at 8 A.M., and every twenty minutes, to 10 P.M.

From New Cross to Blackfriars.—At 7.38 A.M., and every twelve minutes, to 10.41 P.M.; cars, chocolate; lamps, green—Through Queen's Road, High Street, Peckham Road, Church Street, Camberwell New

Road, Walworth Road, London Road, to Blackfriars Road. From Blackfriars Road at 8.30 A.M., and every twelve minutes, to 11.50 P.M.

New Cross to Westminster, viâ *Peckham*.—At 7.42 A.M., and every twelve minutes, to 11 P.M.; cars and lamps, red—Through Queen's Road, High Street, Peckham Road, Church Street, Camberwell New Road, Kennington Road, to Westminster Road. From Westminster at 8.33 A.M., and every twelve minutes, to 11.55 P.M.

From Peckham (Rye Lane) to Blackfriars Bridge.—The same as *New Cross*, which see.

From Stratford to Leytonstone.—At 7 A.M., and every fifteen minutes, to 10 P.M.; cars and lamps, blue—Through Broadway, Stratford and Leytonstone Road. From Leytonstone at 7.18 A.M., and every fifteen minutes, to 10.30 P.M.

From Victoria Station to Vauxhall Bridge.—At 8.50 A.M., and every eight minutes, to 11.15 P.M.; cars, white; lamps, green—Through Vauxhall Bridge Road, by omnibus over Vauxhall Bridge, Harleyford Road, Kennington Oval, and Camberwell New Road.

Short journeys are run at intervals during the day from Highgate and Finsbury Park to the Angel only, and also from Moorgate Street to Abney Park only. See destination boards.

CONSULATE OFFICES AND EMBASSIES.

AMERICA (United States of), 53a Old Broad Street, E.C.; Embassy, 25 Westbourne Place, W.

ARGENTINE REPUBLIC (LA PLATA), 19 Craven Street, Strand, W.C.

AUSTRIA AND HUNGARY, 29 St. Swithin's Lane, E.C.; Embassy, 18 Belgrave Square, S.W.

BELGIUM, 11 Bury Court, St. Mary Axe, E.C.; Embassy, 36 Grosvenor Gardens, Pimlico, S.W.

BRAZIL, 6 Great Winchester Street Buildings, E.C.; Embassy, 32 Grosvenor Gardens, Pimlico, S.W.

BUENOS AYRES. *See* ARGENTINE REPUBLIC.

CANADA, DOMINION OF, Agency-General, 31 Queen Victoria Street, E.C.

CHILI, Gresham House, Old Broad Street, E.C.

COLUMBIA (United States of), 3 St. Helen's Place, E.C.

COSTA RICA, 4 Lime Street, E.C.

DENMARK, 42 Great Tower Street, E.C.; Embassy, 62 Wimpole Street, W.

Consulate Offices and Embassies.

FRANCE, 38 Finsbury Circus, E.C.; Embassy, Albert Gate House, Hyde Park, W.
GERMAN EMPIRE, 5 Blomfield Street, London Wall, E.C.; Embassy, 9 Carlton House Terrace, S.W.
GREECE, 25 Old Broad Street, E.C.; Embassy, 64 Pall Mall, S.W.
GUATEMALA (Republic of), 22 Great Winchester Street, E.C.
HAWAIIAN ISLANDS, St. Michael's Buildings, Cornhill, E.C.
HUNGARY. *See* AUSTRIA.
ITALY, 31 Old Jewry, E.C.; Embassy, 35 Queen's Gate, Kensington, W.
LIBERIA (Republic of), 18 Pinners' Hall, Old Broad Street, E.C.
MEXICO, 4 Adam's Court, Old Broad Street, E.C.
MONTE VIDEO. *See* URUGUAY.
NETHERLANDS, 17 Finsbury Circus, E.C.; Embassy, 40 Grosvenor Gardens, Pimlico, S.W.
NICARAGUA (Republic of), 3 St. Helen's Place, E.C.
PERU, 21 Gower Street, W.C.
PORTUGAL, 10 St. Mary Axe, E.C.; Embassy, 12 Gloucester Place, Portman Square, W.
PRUSSIA. *See* GERMAN EMPIRE.
RUSSIA, 17 Great Winchester Street, E.C.; Embassy, Chesham House, Belgrave Square, S.W.
SALVADOR (Republic of), Wool Exchange, Coleman Street, E.C.
SAN DOMINGO, 18 Coleman Street, E.C.
SIAM, 5 Great Winchester Street Buildings, E.C.
SOUTH AUSTRALIA, Agency-General, 8 Victoria Chambers, Victoria Street, Westminster, S.W.
SPAIN, 21 Billiter Street, E.C.; Embassy, 12 Queen's Gate Place, South Kensington, S.W.
SWEDEN AND NORWAY, 24 Great Winchester Street, E.C.; Embassy, 47 Charles Street, Berkeley Square, W.
SWITZERLAND, 25 Old Broad Street, E.C.
TURKEY, 55 to 58 Ethelburga House, 70 and 71 Bishopsgate Street Within, E.C.; Embassy, 1 Bryanston Square, W.
URUGUAY, Republic of (Monte Video), 49 Lower Belgrave St., S.W.
VENEZUELA (United States of), 42 Moorgate Street, E.C.

STEAMBOATS.

TIMES AND FARES BETWEEN CHELSEA AND LONDON BRIDGE.

Week-day.	*Sunday.*
Chelsea.—Every 10 minutes from 8 to dusk.	Every 10 minutes from 9 to dusk.

Battersea Park.—10 minutes after Chelsea; with tide, one-third less.
Battersea Park, Railway pier. 14 min. later.

Pimlico	24	,,
Nine Elms	27	,,
Vauxhall Bridge Road . .	30	,,
Lambeth	35	,,
Westminster	40	,,
Charing Cross	44	,,
Waterloo	47	,,
Temple	49	,,
Blackfriars (change for Surrey side)	52	,,
St. Paul's	55	,,
London Bridge	60	,,

Fares all the way on week-days, from Chelsea to London Bridge, 2d. Intermediate piers, 1d.

Returning every 10 minutes from Surrey side of London Bridge from 8.30 A.M. to dusk on week-days; and on Sundays every 15 minutes from 9 A.M.

From London Bridge at 10 A.M., and from Chelsea to Kew and Brentford every half hour from 11 to 5, returning every 30 minutes from 12 to dusk.

Fares.—Chelsea to Putney . . . . . 3d.
   ,,   ,, Hammersmith . . . 4d.
   ,,   ,, Kew . . . . . . 6d.
London Bridge to Richmond, 1s.; return, 1s. 6d.
   ,,   ,,   ,, Hampton Court, 1s. 6d.; return, 2s. 6d.

From Woolwich to London Bridge and Westminster every day, from 8 A.M. half hourly to dusk, except in winter, when the service is hourly; returning from Westminster to Woolwich half hourly from 8.10 in summer, 8.40 in winter. *Fares* all the way from Westminster to Woolwich, 6d.

CAB REGULATIONS.

Hiring by time or by distance.—The fare may be by time if so expressed by the hirer at the commencement of the hiring; the fare is, however, always to be reckoned *by distance* when not specified to the contrary.

Fares by time.—When hired and discharged *within the four mile radius*, for any time not exceeding one hour, 2s. for a four-wheeled cab, and 2s. 6d. for a two-wheeled cab. For every fifteen minutes or part thereof above one hour, if a four-wheeled cab, 6d., if a two-wheeled cab, 8d.

If hired beyond the four mile radius, whether discharged beyond it or not, or if hired within but discharged beyond the radius for either a two or four-wheeled, the fare for any time not exceeding one hour is 2s. 6d.; beyond one hour, 8d. for every fifteen minutes or fractional part thereof. A driver is in no case entitled to back fare for the return of his cab after discharged.

Fares by distance.—Within the four mile radius from Charing Cross the fare for one or two persons is 6d. per mile or part of a mile, but no fare is to be less than 1s. Beyond the four mile radius, 1s. per mile or any part of a mile.

If the journey is commenced within the four mile radius and finished *beyond* it, then for every mile completed within the radius, 6d.; for every mile or part of a mile completed beyond the radius, 1s.; but if the entire distance does not exceed one mile, 1s. only can be charged.

If hired beyond the four mile radius, 1s. per mile for the entire distance.

When hired by distance, a driver is not compelled to drive more than six miles, and if required to wait, then 6d. for four-wheeled and 8d. for two-wheeled cabs must be paid for every fifteen minutes, completed either in one or more stoppages. No charge for detentions which do not amount in all to fifteen minutes.

For more than two persons.—Whether by time or distance, when more than two persons are carried, 6d. for each extra person for the whole hiring.

Children.—For each child under 10 years, 3d.

Luggage.—For each parcel carried outside, 2d.; inside no extra charge.

Cab Regulations.

Lost property.—Property left in a cab must be taken by the driver to the nearest police station within twenty-four hours. All inquiries for lost property to be made at the police office, Great Scotland Yard, Parliament Street.

Disputes and penalties.—In the event of a dispute, the hirer may require the driver to drive, without charge, to the nearest Police Court or Station. The penalty for overcharging or for violation of any of these rules is 40s.

CAB FARES.

Reckoned at 6d. per mile, all the following places being within the 4 mile radius.

FARES TO OR FROM (or 4 Wheeled Cabs, 1 or 2 persons; 6d. extra for each additional person)	Euston Station.	Paddington Station.	Broad St. and Liverpool St.	Cannon Street Station.	Charing Cross Station.	London Brdg. Station.	Victoria Station.	Ludgate Hill Station.	Fenchurch St. Station.	Waterloo Station.	King's Cross Station.	Bishopsgate Station.	Bank of Eng., Threadndle. St.
Agel, Islington	1/0	2/0	1/0	1/0	1/6	1/6	2/0	1/0	1/6	1/6	1/0	1/0	1/0
Agricultural Hall, Islington	1/0	2/0	1/0	1/0	1/6	1/6	2/0	1/0	1/6	1/6	1/0	1/6	1/6
Albany Street, Regent's Pk.	1/0	1/6	2/0	2/0	1/6	2/6	2/0	1/6	2/0	1/6	1/0	2/6	2/0
Baker Street, Portman Sq. .	1/0	1/0	2/0	2/0	1/0	2/0	1/0	1/6	2/0	1/6	1/0	2/0	2/0
Bank of England..........	1/6	2/6	1/0	1/0	1/0	1/0	2/0	1/0	1/0	1/0	1/0	1/0	—
Battersea, the Old Church..	3/0	2/6	3/0	3/0	2/0	2/6	1/6	2/6	3/0	2/6	3/0	3/6	3/0
Bayswater, Petersburg Place	2/0	1/0	2/6	2/6	2/0	3/0	2/0	2/0	3/0	2/6	2/0	3/0	2/6
Bedford Square, N.W. corner.	1/0	1/6	1/6	1/6	1/0	1/6	1/6	1/0	1/6	1/0	1/0	1/6	1/6
Belgrave Square, N.W. corner	1/6	1/6	2/0	2/0	1/0	2/0	1/0	1/6	2/0	1/6	2/0	2/6	2/0
Berkeley Sq., N.W. corner ..	1/0	1/0	2/0	1/6	1/0	2/0	1/0	1/6	2/0	1/6	1/6	2/0	1/6
Bishopsgate St.,Houndsditch	2/0	2/6	1/0	1/0	1/6	1/0	2/0	1/0	1/0	1/6	1/6	1/0	1/0
Blackfriars Bdg.,Chatham Pl.	1/6	2/0	1/0	1/0	1/0	1/0	1/6	1/0	1/0	1/0	1/0	1/0	1/0
Bloomsbury Sq., N.W. corner	1/0	1/6	1/6	1/0	1/0	1/6	1/6	1/0	1/6	1/0	1/0	1/6	1/0
Bond Street, Piccadilly.....	1/0	1/6	1/6	1/0	1/0	1/6	1/0	1/0	1/6	1/0	1/6	2/0	1/6
British Museum............	1/0	1/6	1/6	1/0	1/0	1/6	1/6	1/0	1/6	1/0	1/0	1/6	1/0
Brixton, the Church	3/0	3/0	2/6	2/6	2/0	2/0	2/0	2/0	2/6	2/0	3/0	2/6	2/6
Brompton Sq., N.W. corner .	2/0	1/6	2/6	2/0	1/6	2/6	1/0	2/0	2/0	2/0	2/0	2/6	2/6
Brook Street, Davies Street.	1/0	1/0	2/0	1/6	1/0	2/0	1/0	1/6	2/0	1/6	1/6	2/0	1/6
Brunswick Sq., N.W. corner.	1/0	1/6	1/6	1/0	1/0	1/6	1/6	1/0	1/6	1/6	1/0	1/6	1/0
Bryanston Sq., N.W. corner .	1/0	1/0	2/0	2/0	1/6	2/6	1/6	1/6	2/0	2/0	1/6	2/6	2/0
Buckingham Gate, St. J. Pk.	1/0	1/6	2/0	1/0	1/0	1/0	1/0	1/0	2/0	1/0	2/0	2/0	1/6
Cadogan Pier, Chelsea......	2/6	2/0	3/0	2/6	2/0	2/6	1/0	2/0	2/6	2/0	2/6	3/0	2/6
Camberwell Park..........	2/6	3/0	2/0	2/0	2/0	1/6	1/6	2/0	1/6	2/6	2/0	2/0	2/0
Cambridge Heath Gate	2/0	3/0	1/0	2/0	2/0	1/6	3/0	1/6	1/6	2/0	2/0	1/0	1/6
Camden Town, Mot. Red Cap	1/6	1/6	2/0	2/0	1/6	2/0	2/0	1/6	2/0	2/0	1/0	2/0	2/0
Cattle Market, Metropolitan	1/0	2/6	2/0	2/0	2/0	2/0	2/6	1/6	2/0	2/0	1/0	2/0	1/6
Cavendish Sq., N.W. corner .	1/0	1/0	2/0	1/6	1/0	2/0	1/0	2/0	1/6	1/0	2/0	1/6
Chancery Lane, Holborn ...	1/0	2/0	1/0	1/0	1/0	1/0	1/6	1/0	1/0	1/0	1/0	1/0	1/0
Charing Cross, Statue	1/0	1/6	1/0	1/0	1/0	1/6	1/0	1/0	1/6	1/0	1/6	1/6	1/0
Cheapside, Wood Street....	1/6	2/0	1/0	1/0	1/0	1/0	2/0	1/0	1/0	1/0	1/0	1/0	1/0
Chelsea Hospital	2/0	2/0	2/6	2/6	1/6	2/0	1/0	2/0	2/6	1/6	2/6	3/0	2/6
Chesham Place, N.W. corner	2/0	1/6	2/6	2/0	1/0	2/0	1/0	2/0	2/6	1/6	2/0	2/6	2/0
Chester Sq., Pimlico, N.W. c.	2/0	1/6	2/6	2/0	1/0	2/0	1/0	1/6	2/0	1/6	2/0	2/6	2/0
Christ's Hospital	1/6	2/0	1/0	1/0	1/0	1/0	1/6	1/0	1/0	1/0	1/0	1/0	1/0
City Road, Macclesfield St..	1/0	2/0	1/0	1/0	1/6	1/6	2/0	1/0	1/0	1/6	1/0	1/0	1/0
Clapham Common, Plough .	3/0	3/0	2/6	2/6	2/0	2/0	2/6	2/6	2/0	3/0	3/0	2/6
Clerkenwell Green	1/0	2/0	1/0	1/0	1/0	1/0	2/0	1/0	1/0	1/0	1/	1/0	1/0
Commercial Rd., E., Marg. St.	3/0	3/6	1/6	1/6	2/6	1/6	3/0	1/6	1/0	2/6	2/6	1/6	1/6
Corn Exchange, Mark Lane	2/0	2/6	1/0	1/0	1/6	2/0	1/0	1/0	1/6	1/0	1/0
Covent Garden, Russell St. .	1/0	1/6	1/6	1/0	1/0	1/0	1/6	1/0	1/0	1/6	1/0
Custom House	2/0	2/6	1/0	1/0	1/6	1/0	2/0	1/0	1/0	1/0	1/6	1/0	1/0

Cab Fares.

FARES TO OR FROM (2 or 4 Wheeled Cabs, 1 or 2 persons; 6d. extra for each additional person)	Euston Station.	Paddington Station.	Broad St. and Liverpool St.	Cannon Street Station.	Charing Cross Station.	London Brdg. Station.	Victoria Station.	Ludgate Hill Station.	Fenchurch St. Station.	Waterloo Station.	King's Cross Station.	Bishopsgate Station.	Bank of Eng.
Elephant and Castle	2/0	2/6	1/0	1/0	1/0	1/0	1/6	1/0	1/0	1/0	2/0	1/6	1/
Exeter Hall, Strand	1/0	2/0	1/0	1/0	1/0	1/0	1/0	1/6	1/6	1/0	1/0	1/6	1/
EXHIBITIONS.													
Egyptian Hall, Piccadilly	1/0	1/6	1/0	1/6	1/0	1/6	1/0	1/0	1/6	1/0	1/6	2/0	1/
Mdme. Tussaud, Baker St.	1/0	1/0	2/0	2/0	1/0	2/0	1/6	1/6	2/0	1/6	1/6	2/6	2/
Polytechnic Ins., Regt. St.	1/0	1/0	1/6	1/6	1/0	2/0	1/0	1/0	2/0	1/6	1/0	2/0	1/
Royal Albert Hall... ...	1/6	1/0	2/6	2/0	1/6	2/0	1/0	2/0	2/6	2/0	1/6	2/6	2/
Eyre Arms, St. John's Wood	1/6	1/0	2/6	2/6	2/0	3/0	2/0	2/0	3/0	2/6	1/6	3/0	2/
Finchley Road, Swiss Cot...	1/6	1/6	2/6	2/6	2/0	3/0	2/0	2/6	3/0	2/6	1/6	3/0	2/
Finsbury Square, N.W. corner	1/6	2/6	1/0	1/0	1/6	1/0	2/0	1/0	1/0	1/6	1/6	1/0	1/
Fitzroy Square, S.W. corner.	1/0	1/0	2/0	1/6	1/0	2/0	1/6	1/6	2/0	1/6	1/0	2/0	1/
Fleet Street, Fetter Lane...	1/0	2/0	1/0	1/0	1/0	1/0	1/6	1/0	1/0	1/0	1/0	1/0	1/
General Post Office	1/8	2/0	1/0	1/0	1/0	1/0	1/6	1/0	1/0	1/0	1/0	1/0	1/
Gloucester Square, N.W. cor.	1/6	1/0	2/6	2/6	1/6	2/6	1/6	2/0	2/6	2/0	1/6	2/6	2/
Golden Square, Regent St. .	1/0	1/6	2/6	1/6	1/0	1/6	1/0	1/6	1/6	1/0	1/6	2/0	1/
Gower Street, New Road...	1/0	1/6	1/6	1/6	1/0	2/0	1/6	1/6	2/0	1/6	1/0	2/0	1/
Grosvenor Place, Chapel St..	1/6	1/6	2/0	2/0	1/0	2/0	1/0	1/6	2/0	1/6	2/0	2/6	2/
Grosvenor Square	1/0	1/0	2/0	2/0	1/0	2/0	1/0	1/6	2/0	1/6	1/6	2/0	2/
Guildhall, City	1/6	2/6	1/0	1/0	1/0	1/0	2/0	1/0	1/0	1/6	1/6	1/0	1/
Hackney, Wells Street......	2/6	3/6	1/6	2/0	2/6	2/0	3/0	2/0	1/6	2/6	2/0	1/0	1/
Hammersmith Gate	2/6	1/6	3/6	3/0	2/6	3/6	2/0	3/0	3/6	3/0	3/0	3/6	3/
Hanover Square...........	1/0	1/0	2/0	1/6	1/0	2/0	1/0	1/6	2/0	1/6	1/0	2/0	1/
Harley Street,Weymouth St.	1/0	1/0	2/0	2/0	1/0	2/0	1/6	1/6	2/0	1/6	1/0	2/0	1/
Holborn, Hatton Garden ...	1/0	2/0	1/0	1/0	1/0	1/0	1/6	1/0	1/0	1/0	1/0	1/0	1/
Horse Guards, Whitehall...	1/0	1/6	1/6	1/6	1/0	1/6	1/0	1/0	1/6	1/0	1/0	1/6	2/0	1/
HOSPITALS.													
Bethlehem, St. Grg's. Flds.	1/6	2/6	1/6	1/0	1/0	1/0	1/0	1/0	1/0	1/0	1/6	1/6	1/
Charing Cross, Agar Street	1/0	1/6	1/6	1/0	1/0	1/6	1/0	1/0	1/6	1/0	1/0	1/6	1/
Consumption, Brompton.	2/6	2/0	2/6	2/6	1/6	2/6	1/0	2/0	3/0	2/0	2/6	3/0	2/
German, Dalston	2/0	3/0	1/6	2/0	2/6	2/0	3/0	2/0	1/6	2/6	2/0	1/6	1/
Guy's, High St., Borough.	1/6	2/0	1/0	1/0	1/0	1/0	1/6	1/0	1/0	1/0	1/0	1/6	1/
King's College, Portugl. St.	1/0	2/0	1/0	1/0	1/0	1/6	1/6	1/0	1/0	1/0	1/0	1/6	1/
London,Whitechapel Road	2/6	3/0	1/0	1/0	2/0	1/0	2/6	1/6	1/0	1/6	2/0	1/0	1/
London Fever, L'pool Rd.	1/0	2/0	1/0	1/6	1/0	1/6	2/6	1/0	1/6	1/6	1/0	1/0	1/
Middlesex, Charles Street.	1/0	1/6	1/6	1/6	1/0	1/6	1/0	1/6	1/6	1/0	1/0	2/0	1/
Royal Free, Gray's Inn Rd.	1/0	2/0	1/6	1/0	1/0	1/6	2/0	1/0	1/6	1/6	1/0	1/6	1/
St. Bartholomew's, Smthld.	1/6	2/0	1/0	1/0	1/0	1/0	1/6	1/0	1/0	1/0	1/0	1/0	1/
St. Luke's, Old Street....	1/6	2/6	1/0	1/0	1/6	1/0	2/0	1/0	1/0	1/0	1/0	1/0	1/
St. Mary's, Paddington...	1/6	1/0	2/6	2/6	1/6	2/6	1/6	2/0	2/6	2/0	1/6	2/6	2/
St. Thomas', Lambeth ...	1/6	2/6	1/6	1/6	1/0	1/0	1/0	1/0	1/6	1/0	1/6	1/6	1/
University, Gower Street.	1/0	1/6	1/6	1/6	1/0	1/6	1/6	1/6	2/0	1/6	1/0	2/0	1/
Westminster, Broad Sanc.	1/6	2/0	1/6	1/6	1/0	1/0	1/0	1/6	1/6	1/0	1/6	2/0	1/
Houses of Parliament......	1/6	2/0	1/6	1/6	1/0	1/0	1/0	1/6	1/6	1/0	1/8	2/0	1/
Hyde Park Cor., Lamp Post	1/6	1/6	2/0	2/0	1/0	2/0	1/0	1/6	2/0	1/6	2/0	2/6	2/
Hyde Park Gardens	1/6	1/0	2/0	2/0	1/0	2/6	1/0	2/0	2/0	2/0	1/6	2/6	2/
Hyde Park Square, S.W. cor.	1/6	1/0	2/6	2/0	1/6	2/6	1/0	2/0	2/0	2/0	1/6	2/6	2/
Kensal Green, the Church..	2/6	1/6	3/6	3/0	2/6	3/6	2/6	3/0	3/6	3/0	2/6	3/6	3/
Kensington, the Church....	2/0	1/0	3/0	2/6	2/0	3/0	1/0	2/0	3/0	2/6	2/6	3/0	2/

Cab Fares.

ARES TO OR FROM or 4 Wheeled Cabs, 1 or 2 persons; 6d. extra for each additional person)	Euston Station.	Paddington Station.	Broad St. and Liverpool St Station.	Cannon Street Station.	Charing Cross Station.	London Brdg. Station.	Victoria Terminus.	Ludgate Hill Station.	Fenchurch St. Station.	Waterloo Station.	King's Cross.	Bishopsgate Station.	Bank of Eng. Threadnedle. St.
)urn Gate	2/0	1/0	3/0	3/0	2/6	3/0	2/0	2/6	3/0	2/6	2/0	3/0	3/0
gsland Rd., Canal Bridge	2/0	3/0	1/0	1/6	2/0	1/6	2/6	1/6	1/0	2/0	1/6	1/0	1/0
lenhall St., E. India Ho.	1/6	2/6	1/0	1/0	1/6	1/0	2/0	1/0	1/0	1/0	1/6	1/0	1/0
:ester Square, N.W. corn.	1/0	1/6	1/6	1/6	1/0	1/6	1/0	1/0	1/6	1/0	1/6	1/6	1/6
:oln's Inn, Serle Street .	1/0	2/0	1/0	1/0	1/0	1/0	1/6	1/0	1/0	1/0	1/0	1/6	1/0
ibard St., Birchin Lane.	1/6	2/6	1/0	1/0	1/0	1/0	2/0	1/0	1/0	1/0	1/6	1/0	1/0
don Bridge, Adelaide Pl.	2/0	2/6	1/0	1/0	1/6	1/0	2/0	1/0	1/0	1/0	1/6	1/0	1/0
don Docks	2/0	3/0	1/0	1/0	1/6	1/0	2/6	1/0	1/0	1/6	2/0	1/0	1/0
d's Cricket Ground	1/6	1/0	2/6	2/6	2/0	2/6	2/0	2/0	2/6	2/0	1/6	2/6	2/6
vndee Square, N.W. corn.	1/6	1/6	2/0	2/0	1/0	2/0	1/0	2/0	2/0	1/6	2/0	2/6	2/0
lgate Hill, Farringdon St.	1/6	2/0	1/0	1/0	1/0	1/0	1/6	1/0	1/0	1/0	1/0	1/0	1/0
nchester Square, N.W. cor.	1/0	1/0	2/0	2/0	1/0	2/0	1/0	1/6	2/0	1/6	1/0	2/0	2/0
nsion House, City	1/6	2/6	1/0	1/0	1/0	1/0	2/0	1/0	1/0	1/0	1/6	1/0	1/0
rk Lane, Fenchurch St. .	2/0	2/6	1/0	1/0	1/6	1/0	2/0	1/0	—	1/0	1/6	1/0	1/0
.e End Gate............	2/6	3/0	1/6	1/0	2/0	1/0	2/6	1/6	1/0	2/0	2/0	1/0	1/0
orgate St., London Wall.	1/6	2/6	1/0	1/0	1/6	1/0	2/0	1/0	1/0	1/0	1/6	1/0	1/0
w Road, Lisson Grove...	1/0	1/0	2/6	2/0	1/6	2/6	1/6	2/0	2/6	2/0	1/6	2/6	2/0
w Rd., Tottenham Ct. Rd.	1/0	1/0	1/6	1/6	1/0	2/0	1/6	1/6	2/0	1/6	1/0	2/0	1/6
tting Hill Square, N.W.cor.	2/0	1/0	3/0	3/0	2/0	3/0	2/0	2/6	3/0	2/6	2/6	3/0	3/0
t Bailey................	1/6	2/0	1/0	1/0	1/0	1/0	1/6	1/0	1/0	1/0	1/0	1/0	1/0
ford Street, Regent's Circ.	1/0	1/0	1/6	1/6	1/0	2/0	1/0	1/0	1/6	1/0	1/0	2/0	1/6
ford St., Tottenh'm Ct. Rd.	1/0	1/6	1/6	1/6	1/0	1/6	1/0	1/6	1/6	1/0	1/0	1/6	1/0
ford Sq., Hyde Pk., N.W. c.	1/6	1/0	2/6	2/0	1/6	2/6	1/6	2/0	2/6	2/0	1/6	2/6	2/0
ll Mall, George Street ...	1/6	1/6	1/6	1/6	1/0	1/6	1/0	1/0	1/6	1/0	1/6	2/0	1/6
rk Lane, Mount Street...	1/6	1/0	2/0	2/0	1/6	2/0	1/0	2/0	2/0	1/6	1/6	2/0	2/0
:cadilly, Half Moon Street	1/6	1/6	2/0	1/6	1/0	2/0	1/0	1/0	2/0	1/0	1/6	2/0	1/6
rtland Place, Duchess St..	1/0	1/0	1/6	1/6	1/0	2/0	1/0	1/6	2/0	1/0	1/0	2/0	1/6
rtman Square, W.	1/0	1/0	2/0	1/0	1/6	2/0	1/6	2/0	2/0	1/0	1/0	2/0	2/0
AILWAY STATIONS.													
Shoreditch, Great Eastern	2/0	2/6	1/0	1/0	1/6	1/0	2/6	1/0	1/0	1/6	1/6	—	1/0
Fenchurch St., Gt. Eastern	2/0	2/6	1/0	1/0	1/6	1/0	2/0	1/0	—	1/6	1/6	1/0	1/0
King's Cross, Gt. Northern	1/0	1/6	1/6	1/6	1/6	1/6	2/0	1/0	1/6	1/6	—	1/6	1/6
Paddington, Gt. Western.	1/6	—	2/6	2/6	1/6	2/6	1/6	2/0	2/0	2/0	1/6	2/6	2/6
London Bridge, L.B.& S.C.	2/0	2/6	1/0	1/0	1/6	—	1/6	1/0	1/0	1/6	1/0	1/0	
Victoria, Lond. Bri. & C.	1/6	2/0	2/0	2/0	1/0	1/6	—	1/6	1/6	1/0	2/0	2/0	1/6
Ludgate Hill, Chat. & Dov.	1/6	2/0	1/0	1/0	1/0	1/0	1/6	—	1/0	1/0	1/0	1/0	1/0
Victoria, Chatham & Dov.	1/6	2/0	2/0	1/6	1/0	1/6	—	1/6	1/6	1/0	2/0	2/0	1/6
Euston Sq., Lond. & N. W.	—	1/6	2/0	2/0	1/0	2/0	1/6	2/0	1/6	1/0	1/0	2/0	1/6
Waterloo, London & S. W.	1/6	2/0	1/6	1/0	1/0	1/0	1/0	1/0	—	1/6	1/6	1/0	
Charing Cross, South East.	1/0	1/6	1/6	1/0	—	1/6	1/0	1/0	1/6	1/0	1/6	1/6	1/0
St. Pancras, Midland	1/0	1/6	1/6	1/6	1/6	1/6	2/0	1/0	1/6	1/0	1/6	1/6	1/6
egent Circus, Oxford Street	1/0	1/0	1/6	1/6	1/0	2/0	1/0	1/0	1/6	1/0	1/0	2/0	1/6
egent Street, Piccadilly...	1/0	1/6	1/6	1/6	1/0	2/0	1/0	1/0	1/6	1/0	1/0	2/0	1/6
ussell Square, N.W. corner	1/0	1/0	1/6	1/6	1/6	1/6	1/0	1/6	1/6	1/0	1/0	1/6	1/0
. James's Square, N.W. cor.	1/0	1/6	1/6	1/6	1/0	1/6	1/0	1/6	1/6	1/0	1/6	2/0	1/6
. Katherine's Docks......	2/0	3/0	1/0	1/0	1/6	1/0	2/6	1/0	1/0	1/6	2/0	1/0	1/0
. Paul's, Paul's Chain	1/6	2/0	1/0	1/0	1/0	1/0	1/6	1/0	1/0	1/0	1/0	1/0	1/0
oane Square, Sloane Street	2/0	2/0	2/0	2/0	1/0	2/0	1/0	1/6	2/6	1/6	2/0	2/6	2/0
mithfield (W.), Long Lane	1/6	2/0	1/0	1/0	1/0	1/0	1/6	1/0	1/0	1/0	1/0	1/0	1/0

Cab Fares.

FARES TO OR FROM (2 or 4 Wheeled Cabs, 1 or 2 persons; 6d. extra for each additional person)	Euston Station.	Paddington Station.	Broad St. and Liverpool St.	Cannon Street Station.	Charing Cross Station.	London Brdg. Station.	Victoria Terminus.	Ludgate Hill Station.
Stepney Green, K. John's Pal	2/6	3/6	1/6	1/6	2/6	1/6	3/0	1/6
Stoke Newington Rd.Wel.Rd	2/0	3/0	1/6	2/0	2/6	2/0	3/6	2/0
Strand, Wellington Street..	1/0	1/6	1/0	1/0	1/0	1/0	1/6	1/0
Tavistock Square, N.W. cor.	1/0	1/6	1/6	1/6	1/0	1/6	1/6	1/0
Temple Bar	1/0	2/0	1/0	1/0	1/0	1/0	1/6	1/0
THEATRES.								
Adelphi	1/0	1/6	1/6	1/0	1/0	1/6	1/0	1/0
Alhambra, Leicester Sqre.	1/0	1/6	1/6	1/6	1/0	1/6	1/0	1/0
Astley's (Sanger's), Westm	1/6	2/0	1/6	1/0	1/0	1/6	1/0	1/0
Court, Sloane Square	2/0	2/0	2/6	2/0	1/6	2/0	1/0	2/0
Covent Garden, Ital. Opera	1/0	1/6	1/6	1/0	1/0	1/6	1/0	1/0
Criterion, Piccadilly	1/0	1/6	1/6	1/6	1/0	1/6	1/0	1/0
Drury Lane	1/0	1/6	1/0	1/0	1/0	1/6	1/0	1/0
Duke's, Holborn	1/0	2/0	1/0	1/0	1/0	1/0	1/6	1/0
Elephant and Castle	2/0	2/6	1/0	1/0	1/0	1/0	1/6	1/0
Folly, K. Wm. St., Strand	1/0	1/6	1/6	1/0	1/0	1/6	1/0	1/0
Gaiety, Strand	1/0	1/6	1/0	1/0	1/0	1/0	1/0	1/0
Globe, Newcastle St., Strd.	1/0	1/6	1/0	1/0	1/0	1/0	1/6	1/0
Haymarket	1/0	1/6	1/6	1/6	1/0	1/6	1/6	1/0
Holborn Amphitheatre	1/0	1/6	1/0	1/0	1/0	1/6	1/6	1/0
Lyceum, Wellington Street	1/0	1/6	1/0	1/0	1/0	1/0	1/6	1/0
Olympic, Wych Street	1/0	1/6	1/0	1/0	1/0	1/0	1/6	1/0
Opera Comique, Strand	1/0	2/0	1/0	1/0	1/0	1/0	1/6	1/0
Park, Park St., N.W.	1/0	1/6	2/0	2/0	1/6	2/0	2/0	1/6
Philharmonic, Islington..	1/0	2/0	1/0	1/0	1/6	1/6	2/0	1/0
Princess's, Oxford Street	1/0	1/6	1/6	1/6	1/0	1/6	1/0	1/0
Pr.of Wales's, Tottenh.C.R.	1/0	1/6	1/6	1/6	1/0	1/6	1/6	1/0
Royal Alfred, Ch.St., Pdn.	1/6	1/0	2/6	2/6	1/6	2/6	1/6	2/0
Royalty, Dean Street, Soho	1/0	1/6	1/6	1/6	1/0	1/6	1/0	1/0
Sadler's Wells, Islington.	1/0	2/0	1/0	1/0	1/6	1/6	2/0	1/0
St. James's, King Street..	1/6	1/6	1/6	1/6	1/0	1/6	1/0	1/0
Standard, Shoreditch	1/6	2/6	1/0	1/0	1/6	1/0	2/6	1/0
Strand	1/0	2/0	1/0	1/0	1/0	1/0	1/0	1/0
Surrey, Blackfriars Road.	1/6	2/6	1/0	1/0	1/0	1/0	1/0	1/0
Vaudeville, Strand	1/0	1/6	1/0	1/0	1/0	1/6	1/0	1/0
Victoria, New Cut, Lmbth.	1/6	2/0	1/0	1/0	1/0	1/0	1/0	1/0
Thurloe Square, N.W. corner	2/0	2/0	2/6	2/6	1/6	2/0	1/0	2/0
Torrington Square, N.W. cor.	1/0	1/6	1/0	1/6	1/0	1/6	1/6	1/0
Tottenham C. Rd., Francis St.	1/0	1/6	1/6	1/6	1/0	1/6	1/6	1/0
Tower of London	2/0	2/6	1/0	1/0	1/6	1/0	2/0	1/0
Uxbridge Rd., Goldhawk Rd.	2/6	1/6	3/6	3/0	2/6	3/6	2/0	3/0
Vauxhall Bridge, Bridge Rd.	2/0	2/0	2/0	2/0	1/0	2/0	1/0	1/0
Victoria Pk., Bonner's Hi.Gt.	2/6	3/0	1/6	1/6	2/6	1/6	3/0	2/0
Victoria Str., Artillery Row	1/6	2/0	2/0	1/6	2/6	1/6	1/0	1/6
Warwick Square, N.W. corn.	2/0	2/0	2/6	2/0	1/0	2/0	1/0	1/0
Waterloo Brdg., Lancaster Pl.	1/0	2/0	1/6	1/0	1/0	1/0	1/0	1/6
Zoological Gardens, Reg. Pk.	1/0	1/6	2/6	2/6	1/6	2/6	2/0	2/0

THE METROPOLITAN RAILWAYS.

E METROPOLITAN and METROPOLITAN DISTRICT RAILWAYS form an almost
iplete Railway Circle round the Metropolis, and are connected with the Great
stern, Great Northern, Midland, Great Western, South Eastern, London, Chatham
l Dover, and all other lines having a London Terminus. It is intended soon to
nect the Aldgate Station of the Metropolitan Railway with the Mansion House
tion of the District Railway, and then the Circle designated the INNER CIRCLE
l be quite complete. It may also be added that an extension of the St. John's
iod Railway (which joins the Metropolitan Line at Baker Street) has recently been
ned from Swiss Cottage to Willesden, from which point a Railway to Harrow is in
rse of rapid construction, and is expected to be opened for public traffic in the
ing of 1880.
Starting from the present most Easterly Terminus of the Metropolitan Railway at
lgate, Trains are run at intervals of a few minutes throughout the day, from
.M. till Midnight. The following is a List of the Stations now open :—

ALDGATE.
Leadenhall-st., Fenchurch-st., Mark-lane,
icing-lane, the Mint, Eastcheap, the Docks, the
ver, Whitechapel, Commercial Road, Bethnal
en Museum, Minories, Houndsditch. Black-
l Railway Station, and the EAST END OF
NDON, also by Cars of the North Metro-
tan Tramway Co., every few minutes, to
7, Stratford, Leytonstone, Limehouse, Poplar,
East India Docks, &c., &c.

Bishopsgate.
the Great Eastern Railway, Liverpool-st.
ion, Broad-st. Station, Bishop-gate-st., Shore-
h, Victoria Park, the Bank, Royal Exchange,
ck Exchange, London Bridge, &c., &c.
CIAL OMNIBUSES between this Station and
non-st. Station (S.E.R.) meet the Trains.

Moorgate Street Station.
Finsbury, Cheapside, Gresham-st., Guildhall,
asion House, the Bank, Cornhill, Lombard-st.,
g William-st. and London Bridge, Queen
toria-street, Cannon-street, &c., &c.

Aldersgate Street Station.
General Post Office, St. Paul's, Christ's
pital, Smithfield, Goswell-road., St. John's
et-road., Charterhouse-square, Snowhill,
, &c.

Farringdon Street Station.
Metropolitan Meat Market, Clerkenwell, Hatton Garden, Holborn Farringdon
ket, duct, Gray's Inn, Ludgate Hill, Fleet-street,
ncery-lane, Temple, Strand, Blackfriars,
, &c.

King's Cross Station.
Pentonville, Islington, Agricultural Hall,
loway, Barnsbury, Gray's Inn-rd, Foundling
pital, Great Northern and Midland Railways,
&c.

Gower Street Station.
Tottenham Court-rd, Hampstead-rd, Euston-
London and North-Western Railway, Rus-
sq., British Museum, Bloomsbury, Camden
n, Kentish Town, Somers Town, &c.; and,
following Theatres, Prince of Wales', Queen's,
ent Garden, Drury Lane, Adelphi, Vaude-
e. Gaiety, Globe, Lyceum, Olympic, Opera
ique, Strand, The Park ; also Exeter Hall.
IBUSES ply between this Station and the
her Red Cap, Camden Town.

Portland Road Station.
For Albany-st., the Zoological and Botanical
Gardens, Regent's Park East, St. George's Hall,
Polytechnic, Langham Hotel, Regent-st., Oxford-
st., &c., &c. SPECIAL OMNIBUSES between this
Station, Oxford Circus, and Regent Circus meet
the Trains.

Baker Street Station.
For Regent's Park West, Madame Tussaud's,
Baker-st. Bazaar, Portman-square, Manchester-
square, &c. There is a *Branch Line* here with
the following Stations :—

St. John's Wood Road.
For Lord's Cricket Ground, Park Road. Regent's
Park, Primrose Hill, Wellington-road, &c.

Marlborough Road.
For Eyre Arms, Portland Town, Acacia-rd., &c.

Swiss Cottage.
For Belsize Park, Adelaide-road, South Hampstead, &c., &c.

Finchley Road.
West Hampstead.
Kilburn and Brondesbury.
For the Welsh Harp Tavern and Grounds.

Willesden.
For Willesden Green.

Edgware Road Station (Chapel St.).
For Edgware-rd, Marble Arch, Oxford Terrace-
Cambridge Terrace, Paddington Green, Harrow-
rd. South Maida Hill, &c. At this Station the
line bifurcates, the one arm continues the INNER
CIRCLE to South Kensington, Westminster, and
Mansion House, by the Stations as given in
immediate rotation, the other arm conducts by
the several Stations subsequently named, to
HAMMERSMITH (for Kew and Richmond by
Through Trains) and to ADDISON ROAD, Ken-
sington.

Paddington Station.
In Praed-st., opposite the Great Western Hotel,
for Great Western Railway, Hyde Park, East-
bourne-ter., Westbourne-ter., Gloucester-square,
Gloucester-ter., Craven Hill, Hyde Park Gardens,
Norfolk-square, Sussex-square, &c.

Bayswater Station.
In Queen's Road, for Kensington Gardens,
Kensington Palace Gardens, Princes-square,
Paddington Baths, Moscow-rd., in which are the
Bayswater New Synagogue and Greek Church.

THE METROPOLITAN RAILWAYS—continued.

Notting Hill Gate Station.
In High-street, Notting Hill, for Camden Hill, Pembridge-square, Holland Park, Pembridge Gardens, Linden Grove, Ladbroke-rd., &c., &c.

Kensington High Street Station.
Near the Vestry Hall and Old Church, Pro Cathedral, the Carmelites Church, Holland House, Phillimore Gardens, &c., &c.

Brompton (Gloucester Road) Station.
For Cromwell-road, Earls Court, &c., &c.

Earls Court.
For Earls Court Road, &c., &c.

West Brompton.
(Adjoining the West London Railway.)
For Beaufort House, Walham Green, Athletic Club's Ground, Brompton Cemetery, &c., &c. Trains run from this Station to Battersea and Clapham Junction.

South Kensington.
For South Kensington Museum, The Oratory, Horticultural Gardens, Royal Albert Hall, Albert Memorial (South Side), Brompton-rd., Fulham-road, Cromwell-road, Chelsea (West), Thurloe-square, Brompton-square, &c., &c.

Sloane Square.
For Sloane-st., Chelsea (East), Chelsea Hospital, Battersea Park, King's Road, Queen's Road, Royal Court Theatre, Prince's Cricket Ground, Belgravia (West), Eaton-square, &c., &c.

Victoria.
For Crystal Palace, London Chatham and Dover, London Brighton and South Coast Lines, Grosvenor Hotel, Palace Hotel, Belgravia (East), Victoria-rd., Victoria-st., Buckingham Palace, Vauxhall Bridge-rd., &c., &c.

St. James's Park.
For Bird Cage Walk, Royal Aquarium and Imperial Theatre, Victoria-st., Army and Navy Co-Operative Stores, Queen's-sq., Westminster Palace Hotel, Broad Sanctuary, Dean's Yard, Westminster Hospital, &c., &c.

Westminster Bridge.
For Westminster Abbey, Houses of Parliament, Parliament-st., Foreign Office, Home Office, Treasury, India Office, &c., Whitehall, Horse Guards, Great George-st., Old Palace Yard, Thames Embankment, Lambeth Bridge, Westminster Bridge-road, Astley's Theatre, St. Thomas's Hospital, Waterloo Station, &c., &c.

Charing Cross.
For the Thames Embankment, South Eastern Railway, Army and Navy Museum, Society of Arts, the Strand, Trafalgar-sq., National Gallery, St. Martin's-lane, the Folly, Adelphi, Lyceum, Gaiety, Strand, Opera Comique, Globe, Covent Garden, and Drury Lane Theatres, Cockspur-st., Haymarket, Her Majesty's Theatre, Pall Mall, Waterloo Place, &c.

Temple.
For Inns-of-Court, Strand (East), New Law Courts, Fleet-st., &c.

Blackfriars.
For Blackfriars-bridge and Road, Farringdon-Fleet-st., Ludgate-hill Station and Ludgate-h St. Paul's, Queen Victoria-st., Cheapside, &c.

Mansion House Station.
This Station is midway in Cannon Street, near the South-Eastern City Railway Terminus, a is the present City Terminus of the Distr Railway. It is also near St. Paul's, Southwa and London Bridges, the Mansion House, Gui hall, Bank of England, Royal Exchange, and also for the Tower, Royal Mint, &c.

Bishop's Road Station.
This is the first Station on the Line towa Hammersmith after quitting the Edgware Station. It adjoins the Great Western Railw and also serves for Paddington, Westbour Eastbourne, and Gloucester Terraces, Bloomfie rd., &c., &c.

Royal Oak.
For Westbourne Grove, and Westbourne P Road, &c., and the Harrow-road (north).

Westbourne Park.
For Aldridge-road, Tavistock-terrace, &c., and Kensal New Town, and the Artisans' Dwelli in the Harrow-road.

Notting Hill (Ladbroke Grove Roa
For Ladbroke-grove, St. Charles's-square Roman Catholic College, for North Kensing generally, and for Kensal Green and Cemeter &c., &c.

Latimer Road.
For Norland Town, Wormwood Scrubs, &c., The Addison Road (Kensington) Line branc off here. (See below.)

Shepherd's Bush.
For Uxbridge-road, Starch Green, &c., &c.

Hammersmith (Broadway Statio
For the River Thames, Hammersmith Bri Barnes, Putney, and Mortlake, &c., &c., and SPECIAL OMNIBUSES TO BARNES.

Uxbridge Road (Kensington Lin
For Norland Road, Holland Road, &c., &c.

Kensington (Addison Road).
For Hammersmith-rd., St. Mary Abbot's-and North-West Kensington. From here Trains leave for Crystal Palace, Chelsea, Ba sea, Richmond, &c.

Kew Gardens and Richmond by Through Trains from all Metropolitan Statio

LONDON: PRINTED BY W. CLOWES AND SONS, STAMFORD STREET AND CHARING CROSS.

ADVERTISER.

SCHWEITZER'S
COCOATINA,
ANTI-DYSPEPTIC COCOA OR CHOCOLATE POWDER.

Guaranteed  Strongly recommended

Pure Soluble Cocoa, By the Faculty

Without Admixture. For Family Use.

Cocoatina is the highest class of Soluble Cocoa or Chocolate in a concentrated form.

It consists solely of the finest Cocoa Beans, without sugar or spice; the *excess* of fat being extracted mechanically, which not only renders it more delicate and digestible, but increases the proportion of flesh-forming and nourishing properties.

Made instantaneously with boiling water, palatable without Milk.

THE FACULTY pronounce it "the most nutritious, perfectly digestible Beverage for BREAKFAST, LUNCHEON, or SUPPER, and invaluable for Invalids and young Children."

Cocoatina will bear the strictest Chemical Test.

It is prescribed with great success for delicate Females and Children when all other food is rejected; and is celebrated for its restorative, qualities in cases of Debility and imperfect Digestion.

Highly commended by the entire Medical Press.

Being absolutely free from sugar (the *excess* of fat), or any admixture, it keeps better in all climates, and is four times the strength of Cocoas *thickened yet weakened* with arrowroot, starch, &c., *and in reality cheaper than such mixtures;* one tea-spoonful being sufficient for a cup of Cocoa (*the cost of which is less than a halfpenny*), and two or more for a cup of Chocolate.

Cocoatina à la Vanille,

Is the most delicate, digestible, cheapest Vanilla Chocolate, and may be taken when richer Chocolate is prohibited.

DIRECTIONS FOR USE ON THE LABEL OF EVERY PACKET.

Sold in air-tight Tin Packets only, at 1s. 6d., 3s., 5s. 6d., 10s. 6d., and 20s. by Grocers, Chemists, Confectioners, &c.

Sole Proprietors—H. SCHWEITZER & CO., 10, Adam St., London, W.C.

ADVERTISER.

J. H. STEWARD,

OPTICIAN TO THE
BRITISH AND FOREIGN GOVERNMENTS,

The National Rifle Associations of England, Ireland, Canada, and America; and The National Artillery Association.

BY APPOINTMENT.

STEWARD'S CELEBRATED BINOCULAR
OPERA, FIELD, TOURIST'S, & MARINE GLASSES.

THE "DUKE" BINOCULAR FIELD GLASS.

The most Powerful made, having PERFECT DEFINITION, GOOD LIGHT, and FIELD OF VIEW.
As supplied to SIR GARNET WOLSELEY'S STAFF-OFFICERS.

Sole Maker of
THE CELEBRATED LORD BURY TELESCOPE, £3 10s.

Illustrated Catalogues gratis, post-free.

ADDRESSES:
406 & 66 STRAND, 456 WEST STRAND, 54 CORNHILL,
LONDON.

LAMPLOUGH'S
PYRETIC SALINE.

An Effervescing and Tasteless Salt. A most

Invigorating, Vitalizing and Refreshing Tonic,

Gives instant relief in Headache, Sea or Bilious Sickness, Indigestion, Constipation, Low Spirits, Lassitude, Heartburn, Feverish Colds; and quickly cures the worst form of

TYPHUS, SCARLET, JUNGLE, AND OTHER FEVERS,

Prickly Heat, Small Pox, Measles, Eruptive or Skin Complaints,

And various other Altered Conditions of the Blood.

The testimony of Medical Gentlemen and the Professional Press has been unqualified in praise of

LAMPLOUGH'S PYRETIC SALINE,

As possessing most important elements calculated to restore and maintain
HEALTH WITH PERFECT VIGOUR OF BODY AND MIND.

DR. PROUT.—" Unfolding germs of immense benefit to mankind."
DR. MORGAN.—" It furnishes the Blood with its lost Saline constituents."
DR. TURLEY.—" I found it act as a specific, in my experience and family, in the worst form of scarlet fever, no other medicine being required."
DR. S. GIBBON (formerly Physician of the London Hospital).—" Its usefulness in the treatment of disease has long been confirmed by medical experience. I have been in the habit of using it in private practice for many years. In hot climates it is of especial value."
DR. SPARKS (Government Medical Inspector of Emigrants from the Port of London).—" I have great pleasure in bearing my cordial testimony to its efficacy in the treatment of many of the ordinary and Chronic forms of Gastric complaints and other forms of Febrile Dyspepsia."
DR. J. W. DOWSING.—" I used it in the treatment of forty-two cases of Yellow Fever, and I am happy to state I never lost a single case."
DR. W. STEVENS.—" Since its Introduction, the fatal West India Fevers are deprived of their terrors."
RAWUL PINDEE, PUNJAUB, INDIA.—"Solely from the ascertained merits of your preparation, after use in the Fever-Stricken Districts by which we are surrounded, we firmly believe that the use of your PYRETIC SALINE will do more to prevent Fever than all the Quinine ever imported can cure."
HER MAJESTY'S REPRESENTATIVE, the GOVERNOR OF SIERRA LEONE, states:—" It is of great value, and I shall rejoice to hear it is in the hands of all Europeans visiting the Tropics."

In Patent Glass-stoppered Bottles, **2/6, 4/6, 11/- and 21/-** *each.*

LAMPLOUGH'S CONCENTRATED LIME JUICE SYRUP,

From the Fresh Fruit, as imported for the Hospitals; a perfect luxury; forms, with the addition of Pyretic Saline, a most delicious and invigorating beverage for Total Abstainers, the Delicate and Invalid; of special service in Scrofula, Fevers and Rheumatism, and a low or altered condition of the system. In Patent glass-stoppered Bottles, at 2/- and 4/6 each.

May be obtained of all Chemists, and of the Proprietor,

H. LAMPLOUGH, Consulting Chemist, 113, Holborn, London, E.C.

ADVERTISER.

BRIDAL TROUSSEAUX,
£50, £60, and £100.

LAYETTES,
£20 and £40.

Price List of Wedding & Indian Outfits & Baby Linen, post-free.

CHEQUES CROSSED LONDON AND WESTMINSTER BANK, ST. JAMES'S SQUARE.

Mrs. ADDLEY BOURNE,
Ladies' Outfitter, Corset and Baby Linen Manufacturer,
37, PICCADILLY,
Opposite St. James's Church, London.

MÉDAILLE D'OR.
EXPOSITION UNIVERSELLE,
1878.

MANUFACTURE
DE
PIANOS & ORGUES.

MAISON FONDÉE EN 1832,
PAR
AL. DEBAIN,
INVENTEUR DE L'HARMONIUM,
U PIANO MÉCANIQUE, etc.
GRAND PRIX DE ROME.
Membre du Jury aux Expositions
Hors Concours.
MAINTENANT EN SOCIÉTÉ,
SOUS LA RAISON SOCIALE
DEBAIN & CIE.,
Usine a St-Ouen.
Près le chemin de fer du Nord.
MAGASINS DE VENTE,
A PARIS,
ET
41, RATHBONE PLACE,
OXFORD STREET,
A LONDRES.

ANCIENNE MAISON PATRONNEE
DES SOMMITES MUSICALES.

Rossini.	Moscheles.	Fessy.
Auber.	A. Adam.	Gejan.
Halevy.	A. Thomas.	Boely.
Berlioz.	Lefèbure.	Bertini.
Benedict.	Caraffa.	etc., etc.

FOURNISSEUR BREVETÉ DE LL. MM.

La Reine d'Angleterre.	Le Sultan de Turquie.
Le Roi Louis-Philippe.	Le Vice-Roi d'Égypte.
L'Empereur Napoleon III.	Le Roi de Hanovre.
L'Emp renr de Russie.	La Reine Christine.
L'Empereur de Brésil	La Reine Isabelle.
Le Roi de Hollande.	Le Roi de Cambridge.
Le Roi d'Italie.	Le Schah de Perse.
Le Roi de Portugal.	La Reine d'Oude, etc., etc.

J. STUTTAFORD,
Seul Representant, a Londres.

Gold Medal, Paris Exhibition,
1878.
DEBAIN & CO.
(*Fournisseurs, by Brevet, to Her Majesty*),
41, RATHBONE PLACE,
OXFORD STREET, LONDON, W.
(Late 357, OXFORD STREET).

HARMONIUMS,
SIMPLE AND PERCUSSIVE
(DEBAIN, Inventor),
From 8 to 200 Guineas.

ORGANOPHONES
(DEBAIN, Inventor),
From 40 to 200 Guineas.

PIANOS-MÉCANIQUES
(DEBAIN, Inventor),
From 100 Guineas.

PIANOS,
Seven Octaves, Trichord, Check Action
Plinth and Consoles, &c.
(Suitable for Export).
From 31 to 180 Guineas.

MUSIC SEATS
(*Metal Tube Frames, Gilt with the best Gold Bronze*).

Harmonium Chairs, 31s. 6d.
Piano Stools, "Ionic," without screw, 42s.
Piano Stools, "Trépied," with screw, 63s.

Lists and Drawings on Application.

DEBAIN & CO.,
41, Rathbone Place, Oxford St.,
LONDON, W.
J. STUTTAFORD, Representative.

ESTABLISHED 1680.
JAMES HOW & CO.
(Successors to GEO. KNIGHT & SONS),

CHEMICAL AND PHILOSOPHICAL INSTRUMENT MAKERS
to Her Majesty's Government.

73, FARRINGDON ST., LONDON
(Late of 2, Foster Lane, and 5, St. Bride Street).

BINOCULAR OPERA, FIELD, & MARINE GLASSES,
Meteorological Instruments, Barometers, Thermometers, &c.

MICROSCOPES AND MICROSCOPIC APPARATUS.
How's Student's Microscope, £5 5s.   How's Microscopic Lamp.
Preparations illustrating all branches of Microscopical Science.
Apparatus for ELECTRICITY and MAGNETISM, OPTICS, HEAT, MECHANICS, HYDROSTATICS, PNEUMATICS, &c.

Chemical Apparatus, Glass, Porcelain, &c.
Chemicals of the Greatest Attainable Purity.
PHOTOGRAPHIC APPARATUS AND MATERIALS.

MAGIC LANTERNS AND DISSOLVING VIEW
APPARATUS.
Every description of Slides for the Magic Lantern kept in STOCK, including Views in Great Britain, France, Switzerland, Italy, Egypt, the Holy Land, America, &c., the Zulu War, Humorous Subjects, Fairy Tales, &c.

Lantern Slides specially adapted for the Illustration of SCIENTIFIC LECTURES. HOW'S Series of Geological Illustrations; a New Series of Physiological Slides as used by Dr. B. W. RICHARDSON, F.R.S.; Enlarged Photographs of Microscopic Objects by Dr. MADDOX.

MATHEMATICAL DRAWING INSTRUMENTS.
TELESCOPES, SPECTROSCOPES, POLARISCOPES, &c.
Spectacles to suit all defects of Vision.

Catalogues on Application.

W. TARN & CO.,
GENERAL HOUSE FURNISHERS AND SILK MERCERS.

DEPARTMENTS.

Drawing Room Furniture.
Dining Room Furniture.
Bedroom Furniture.
Bedding.
Office Furniture.
Carpets of all Descriptions.
Floor Cloths, &c.
Household Drapery.
Table Linen, &c.
Cornices, Poles, Fringes, &c.
Silks, Velvets, &c.

Mantles, Shawls, &c.
Lace, Ribbons, and Haberdashery.
Furs, Parasols.
Hosiery, Gloves.
Bonnets, Millinery, &c.
Ladies' Outfits and Baby Linen.
Children's Dresses.
Dress Materials.
Costumes and Dressmaking.

Ladies' Boots and Shoes.

FAMILY MOURNING.

Stocks Large, Choice, and Well-assorted in Prices, Colours, and Qualities.

OUR SILKS, VELVETS, RIBBONS, and TRIMMINGS are carefully purchased, having thoughtful attention given to the Matching and the Blending of the Colours. Our Extensive Premises, Large Stock, and Numerous Staff enable us to carry out Orders to any extent with promptness, combined with moderate charges.

PATTERNS SENT FREE.

Country Orders, if Accompanied by a Remittance, will Receive Prompt Attention.

A Furniture Catalogue containing 550 Drawings on application.

NEWINGTON CAUSEWAY & NEW KENT ROAD, S.E.

THOMAS ALDRED,

Archery Manufacturer to the Royal Family of England and Principal Crowned Heads of Europe,

AND

HOLDER OF SIX PRIZE MEDALS,

Begs to state that his Goods are of first-rate excellence, at the most moderate prices.

SPECIAL TO AMERICAN ARCHERS.

The Members of Archery Clubs in the United States are respectfully invited to become purchasers of THOMAS ALDRED'S celebrated Archery Goods. T. A. manufactures *the best goods only*, and has the honour of supplying the great bulk of the Members of the principal Clubs and Societies of Great Britain, and the Committees of the Public Toxophilite Matches in England.

WHOLESALE, RETAIL, AND FOR EXPORTATION.

Manufactory: 126, Oxford Street, London.

Catalogues of Prices gratis.

TURKEY, PERSIAN,
AND OTHER
ORIENTAL CARPETS, RUGS, MATTINGS,
ETC.

CARDINAL & HARFORD,
IMPORTERS,
LEVANT CARPET WAREHOUSE,
108 & 109, HIGH HOLBORN, LONDON, W.C.

Price Lists and Estimates on application.

COOPER'S
CANTHARIDINE
AND
ROSEMARY CREAM.

Answers the combined purpose of Pomade, Stimulating Lotion, and Hair Cleaner; being comparatively free from Oil, it is particularly approved of by Ladies, and is unequalled for the Whiskers.

In Bottles, 1s. and 2s.

RELIABLE
MARKING INK.
PRICE 1s.

This Ink has four great advantages:
1. It does not destroy the Linen
2. It may be used with any kind of Pen.
3. The Bottles are sent out full and are always ready for use.
4. It is half the price of other Marking Inks.

Wm. T. Cooper, Chemist,
Maker, 28, Oxford Street, W.

ADVERTISER. ix

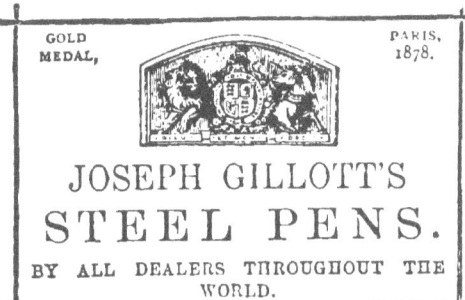

JOSEPH GILLOTT'S
STEEL PENS.
BY ALL DEALERS THROUGHOUT THE WORLD.

TURKEY AND EASTERN
CARPET DEPÔT,

10, Paternoster Buildings, Newgate St., London, E.C.

CRANWELL & CO., IMPORTERS.

The Benevolent or Strangers' Friend Society,

WHICH HAS FOR NEARLY A CENTURY

RELIEVED THE SICK AND DISTRESSED POOR AT THEIR OWN ABODES, IN LONDON AND ITS VICINITY,

BEARS THE FOLLOWING PROMINENT FEATURES:

1. It is unrestricted in its Benevolence. It regards neither Creed nor Country. As far as its means will allow, it visits and relieves EVERY CASE THAT COMES UNDER ITS NOTICE.
2. It is neither Sectarian nor Proselyting. It never says, "You must come to my church or my chapel."
3. Its Agents shun no locality.
4. Its Operations are never suspended.
5. No case is relieved until after special and searching inquiry
6. The Accounts are audited every month.

Lastly. The expenses of Management are small.

SMALL SUMS GIVEN WEEKLY FOR A MONTH OR TWO HAVE RESTORED THOUSANDS OF FAMILIES TO COMFORT AND COMPETENCE.

Every Information gladly afforded to Members.

SUBSCRIPTIONS and DONATIONS will be thankfully received by Messrs. HOARE, Bankers, Fleet-street; J. S. BUDGETT, Esq., the Treasurer, Ealing Park, W.; and by W. J. CHAMPION, the Secretary, at the Office of the Society, 7, EXETER HALL, STRAND, W.C.

Private Residential Family Club,

ALEXANDRA MANSIONS,
1 & 3, HARRINGTON ROAD,
SOUTH KENSINGTON, S.W.
(Facing CROMWELL PLACE).

Established as a Residential Club for Families, and Visitors to Town, combining the privacy and comfort of a well-appointed Home, thereby avoiding the responsibility of housekeeping, the discomfort of Lodgings, or the expense of an Hotel.

The situation is one of the best in London, being ¼ minute's walk from South Kensington Station.

Strict references are required, as the Club is conducted as a first-class Private Residence.

Arrangements can be made for Private Sitting Room and Permanent Residence.

For further particulars apply to

THE PROPRIETOR, ALEXANDRA MANSIONS,
1 & 3, *Harrington Road, South Kensington, S.W.*

TERMS: Per Week.
Single Room and Board . . . . 2 to 4 guineas.
Double do.   do.   . . . . 4 to 6   „
Club Subscriptions (including Newspapers and usual extras) 5s.

SAMARITAN FREE HOSPITAL
FOR WOMEN AND CHILDREN.

Lower Seymour Street, Portman Square, W.

Dorset House Branch, 1, Dorset Street, Manchester Square.

Patroness—HER ROYAL HIGHNESS THE DUCHESS OF CAMBRIDGE.
President—THE RIGHT HON. THE LORD LEIGH.
Vice-Presidents—

Most Hon. THE MARQUIS OF HERTFORD.
The Right Hon. THE EARL DUCIE.
Right Hon. LORD MANNERS.
The Right Hon. THE LORD SELBORNE.
SIR GEORGE BAKER, Bart.
SIR CHARLES ROWLEY, Bart.
SIR THOS. CHAMBERS, Q.C., M.P., Recorder of London.

Chaplain—The Rev. FRANCIS J. HOLLAND, M.A.
Chaplain, Dorset House—Rev. JAMES HUTCHONS, M.A.
Treasurer—RICHARD B. WADE, Esq. | **Hon. Sec.**—J. LIVINGSTON JAY, Esq.

HONORARY MEDICAL OFFICERS.
SIR WILLIAM JENNER, Bart., K.C.B., M.D.
Consulting Physicians—R. GREENHALGH, M.D.; H. SAVAGE, M.D., F R.C.S.
Consulting Surgeon—T. SPENCER WELLS, F.R C.S.
Physicians for In-Patients—C. H. F. ROUTH, M.D.; W. R. ROGERS, M.D.
Physicians for Children In-Patients—W. H. DAY, M.D.; A. WYNN WILLIAMS, M.D.
Surgeons for In-Patients—
G. GRANVILLE BANTOCK, M.D., F.R.C.S., Edin.; J. KNOWSLEY THORNTON, M.B., M.C.
Physicians for Out-Patients—
A. WYNN WILLIAMS, M.D.
PERCY BOULTON, M.D.
W. H. DAY, M.D.
F. H. CHAMPNEYS, M.A., M.B.
Surgeons for Out-Patients—
W. A. MEREDITH, M.B., M C ; ALBAN H. G. DORAN, F.R.C.S.

OBJECTS OF THE HOSPITAL.
An In-department for the reception of poor Women afflicted with diseases peculiar to their sex, where they have home comforts and hospital treatment without publicity.
Children received as In-Patients at the Branch.
An Out-department for such diseases of Women and all diseases of Children.
To furnish attendance to Poor Married Women at their own Homes during their confinement.
There are 52 Beds in the Hospital and its Branch, 16 being for Children.
Since its foundation no less than **229,362** Women and Children have been treated in the Out-department, and **5,431** Women admitted as In-Patients, of whom **547** were operated upon for Ovarian Tumour, with **422** recoveries, and only **125** deaths.
Admission Free, without Letter of Recommendation.
Bankers—SIR SAMUEL SCOTT, BART., & Co., 1, Cavendish Square.
CONTRIBUTIONS are earnestly solicited, and may be paid to Messrs. BARCLAY & Co., 54, Lombard Street; Messrs. COUTTS & Co., 59, Strand; Messrs. GLYN & Co., 67, Lombard Street; Messrs. RANSOM & Co., 1, Pall Mall East; Messrs. HATCHARD, Piccadilly; or to
GEORGE SCUDAMORE, *Secretary*.

ADVERTISER.

EFFERVESCING LOZENGES.

Simple Effervescing Lozenges, or Solid Thirst Quenchers, for quenching thirst without drinking.
Phosphate of Iron Effervescing Lozenges. The most certain preparation of Iron for Children.
Soda and Bismuth Effervescing Lozenges, one after each meal.
*Astringent Voice Effervescing Lozenges, made from the well-known Red Gum of Australia, do not contain any irritant stimulant. *Chlorate of Potash Effervescing Lozenges. * These are analogous to Gargles in their action."—*Lancet.*
From their slowly dissolving in the mouth, their constituents become very intimately mixed with the saliva, and medicines thus administered are much more readily taken up by the system. In Bottles, 1s.; by Post, 1s. 2d. Patentee and Manufacturer—
W. T. COOPER, Chemist, 26, Oxford Street, London.

BROWN AND GREEN'S

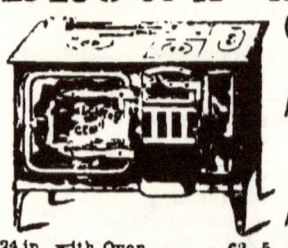

Celebrated Gem Cooking Stove.
**GREAT SAVING OF COAL,
AND CURE FOR SMOKY CHIMNEYS.**
Prices on Application

**BROWN AND GREEN'S
PRIZE MEDAL KITCHENERS**

		£ s.
24 in., with Oven		2 5
30 in. ,, Oven & Boiler		3 5
36 in. ,, Oven & Boiler		5 0

Smaller and Larger Sizes.

London Warehouse:—72, Bishopsgate St.
Manufactory:—LUTON.

THE RENT GUARANTEE SOCIETY (Limited)

Undertakes the Collection of Tithes, Mortgages, Interest, and Dividends; Weekly, Monthly, and Quarterly Rents; also the entire Management of Property, Re-Letting, Superintending all Repairs, and Paying all Outgoings.

Offices:--66, CANNON STREET, E.C.

BARCLAY & SON,
138, REGENT STREET, LONDON.
To Her Majesty and H.R.H. the Prince of Wales.

DUPLEX LAMPS.	A 1 KEROSINE OIL.
MODERATOR LAMPS.	WAX, SPERM,
READING LAMPS.	AND
MICROSCOPE LAMPS.	PARAFFINE
BEST COLZA OIL.	CANDLES.

Illustrated Catalogues Post Free.

North British and Mercantile Insurance Company,
LONDON AND EDINBURGH.
ESTABLISHED 1809.
Incorporated by Royal Charter and Special Acts of Parliament.

SUBSCRIBED CAPITAL .. £2,852,566 STERLING.
FIRE RESERVE FUNDS (1877) .. .. £1,099,642.

HEAD OFFICES { 61 THREADNEEDLE STREET, LONDON.
64 PRINCES STREET, EDINBURGH.

BOARD OF DIRECTORS IN LONDON.
Chairman—JOHN WHITE CATER, Esq.

RICHARD BARING, Esq.
RICHARD BRANDT, Esq.
ALEX. H. CAMPBELL, Esq.
EDWARD COHEN, Esq.
P. DU PRÉ GRENFELL, Esq.
QUINTIN HOGG, Esq.
Hon. HUGH MCCULLOCH.

CHARLES W. MILLS, Esq.
JUNIUS S. MORGAN, Esq.
GEORGE GARDEN NICOL, Esq.
JOHN SANDERSON, Esq.
Baron JOHN H. W. SCHRÖDER.
GEORGE YOUNG, Esq.

Manager of Fire Department—
G. H. BURNETT.
Foreign Sub-Manager—P. WINSOR.

Manager of Life Department—
HENRY COCKBURN.
Secretary—F. W. LANCE.

General Manager—DAVID SMITH, F.R.S.E.

United States Branch.
CENTRAL OFFICE, 54 WILLIAM STREET, NEW YORK.

BOARD OF DIRECTORS IN NEW YORK.
Chairman—SOLON HUMPHREYS, Esq., Merchant.

C. H. DABNEY, Esq., Merchant.
DAVID DOWS, Esq., Merchant.
SIMEON B. CHITTENDEN, Esq., Merchant.

E. P. FABBRI, Esq., Merchant.
T. ROOSEVELT, Esq., Merchant.
EZRA WHITE, E q.

Managers—C. E. WHITE, and SAMUEL P. BLAGDEN.
Bankers—Messrs. DREXEL MORGAN & Co. *Solicitors*—LORD, DAY, & LORD.

THIS COMPANY insures against Fire nearly every description of Property in all parts of the world, at the lowest rates of Premium corresponding to the risk.

Insurances effected for Seven Years by prepayment are charged for Six only.

Losses settled with promptitude and liberality at the Branches and Principal Agencies.

As an instance of the standing of the Company, it may be mentioned that during the last decade of years (1866 to 1877) the Fire Premiums, after deducting re-insurances, amounted to £7,145,137, while losses to the extent of 350,523 were indemnified.

THE
ST. MARYLEBONE FEMALE PROTECTION SOCIETY,

157-9, MARYLEBONE ROAD, LONDON, N.W.

Patroness.
HER ROYAL HIGHNESS THE DUCHESS OF CAMBRIDGE.
Treasurer.
JOHN DEACON, Esq., 20, Birchin Lane, E.C.
Sub-Treasurer.
RICHARD B. WADE, Esq., 13, Seymour Street, Portman Square, W.
Honorary Physician.
Dr. FRANCIS H. CHAMPNEYS, M.A., 11, Wyndham Place, Bryanston Square, W.
Secretary.
GEORGE SCUDAMORE, 157, Marylebone Road, N.W.
Matron.—MRS. H. ALSOP.
Bankers.
SIR SAMUEL SCOTT, Bart., & Co., 1, Cavendish Square, W.; Messrs. WILLIAMS, DEACON, & Co., 20, Birchin Lane, E.C.; The NATIONAL PROVINCIAL BANK OF ENGLAND, Bishopsgate Street, E.C.; and the St. Marylebone Branch, 53, Baker Street, W.

THIS SOCIETY, founded in 1838, seeks to reclaim Young Women from all parts of the Country, who have, by one false step, fallen from the path of virtue. They are cared for in their trouble if expecting to become mothers; and, after suitable training, are placed in service, where needful help is given them in supporting their infants, les , through want, they should fall again into sin. This is the more necessary from the extreme youth of many of the applicants, which prevents their earning sufficient to maintain their infants.

DURING THE PAST YEAR 84 WOMEN AND 72 BABIES FOUND A HOME AND PROTECTION IN THIS INSTITUTION.

Subscriptions and Donations are earnestly solicited.

Cheques should be "crossed" Messrs. Sir S. SCOTT, Bart., & Co. Post-office Orders payable to GEORGE SCUDAMORE, at the Western Branch District Post-Office, Vere Street, Oxford Street, W.

Demy 16mo., cloth, price One Shilling.

HEALTH PRIMERS.

EDITORS:

J. LANGDON DOWN, M.D., F.R.C.P., HENRY POWER, M.B., F.R.C.S.,
J. MORTIMER-GRANVILLE, M.D., JOHN TWEEDY, F.R.C.S.

Under this title is being issued a Series of SHILLING PRIMERS on subjects connected with the Preservation of Health, written and edited by eminent medical authorities.

The list of Contributors includes the following names:—

W. H. ALLCHIN, M.B., F.R.C.P., F.R.S.E.; G. W. BALFOUR, M.D., F.R.C.P.E.; J. CRICHTON BROWNE, M.D., LL.D., F.R.S.E.; SIDNEY COUPLAND, M.D., M.R.C.P.; JOHN CURNOW, M.D., F.R.C.P.; J. LANGDON DOWN, M.D., F.R.C.P.; ROBERT FARQUHARSON, M.D., Edin., M.R.C.P.; TILBURY FOX, M.D., F.R.C.P.; J. MORTIMER-GRANVILLE, M.D., F.G.S., F.S.S.; W. S. GREENFIELD, M.D., F.R.C.P.; C. W. HEATON, F.C.S.; HARRY LEACH, M.R.C.P.; G. V. POORE, M.D., F.R.C.P.; HENRY POWER, M.B., F.R.C.S.; W. L. PURVES, M.D., F.R.C.S.; J. NETTEN RADCLIFFE, Ex-Pres., Epidl. Soc., &c.; C. H. RALFE, M.A., M.D., F.R.C.P.; S. RINGER, M.D., F.R.C.P.; JOHN TWEEDY, F.R.C.S.; JOHN WILLIAMS, M.D., F.R.C.P.

The following Volumes are now ready:—

Premature Death; its Promotion or Prevention.
Alcohol: Its Use and Abuse.
Exercise and Training.
The House and its Surroundings.
Personal Appearances in Health and Disease.
Baths and Bathing.
The Skin and its Troubles.
The Heart and its Functions.

To be followed by:

The Nerves.	The Throat and Voice.
The Ear and Hearing.	Temperature in Health and Disease.
The Head.	
Clothing and Dress.	Health of Travellers.
Water.	Health in Schools.
Fatigue and Pain.	Breath Organs.
The Eye and Vision.	Foods and Feeding.

London: DAVID BOGUE, 3, St. Martin's Place, W.C.

BOGUE'S HALF-HOUR VOLUMES.

THE GREEN LANES: A Book for a Country Stroll. By J. E. TAYLOR, F.L.S., F.G.S. Illustrated with 300 Woodcuts. Fifth Edition. Crown 8vo., cloth, 4s.

THE SEA-SIDE; or, Recreations with Marine Objects. By J. E. TAYLOR, F.L.S., F.G.S. Illustrated with 150 Woodcuts. Fourth Edition. Crown 8vo., cloth, 4s.

GEOLOGICAL STORIES: A Series of Autobiographies in Chronological Order. By J. E. TAYLOR, F.L.S., F.G.S. Numerous Illustrations. Fourth Edition. Crown 8vo., cloth, 4s.

THE AQUARIUM: Its Inhabitants, Structure and Management. By J. E. TAYLOR, F.L.S., F.G.S. With 238 Woodcuts. Second Edition. Crown 8vo., cloth extra, 6s.

THE MICROSCOPE: A Popular Guide to the Use of the Instrument. By E. LANKESTER, M.D., F.R.S. With 250 Illustrations. Sixteenth Thousand. Fcap. 8vo., cloth plain, 2s. 6d.; coloured, 4s.

THE TELESCOPE: A Popular Guide to its Use as a means of Amusement and Instruction. By R. A. PROCTOR, B.A. With numerous Illustrations on Stone and Wood. Fifth Edition. Fcap. 8vo., cloth, 2s. 6d.

THE STARS: A Plain and Easy Guide to the Constellations. By R. A. PROCTOR, B.A. Illustrated with 12 Maps. Tenth Thousand. Demy 4to. boards, 5s.

ENGLISH ANTIQUITIES. By LLEWELLYNN JEWITT, F.S.A. *Contents:* Barrows, Stone Arches, Cromlechs—Implements of Flint and Stone—Celts and other Instruments of Bronze—Roman Roads, Towns, &c.—Tesselated Pavements, Temples, Altars—Ancient Pottery—Arms and Armour—Sepulchral Slabs and Brasses—Coins—Church Bells—Glass—Stained Glass—Tiles—Tapestry—Personal Ornaments, &c. With 300 Woodcuts. Second Edition. Crown 8vo., cloth extra, 5s.

ENGLISH FOLK LORE. By the Rev. T. F. THISELTON DYER. *Contents:*—Trees—Plants—Flowers—The Moon—Birds—Animals—Insects—Reptiles—Charms—Birth—Baptism—Marriage—Death—Days of the Week—The Months and their Weather Lore—Bells—Miscellaneous Folk Lore. Crown 8vo., cloth, 5s.

PLEASANT DAYS IN PLEASANT PLACES. Notes of Home Tours. By EDWARD WALFORD, M.A., late Scholar of Balliol College, Oxford, Editor of "County Families," &c. *Contents:*—Dorney and Burnham—Shanklin—Hadleigh—St. David's—Winchelsea—Sandwich—St. Osyth's Priory—Richborough Castle—Great Yarmouth—Old Moreton Hall—Cumnor—Ightham—Shoreham and Bramber—Beaulieu—Kenilworth—Tattershall Tower—Tower of Essex. Illustrated with numerous Woodcuts. Second Edition. Crown 8vo., cloth extra, 5s.

IN PREPARATION, UNIFORM WITH THE ABOVE,

HOLIDAYS IN HOME COUNTIES. By EDWARD WALFORD, M.A. With numerous Illustrations. Crown 8vo., cloth extra, 5s.

London: DAVID BOGUE, 3, St. Martin's Place, W.C.